Facing West

Kyung-Chik Han and Bob Pierce, cofounders of World Vision. Pastor Han built
the humanitarian and churchly institutions that became the foundation of World
Vision before Pierce ever arrived in Korea. As Pierce's star began to rise in the West,
however, Han's efforts were trivialized. In America, he was typically known as Pierce's
interpreter.

Facing West

*American Evangelicals in an Age
of World Christianity*

DAVID R. SWARTZ

OXFORD
UNIVERSITY PRESS

OXFORD
UNIVERSITY PRESS

Oxford University Press is a department of the University of Oxford. It furthers
the University's objective of excellence in research, scholarship, and education
by publishing worldwide. Oxford is a registered trade mark of Oxford University
Press in the UK and certain other countries.

Published in the United States of America by Oxford University Press
198 Madison Avenue, New York, NY 10016, United States of America.

Library of Congress Cataloging-in-Publication Data
Names: Swartz, David R., author.
Title: Facing West : American evangelicals in an age of world Christianity/
David R. Swartz.
Description: New York, NY, United States of America : Oxford University
Press, 2020. | Includes bibliographical references and index.
Identifiers: LCCN 2019045483 (print) | LCCN 2019045484 (ebook) |
ISBN 9780190250805 (hardback) | ISBN 9780190250829 (epub) |
ISBN 9780190250836 (online)
Subjects: LCSH: Missions—History—21st century. | Evangelicalism—United States.
Classification: LCC BV2120 .S93 2020 (print) | LCC BV2120 (ebook) |
DDC 277.3/083—dc23
LC record available at https://lccn.loc.gov/2019045483
LC ebook record available at https://lccn.loc.gov/2019045484

1 3 5 7 9 8 6 4 2

Printed by Integrated Books International, United States of America

Contents

Acknowledgments

My acknowledgments reflect the expansive geography of this book. I am the grateful recipient of help and hospitality from friends, scholars, activists, preachers, and humanitarians who span the globe.

For help with material on Chicago, I am grateful to Joel Carpenter and Tim Gloege. On Korea, I am grateful to Jin Jeon, Jong-sam Park, Hoon Song, Inyeop Lee, and Marilee Pierce Dunker. On India, Skip Elliott, David Hollinger, and Art McPhee. On Lausanne, Al Tizon and David Kirkpatrick. On the Philippines, Steve Gray, Steve Offutt, and David King. On Guatemala, Bob Brenneman and Virginia Garrard-Burnett. On Uganda, Jason Bruner, Tim Gloege, John Maiden, and Ruth Ann Reese. On Boston, Alice and Tim Colegrove, Michelle and Jim Harper, and Gina Zurlo.

For inviting me to test-drive ideas in public lectures, I am grateful to Esther Jadhav, Greg Haseloff, Dan Strait, Paul Nesselroade, and David Rightmire at Asbury University; Gregg Okesson and the faculty and graduate students of the E. Stanley Jones School at Asbury Theological Seminary; Mark Edwards at Spring Arbor University; and Uta Balbier, Hans Krabbendam, Kendrick Oliver, and Axel Schäfer at workshops in the United Kingdom, the Netherlands, and Germany on global evangelicalism. For helpful critiques at conferences, I thank commentators from the Organization of American Historians, University of Southampton in the United Kingdom, Kangnam University in Seoul, Indiana University-Purdue University at Indianapolis, Pepperdine University, the Communal Studies Association, the Society for the Scientific Study of Religion, the Conference on Faith and History, the United Nations Development Programme in Bangkok, Princeton Theological Seminary, Lipscomb University, and the University of California at Berkeley.

For help during sabbatical research in Thailand, I thank Christa Crawford, Clint Baldwin, Ayi Bechegoo, Liz Hilton, Carrie Stoltzfus, Adele Pucci, Candice and Tom Mast, Todd Johnson, Kimberly Wheeler, Paul Buckley, Paul Utley, Pik at our *mooban* café, Amy Collins, Carter Quinley, Sarah Lapa, Kara and Craig Garrison, Tawee Donchai, Lori Rowe, Brett Steffen, Evan McCall, and the surgeon in Chiang Mai who fixed my tooth.

Closer to home, I am grateful to scholars who engaged substantively with this manuscript. They include James Bielo, Darren Dochuk, David Kirkpatrick, Melani McAlister, George Marsden, Mark Noll, and Steve Offutt. For more extensive readings, I am especially grateful to Joel Carpenter, Tim Gloege, Kevin Miller, Nathan Showalter, Steve Swartz, and Phyllis Miller Swartz.

For help in securing sources at archives and elsewhere, I thank Steve Gray of World Vision International, Suzanne Gehring of Asbury University, Grace Yoder of Asbury Theological Seminary, Rich Elliott of Park Street Church in Boston, Doris Wagner of Global Spheres, Hoon Song at the Kyung-Chik Han Foundation, Alison Barfoot of the Anglican Church of Uganda, Jeff Bass and Judy Hall of Emmanuel Gospel Center, Alyson Thomas of Fuller Theological Seminary, Reuben Sairs at Rosedale Bible College, Brooke Guthrie of Duke University, and Katherine Graber and Bob Shuster at the Billy Graham Center Archives.

For friendship and conversation related to this project, I thank Clint Baldwin, Kevin Bellew, Sarah Bellew, Kevin Brown, Carolyn DuPont, Skip Elliott, Luke Embree, Nathan Miller, Steve Offutt, Erin Penner, Sydney Penner, Andy Reynolds, Kirk Sims, Josh Smith, and Henry Zonio. I am also grateful to my colleagues at the Anxious Bench blog: Beth Allison Barr, Melissa Borja, Kristin Kobes DuMez, Chris Gehrz, Agnes Howard, Tal Howard, Philip Jenkins, John Turner, and Andrea Turpin. Their writing inspires me.

For wise counsel and for shepherding this book to publication, I thank Theo Calderara, Drew Anderla, Salma Ismaiel, Shalini Balakrishnan, and anonymous referees at Oxford University Press.

For permission to publish portions of already-printed essays and articles, I thank Cascade Books, Oxford University Press, Palgrave Macmillan, *Religions, The Review of Faith & International Affairs*, and the *Journal of American Studies*.

For institutional support and generous funding to complete this project, I thank Jon Kulaga, Tim Campbell, Steve Clements, and Bonnie Banker at Asbury University as well as the Society for the Scientific Study of Religion for a Jack Shand Research Grant.

My family deserves the most thanks of all. I am grateful to Lisa Weaver Swartz, a wise conversation partner and a delightful companion. And though this book would have appeared several years earlier without them, I am grateful to my children, whose courage, enthusiasm, and unending questions made travel in Southeast Asia and life in general much richer. I dedicate this book to Andrew, Jonathan, Benjamin, and Anna. May you grow up to be citizens of the whole world.

Introduction

Located just blocks from Korea's National Assembly and nestled amid the soaring skyscrapers of Seoul's financial district, World Vision's nine-story office building occupies prime real estate. I sat in a conference room on the building's top floor filled with sturdy vintage furniture from the 1970s, ready to begin research on the origins of one of the largest humanitarian organizations in the world. I expected to confirm and add Korean texture to the accepted narrative: that a larger-than-life American evangelist named Bob Pierce, undone by sights of Marxist cruelties in the early 1950s, had helped bring Korea out of its wartime devastation. In this story Pierce, alongside the U.S. Army, had started schools, orphanages, and churches that lifted the nation to democratic and capitalist heights. World Vision's founding myth has stood for well over half a century, and I anticipated hearing it repeated yet again.

But Jong-Sam Park, the just-retired president of World Vision Korea, told a different story. The silver-haired executive fielded my persistent questions about Bob Pierce, but he was much more interested in talking about a Korean pastor I had never heard of. Kyung-Chik Han, Park said, had helped him during the Korean War when Park was a refugee child who slept on the streets of Seoul covered only by a straw mat. I listened impatiently, hoping to return to my questions about American missionaries and World Vision's founding. But when I tried to guide him back, he grew exasperated. Han, he exclaimed, was the founder of World Vision. "Of World Vision Korea?" I tried to clarify. "No, the whole thing," replied Park, relishing this opportunity to reorient the perspective of a young scholar who seemed bent on telling a narrative of American triumphalism.[1]

This meeting opened a line of research that led to the stately Young Nak Presbyterian Church. At this congregation of 60,000 located in the heart of Seoul, I spoke with a Korean historian with graduate training from Boston University. He led me through an impressive museum display about Han and confirmed Park's assertion that Han was, in fact, a prominent historical figure who profoundly shaped the direction of World Vision. He also gave me files that contained thousands of pages of sermons, memoirs, and secondary literature, all of which had just been translated into English. These Korean sources showed that Han had built the medical, educational, and churchly institutions that became the foundation of World Vision before Pierce ever arrived in Asia (see Figure I.1). The American evangelist, it turns out, was plugging into an

Facing West. David R. Swartz, Oxford University Press (2020). © Oxford University Press.
DOI: 10.1093/oso/9780190250805.001.0001

Figure I.1. Kyung-Chik Han and Bob Pierce, cofounders of World Vision, distributing food and clothing during the Korean War in the early 1950s. Courtesy of the Kyung-Chik Han Foundation, Seoul, Korea.

existing humanitarian network already constructed by Koreans. As Bob Pierce's star began to rise in the West, however, Han's contributions were trivialized. In America, he was typically known as Pierce's interpreter.[2]

Upon reflection, this new and striking narrative made sense of evidence that had already passed before my unseeing eyes. American archival sources described the two men appearing on stage together throughout the early 1950s in Seoul. Han may have interpreted Pierce's sermons into Korean for his parishioners, but Han also spoke in his own voice as the pastor of the largest Presbyterian church in the world—and as the architect of hundreds of humanitarian initiatives that were becoming the foundation of World Vision. Sources also showed that the partnership was evident in America. On a cold November evening in 1954 at Chicago's Orchestra Hall, where Han earlier had appeared on stage, the irrepressible Pierce acknowledged his colleague's evangelistic and humanitarian bona fides. Han, he said, was expertly distributing rice and the gospel to "war weary" Koreans. In this moment, a terrifying time in the Cold War when it appeared as if the United States and the Soviet Union might destroy each other with nuclear weapons, Pierce proclaimed hope for Asia, partly because of Han's work on the Korean peninsula. Pierce called him "a man of God, full of the Holy Ghost, the real soul-winner." But Pierce didn't put all his hope in Han—or in God. He praised American bombers over Seoul, and he pledged to do his own part. "I don't expect to die in hospital sheets, I expect to die at the hand of a Communist."

Pierce ended his sermon with a plea that was part sales pitch and part altar call. "How I pray tonight that there be someone who will answer the call and give God your heart, to fill you with the Holy Ghost, and break your heart . . . I have 600 children waiting adoption this month. Their pictures are already taken, their names [could be] filed within ten days, if you will write on that envelope, 'I will adopt a child' and covenant with God that you will send ten dollars a month for a year." With business-like efficiency, volunteers collected the pledges, hurried the crowd out, and ushered a new one in. Then they did the presentation all over again. The money given in Chicago that evening went to a brand-new organization called World Vision that would grow from 240 sponsorships of children in 1954 to 3.5 million sponsorships in 2015. By 2019 combined revenues for World Vision International, the global umbrella organization, was $2.75 billion.[3]

At that moment in Chicago, the notion that World Vision was the brainchild of two men was already starting to fade. And as Bob Pierce became a legend and friend to presidents around the world, Han disappeared from the American imagination, nudged off the stage by a formidable Christian Americanism and Pierce's big personality. Despite his reputation among Koreans as a cofounder of World Vision, Han's obscurity in the United States was nearly complete by the end of the 1950s. The narratives of these two men—one American, one Korean—reflect contemporary debates about American identity and exceptionalism. Han's story stresses that the United States is simply one nation among many others. In contrast, Pierce, a transcendent figure who sought to save the world from Marxists, suggests that America is a nation to save all nations.

This latter version has become standard history. I had arrived in Korea having read numerous English-language memoirs, scholarly articles, and books on World Vision. None of them—with the exception of several brief reflections by Pierce himself and his daughter Marilee Pierce Dunker—mentioned Han, a towering figure in Korean church history who taught Bob Pierce about social justice. So it was not until I spoke with Jong-Sam Park that my understanding of World Vision's origins was transformed. This book, then, represents an attempt to heed Tite Tiénou's admonition to move beyond provincial imperial narratives by listening well. Conversations with Korean humanitarians in Seoul, Thai activists in Chiang Mai, and Nigerian immigrants in Boston—alongside close readings of non-American written sources—helped me recover these transnational stories. Moving beyond traditional borders offers new insights into an evangelical tradition that imagines itself as simultaneously American and part of a global communion.[4]

In recent decades scholars have called for the integration of both religion and transnationalism into American narratives fixated on politics and confined within national boundaries. Until recently these pleas have largely gone unanswered. About American history broadly conceived, Luke Clossey and Nicholas

Guyatt write, "We're overwhelmingly interested in ourselves. Europe, the U.S., and Canada are the subject of more than three-quarters of all historical research in Britain and North America." The same is true in the field of religious history. In a recent span of ten issues of *Church History*, only three articles out of over sixty focused on the history of Christianity since 1500 in Asia, Africa, or Latin America. Even fewer have scrutinized religious movements that move from South to North and East to West.[5]

Much of the transnational literature that does exist emphasizes imperialistic aspects of Western religion. Popular depictions of "ugly Americans" and intolerant missionaries buttress a long tradition of critical scholarship. It is a historiographical strain, says André Corten, that understands evangelicalism "as a bridgehead of American imperialism, the alarming proliferation of churches being understood in terms of the millions of dollars spent buying converts." Pierce's Korea is a morality tale for these scholars. American missionaries, they argue, sparked revival in the 1910s, and then the war machine in the 1950s remade Korean Christianity in America's image. Korean and American critics alike suggest that resurgent Korean Christianity midwifed a rapacious consumerism that now seethes in Seoul's high-rise towers. The imposition of American mores, it could be argued, extended even to historical narratives. The birth of World Vision became an all-American story as the Western gaze erased memories of Han. Mission proceeded from "the West to the rest."[6]

Other scholarship stresses the burgeoning of global evangelicalism. Religious demographers Gina Zurlo and Todd Johnson note that the growth rate of Christians in Asia and Africa from 1900 to 2000 was nearly double that of the general population. In 1900 the Global North contained 82 percent of all Christians; by 2020 it will contain only 33 percent. Significantly, these evangelical advances abroad did not truly accelerate until the postcolonial era. Jehu Hanciles writes, "Attempts to impose Western Christian institutions and expressions not only failed, but they also stimulated ethnic consciousness and unleashed powerful non-Western initiatives (ecclesiastical and political) that subverted structures of foreign domination." Korean evangelicalism embodies this growth. By the 1990s World Vision Korea had been transformed from a recipient nation to a top-five contributing partner of World Vision International. By the turn of the twenty-first century, nearly half a million people were attending a single church in Seoul—the Yoido Full Gospel Church—which was more than can be claimed by entire North American denominations such as the Christian Reformed Church, the Evangelical Free Church, or the Presbyterian Church in America. Korea represents a staggering transfer of religious vitality from the West to the East.[7]

While this book takes American evangelicalism as its subject, it recognizes evangelicals from the Majority World as religious actors in their own right. When the United States is put in a global context—that is, when C. Peter Wagner is put in relationship with Claudio Freidzon of Argentina, when Bob Pierce is paired with Kyung-Chik Han of Korea, and when Pasadena, California, is one node of a sprawling global network that includes Manila and Cochabamba—different American evangelical stories emerge. As numerous scholars have noted, Fuller Theological Seminary hosted a domestic battle for an inerrant Bible. But it was also the site of an international encounter with Pentecostal supernaturalism in the 1970s and a laboratory for international development studies in the 1980s. As a small, but growing, set of scholarship shows, using a global lens illuminates important aspects of American evangelicalism sometimes obscured by accounts of national politics, theology, and business culture.[8]

This book, at base, contends that encounters abroad have deeply shaped certain sectors of American evangelicalism. To be sure, the United States, aided by this religious group, exercised immense economic, military, and cultural power. Evangelicals imagined themselves as a hedge against godless communism as they did things for and to other peoples. But this single story overplays American agency. Transnational networks were pluralistic, participatory, and multidirectional enterprises. Relationships, however unequal, often featured exchange. Sometimes global Christians, working with World Vision, the Latin American Theological Fraternity, the Lausanne movement, InterVarsity Christian Fellowship, and the World Evangelical Fellowship, resisted and refashioned empire. As international telephone traffic quadrupled between 1991 and 2004, as air passengers from the United States grew from ten million in 1975 to sixty million in 2000, as the Internet shrank time and space, and as a remarkable 62 percent of active church members in the United States traveled or lived in another country, American Christians sometimes returned home thinking more critically about their own heritage and assumptions. In the meeting of East and West, influence flowed in multiple directions. Sometimes the "empired" struck back.[9]

In addition to this overarching thesis about reflexivity, *Facing West* makes three ancillary claims. First, transnational encounters often have not fit American political and cultural categories. Sometimes influence took progressive shape. Global Christians and missionaries often pushed back against a racially segregated Christian Americanism that fused personal piety, free enterprise, anticommunism, and patriotism. In the 1950s and 1960s many of them joined the civil rights movement. In the 1970s others challenged rationalized methods of evangelization. In the 1980s still others urged more structural solutions to world hunger and poverty. Charting practices of race, mission, and social justice complicates scholarship that depicts missionaries and their converts solely as purveyors of American-style consumer capitalism. That said, Majority World evangelicals have not been exemplars of progressive humanism. Many have contended that Pentecostal renewal, more than economic development, is the key to social transformation. Others have leveled vigorous critiques of sexual practices in America, specifically regarding abortion, contraception, homosexuality, and divorce.[10]

Han embodied this global heteropraxy. As a pastor to persecuted and poverty-stricken Koreans, he pressed for social justice in ways that seemed liberal to many Americans. At the same time, the intensely anticommunist Han reinforced American evangelical Cold War bona fides. He practiced a staunch nationalism and exhibited authoritarian tendencies, a feature of world Christianity that American progressives do not like to highlight. Half a century later, the organization Han cofounded, even as it displays some socially progressive stances, continues to maintain a conservative view of marriage. In fact, my visit to Seoul took place just weeks after the 2014 World Vision firestorm over whether to hire Christians in same-sex relationships. My minders in Seoul made it very clear that Korean evangelicals did not support the initial decision from Seattle to allow gay marriage for its employees. Within hours of the announcement, World Vision Korea had received hundreds of dissenting phone calls from constituents. In response, the organization communicated its dissent to World Vision headquarters in the United States and posted a strongly worded statement on its website. This Korean response was not uniform globally. Latin American evangelicals, for instance, express much more ambivalence about same-sex marriage. Nonetheless, backlash in Korea and elsewhere, especially as it was highlighted by American conservatives, was a key reason why World Vision U.S. reversed its decision just days later. Majority World evangelicals—representing complex combinations and variations of authoritarianism, sexual mores, social justice commitments, cultural sensitivity, prosperity gospel sermonizing, and supernatural charisma—simply do not fit the archetypal conservative–progressive binary as it stands in the United States. Christians from abroad hold the potential to shake up established patterns by showing American evangelicals that it is possible to be a Pentecostal social justice warrior.

Second, this book contends that migration and demographic realignments are intensifying the impact of the global reflex. From the shambles of the Korean War, Han helped oversee a missionary force that grew to about 19,000 by the mid-2000s. Han's original Young Nak Presbyterian Church has grown to over 500 Young Nak daughter congregations worldwide. An even larger Asian diaspora has built large churches and shaped university ministries throughout the United States. Global encounters thus continue apace as massive numbers of immigrants from around the world seek to reinvigorate a white American evangelicalism that is in demographic free fall. The current influence of international Christians may seem modest compared with 2045, when demographers project that the United States will become a minority-majority nation. It is possible that support for Donald Trump in the 2010s may be perceived in the 2040s as a last gasp of white Christian Americanism within a profoundly multicultural movement.[11]

Third, this book, despite its narration of important demographic shifts, shows that evangelical cosmopolitanism is not pervasive at present. Its elite representatives stand as an embattled minority that struggles to convince constituents of new insights. While global Christians have opened up a broader range on the cultural, political, and theological spectrum within traditionalist conservative, moderate, progressive, and college-educated sectors, Christian Americanism persists. White Americans remain at the helm of most international initiatives, and even multicultural organizations led by nonwhites are often circumscribed by cultures of whiteness. Most jarring for boosters of multicultural evangelicalism was Trump's political ascendance in 2016. Many white evangelicals—and even some nonwhite evangelicals—cheered the president's jingoistic America-first salvos. The election exposed a conspicuous populist–establishment divide. Indeed, evangelicalism has always been a vast marketplace propelled by populist energies more than top-down structures. A decentralized ecclesiology has rewarded charisma and entrepreneurial activity. A persistent individualism has pushed the laity to defy authority and follow their own instincts. A populist sensibility has encouraged a distrust of the analyses of experts and an elevation of the opinions of rank-and-file believers. As their numbers decline in the twenty-first century, many populist evangelicals feel left out of an America they feel once belonged to them. Despite the efforts of establishment cosmopolitans, populists often resist or tame Majority World encounters that threaten Christian Americanism. The global reflex often stalls when it reaches America's shores.[12]

There are limitations to sweeping global histories that span six continents. American evangelicals and scholarly critics alike often resort to telling single stories of Majority World Christians as either benighted savages or naïve innocents—and of American internationalists as either cold imperialists or compassionate saviors. But globetrotting evangelicals, when understood in the fullness of their contexts and complexities, consistently defy these tropes. Bob Pierce emerges as a compassionate authoritarian who peddled American exceptionalism and practiced a humanitarianism ahead of his time. Likewise, Kyung-Chik Han appears as a Christian nationalist who abetted dictatorial regimes in Korea even as he pioneered programs of social justice. Endless variants of these idiosyncratic figures preach and pray and worship in hundreds of nations around the world. This book, then, is suggestive, not comprehensive. It does not narrate a definitive history of global evangelicalism. Rather, it is a transnational history of American evangelicalism that charts a phenomenon of reflexivity. It considers how encounters in Korea, India, Switzerland, the Philippines, Guatemala, Uganda, and Thailand shape religion in places like Kentucky and California. New narratives emerge when we face West, when we consider that evangelical networks not only go out to, but also come from, the ends of the earth.

Notes

1. Author interview with Jong-Sam Park, Seoul, Korea, May 20, 2014; Kirsty Taylor, "It's Time to Give from Experience," *Korea Herald*, July 13, 2011.
2. Author interview with Hoon Song, Seoul, Korea, May 21, 2014.
3. "Sermon by Dr. Bob Pierce," November 5, 1954, pgs. 2, 23–25, in folder "Admin-Bob Pierce Sermons," World Vision International Archives, Monrovia, Calif.
4. Tite Tiénou, "Christian Scholarship and the Changing Center of World Christianity," in Susan Felch, ed., *Christian Scholarship . . . For What?* (Grand Rapids, Mich.: Calvin College, 2003), 93–94.
5. Thomas Bender, *A Nation among Nations: America's Place in World History* (New York: Hill & Wang, 2006); Ian Tyrrell, *Transnational Nation: United States History in Global Perspective since 1789* (New York: Palgrave, 2007); Luke Clossey and Nicholas Guyatt, "It's a Small World After All: The Wider World in Historians' Peripheral Vision," *Perspectives on History*, May 1, 2013.
6. Critical depictions include William Lederer, *The Ugly American* (New York: Norton, 1958); Barbara Kingsolver, *The Poisonwood Bible* (New York: Harper, 1999); Steve Brouwer, Susan Rose, and Paul Gifford, *Exporting the American Gospel: Global Christian Fundamentalism* (New York: Routledge, 1996); David Stoll, *Is Latin America Turning Protestant?: The Politics of Evangelical Growth* (Berkeley: University of California Press, 1990), xv; Jeff Sharlet, *The Family: The Secret Fundamentalism at the Heart of American Power* (New York: HarperCollins, 2008); Bethany Moreton, "The Soul of Neoliberalism," *Social Text* 25, No. 3 (Fall 2007): 103–23; Soren Hvalkof and Peter Aaby, *Is God an American? An Anthropological Perspective on the Missionary Work of the Summer Institute of Linguistics* (Copenhagen: International WorkGroup for Indigenous Affairs, 1981). For "bridgehead," see Andre Corten and Ruth Marshall-Fratani, *Between Babel and Pentecostalism in Africa and Latin America* (Bloomington: Indiana University Press, 2001), 6. For contrarian arguments that American missionaries reinforced indigenous cultures, sparked democratization, and behaved more civilly than diplomats, armies, engineers, and corporations, see Lamin Sanneh, *Translating the Message: The Missionary Impact on Culture* (Maryknoll, N.Y.: Orbis, 2008); Mark Noll, *From Every Tribe and Nation: A Historian's Discovery of the Global Christian Story* (Grand Rapids, Mich.: Baker Academic, 2014), 8; Robert Woodberry, "The Missionary Roots of Liberal Democracy," *American Political Science Review* 106, No. 2 (March 2012): 244–74.
7. On demographic data, see Todd M. Johnson and Gina A. Zurlo, eds., *World Christian Database* (Leiden/Boston: Brill, accessed May 2018); Todd M. Johnson and Kenneth R. Ross, eds., *Atlas of Global Christianity* (Edinburgh: Edinburgh University Press, 2009). On Yoido Full Gospel Church, see Mark Noll, *The New Shape of World Christianity: How American Experience Reflects Global Faith* (Downers Grove, Ill.: InterVarsity Press, 2009), 20–21. On World Vision Korea, see Haemin Lee, *International Development and Public Religion: Changing Dynamics of Christian Mission in South Korea* (Eugene, Ore.: Pickwick Publications, 2016), 42. On the flowering of Christianity in the postcolonial era, see Lamin Sanneh, *Whose Religion Is*

Christianity?: The Gospel Beyond the West (Grand Rapids, Mich.: Eerdmans, 2006), 18, 35; Jehu Hanciles, *Beyond Christendom: Globalization, African Migration, and the Transformation of the West* (Maryknoll, N.Y.: Orbis Books, 2008), 377. Also see Philip Jenkins, *The Next Christendom: The Coming of Global Christianity* (New York: Oxford University Press, 2002); Dana Robert, *Christian Mission: How Christianity Became a World Religion* (Oxford, UK: Blackwell, 2008); Andrew Walls, *The Missionary Movement in Christian History* (Maryknoll, N.Y.: Orbis, 1996).

8. For a sample of recent scholarship that puts American religion in global perspective, see Paul Freston, *Protestant Political Parties: A Global Survey* (Burlington, Vt.: Ashgate, 2004); Doris Buss and Didi Herman, *Globalizing Family Values: The Christian Right in International Politics* (Minneapolis: University of Minnesota Press, 2003); Erica Bornstein, *The Spirit of Development: Protestant NGOs, Morality, and Economics in Zimbabwe* (Palo Alto, Calif.: Stanford University Press, 2006); David King, *God's Internationalists: World Vision and the Age of Evangelical Humanitarianism* (Philadelphia: University of Pennsylvania Press, 2019); Andrew Preston, *Sword of the Spirit, Shield of Faith: Religion in American War and Diplomacy* (New York: Knopf, 2012); Mark Hutchinson and John Wolffe, *A Short History of Global Evangelicalism* (Cambridge, UK: Cambridge University Press, 2012); Sarah Miller-Davenport, "'Their Blood Shall Not Be Shed in Vain': American Evangelical Missionaries and the Search for God and Country in Post-World War II Asia," *Journal of American History* 99, No. 4 (March 2013): 1109–32; Brian Stanley, *The Global Diffusion of Evangelicalism* (Downers Grove, Ill.: InterVarsity Press, 2013); Emily Conroy-Krutz, *Christian Imperialism: Converting the World in the Early American Republic* (Ithaca, N.Y.: Cornell University Press, 2015); Michael Thompson, *For God and Globe: Christian Internationalism in the United States* (Ithaca, N.Y.: Cornell University Press, 2015); Heather Curtis, *Holy Humanitarians: American Evangelicals and Global Aid* (Cambridge, Mass.: Harvard University Press, 2018); Melani McAlister, *The Kingdom of God Has No Borders: A Global History of American Evangelicalism* (New York: Oxford University Press, 2018); Lauren Turek, *To Bring the Good News to All Nations: Evangelical Influence on Human Rights and U.S. Foreign Relations* (Ithaca, NY: Cornell University Press, 2020).

9. On the "global turn" and reflexivity, see Daniel Rodgers, *Atlantic Crossings: Social Politics in a Progressive Age* (Cambridge, Mass.: Harvard University Press, 1998); Mary Dudziak, *Cold War Civil Rights: Race and the Image of American Democracy* (Princeton, N.J.: Princeton University Press, 2000); Thomas Borstelmann, *The Cold War and the Color Line: American Race Relations in the Global Arena* (Cambridge, Mass.: Harvard University Press, 2001); Amy Kaplan, *The Anarchy of Empire in the Making of U.S. Culture* (Cambridge, Mass.: Harvard University Press, 2002); Kristin L. Hoganson, *Consumers' Imperium: The Global Production of American Domesticity, 1865–1920* (Chapel Hill: University of North Carolina Press, 2007); Andrew Preston and Doug Rossinow, *Outside In: The Transnational Circuitry of U.S. History* (New York: Oxford University Press, 2016). For numbers on the shrinking globe, see Robert Wuthnow, *Boundless Faith: The Global Outreach of American Churches* (Berkeley: University of California Press, 2009), 3–4.

For the beginnings of a historiography on how global encounters have shaped American religion, see Jane Hunter, *Gospel of Gentility: American Women Missionaries in Turn-of-the-Century China* (New Haven, Conn: Yale University Press, 1984); Patricia R. Hill, *The World Their Household: The American Women's Foreign Mission Movement and Cultural Transformation, 1870–1920* (Ann Arbor: University of Michigan Press, 1985); Daniel H. Bays and Grant Wacker, eds., *The Foreign Missionary Enterprise at Home: Explorations in North American Cultural History* (Tuscaloosa: University of Alabama Press, 2003); Thomas Oden, *How Africa Shaped the Christian Mind: Rediscovering the Seedbed of Western Christianity* (Downers Grove, Ill.: InterVarsity Press, 2010); Jay Case, *An Unpredictable Gospel: American Evangelicals and Global Christianity* (New York: Oxford University Press, 2012); David Hollinger, *Protestants Abroad: How Missionaries Tried to Change the World but Changed America* (Princeton, N.J.: Princeton University Press, 2017).

10. On how evangelical politics is "not usually dogmatically neoliberal, as the American right would like," see Paul Freston, *Evangelicals and Politics in Asia, Africa, and Latin America* (Cambridge, UK: Cambridge University Press, 2001), 293. On global economic inequalities, see Neil Ormerod and Shane Clifton, *Globalization and the Mission of the Church* (London: T&T Clark, 2009), 50.

11. On the burgeoning numbers of Korean missionaries, see Jehu Hanciles, "Transformations within Global Christianity and the Western Missionary Enterprise," *Mission Focus* 14 (2006): 8.

12. Robert P. Jones, *The End of White Christian America* (New York: Simon & Schuster, 2016); Kay Higuera Smith, Jayachitra Lalitha, and Daniel Hawk, eds., *Evangelical Postcolonial Conversations* (Downers Grove, Ill.: InterVarsity Press, 2014).

PART I
CHRISTIAN AMERICANISM

1

Chicago 1945

Youth for Christ and World War II

Either communism must die or Christianity must die.

—Billy Graham[1]

The crowd was in a celebratory mood. On Memorial Day 1945, only three weeks after victory over Germany and three months before an anticipated victory over Japan, 75,000 people gathered in Chicago for a religious event that boiled over with patriotic fervor (Figure 1.1). Attendees sang the national anthem. The United States Marine Color Guard marched through Soldier Field and posted American flags around the stadium. Lieutenant Robert Evans of the U.S. Navy appealed to the crowd to buy war bonds. The throng sang "Anchors Aweigh," "The Marine's Hymn," and "Army Air Corps." Everything about the moment suggested the successful prosecution of a messianic mission. Americans were freeing the world from Japanese totalitarianism, German Nazism, and Italian fascism.[2]

But now another threat loomed. The Soviet Union, though still an ally in World War II, was ruled by an atheistic Marxist ideology that threatened free enterprise and Christian faith. The fifty entrepreneurs who funded the Soldier Field rally called themselves "The Business World Committee." They manufactured glass, roofing supplies, insulation, and appliances—and they preached against centrally planned economies. The New Deal, many had been declaring for over a decade, was veering too close to socialism. To some of them, President Franklin Roosevelt represented the Marxist threat at home. For Herbert Taylor, president of Club Aluminum and a speaker at the rally, true citizenship meant integrity, entrepreneurship, and freedom for the world's peoples, especially those in the iron grip of totalitarianism.

On this Memorial Day in Chicago, freeing people and enterprise from totalitarianism was inextricably linked to Christian faith. Youth for Christ (YFC), an important evangelical organization still in its infancy, had organized the rally. The patriotic homages were sacralized by an hour-long pageant paying tribute to a different set of conquering heroes: American missionaries. Their locations—China, India, Russia, Mexico, Africa, and the United States—would become critical sites in the emerging Cold War. Billy Graham, still relatively unknown,

Facing West. David R. Swartz, Oxford University Press (2020). © Oxford University Press.
DOI: 10.1093/oso/9780190250805.001.0001

Figure 1.1. 75,000 people attended the 1945 Memorial Day rally at Soldier Field that combined patriotism and evangelistic fervor. In this scene, nurses created a "living" cross that marched across Soldier Field. Courtesy of the Billy Graham Center Archives, Wheaton, Ill.

joined in as attendees in the stadium tenderly sang "Just As I Am," followed by a triumphant rendition of "All Hail the Power of Jesus' Name." Then the spotlight was thrown on the American and Christian flags as a deep bass voice sang "God Bless Our Boys." Celestial and worldly symbols blended in a striking pageant of tanks, planes, jeeps, three white crosses, and an enormous neon sign that blazed "Jesus Saves." The perimeter featured angelic figures blowing golden trumpets upon the colonnades of Soldier Field. These apocalyptic images from the Book of Revelation inspired hundreds to make "decisions for Christ." Many more pledged to carry the "good news" of the Gospel to the ends of the earth. "Where He Leads," one of the closing hymns intoned, "I Will Follow."[3]

The three-hour display ended with a dramatic rehearsal of the great commission to go forth and make disciples of all nations. The stadium lights were extinguished, except for a piercing beacon light on an elevated lighthouse at the center of the field. As a choir of 5,000 youth sang "We Shall Shine as the Stars in the Morning," the lone light slowly swept the stands, illuminating tens of thousands of evangelicals eager to share their revived faith. As the lights flickered back on to deafening applause, these youths were released to free souls, people, and enterprise around the world in the service of Christian Americanism.[4]

I. Narrating a New Evangelicalism

The white men who engineered the spectacle in Chicago called themselves "new evangelicals." To be sure, there was much about them that was not new at all. Since D. L. Moody's turn toward respectability in the late nineteenth century, conservative evangelicals had consistently emphasized evangelism, theological orthodoxy, and cross-denominational fellowship. They also sought to engage broader society. In the first decades of the twentieth century, writes historian Timothy Gloege, they helped develop new business practices associated with modern consumer capitalism. In the 1920s and 1930s, Aimee Semple McPherson, a preacher in Los Angeles, built a media empire using spellbinding pageantry that rivaled the spectacle in Chicago. In 1936 evangelist Charles Fuller signed an agreement with Mutual Broadcasting and was soon delivering on-air sermons to tens of millions coast to coast. The new evangelicals were continuing a long tradition of creating and distributing culturally relevant religious content. But in the wake of World War II, as they sought to expand the coalition of theological conservatives, they began to tell a new story. Wanting to distinguish themselves from subversive isolationists, hard-edged populists, and marginal fundamentalists whom they found embarrassing, Herbert Taylor and Billy Graham announced that they were launching an innovative religious movement, one suited for the modern age.[5]

World War II gave them a strong start. As historian Matthew Sutton puts it, the war "provided an opportunity for redemption" and a chance to "reform their nation along godly lines." In a Saturday evening sermon at Orchestra Hall in Chicago held two weeks after the Memorial Day rally, Youth for Christ founder Torrey Johnson framed the new movement around its theological and ecclesiastical location. First, he rejected religious liberalism, connecting what he saw as a theological scourge to the atrocities of Nazism. "I know what higher criticism can do. . . . Germany today is in disgrace—a nation that has rejected the Word of God and has turned its back upon Jesus Christ." It has "brought about Dachau and Buchenwald, and the concentration camps of the present day." Liberals do not preach the Gospel of Jesus Christ, he suggested, and consequently cannot change the world for the good.[6]

Second, Johnson urged the new evangelicals to keep their distance from separatist fundamentalism. When asked by a *Time* magazine reporter about the anti-Semitic evangelist Gerald Winrod of Wichita, Kansas, Johnson said he did not know the man—and most definitely did not approve of his views. Moreover, Johnson felt that the efforts of fundamentalists to preserve doctrinal purity too often turned into petty narcissism. He instead envisioned a movement that would transcend denominations. "I believe that God has raised up Youth for Christ," he declared at Orchestra Hall, "to bring together churches and people who otherwise couldn't get together." For Johnson, one thing was paramount: the spread of the Gospel. Speaking to the hundreds of soldiers in the crowd, he said, "You fellows KNOW more than any other people in the world, that the Gospel of Jesus Christ is THE THING; It's the ONLY THING; it's the thing that has brought all of the blessings of Western Civilization to us." "In these days that lie ahead," he continued, "as we penetrate every part of the English world and as we ask God to give us the spirit of cooperation and good-will with churches, schools, and leaders here and there, we must press the battle on the Mission Field." Youth for Christ, according to historian Joel Carpenter, "became the spearhead of a postwar evangelistic thrust and the first dramatic sign that evangelicals were 'coming in from the cold.'" Avoiding what they understood to be the extremes of fundamentalism and liberalism, the planners of the Soldier Field rally sought to build a broad coalition that would spread the Gospel.[7]

To do so, they used language the world could understand. Torrey Johnson might be the pastor of Midwest Bible Church, but he was not a "conventional minister," reported the *Chicago Tribune*. "He wears light-colored, dapper clothes and even sometimes a Sinatra bow tie." His conversational style was breezy. Intrigued that young people actually were flocking to a religious event, the *Tribune* dubbed the crowd the "bobby sox brigade." Johnson's production included Rose Arzoomanian, a soprano soloist who won a national singing contest on the CBS radio program *Hour of Charm*. He recruited Gil Dodds, a runner known as the "Flying Parson" who held the world record for the indoor mile. Porter Barrington, pastor of the First Baptist Church of Hollywood, told *Newsweek* that "the [Soldier Field] spectacle out-colossaled the movies." Johnson downplayed the pageant, saying that American youth wanted to go beyond "boogie-woogie and jitterbugging—they want something that is REAL!" But Youth for Christ's savvy marketers clearly anticipated the cultural mood of a war-weary and entertainment-starved nation ready for a victory party replete with tanks, athletic displays, neon signs, and flags. Promotional materials in the *Tribune* and on WGN radio proclaimed the new methodology: "Geared to the Times, Anchored to the Rock." In contrast to what they characterized as the culture-rejecting posture of fundamentalism, these evangelicals embraced the neon.[8]

Public institutions reciprocated. As the Memorial Day rally approached, Torrey Johnson was inundated with enthusiastic telegrams. Illinois governor Dwight Green and Chicago mayor Edward Kelly pledged their support. Four years before he would instruct his newspapers to "puff Graham," the publisher Randolph Hearst sent telegrams to his twenty-two newspapers, telling them to cover Youth for Christ. "Don't just write one or two articles," he wrote. Print articles "continually" with "illustrated accounts of what occurred." Youth for Christ's work was "commendable and in every way desirable," in part because "it will be one of the most valuable influences in overcoming juvenile delinquency." Johnson's efforts enjoyed widespread civic support in Chicago.[9]

The new evangelicalism, as it angled for relevance and influence, understood itself as fully participating in the "American Century." Henry Luce, a publishing mogul and the founding editor of *Time*, *Sports Illustrated*, *Fortune*, and *Life* magazines, popularized the phrase in 1941. Making a case for American entry into World War II, Luce argued for a recovery of America's historic ambitions. Earlier centuries had "teemed with manifold projects and magnificent purposes." As Europe disintegrated and with the Pacific under attack, America stood ready. "We must undertake now to be the Good Samaritan of the entire world," he wrote, exerting "the full impact of our influence, for such purposes as we see fit and by such means as we see fit." Luce, who grew up the son of missionaries in China, predicted that this extension of manifest destiny would result in "the first great American Century." Biographer Alan Brinkley described Luce's vision as "an almost evangelical commitment to righting the wrongs of the world." Evangelicals themselves, in a 1958 report in *Christianity Today*, crowed that they comprised 39 percent of Protestant ministers, outranking all comers, including fundamentalists (35 percent), liberal (14 percent), and neo-orthodox (12 percent). Seeing themselves as guardians of America's spiritual vision and extenders of liberty and Christian faith, evangelicals affirmed Luce's nationalistic vision.[10]

The most important evangelical institutions helped plan and execute the Soldier Field rally. They included Moody Bible Institute (sometimes called the "West Point of Christian Service"), Wheaton College (sometimes called the "Harvard of evangelicalism"), and the Salvation Army. Eventually superseding them all was a young minister at First Baptist Church in suburban Western Springs, Illinois. Billy Graham impressed observers with "fire and such exuberance and fidelity to preaching the Word of God" that he was recruited to preach at Youth for Christ's first rally in 1944. He became Youth for Christ's first full-time staff member the following year. Four years after that, Henry Luce attended a Graham crusade in Columbia, South Carolina. Thereafter, the mogul threw the full weight of his publishing empire behind the young all-American evangelist who viewed the nation in similarly providential and redemptive ways. After Luce's endorsement, writes William Martin, "Billy could go wherever he wanted and set his own terms." But in 1945, a still-unknown evangelist stood at Soldier Field. Youth for Christ was Graham's institutional home before he became an institution himself.[11]

Other soon-to-be evangelical icons were at Soldier Field too. Recent Wheaton graduate Carl F. H. Henry, who soon would publish *The Uneasy Conscience of*

Modern Fundamentalism (1947), served as publicity director for the event. He went on to teach at Fuller Theological Seminary and serve as the first editor of *Christianity Today*, an evangelical standard that almost immediately outpaced rival *Christian Century* in its reach. Also present at the rally was Charles Fuller, a radio evangelist and eponymous founder of the premier evangelical seminary. In fact, Fuller was the main speaker at a reprise of the Memorial Day rally a year later. Robert Cook, a Chicago-area pastor and brother-in-law of Torrey Johnson, served on the advisory council of Youth for Christ in the mid-1940s and then succeeded Johnson as president. Later he became president of the National Association of Evangelicals (NAE). Bob Pierce, a minister in the Los Angeles branch of Youth for Christ, also attended the Chicago rally. He would go on to lead evangelistic tours of China and Korea and cofound the humanitarian organization World Vision. The rally's full-throated Christian Americanism was voiced by a new generation of emerging men who would populate the highest levels of the movement.[12]

They also sought to populate the highest levels of a nation they viewed as once belonging to them. Building evangelical institutions to compete with secular institutions, locating *Christianity Today* just down the street from the White House, and conducting crusades in the heart of liberal cities such as Los Angeles and New York City reflected the bold aspirations of this movement. In fact, Boston pastor Harold Ockenga's first presidential address as head of the NAE rivaled the grandiosity of Henry Luce's "American Century" speech. The new organization, he declared, "is the only hopeful sign on the horizon of Christian history today. If we who are gathered here meet our responsibility this week it may well be that the oblique rays of the sun are not the rusty red of its setting but are the golden rays of its rising for a new era." American successes in World War II, coupled with the threats of an emerging Cold War, emboldened these evangelicals to accelerate an ambitious global vision that emphasized liberty. It sought to free people from authoritarian tyranny, to free markets from Marxism, and to free souls from hell.[13]

II. Spiritual Liberty

It was spiritual liberation that most animated the new evangelical project. At their core, these conservative Christians were supernaturalists motivated by a desire to tell non-Christians about the one true God. This notion of Christian expansion lay at the heart of the momentous 1910 Edinburgh World Missionary Conference. Suffused with military metaphors and motivated by a sense of global need, the Edinburgh conference struck a notably aggressive and exclusive tone. Only Jesus, not Muhammad, could save lost souls. The Western Church, intoned

John Mott, author of *The Evangelization of the World in This Generation* (1900), needed to "deliberately and resolutely attack some of these hitherto almost impregnable fortresses" in the Middle East and Asia with the truth of the Gospel. The 1,216 delegates anticipated that "the world was on the eve of a new transfiguration destined to inaugurate the kingdom of God in its fullness."[14]

This golden age of missionary work soon diminished. The Student Volunteer Movement (SVM), founded by Mott and others closely associated with the Edinburgh conference, rapidly declined. The massive conflict between Christian nations in World War I annihilated fifteen million soldiers and birthed a new mood of cynicism and secularism. War crippled the missionary enterprise, notes historian Nathan Showalter, and the number of SVM student missionaries dropped precipitously from a high of 2,700 students to 252 by 1928. Between wars, economies collapsed, and spending on missions by all North American Protestants fell from $6.9 million in 1929 to $4.5 million in 1936. After several decades of evangelistic stagnation, the new evangelicals were poised to reinvigorate the missionary enterprise.[15]

While they simplistically blamed liberals for the decline, there was something to their critique. Mainliners were moving away from forthright evangelization to a program of spreading "American civilization." The 1932 publication *Re-Thinking Missions*, for example, reflected a profound mainline ambivalence over missionary work. William Hocking, who wrote the first four chapters of the book, emphasized religious cooperation, avoided "any definite Christological propositions," and questioned "the unique deity of Jesus Christ." Hocking was much more concerned about the threat of secularism than the challenge of other religions, and he urged missionaries "to seek with people of other lands a true knowledge and love of God, expressing in life and word what we have learned through Jesus Christ, and endeavoring to give effect to his spirit in the life of the world." *Re-Thinking Missions*, in stressing ecumenical unity over exclusivity, challenged evangelical certitudes. According to historian Timothy Yates, it emphasized how "Christian, Buddhist, Hindu and Confucianist could open to one another the treasures of their discoveries, so mutually advancing in truth and authenticity." The innovative publication did not emphasize the cross, the atonement, the resurrection, or the Holy Spirit.[16]

In response, Charles Trumbull, the Presbyterian editor of the *Sunday School Times*, bemoaned "our Modernistic Mission Board." In the wake of *Re-Thinking Missions*, he and other evangelicals denounced mainline ambivalence and set out to reinvigorate American missions. Some, like the Methodist missionary E. Stanley Jones who maintained that the gospel really was unique and that Gandhi really needed to be converted, worked from within mainline denominations. These institutions, however, were sometimes hostile to evangelistic efforts. Liberal parent organizations such as the World Sunday School

Association, for example, refused to fund the more conservative Sunday School Union. Wanting to conserve the missionary spirit and traditional doctrine of the Edinburgh Conference, many conversionist-oriented mainliners increasingly withdrew to establish their own "faith missions." Fifty-six new agencies were established between 1918 and 1945. They thrived immediately. Numbers of missionaries within the Sudan Interior Mission increased from forty-four to 494 between 1920 and 1945, and income rose from $29,000 to $388,000 between 1917 and 1941. Eventually, many of them banded together to form the Interdenominational Foreign Missions Association (IFMA) and the Evangelical Foreign Mission Association (EFMA). This missionary work, though it burgeoned in terms of money, communication, and organizational structures, was not rooted in rigorous theological reflection. In 1945, the year of the Soldier Field rally and the founding of EFMA, it did not seem necessary. According to one practitioner, "The strategy amounted to one major command of Jesus to his disciples: Go!"[17]

The sermons of evangelical titan Harold Ockenga drove this evangelistic impulse. He organized a week-long annual conference with over fifty missionary speakers. In the spring of 1946, the conference raised $75,000. A year later at the inaugural address of the founding of Fuller Theological Seminary, Ockenga declared his unrelenting focus on missions. Ockenga preached, "The Lord Jesus laid down His program, and the trouble with so many of us is that we don't follow His program. Here it is in all of its simplicity. He placed missions first. . . . We must have hearts full of passion and zeal, that are on fire for Jesus Christ to win souls." A premillennial eschatology, which suggested that the apocalypse was at hand, underlay the zeal. Souls urgently needed to be saved, and it seemed possible to Ockenga and his colleagues, according to historian Dana Robert, that "their generation would be the one to preach the gospel from one end of the world to another."[18]

The pageant at Soldier Field reflected this postwar surge. The headquarters of Youth for Christ, an affiliate of EFMA, featured a world map with this challenge: "Go ye into all the world and preach the Gospel to every creature." The organization even deployed "invasion teams" for half-year mission tours of the world. Torrey Johnson, Youth for Christ's organizer, preached, "By the Grace of God we'll see to it, if it is humanly possible, to bring the Gospel of Jesus Christ to the ends of the earth, until the last one shall have heard, everyone shall have had an opportunity, and those souls for whom Jesus died shall have come weeping their way to the Foot of the Cross of Calvary." At the altar call of this rally, several hundred committed themselves to Christ and to the missionary task. Indeed, Youth for Christ produced the "greatest generation of missionary recruits in the history of the church," writes Joel Carpenter. Between 1952 and 1960, according to missiologist Scott Moreau, the number of evangelical missionaries increased by nearly 150 percent. Mainline missionaries, by contrast, grew by only 4.5 percent in this period before dropping precipitously from 8,279 to 4,817 between 1969 and 1979 as fewer enlisted and as many deserted to evangelical agencies. As historian Grant Wacker notes, the ideas of Hocking in *Re-Thinking Missions* "may have resonated in the walnut-paneled classrooms of the old-line seminaries, but they played wretchedly in Peoria." By the 1980s over 30,000 evangelicals, hoping to save millions from their sins, had taken over the missionary enterprise.[19]

III. Political Liberty

Evangelistic ambitions took on geopolitical import as soldiers and missionaries encountered hostile regimes around the world. Having just defeated Germany, Italy, and Japan, American evangelicals in the 1950s bumped up against the red tide of communism in Latin America, Africa, and Asia. Political and economic systems mattered, even if only to preserve space for conversions. Christian anticommunists sought to free bodies as well as souls.

This ramped-up dedication to global responsibility was not without misgivings. Some worried about the corrupting influences of war. After visiting occupation forces in Europe in 1947, Ockenga and a delegation of American clergy returned aghast at the moral laxity of the military. They had learned about venereal disease, drunkenness, vulgarity, pornography, and black market trading in the ranks. Out from under the moral care of their congregations, increasing numbers of young people were being exposed to unholy living. Others condemned what they called "the militarization of the nation in peacetime." The NAE publication *United Evangelical Action* declared that the Universal Military Training and Service Act, passed in 1951, was "capitalizing on the anxieties of the present world crisis to introduce a system of militarism strangely like those inflicted upon the people in the Old World." In the end, though, evangelicals conceded the need for national defense. They determined that the military had done good work in defeating the Nazis and fascists, and returning soldiers were greeted as conquering heroes. The immoral behavior of soldiers, while troubling, could be fixed by chaplains offering spiritual instruction. In fact, the NAE pursued chaplaincy with vigor, and Ockenga was appointed as chairman of the Commission for Army and Navy Chaplaincies.[20]

Robert Evans, who served as a chaplain in the navy, exemplified evangelical global obligations. A child of missionaries and a graduate of Wheaton College, he was wounded in the D-Day invasion at Normandy. After the war, Evans served as a Youth for Christ executive secretary. At the Soldier Field rally, he sold war bonds—more, according to one booster, "than at any other large meeting in the history of the United States." Evans went on to become a Youth for Christ missionary to Europe in the 1950s and then the founder of Greater Europe Mission. For those who saw the United States as a God-ordained bulwark against the forces of darkness, Evans's wartime bravery and piety modeled evangelicals' twin aims of political and spiritual freedom. In a *Moody Monthly* article, a Baptist minister in Washington, D.C., intoned, "Oppressed peoples around the earth have come to look upon America and its ideals as a hope for civilization." Christian America should operate as a "moral and spiritual leader in world affairs."[21]

Billy Graham lifted this already-soaring nationalistic rhetoric to new heights. His emergence coincided with the first frightening years of anxiety over Soviet aggression. According to biographer Steven Miller, Graham was "the quintessential Cold War revivalist. From the very beginning of postwar tensions with the Soviet Union, he linked his evangelism to the destiny of the United States and its leaders." At a 1947 "Christ for This Crisis" crusade in Charlotte, North Carolina, Graham preached sermons entitled "The End of the World" and "Will God Spare America?" He declared that communism was "Satan's religion," a "great anti-Christian movement." In 1952 Graham mailed the book *Communism and Christ* to every member of Congress and to the presidential cabinet. Communism, it delineated, had its very own trinity: "Marx the Lawgiver, Lenin the Incarnate Truth, Stalin the Guide and Comforter." At a 1954 crusade in London, Graham distributed calendars that read, "What Hitler's bombs could not do, socialism with its accompanying evils shortly accomplished." Graham later said it was a misprint—that it should have read "secularism"—but the text did accurately reflect the evangelist's hawkish sensibilities in the early years of his career.[22]

As Graham and others sought to stop the red tide, they scrupulously analyzed global headlines for "signs of the times." In major periodicals such as *Moody Monthly*, the *Sunday School Times*, and the *Pentecostal Evangel*, coverage increasingly extended beyond devotional writings and missionary activity to politics. The Cold War in particular, historian Mark Noll points out, became "a major fixation." Articles railing against "Marxist materialism" appeared regularly in the early years of the postwar era. In *Christianity Today*, read by hundreds of thousands, prominent politicians bemoaned communist expansion and antidemocratic policies. In its pages FBI Director J. Edgar Hoover and Walter Judd, a former missionary and Republican congressman from Nebraska, lamented the West's failure of nerve in the Suez crisis. The NAE's *United Evangelical Action* newsletter carefully observed developments in China and the Soviet Union, condemning Marxist atrocities of religious and political persecution. "When

God is out," explained one representative article, the "tragic sequel is Bureaucracy, Dictatorship and Regimentation. Then the individual exists for the State and not the State for the individual." Evangelical publishers advertised countless books with titles such as *Communism: Its Faith and Fallacies* (1962), *How to Fight Communism Today* (1962), and *Know Your Enemy: Communism* (1961). A popular Vacation Bible School curriculum produced by Scripture Press in Wheaton, Illinois, boasted that it could make "our youth . . . strong in the Lord and the power of His might." "Our answer to Khrushchev," the ad copy read, "is Patriots for Christ for '62 VBS." This felt urgency was rooted in fear that Marxists might win out in Western Europe as France, Britain, and Italy struggled to recover from the devastation of World War II.[23]

In the immediate postwar years, then, evangelicals set out to save Europe all over again. Youth for Christ's Torrey Johnson wired a German pastor, "If Germany goes communistic, then you can write France, Italy, Spain, and Portugal off. . . . and you can shove England down the road of socialism." Hoping that spiritual conversion could fend off communist incursions, Youth for Christ sent dozens of its "invasion teams" to Great Britain, Scandinavia, France, the Netherlands, Germany, Greece, and Italy; the Caribbean and South America; and India and China. These touring evangelists, alongside a relief program launched by the nascent NAE, essentially functioned as spiritual relief workers supporting an evangelical Marshall Plan to save susceptible nations. General Douglas MacArthur encouraged the partnership. He invited Youth for Christ and Southern Baptist evangelists to come to Japan to "provide the surest foundation for the firm establishment of democracy."[24]

The war for democracy offered inspiration and resources for evangelism. At a 1945 conference in Winona Lake, Indiana, Merv Rosell argued that the intensity of warfare should be similarly utilized by missionaries. He preached, "Just as 'men expect to win a great war in one generation' and spare no expense in doing so, so we could make the gospel available to every human being in the world in our generation. There are days ahead when youth will conquer for Christ . . . even though the triumph may cost blood . . . and taste the sweetness of world-wide victory!" He ended by challenging his congregation to participate in "God's global 'Go,' Christian conquest, and God's 'gigantic world plan.'" Another minister, Robert Hall Glover, suggested that World War II "furnishes an exact parallel to the missionary enterprise. As we provide munitions and supplies to our soldiers, so must we do in the missionary enterprise that 'is another conflict, on a world-wide scale.'" The martial language and strategies learned from World War II could be applied to the spiritual realm.[25]

When Chicago-area churchgoers converged on Soldier Field in 1945, their dramatic display of Christian Americanism represented a deep and broad impulse. In a patriotic segment that lasted over an hour, "Taps" was played, and

Boy Scouts placed a wreath in memory of "those who have given their lives in all the wars of the United States." Tributes were offered to Army Lieutenant Colonel Stoll, who participated in the first wave of the New Guinea invasion in World War II, and to Robert Nelson, vice-president of the ARMA Corporation, which employed 8,000 people to build precision equipment for the Navy. The crowd sang the national anthem, followed by the "Battle Hymn of the Republic." Reserve Officers' Training Corps (ROTC) units from local high schools and a Marine color guard posted American flags around the stadium. Prayers were said for the armed forces, and the audience was implored to purchase war bonds. A patriotic defense of American democracy was central to the evangelical project at mid-century.[26]

IV. Economic Liberty

Efforts to free souls and bodies were accompanied by attempts to free markets from central control. The capitalistic impulse was not always the default position. In the late nineteenth and early twentieth centuries, Jeffersonian evangelicals were concerned about concentrations of wealth and power, and southern and western populists fulminated against big business as much as big government. Continuing into the Great Depression, some activists, according to historian Darren Dochuk, "combined calls for Christian revival and morality with a critique of capitalism and economic injustice." The coming of the Cold War, however, dampened these critiques and tightened the alliance between religious conservatism and capitalism. Evangelicals linked Marxism to atheism, and they tied Christian faith to American free enterprise. In the 1930s some began to describe the New Deal as a communistic incursion. Auto parts dealer George Pepperdine, fueled by his commitment to Christ and capitalism, even started his own college, rooting it in opposition to socialism. Organizations like the Business Men's Evangelistic Clubs and Christian Business Men's Committee International, according to Sarah Hammond, further tried "to steer the masses to Christ and free enterprise from the top down." The success of World War II and the missionary surge of the postwar years seemed to offer evangelicals an opportunity to spread the gospel of economic liberty.[27]

Herbert Taylor, another key organizer of the Soldier Field rally, embodied this entrepreneurial spirit. Concerned that liberal ministers in Chicago were not preaching "a real gospel message," yet criticized by fundamentalists for being "a Methodist do-gooder" and "not sufficiently a Bible-banger," Taylor traversed the middle path of the evangelical movement. A veteran of the Navy, he helped distribute food and water in France, and when the war concluded, he was offered two jobs: a ministry position with the YMCA or a sales job with the Sinclair Oil

Company. Taylor chose business. He explained, "God presented me with a plan, his particular plan for me." The plan called for making a fortune by the age of forty-five, then donating his time and money to ministry.[28]

This is precisely what happened. In Oklahoma Taylor thrived as a lease broker in the oilfields, as an insurance salesman, and as a real estate broker. The *Daily Oklahoman* called him "Sign-'em-up Taylor" for his efforts in spearheading a drive for paved roads in the county. Taylor then moved to Chicago, where he worked way up the corporate ladder to the vice presidency of the Jewel Tea Company, one of the largest direct-sales tea companies in the United States. He then took over Club Aluminum Products, which sold high-end cookware, and rescued the company from bankruptcy in the bleak years of the Great Depression. His command of debt restructuring and the new method of direct sales to department stores and grocery chains proved wildly successful. The young CEO saved 250 jobs and canceled Club Aluminum's $400,000 debt within five years.[29]

Taylor credited his management style and disciplined workforce. He sought to cultivate good character and good products by asking a series of questions whenever presented with a proposal: Is it the truth? Is it fair to all concerned? Will it build goodwill and better friendships? Will it be beneficial to all concerned? He dubbed these questions the "Four-Way Test." Citing Jeremiah 9:23–24, he explained that the test was a way of "pointing people to God and to a responsible, satisfying way of life." It promoted eternal values of honesty and faith. According to his biographer, the test was "a visible symbol permeating every nook and cranny of the company." It appeared in annual reports to stockholders, on the backs of salesmen's calling cards, and as car window stickers. Employees were required to memorize and recite it. It worked so well that national and international levels of the Rotary Club adopted the test in the 1950s as its organizing principle and mantra. Taylor, rewarded handsomely for his managerial and entrepreneurial genius, accumulated—and gave away—fantastic amounts of personal wealth. As an indication of his prominence and influence, *Newsweek* magazine featured Taylor on its cover in 1955.[30]

Corporate paternalism required as much of the corporation as of the workers. Taylor sought direct contact with his employees in order to learn their frustrations and desires. He incentivized ingenuity, high character, and service with profitsharing. In fact, stockholders sometimes criticized Taylor for being more generous with employees than themselves. To be sure, Taylor opposed labor unions on principle, but he nevertheless made contributions to the welfare funds of unions. Taylor and other evangelical industrialists saw themselves as bridging the gap between management and labor. The National Association of Evangelicals called this important task "industrial chaplaincy." In an age of bitterly antagonistic labor battles, its Commission on Industrial Chaplaincy suggested that employer generosity could eliminate tension between

Figure 1.2. Herbert Taylor, who helped fund and organize the Memorial Day rally, was president of Club Aluminum and Rotary International. He also served on the executive board of the National Association of Evangelicals. He is seated on the far left at this meeting of the NAE in the late 1940s. Courtesy of the Billy Graham Center Archives, Wheaton, Ill.

management and labor by balancing pastoral care and free-market principles. One of its early brochures pictured a Bible beaming warm rays over a factory full of workers. The image—as theological as it was social and economic—included the CEO as a benevolent godlike figure who showered fair and attentive interest on the lowliest assembly line worker. Sin was depicted as a group of humans on strike against God. As historian Sarah Hammond recounts, "Evangelical businessmen believed, with no sense of contradiction, that God's grace was unearned, yet a sign of virtue; spiritual, yet manifested in money; everlasting, yet easily lost; a joy, yet a yoke to bear. The 'man of leadership' could never stop working for God, lest he fall from grace." Industrial chaplaincy could reconcile warring parties and transform the hard edges of capitalism into a benevolent and prosperous system of free enterprise.[31]

The paternalistic energies of God's businessmen extended beyond the corporation. Taylor launched community service projects on the deprived Near North

Side of Chicago. He served bread and soup at a storefront mission and claimed to have reduced recidivism 40 percent by placing delinquents in Rotary homes. At the age of forty-seven, Taylor set up a major philanthropic organization called the Christian Workers Foundation (CWF). Funded through the sale of 25 percent of Club Aluminum's stock, the CWF contributed to hundreds of evangelical organizations including InterVarsity Christian Fellowship, Young Life, Christian Service Brigade, Child Evangelism Fellowship, and Fuller Theological Seminary. Taylor provided significant outlays at first and then tried to wean them from dependency. He was on forty-five boards and committees during his life, including service as the founding treasurer of the NAE, which he organized to function like a modern corporation. Taylor's entrepreneurial vision, which emphasized individualistic, ground-level solutions to social problems above government solutions, sought to serve the twin mandates of profit and paternalism.[32]

Taylor's economic philosophy fell outside the mid-century liberal consensus. Excepting military buildups, most evangelicals opposed government activism. To philanthropists George Pepperdine and R. G. LeTourneau, owner of an earthmoving company, the New Deal was a "most benevolent dictatorship . . . but a dictatorship it is, all the more impressive in that it has been forced upon a great nation, not by the force of arms, but by the force of circumstances." Harold J. Ockenga condemned Roosevelt's "managerial revolution" as one cause of the "break-up of the moral fiber of the nation." Taylor, who made small but regular donations to Republican candidates, joined in these critiques. As such, Taylor and his capitalist colleagues were important members of an emerging coalition of Wheaton and Moody evangelicals from the North and a growing demographic from the Sunbelt. Together they added to a broader conservative coalition that included Ayn Randian libertarians, small-government Hayekians, and anti-Keynesian economists. Taylor was not a political activist himself, and he demonstrated a willingness to support centralized structures in times of national emergency such as depression and war. As a general principle, however, he sought to spread the gospel of spiritual, political, and economic liberty through the nation and the world.[33]

Taylor's behind-the-scenes role in the NAE underscored the significance of business and free enterprise to the new evangelical project. Responsive to market forces, Taylor's Club Aluminum sponsored "Club Time" broadcasts on ABC. Soloist George Beverly Shea starred, leading hymns and Scripture readings to impressive radio ratings. Taylor's role at the Soldier Field event was likewise simultaneously obscure and significant. The flashier Torrey Johnson headlined the event, but Taylor led the committee that financed it. Programs for the rally noted that Taylor, President of the Club Aluminum Corporation of America, had been "in full charge of the U.S. Government aluminum program after the outbreak of World War II." They also thanked dozens of other Christian businessmen: Philip

Benson, President of the Dime Savings Bank of Brooklyn; William Erny, a Chicago paper box manufacturer; Carl Gunderson, a Chicago construction contractor and leader of the Christian Business Men's Committee; Freelin Carlton, manager of the Sears department store on State Street; and Cornelius Ulrich, director of the Central Broadcasting Agency in Chicago. They gave money, arranged for marketing, organized the event, and served as ushers. These businessmen embodied the evangelical testimony for Christ and capitalism.[34]

The extravaganza at Soldier Field launched a far-flung movement. In the months that followed, Youth for Christ produced similar events in New York, Seattle, Philadelphia, Washington, St. Louis, and Minneapolis. Over the next several years, its evangelists fanned out to nearly fifty countries. By the late 1940s, regular meetings were being held in thousands of towns and cities with an estimated weekly attendance of one million people. They were highly orchestrated, sophisticated events produced for radio and presided over by young, cool preachers. Each of the gatherings reflected the most salient characteristics of postwar American evangelicalism: piety, missionary work, cultural relevance, business, anticommunism, and patriotism. Many other organizations, including the Far Eastern Gospel Crusade, Frank Vereidi's International Committee on Christian Leadership, and the National Prayer Breakfast, pursued the same Christian American endeavor.[35]

To be sure, there was a spectrum of evangelicals during the Cold War. Not all shared Billy Graham's patriotic intensity. In the NAE's *United Evangelical Action* magazine, missionary executive A. C. Snead cautioned, "We must go to the mission field, not as Americans or Canadians, or those of any other land, but as representing the Lord Jesus Christ. We are to go, not to demand that those of Africa or the East should take our western civilization, but rather that we may present to them the living Christ, who Himself was born in Asia and became the Savior of all men. Remember, when we go to other lands as missionaries, we are the 'foreigners,' not they." Even true believers in Christian Americanism emphasized the imperative of faith more than the imperative of capitalism. Graham repeatedly declared that God loved the Soviets as much as he loved Americans.[36]

Other tensions also marked their close identification with the nation. First, evangelicals nurtured what Grant Wacker calls a "custodial ideal." They claimed a Christian heritage for the nation and a compulsion to sustain national morality even as they nurtured an otherworldly faith. Second, in attaching the blessings of business and democracy so closely to Christian faith, they were vulnerable to accusations of hypocrisy. They often spread American civilization as much as mainliners did, even though this sometimes distracted from their gospel message. Third, evangelicals benefitted inordinately from government funding, even as they viscerally preached an antigovernment gospel. Receiving educational aid, healthcare, and foreign-aid monies to spread their vision abroad, their work was subsidized by what Eisenhower would later call the military–industrial complex.[37]

These tensions, however, were obscured by the blinding optimism on display at Soldier Field. Christian Americanism was the dominant paradigm through which Cold War era evangelicals understood the world. The men who planned it—Torrey Johnson, Bob Pierce, Cliff Barrows, Herbert Taylor, and Billy Graham—would become household names over the next decades, and their ideas would predominate through the 1950s and 1960s. The future would also present stark challenges: the decolonization of the so-called Third World; genocides in Cambodia and the Soviet Union; an expanding Marxist presence around the world; the anxieties of the nuclear age; and a surge of Islam, Buddhism, and other non-Christian religions. Even global converts of empire would rise up to confront this powerful matrix of Christianity, democracy, and free enterprise.

Notes

1. Billy Graham, "Satan's Religion," *American Mercury*, August 1954, 41–46.
2. Draft of rally program, April 1945, in Box 27, Folder 14, Torrey Johnson Collection, Billy Graham Center Archives, Wheaton, Ill.; Torrey Johnson interview, August 14, 1985, Audio tape 6, Torrey Johnson Collection, BGCA.
3. Victory Youth Rally program, in Box 72, Folder 1, Herbert J. Taylor Collection, BGCA; William F. McDermott, "Bobby-Soxers Find the Sawdust Trail," *Collier's*, May 26, 1945, 23, copy in Photo Album I, Torrey Johnson Collection, BGCA.
4. James O. Supple, "Patriotic Note Marks Service at Soldier Field," *Chicago Sun*, May 31, 1945, in Photo Album I, Torrey Johnson Collection, BGCA; James Hefley, *God Goes to High School* (Waco, Tex.: Word Books, 1970), 25.
5. On evangelical isolationism in WWI, see Matthew Sutton, *American Apocalypse: A History of Modern Evangelicalism* (Cambridge, Mass.: Harvard University Press, 2014), 52–68, 266; Markku Ruotsila, *The Origins of Christian Anti-Internationalism: Conservative Evangelicals and the League of Nations* (Washington, D.C.: Georgetown University Press, 2008). On Fuller and McPherson, see Sutton, *American Apocalypse*, 122–23; Sutton, *Aimee Semple McPherson and the Resurrection of Christian America* (Cambridge, Mass.: Harvard University Press, 2007). On the persistence of corporate evangelicalism through the first half of the twentieth century, see Timothy Gloege, *Guaranteed Pure: The Moody Bible Institute, Business, and the Making of Modern Evangelicalism* (Chapel Hill, N.C.: University of North Carolina Press, 2015).

6. For "reform their nation," see Matthew Sutton, *American Apocalypse*, 52–68, 266. Johnson sermon transcript, June 16, 1945, pp. 3–4, in Box 27, Folder 14, Torrey Johnson Collection, BGCA.

7. On Johnson and Winrod, see Joel Carpenter, "Youth for Christ and the New Evangelicals' Place in the Nation," 137–38, in Rowlan Sherrill, ed., *Religion and the Life of the Nation: American Recoveries* (Urbana: University of Illinois Press, 1991). For "I believe," see Johnson sermon transcript, June 16, 1945, 2–3. For "spearhead of a postwar evangelistic thrust," see Carpenter, "Youth for Christ," 129.

8. "Wanted: A Miracle of Good Weather and the 'Youth for Christ' Rally Got It," *Newsweek*, June 11, 1945. For "boogie-woogie," see Torrey Johnson sermon transcript, June 16, 1945, 2. On savvy marketing, see Torrey Johnson to "Dear Co-Worker," July 2, 1945, in Box 72, Folder 2, Herbert J. Taylor Collection, BGCA. For "geared to the times," see Torrey Johnson to "Christian Friend and Prayer Warrior," October 1944, in Box 72, Folder 1, Herbert J. Taylor Collection, BGCA. For more on the rise of Youth for Christ, see Joel Carpenter, ed., *The Youth for Christ Movement and Its Pioneers* (New York: Garland Publishing, 1988).

9. W. R. Hearst to "Editors of All Hearst Papers," June 10, 1945, in Box 29, Folder 2, Torrey Johnson Papers, BGCA.

10. Henry R. Luce, "The American Century," *Life*, February 17, 1941, 61; Alan Brinkley, *The Publisher: Henry Luce and His American Century* (New York: Vintage Books, 2011), 269. On evangelical religious predominance, see "What Protestant Ministers Believe," *Christianity Today*, March 31, 1958, 30; Elesha Coffman, *The Christian Century and the Protestant Mainline* (New York: Oxford University Press, 2013), 200.

11. On Graham and Youth for Christ, see Dunlop interview, Tape 3, Merrill Dunlop Collection, BGCA. On Graham and Luce, see William Martin, "Billy Graham," 82, in David Harrell, ed., *Varieties of Southern Evangelicalism* (Macon, Ga.: Mercer University Press, 1981), 82.

12. Carl F. H. Henry, Youth for Christ press release, March 1945, in Box 27, Folder 14, Torrey Johnson Collection, BGCA; "The Greatest Youth Gathering in History: The 1945 Youth for Christ Rally at Soldier Field" exhibit, BGCA.

13. On evangelical cultural ambitions, see Joel Carpenter, *Revive Us Again: The Reawakening of American Fundamentalism* (New York: Oxford University Press, 1997). Ockenga quoted in Sarah Ruble, *Gospel of Freedom and Power: Protestant Missionaries in American Culture after World War II* (Chapel Hill, N.C.: University of North Carolina Press, 2012), 58.

14. For Mott and Edinburgh, see Timothy Yates, *Christian Mission in the Twentieth Century* (Cambridge: Cambridge University Press, 1994), 31. For "new transfiguration," see Brian Stanley, "Twentieth-Century World Christianity: A Perspective from the History of Missions," 52–53, in Donald Lewis, ed., *Christianity Reborn: The Global Expansion of Evangelicalism in the Twentieth Century* (Grand Rapids, Mich.: Eerdmans, 2004).

15. On the decline of SVM, see Nathan D. Showalter, *The End of a Crusade: The Student Volunteer Movement for Foreign Missions and the Great War* (Lanham,

Md.: Scarecrow Press, 1997); Robert T. Handy, *A Christian America: Protestant Hopes and Historical Realities* (New York: Oxford University Press, 1971), 201. On the decline in missions spending, see K. S. Latourette, *A History of the Expansion of Christianity* (London: Harper & Brothers, 1947), 7: 289.

16. William Hocking, *Re-Thinking Missions: A Laymen's Inquiry after One Hundred Years* (New York: Harper, 1932) 44, 70. On Hocking's concern about secularism, see David Hollinger, *Protestants Abroad: How Missionaries Tried to Save the World But Changed America* (Princeton, N.J.: Princeton University Press, 2017), 70. Latourette quoted in Yates, *Christian Mission*, 91–92. Trumbull quoted in Patterson, "The Loss of a Protestant Missionary Consensus," 84, in Joel Carpenter and Wilbert Shenk, eds., *Earthen Vessels: American Evangelicals and Foreign Missions, 1880-1980* (Grand Rapids, Mich.: Eerdmans, 1990).

17. On liberal hostility, see Yates, *Christian Mission*, 83–84; Scott Moreau, "Evangelical Missions Development, 1910 to 2010," 8, in Beth Snodderly and Moreau, eds., *Evangelical and Frontier Mission Perspectives on the Global Progress of the Gospel* (Oxford: Regnum Books, 2011), 8. On evangelical criticism of liberal ambivalence toward missions, see J. Elwin Wright, "The Federal Council and the Universalist Church," *United Evangelical Action*, December 15, 1944, 6. On the rise of "faith missions" and the formation of IFMA, see Joel Carpenter, "Propagating the Faith Once Delivered: The Fundamentalist Missionary Enterprise, 1920-1945," 94–100, 122–27, in *Earthen Vessels*; Rodger Bassham, *Mission Theology, 1948-1975* (Pasadena, Calif.: William Carey Library, 1979), 181. On the urgency of the missions task, see Harold Lindsell, *A Christian Philosophy of Missions* (Wheaton, Ill.: Van Kampen Press, 1949). For "Go!" see Charles Van Engen, "A Broadening Vision: Forty Years of Evangelical Theology of Mission," 210, in *Earthen Vessels*.

18. On Ockenga and missions, see Daniel Fuller, *Give the Winds a Mighty Voice: The Story of Charles E. Fuller* (Waco, Tex.: Word Books, 1972), 195, 209–10. For "one end of the world to another," see Dana Robert, "The Crisis of Missions: Premillennial Mission Theory and the Origins of Independent Evangelical Missions," 31, in *Earthen Vessels*.

19. On Youth for Christ's evangelical cooperation, see Pierard, *Earthen Vessels*, 171. For "invasion teams," see David King, "Seeking a Global Vision: The Evolution of World Vision and American Evangelicalism" (PhD diss., Emory University, 2012), 37. For "By the Grace of God," see Johnson sermon transcript, June 16, 1945, pp. 3– 4. For "greatest generation," see Carpenter, "Geared to the Times, but Anchored to the Rock," *Christianity Today*, November 8, 1985, 44. For numbers on the rise of evangelical missionaries, see Moreau, "Evangelical Missions Development," 12; David Howard, *The Dream That Would Not Die: The Birth and Growth of the World Evangelical Fellowship, 1846-1986* (Exeter, UK: Paternoster Press, 1986), 173. For more on mainline missionaries and "played wretchedly," see Stoll, *Is Latin America Turning Protestant?* (Berkeley: University of California Press, 1990), 72; Hollinger, *Protestants Abroad*, 86–89.

20. On evangelical ambivalence on the military in the 1940s and early 1950s, see Anne Loveland, *American Evangelicals and the U.S. Military, 1942-1993* (Baton Rouge: Louisiana State University Press, 1996), 1–15; "4 U.S. Clergymen Urge Haste

on AID," *New York Times*, October 5, 1947, 2. For objections to militarization, see "NAE Convention Resolutions," *United Evangelical Action*, July 1, 1952, 8; "Military Training," *UEA*, January 15, 1955, 11; "What of UMT?" *UEA*, February 15, 1952, 7. On evangelical chaplaincy, see Loveland, *American Evangelicals and the U.S. Military*, 16–32; Homer Rodeheaver, "Soul Saving in Army Camps: Our Greatest Evangelical Opportunity," *UEA*, January 2, 1945, 5; "NAE Chaplains in Active Service," *UEA*, April 1959, 12; James DeForest Murch, "Forward March! God Wills It!" *UEA*, June 1, 1954, 21; "Evangelical Chief of Army Chaplains," *UEA*, July 15, 1958, 10.

21. Pierard, "Pax Americana and the Evangelical Missionary Advance," 171, in *Earthen Vessels*; Torrey Johnson interview, Tape 6, August 14, 1985, Torrey Johnson Collection, BGCA. Luther J. Holcomb, "Christian America's Contribution to World Peace," *Moody Monthly*, October 1946, 98, 126.

22. On Charlotte, see Steven Miller, *Billy Graham and the Rise of the Republican South* (Philadelphia: University of Pennsylvania Press, 2009), 22. For "Marx the Lawgiver," see Charles Lowry, *Communism and Christ* (New York: Morehouse-Gorham, 1952), 37. On Graham in London, see David Aikman, *Billy Graham*, 86.

23. For "major fixation," see Mark Noll, "The View of World-Wide Christianity from American Evangelical Magazines, 1900-2000," 367–68, in *Making History for God: Essays on Evangelicalism, Revival and Mission in Honour of Stuart Piggin*, eds. Geoffrey R. Treloar and Robert D. Linder, eds. (Sydney: Robert Menzies College, 2004). On Baptist anticommunism, see *Southern Civil Religions in Conflict: Civil Rights and the Culture Wars* (Macon, Ga.: Mercer University Press, 2002). For other anticommunist screeds, see J. Edgar Hoover, "Communism: The Bitter Enemy of Religion," *Christianity Today*, June 22, 1959, 3–5; Walter H. Judd, "World Issues and the Christian," *Christianity Today*, June 23, 1958, 6; Hoover, "Storming the Skies: Christianity Encounters Communism," *Christianity Today*, December 21, 1962, 3–5. For "when God is out," see "Christianity and Democracy," *UEA*, December 1, 1944, 8; "Churches Gain Freedom, but Communists Still Anti-Religious," *UEA*, December 1, 1944, 6. For VBS curriculum, see "Patriots for Christ," *Christianity Today*, March 2, 1962, 23.

24. On evangelical material and spiritual relief, see "NAE Commences Shipments of Relief Goods to War-Torn Europe," *UEA*, March 19, 1945, 1; J. Elwin Wright, "Park Street Church in Boston Leads Way in Foreign Relief," *UEA*, October 15, 1944, 1. MacArthur quoted in Pierard, "Pax Americana," 174.

25. Rosell and Glover quoted in Pierard, "Pax Americana," 168.

26. Draft of rally program, c. April 1945, in Box 27, Folder 14, Torrey Johnson Collection, BGCA.

27. Darren Dochuk, *From Bible Belt to Sunbelt: Plain-Folk Religion, Grassroots Politics, and the Rise of Evangelical Conservatism* (New York: W.W. Norton, 2010), 10, 123; Sarah Hammond, "'God's Business Men': Entrepreneurial Evangelicals in Depression and War" (PhD diss., Yale University, 2010).

28. For "Methodist do-gooder" and Taylor's ecclesiastical location, see Paul Heidebrecht, "Pragmatic Evangelical: Herbert Taylor, 1893-1978," *Methodist History* 26, No. 2 (January 1988): 111. For more on Taylor, see Darren Grem, *The Blessings of*

Business: How Corporations Shaped Conservative Christianity (New York: Oxford University Press, 2016), 13–48.

29. On his early career, see Herbert Taylor, *God Has a Plan for You* (Old Tappan, N.J.: Revell, 1968), 21–44.

30. For "satisfying way of life," see Paul Heidebrecht, *God's Man in the Marketplace: The Story of Herbert J. Taylor* (Downers Grove, Ill.: InterVarsity Press, 1990), 58. On the expansion of the Four-Way Test to the Rotary Club, see Heidebrecht, *God's Man*, 49–57. See "Rotary President: 50 Years to the Good," *Newsweek*, February 28, 1955, 25–32.

31. On Taylor's paternalism, see Heidebrecht, *God's Man*, 40–41, 67–71; Taylor, *God Has a Plan*, 16, 27–28. For the Commission on Industrial Chaplaincy and "man of leadership," see Hammond, "God's Business Men," 252–53, 273.

32. On Taylor's community work, see Heidebrecht, *God's Man*, 47–48, 61, 67–68. On the NAE as a modern corporation, see Hammond, "God's Business Men," 243.

33. For "most benevolent dictatorship" and Taylor's flexible conservatism, see Hammond, "God's Business Men," 179. Ockenga quoted in Hammond, "God's Business Men," 203. On his conservative advocacy in Washington, see Taylor, *God Has a Plan*, 43. On the contributions of evangelical corporatism to Christian Americanism, see Kevin Kruse, *One Nation under God: How Corporate America Invented Christian America* (New York: Basic Books, 2015). On the rise of Sunbelt evangelicalism, see Dochuk, *From Bible Belt to Sunbelt*, 64, 114–18, 129, 184–86.

34. On "Club Time," see Heidebrecht, *God's Man*, 74–48. On members of "The Business World" committee, see Victory Youth Rally program, in Box 72, Folder 1, Herbert J. Taylor Collection, BGCA; Hammond, "God's Business Men," 124; Heidebrecht, *God's Man*, 96–97. On Youth for Christ's marketing savvy, see Hefley, *God Goes to High School*, 25, 28; Torrey Johnson and Robert Cook, *Reaching Youth for Christ* (Chicago: Moody Press, 1944), 18.

35. On the expansion of Youth for Christ in the late 1940s, see Carl F. H. Henry news release, Youth for Christ Committee, in Box 27, Folder 14, Torrey Johnson Collection, BGCA; Victory Youth Rally program, in Box 72, Folder 1, Herbert J. Taylor Collection, BGCA; William F. McDermott, "Bobby-Soxers Find the Sawdust Trail," *Collier's*, May 26, 1945, 23; copy in Photo Album I, Torrey Johnson Collection, BGCA; "Youth for Christ Rallies Under Way," *Los Angeles Times*, February 11, 1951, 45; Carpenter, "Youth for Christ," 129. On other exemplars of Christian Americanism, see Sarah Miller-Davenport, "'Their Blood Shall Not Be Shed in Vain': American Evangelical Missionaries and the Search for God and Country in Post-World War II Asia," *Journal of American History* 99, No. 4 (March 2013): 1109–32.

36. A. C. Snead, "The Foreign Missionary in a Changing World," *UEA*, May 1, 1948, 3–4; Molly Worthen, "The Intellectual Civil War within Evangelicalism," *Religion & Politics*, December 3, 2013.

37. On the custodial ideal, see Carpenter, "Youth for Christ," 143. On a broader Christian nationalism that included mainline Protestantism, see George Marsden, *The Twilight of the American Enlightenment: The 1950s and the Crisis of Liberal*

Belief (New York: Basic Books, 2014). On evangelicals and the federal government, see Axel R. Schäfer, *Piety and Public Funding: Evangelicals and the State in Modern America* (Philadelphia: University of Pennsylvania Press, 2012); Jonathan Herzog, *The Spiritual-Industrial Complex: America's Religious Battle against Communism in the Early Cold War* (New York: Oxford University Press, 2011).

2

Seoul 1952

World Vision and the Korean War

Let my heart be broken with the things that break the heart of God.
—Bob Pierce[1]

Evangelist Billy Graham spent Christmas Day of 1952 far away from his wife
and cozy log home in Asheville, North Carolina. On a mission with Youth for
Christ in the trenches of war-torn Korea, he visited American troops on patrol
near a snow-covered hill held by communist forces along the bleak 155-mile
front. As artillery thundered all around, he declared to nearly 5,000 soldiers,
"You are not forgotten. Millions of Americans are praying for you. Millions of
Americans know that you are fighting for the freedom of the world." Each un-
shaven soldier, said Graham, was a "rugged he-man. Every one was a courageous
red-blooded American." Haggard in their grimy winter uniforms, they listened
warily with helmets on and rifles in hand. They had just left their positions
under the cover of darkness, and now they sat on sandbags holding Bibles torn
by shrapnel on a hillside overlooking the stage of "Bulldozer Bowl." This iconic
structure had been the site of happier times when an American surge had nearly
retaken the Korean peninsula and would be again a year later when Marilyn
Monroe sashayed onto the stage in a slinky, plum-colored sequined dress. At
this moment, though, the men were emotionally unsteady and vulnerable in
an unforgiving terrain. At least a third of the men assented to the invitation to
"accept Christ." Graham later told audiences back home how touched he was as
the young soldiers approached the altar. "When I saw the tiredness in their eyes,
the lines on the faces that should have been young, I had to turn away," he said.
"I was weeping."[2]

Developments in Asia were chastening the intense global optimism expressed
at Soldier Field in 1945. As battle-weary soldiers entered their third awful year
of fighting in the Korean War, it was hard to believe that Ruth Graham, the
evangelist's wife, had once been a high school student in nearby Pyongyang. In
the 1930s that city, sometimes called "the Jerusalem of the East," was considered one of Asia's major centers of Christianity. It was equally difficult to imagine that Ruth's family had worked as missionaries in China, when that great

Facing West. David R. Swartz, Oxford University Press (2020). © Oxford University Press.
DOI: 10.1093/oso/9780190250805.001.0001

nation seemed to be heading in a more Christian and democratic direction. But conditions had shifted dramatically. Missionaries had been expelled from China by Mao in 1949, and American and United Nations forces could not make progress against the Chinese and North Korean soldiers. Since 1951, Seoul had changed hands three times, the city had been leveled, civilians were starving in the streets, and churches were in disarray.

Danger remained even in American-controlled Pusan. In the far south of Korea where Graham and his Youth for Christ colleague Bob Pierce began their revival tour, the communist presence was palpable. As the evangelists issued their first altar call for sinners to step forward to repent, the streetlights failed, and the meeting was plunged into darkness. Worried that saboteurs were about to strike, organizers called off the rest of the meeting, and the crowd went home. At another event, Graham had just finished a "fire and brimstone" sermon to 8,000 people when fires broke out in six small buildings nearby. At yet another event, one hundred guards armed with machine guns surrounded the makeshift platform, which held Graham and Korea's vice-president Ham Tai Young. They were there for good reason—this had been the site of an assassination attempt on Korean President Syngman Rhee months earlier, and communist agents had threatened to attack the revival. Graham projected bravado, telling a reporter that "if I am bumped off, it will be God's will."[3]

The evangelist also worried about the casualties of war. On his way from Pusan to Seoul, Graham encountered roads and cities jammed with millions of men, women, and children on foot. In reports sent to the United States, he detailed the horror: "On the streets you hear no laughter. Lepers mingle with the crowds calling for alms. Disease is rampant. I saw children walking through the streets wearing nothing but a tattered piece of burlap and carrying a can, begging for food." At one revival service in Seoul, the 34-year-old North Carolina preacher spoke in the bitter cold to impoverished women bundled in threadbare clothes. As their breath turned to steam, described one newspaper report, the women "coughed and sniffled as the American whose name they can't pronounce spoke to them in the bare, dimly lit church." During another service, Graham was whisked into a sandbag bunker as antiaircraft guns tried to fend off communist bombers. American soldiers were in bad shape too. Graham prayed over a GI who uttered "haunting groans" as blood leaked out of his body. He comforted another whose eyes had been shot out. He held the hands of dozens of men as they died.[4]

The armies that had inflicted those wounds were formidable. Communist forces in Korea, Graham declared, were "deeply entrenched—their mortar fire and artillery fire excellent and deadly efficient. . . . There is no easy way to solve the problem. We can't pull out." Upon his return to Dallas five weeks later, Graham echoed President-elect Eisenhower's assessment that "we are really in a bear trap in Korea. . . . Only prayer can win for us in Korea." This assessment reflected the high anxiety about the Marxist threat shared by Graham and millions of American evangelicals. Graham compiled hundreds of stories of communist atrocities. In one case, he said, a lone pastor "survived entombment in a cave where 300 Christians were executed." Graham returned home with stiff warnings from American GIs. The most-asked question by our troops, he told American civilians, was "Why do we let Communists run loose here at home while the Communists are killing our men in Korea?"[5]

Conditions were so bad, Graham concluded, that spiritual transformation might be the only solution. He urged evangelicals to pray for their communist enemies, and he implored his friend Eisenhower to institute a national day of prayer. Perhaps this, more than tanks, could bring "a miraculous end" to the deadlocked war. In fact, it was already making a difference, reported Graham. He saw no girlie pinups, only Bibles, in the barracks. He described high rates of "decisions for Christ" among the troops. Even a quarter of the communist prisoners of war, he claimed, had professed faith in Christ. In a sermon delivered in Hawaii on the trip home, Graham revealed his strategy: keep America spiritually robust by insisting that "the only true moral code is the gospel of Jesus Christ." "I believe that America is truly the last bulwark of civilization," he preached. "If America fails, Western culture will disintegrate. America is only as strong as her moral and spiritual forces." Once America was stabilized, it must "help other nations adopt a moral code." The world was a spiritual battleground as much as a military one.[6]

Youth for Christ's tour of Korea also revealed important social emphases. Graham repeatedly praised the racial integration of American forces. "It was thrilling to see a Negro GI, a Caucasian GI, and a Korean native marching side by side up the aisle to commit themselves to Christ." Praising the kindness of American soldiers toward Korean children, he declared that the United States had sent "the most compassionate army in American history." Graham and Pierce themselves participated in humanitarian activities, visiting Tabitha House, a home for war widows. As the war progressed, Pierce would raise funds in America on behalf of a Korean pastor, Kyung-Chik Han, who tutored Pierce on organizing and dispensing humanitarian aid. Together Pierce and Han would establish World Vision, a humanitarian organization founded in the crucible of war (Figure 2.1). For American evangelicals in the immediate postwar era, defeating communism, caring for orphans, and spreading the gospel were companion efforts. Each utilized a vocabulary of liberty. America would protect the liberties of peoples threatened by the tyranny of communism. Then they would be positioned to receive spiritual liberties offered by Christ. If Youth for Christ rallies in the 1940s reflected the ideals of white evangelicals in the postwar period, revivals in Seoul offered them a chance to pursue their salvific ambitions on a global stage.[7]

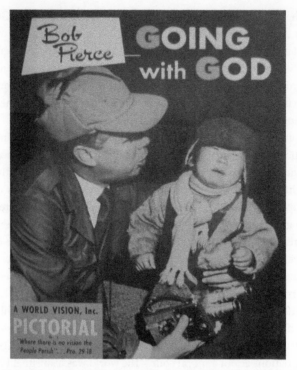

Figure 2.1. Bob Pierce, combining evangelism and humanitarianism, was said to have founded World Vision in Korea. Courtesy of World Vision International Archives, Monrovia, Calif.

Even the way this story has been told reflects a messianic impulse. In the conventional telling of World Vision's birth, Bob Pierce singlehandedly founded the organization, wedding American exceptionalism to evangelical mission. In this myth of origin, Christian Americanism saved Korea and added social justice to its anticommunist arsenal. But this is not the whole story. Viewing World Vision's early years through a global lens illuminates the role of Kyung-Chik Han, a monumental figure in Korean history who has been forgotten in the United States. The pages that follow tell the story of World Vision's birth twice: first with Pierce, then with Han, as the protagonist. The astonishing disjuncture in these two accounts demonstrates the persistent power of Christian American narratives. It also shows how transnational approaches can recover historical figures erased from those narratives.

I. Christian Americanism in Asia

Evangelicals operating in Asia enjoyed the strong support of the U.S. military. In late 1945, just months after Japan's surrender, General Douglas MacArthur stripped Shintoism of state support. In early 1946 he told a reporter that missionaries enjoyed "an unparalleled opportunity" to spread the Christian faith to the Japanese people. In 1948 *Moody Monthly* quoted MacArthur as saying, "You can't have true democracy without Christianity." Soon after, a Youth for Christ publication quoted MacArthur calling for 10,000 missionaries and ten million Bibles. Ruling as a virtual overlord in Japan until 1951, MacArthur saw Christianity as a vital resource in "democratization" and did much to aid missionary work. He gave Methodist missionary E. Stanley Jones the "red carpet treatment" at headquarters in Tokyo and offered him the use of military transportation. Jones got up three times to leave, but MacArthur, he said, "wouldn't let me go." The general told the missionary, "Where you sent one missionary, now send a hundred." As the Cold War ramped up, Japan, with its proximity to China and the Soviet Union, was perfectly positioned to act as a bulwark against communism.[8]

Graham, Pierce, and thousands of missionaries took up the general's invitation to preach about God and democracy. Many did so in postwar Japan, but even more fanned out to other vulnerable Asian sites. Before Mao's victory in 1949, they joined a long tradition of successful work in China led by missionary celebrities such as Hudson Taylor, Samuel Moffett, "Lottie" Moon, and thousands of missionaries sent by China Inland Mission and recruited by the Student Volunteer Movement. They converted hundreds of thousands, including Sun Yat-sen, who was, according to historian Tu Yichao, "a part-time missionary before he became a professional revolutionary," and his nationalist successor Chiang Kai-shek, the president of the first Republic of China. Chiang had been baptized by an American missionary and later married the daughter of a Chinese Methodist missionary. Billy Graham's father-in-law, L. Nelson Bell, a primary force behind the 1956 launch of *Christianity Today*, had been a medical missionary to China from 1916 to 1941, a stretch during which Graham's wife was born. Bell became a fervent booster of Chiang Kai-shek and the Nationalists and was instrumental in making connections between China's ruling elite and America's evangelicals while Chiang was still in power. A still-unknown Bob Pierce, before entering Korea, was a Youth for Christ missionary in China. In 1947 he produced one of the first films on Christian missions in China, and led four months of evangelistic rallies. He attracted audiences in the thousands and earned a reputation as a fiery evangelist. China loomed large in the American imagination, and most American evangelicals, according to historian Miles Mullin, knew someone who had been in China.[9]

In the late 1940s Pierce and Bell began issuing alarming reports from China. In instances that recalled the harrowing Boxer Rebellion of 1900 and the executions of John and Betty Stam, the so-called "foreign devil" missionaries beheaded by communist rebels in 1934, Christians were under attack yet again. In 1949 the Chiangs and all Western missionaries were pronounced the "running dogs of imperialism" and expelled by Mao's Red Army. E. Stanley Jones, who had worked closely with General Chiang and was completing an evangelistic tour through Shanghai, Chengtu, Amoy, and Canton, barely made it home, catching one of the last flights out of China on May 2, 1949, just "a little ahead of the Communist flood." Most Chinese Christians did not escape. Eight thousand were killed, and the atrocities accelerated in 1950 and 1951 as Mao consolidated power. In one particularly tragic episode, nearly one hundred China Inland Mission pastors were dragged to death, crucified, or shot en masse in the streets. In another, Southern Baptist missionary doctor Bill Wallace was arrested, tortured, and murdered. Dave Morken, the last "YFC man" to leave the China mainland, was among the fortunate survivors. He was held captive by the communists in Shanghai for several weeks before being released. Aspirations for Christianity and democracy in Asia seemed fragile indeed. American evangelical anticommunism was grounded in the visceral experience of communist atrocities.[10]

Missionaries also operated out of a sense of possibility. The Chiangs—and the Nationalist government of a million soldiers and civil servants—relocated to the island of Formosa (soon renamed Taiwan), just eighty miles off the coast of China, poised to retake the mainland should Mao falter. There were concerns that the Chiangs were dictatorial and lacked "real spiritual insight," and so they carefully cultivated images as pious believers. Connections with Youth for Christ leadership were key to developing this reputation. Chiang invited the organization's evangelists to his island. A friendship grew between Madame Chiang and Ruth Graham, and Bob Pierce and Billy Graham traveled with Chiang on tours of Asia. Graham was charmed by Chiang, who smiled through their initial meeting, causing the evangelist to gush, "I doubt if there are two statesmen in the world today that are more dedicated to Christ and His cause than Generalissimo Chiang Kai-shek and his wife." Meanwhile, Youth for Christ evangelists claimed to convert several thousand Formosans and Chinese refugees each month, and a total of 30,000 Nationalist Chinese enrolled in follow-up Bible study. The Chiangs filled American boosters with the hope of indigenous uprisings on the mainland, an alluring and conceivable prospect given the broader dissolution of colonial empires in this period.[11]

Evangelicals became important members of a burgeoning "China Lobby" that pushed for an aggressive rollback of communist gains in Asia. Bell, Pierce, and Graham joined publisher Henry Luce, himself born to missionary parents in China, in warning of Mao's impending victory. They also joined Alfred Kohlberg, a Chinese textile importer and member of the far-right John Birch Society; Albert Wedemeyer, commander of U.S. forces in China and Chiang's chief of staff in the struggle against Mao; and Walter Judd, a Republican congressman from Minnesota and former medical missionary to China. The ideological windfall of persecution reports—and the growing intensity of the Cold War—linked missionaries ever more tightly to the government, which valued missionaries as an important source of knowledge about local conditions throughout Asia. In turn, Secretary of State John Foster Dulles, according to journalist David Aikman, appreciated how Graham's crusades often "created ripples of goodwill in countries whose governments were actually quite skeptical of Washington." The collaboration strengthened in the early 1950s. Religious groups handled 70 percent of the U.S. government's food distribution around the world, and the Defense Department aided the efforts of evangelical missions. In 1952 General Mark Clark and the Pentagon essentially sponsored Graham's Christmas trip to the troops in Korea. The Army provided all transportation, lodging in officers' billets, even the platforms on which Graham preached his fiery sermons. The China Lobby networked missionaries, publishers, industrialists, and generals in a powerful matrix of Christian Americanism.[12]

No figure better represented the Wheaton–Washington axis than John Broger, a naval officer and founder of the Far East Broadcasting Company (FEBC). Broger, who would go on to earn an honorary doctorate from Wheaton College after installing twenty-eight transmitters in Asia that broadcasted in seventy-two languages to millions of people, was an authentic member of the so-called "greatest generation." Before launching FEBC with two Pentecostals in Los Angeles, the tall, mustachioed naval officer served as an American aide to Filipino guerrillas in World War II. A graduate of Southern California Bible College, he nurtured ties with the John Birch Society. Like Pierce and a host of others, he traveled a well-trod path to China, where he sought to establish a radio station. After being expelled from Shanghai, he was welcomed to Formosa by Chiang Kai-shek. From there Broger took FEBC to a Filipino jungle, where he previously had worked for the U.S. Army. In 1948 KZAS, "Call of the Orient," debuted with a live rendition of "All Hail the Power of Jesus's Name." Over the next decades, FEBC extended its range to all of Southeast Asia and into the Soviet Union.[13]

From the religious conversion of Asians, Broger turned to the political conversion of Americans. While president of FEBC, he worked as a hired consultant for the Joint Chiefs of Staff. Then in 1950 he moved from Manila to Washington to work for Admiral Arthur Radford, a "zealous Presbyterian admiral" who chaired the Joint Chiefs. During the 1950s Broger worked as an expert Cold War propagandist—and did so with the passion of a soldier hardened by battle on the front lines of the Cold War. His specialty was "troop indoctrination," and he utilized an influential pamphlet called "Militant Liberty." The document itself, while a standard articulation of domino theory, was fairly nuanced, recognizing the variability of local conditions, definitions of liberty, the need for patience— and the possibility that capitalism too could descend into a ruthless, animalistic struggle for power. At the same time, it represented a rigorous rally for democracy by man who came to be called "God's Gestapo." Broger asserted the need for an "aggressive vigilance" in order to "vanquish communist ideology."[14]

In the late 1950s Broger began to popularize the notion of "militant liberty" among the civilian population. As deputy director of Armed Forces Information and Education, he recruited John Wayne in the mid-1950s to play a navy flier confronting naïve pacifists in Congress. *Wings of Eagles*, financed in part by The Fellowship, a secretive bipartisan organization for politicians in Washington, D.C., was screened in the armed forces, schools, and civic organizations. Broger himself toured the country as a popular speaker, enjoying friendly audiences among evangelicals captivated by his World War II heroism, missionary experience, and feisty anticommunism. The crucible of Cold War Asia accelerated Christian Americanism at home and abroad.[15]

II. An American History of World Vision

World Vision, which would become the largest evangelical organization in postwar America, reflected these Cold War commitments. Founder Bob Pierce was born in 1915 in a small town in central Iowa and, like so many others in the interwar period, moved to Southern California. Suffering from an unstable childhood and rocky marriage, Pierce boasted a dramatic conversion narrative. His charisma then took him on a fast track through the surging Sunbelt world of Angeleno Baptists and Nazarenes as a youth pastor and regional evangelist. In 1944 Pierce signed up to preach for Youth for Christ.[16]

Pierce's first international trip—to China in the summer of 1947—fueled the young evangelist's revivalist aspirations. He arrived bearing a Bible, a gift from Billy Graham, for the embattled Chiang Kai-shek. Then, as civil war raged, he was said to have notched 17,852 "decisions for Christ" in a stunningly successful four-month evangelistic tour. But on his second trip in 1948, the specter of communism turned into a ghastly spectacle. Pierce witnessed Mao's destruction of hospitals, schools, and missionary compounds. Hundreds of Chinese pastors, new friends of the young evangelist, were murdered, and Pierce, sometimes only miles from the front, escaped just before the Red Army took all of mainland China. After preaching to nearly 15,000 near the old palace in Peking, Pierce fled to Formosa along with Chiang Kai-shek.[17]

With China lost, Pierce set his sights on Korea. A visit in the spring of 1950, however, reinforced his sense of alarm. As he preached to tens of thousands of South Koreans, communist forces massed on the other side of the 38th parallel. Then, just weeks after Pierce returned to the United States, they invaded, sparking the Korean War. The attack engulfed Seoul and pushed the South Koreans to the coast at Pusan. By January 1951 communists held more than 90 percent of the Korean peninsula. A daring intervention at Incheon in February by General Douglas MacArthur, who Pierce called an "old soldier whose greatness and wisdom shall not fade away," led not only to the recapture of Seoul, but also the advance of U.S. and United Nations forces to the Yalu River on the border of Korea and China. But then a sudden intervention by Chinese fighters reversed the progress. Seoul became a battlefield yet again, leaving it a bleeding and battered city. The war persisted for two more gory years, when a 1953 armistice established a demilitarized zone at almost the same line where the devastation had begun three years earlier. According to Pierce, it was a "story written in the blood of young men." In Korea, as in China, Pierce's anticommunism was rooted in a narrative of combat and razor-thin survival against a brutal enemy. World Vision would emerge as an existential response to the anxieties of the Cold War Pacific theater.[18]

Pierce maintained a peripatetic pace in those years of military action. Watching helplessly from his home base in the United States, he began to raise money. At the 1950 Youth for Christ convention in Winona Lake, Indiana, Pierce told dramatic stories of Christian martyrdom at the hands of communists. Billy Graham, who heard Pierce speak, told the crowd, "I had planned to buy a Bel Air Chevy, but instead I'm giving the money to Bob Pierce for the Koreans." At a Graham crusade in Portland, Oregon, just a month after the communist incursion, Pierce's testimony prompted many of the 8,000 attendees to press money in his hands to support Korean Christians. These exchanges were repeated at evangelistic crusades across the country through the summer and fall of 1950. By September Pierce had set up bookkeeping in a tiny room of Youth for Christ's offices in Portland, Oregon, adopted the statement of faith of the National Association of Evangelicals, and signed articles of incorporation for "World Vision."[19]

Pierce also returned to Korea in the late summer of 1950, catching the last civilian flight until the war ended several years later. At the invitation of South Korean president Syngman Rhee, he continued his spiritual offensive. In a series of evangelistic crusades, Pierce persuaded 25,000 Korean civilians, Korean soldiers, and American soldiers "to turn from the darkness of heathenism and unbelief unto the glorious light of the Gospel." He was helped by South Korean soldiers who, according to another missionary, "had canvassed the entire town and with gun in hand had 'invited' every soul to attend the meeting." The result—lots of conversions and significantly reduced communist activity in the region—seemed to justify Rhee's support. "Youth for Christ's type of evangelism," the president predicted, "will help hold back the flood of atheism which is flowing through the Far East." The geopolitical translation of Rhee's spiritual judgment was not difficult: missionaries could aid military efforts to stop godless communism.[20]

Pierce reinforced this message to American audiences through film. As he circulated through Korea as a missionary and as an embedded war correspondent for the *Christian Digest*, he collected amateur footage of the hostilities with a silent motion picture camera. The resulting films became a masterful fundraising tool and reflected the religious and political sensibilities of evangelical culture in the 1950s. *Dead Men on Furlough* (1954) (Figure 2.2) portrayed an idyllic Christian Korean culture under siege by the "red horde." Using a combination of B-list Hollywood actors, Korean immigrants living in Los Angeles, and newsreel footage of American soldiers advancing through the mountains and marshes of Korea, the film told the story of Pastor Chai, a courageous soul who ran a medical clinic before "the Reds" imprisoned him and held his wife and baby hostage. Before he was shot, Pastor Chai made the case for American intervention: "There are still too many who believe we can deal with the communists. You must tell them what you have seen here. You must remember every ugly act of these godless men. You must tell this story far and wide so it will reach men who hate evil and will take action until it is too late."[21]

This was a standard midcentury morality tale. It was also deeply personal to Pierce, whose Cold Warrior mentality was grounded in the torture and deaths of his many Chinese and Korean friends. These Asian Christians, Pierce explained, were exemplars of spiritual integrity who woke at 4:30 a.m. every day to pray at church and who serenely submitted to martyrdom. "With heroes such as this . . . is it any wonder that the Korean church stands true?" Justice—and concern for the future of the world—demanded action. "An aroused free world rose to the challenge," Pierce narrated in *Dead Men*. "It took G.I. blood to inform . . . a good many evangelical Christians that the peninsular nation of Korea is one of great significance in the confused pattern of present-day world history." The implication was that American intervention might well be needed to save the world.[22]

In *The Red Plague* (1957) Pierce described the global threat beyond Korea. In its survey of the vulnerabilities of Japan, Thailand, Malaya, Burma, India, and nations in Africa, the thirty-minute film used striking graphics and dramatic pauses to alert Americans to "the godless religion spawned in hell." As a tide of color bled across a map from the Soviet Union into Southeast Asia, Pierce intoned the following words: "Like a deadly red plague spreading out in all directions, the massive force of Communism has spread over the globe until today it claims over

Figure 2.2. Borrowing language from Lenin to suggest how dangerous it was to be a Korean Christian, World Vision circulated this 1954 film throughout the United States to raise money. Courtesy of World Vision International Archives, Monrovia, Calif.

one third of the world's population. China . . . Japan . . . Africa . . . India . . . all have succumbed to its insidious workings in greater or lesser degree; and wherever Communism holds sway, the forces of Christianity and Christian missions are bitterly opposed and, where possible, eliminated." Even the United States was vulnerable. "At this very moment," Pierce warned, "there are principalities and powers working feverishly to deprive *you* of your right to worship God." The evangelist's plea for intervention, with its declaration of guilt and possibility of redemption, sounded much like an altar call: "In less than 50 years communism has done what Christianity has failed to do in 2,000 years. And it is our fault. Yours and mine. We have failed to make missions a matter of personal concern. What to do about it? Ask God on bended knee for an opportunity of service."[23]

Indeed, mid-century evangelicals contended that revival offered the strongest defense against totalitarian regimes. As Korea remained on the edge of survival in the years after the war with "Communist jet bombers poised only twenty seconds away," Pierce fought back with spiritual ammunition. His 1957 Seoul Crusade drew nearly 300,000 people and boasted "3,115 first-time decisions for salvation." Pierce remained most committed to Korea, but he also regularly made his way to other critical Cold War sites. Between 1950 and 1960 Pierce traveled over 2.5 million miles on regular trips through Japan, Formosa, Hong Kong, India, Thailand, and Korea. He declared, "If Christian Americans fail these strategic points today, then all Asia may be lost to the witness of Christ tomorrow."[24]

Pierce's evangelistic wanderlust was not unusual—thousands of missionaries circulated throughout the Asian front of the Cold War—but his response to the suffering was. While evangelicals had long built hospitals and schools in the Majority World, the fundamentalist-modernist controversies of the 1920s had moved them away from language that too closely resembled the social gospel, which was tainted by its association with theological liberalism. Pierce's observations of physical suffering and poverty in China and Korea, however, provoked him to reengage humanitarianism both theologically and rhetorically. In characteristic evangelical fashion, a personal encounter, which became World Vision's founding myth, sparked Pierce's transformation. On his first trip to China in 1947, he met a young Chinese girl named White Jade who had been beaten and disowned by her father after she converted to the Christian faith. Effectively an orphan, White Jade had no place to go. Local Christians in Fujian province did not have the capacity to care for yet another orphan, and so Pierce gave away all his remaining cash—five dollars—and pledged the same amount each month thereafter. White Jade had broken his heart. In 1951, after seeing more suffering in Korea, Pierce wrote the following sentence on the inside cover of his Bible: "Let my heart be broken with the things that break the heart of God." This phrase became World Vision's spiritual mantra, and the experience with White Jade birthed its child sponsorship program. "I went to change them," he said, "but instead I was the one that returned changed," he told audiences across the United States.[25]

World Vision grew quickly. In 1951 alone the organization, run by a skeleton staff and fueled by Pierce's large personality, raised and spent nearly $80,000 to fund hospitals, purchase jeeps for missionaries, and provide training for South Korean military chaplains. In order to distribute these funds, Pierce recruited

Korean political leaders and a diverse set of evangelical missionaries from Presbyterian, Pentecostal, Southern Baptist, and holiness traditions. To raise more money, he returned frequently to the United States. On preaching tours, he captivated audiences for hours at a time. "It was nothing for this gifted man of God to raise a hundred thousand dollars in a single meeting," said one supporter. He seemed unstoppable, and Pierce's travels and projects were as unpredictable as the mysterious movements of the Holy Spirit, which he said led him. Boosters, including singer Cliff Barrows, prominent pastor Richard Halverson, evangelist Jack Shuler, Lieutenant General William K. Harrison, U.S. Senator Frank Carlson, and educator Henrietta Mears, began to line up behind him. His longtime Youth for Christ colleague Billy Graham, who was emerging as a star evangelist in the United States, dubbed Pierce "America's missionary ambassador to the Far East."[26]

Pierce's star shone even brighter as Korean orphans began to provide World Vision with its defining identity. American evangelicals could sponsor an orphan for ten dollars a month to help with food, clothing, education, and religious teaching. As Pierce made pitches on behalf of "my orphanages," annual fundraising jumped from $57,000 in 1954 to over $450,000 in 1956. By the late 1960s World Vision had become a humanitarian behemoth recognizable even to nonreligious Americans. By the 2010s it boasted 40,000 employees, a budget of $2.6 billion, and offices in over one hundred countries. Pierce appeared to be the force of nature that set it in motion.[27]

III. A Korean History of World Vision

That's one version. But from Korea itself, there is another, very different narrative, one that resists American triumphalism. Accompanying Pierce and Graham on their entry into Seoul from Pusan at Christmas 1952 was a Korean pastor named Kyung-Chik Han (Figure 2.3). Identified by Graham as "our interpreter," Han was actually the prominent minister of Young Nak Church, which towered over the city atop a high central ridge. He had barely escaped Seoul two years earlier after a second communist invasion, and conditions remained awful upon his return. Though the massive granite structure of Young Nak remained, the rest of Seoul was in rubble. Eighty percent of the buildings had been destroyed, and martial law persisted. The tragic scenes in Seoul, however, belied the vitality of Korean Christianity, and Graham's modest description of Han belied the Korean pastor's reputation in his homeland as "a majestic figure standing at the center of the one hundred years of Korean Church History." Warmly called "Pastor Han" by Korean Christians, to this day he is left out of Western narratives, despite his reputation among Koreans as a cofounder of World Vision.[28]

Figure 2.3. Kyung-Chik Han spent nearly a decade in the United States, studying at Emporia State University and Princeton Theological Seminary, before returning to Korea, where he launched the dozens of humanitarian efforts that became World Vision. Courtesy of the Kyung-Chik Han Foundation, Seoul, Korea.

Han's rise to prominence was unlikely. Born into a Confucian family in 1902, just before Japan's brutal colonization of Korea, Han grew up in Saetmal, a tiny settlement of twenty-five families located twenty-five miles north of the capital city of Pyongyang. Revival swept through the poverty-stricken village the year after Han's birth, and his family was converted to Christianity by the highly regarded missionary Samuel Moffett. The Pyongyang Great Revival of 1907 Christianized the region even more. The number of Protestants alone jumped from about 30,000 to over 160,000 between 1904 and 1909. After Buddhist and Confucian supremacy in the nineteenth century and before the gritty urban center became the capital city of an atheistic North Korea, Pyongyang was the "holy city" of Korean Protestantism for nearly four decades.[29]

Han's rise mirrored that of Korean Christianity. Church leaders immediately saw his potential, noting his amiable bearing, exceptional intelligence, and vital faith. Han was studying to be a chemist when he heard God's voice calling him to preach the gospel, and he complied. In the late 1920s his church sent him to study at Princeton Theological Seminary with J. Gresham Machen, the premier fundamentalist theologian in America. Compelled by Machen's intellect and theology, but nonplussed by his pugnacious separatism, Han occupied a middle theological space characterized by a gentle ecumenical conservatism. He distrusted neo-orthodox theologian Karl Barth, who was anathema to many theological conservatives, but Han also felt that social justice should be pursued. While at Princeton he toured the University Settlement Neighborhood Guild and Jane Addams's Hull House in Chicago. He began a lifelong practice of reading the *New York Times* and science magazines, which often informed his sermons. Even in those early years of training, as he cultivated skills that would make him a renowned leader in Korea, observers praised his incisive sermons delivered with authenticity, empathy, and a crisp, dignified voice.[30]

These qualities served Han well as he began his first pastorate in 1933 in Sinuiju, a large northern city at the border of China. If Bob Pierce's humanitarianism was built on the intensely emotional response of a privileged American's shock at foreign poverty, Han's was rooted in the prolonged shepherding of a suffering flock. His thirteen years in the far north were a productive, if worrisome time, as his large congregation dealt with an oppressive social environment. Mounting Japanese imperialism restricted Christian activities. Han, a devoted patriot who still deeply mourned the collapse of the Chosun Dynasty and commonly wore a *durumagi* (a traditional Korean overcoat) and black rubber shoes, was regarded with suspicion by the Japanese when he returned from the United States. Authorities forced him to bow to a Shinto shrine, an act he regretted for the rest of his life. They also tortured him and put him under police surveillance. Other Koreans, not only Christian leaders, were oppressed too. The economy struggled, and there were few political freedoms. Amid these difficulties, Han oversaw the construction of a church building, an orphanage, and a nursing home. He was emerging as an important voice in religious and civic affairs.[31]

The year 1945 marked the end of one threat and the crushing start of another. Japan surrendered to Allied forces, which appeared to inaugurate a new era of Korean independence under a benign American sphere of influence. These were thrilling months as Koreans littered the streets with discarded Shinto shrines that had been imposed in every home. Han even got a taste of self-rule when he formed the Sinuiju Self-Government Association during the political transition. But the stirring challenge of organizing young men into a police force gave way to despair. American rule in the north of Korea did not materialize as he had expected. Instead, the 38th parallel was established with Soviet oversight of Sinuiju and all other areas north of Seoul. Devastated by this development, Han resisted. He launched a new political party, the Christian Social Democratic Party (SDP), which sought to establish "democratic government and social improvement according to the Christian spirit." The Russians immediately cracked down. As the SDP crumbled, Koreans in the north suffered summary executions, land seizure, and torture. Forced to flee after an order was issued for his arrest, Han disguised himself and fled. After a long and arduous journey southward on mountain trails, he managed to cross the still-leaky border in late 1945.[32]

Han's leadership continued in Seoul, where conditions, exacerbated by a crush of refugees from the north, were as bad as in Sinuiju. Han was driven to despair as he walked amid the beggars, homeless people, and prostitutes. "I cannot control my heart," he mourned in a sermon entitled "A Gospel of the Propertyless." Immediately he began securing tents, assigning work duties, and organizing temporary cooperatives and schools. Within months he presided over the first church meetings of twenty-seven displaced North Koreans. Within half a year, Young Nak Presbyterian Church boasted over one thousand members. Within two years, 4,300 members worshiped in tents as the refugees built a giant stone structure by hand with $20,000 worth of materials donated by American Christians. All the while, Han continued his humanitarian work. In 1947 he built the Borinwon orphanage. He established a widow's home called Mojawon, Hapsil Children's House, Youngnak Children's House, and departments of funeral services and education. In 1948 he was elected chair of South Korea's Laborers and Farmers Committee. He delivered impassioned speeches on behalf of Seoul's 4.6 million refugees and helped create a special voting zone for them. "To help the poor and the weak people must be the first," declared Han.[33]

On June 25, 1950, tragedy struck yet again. Just weeks after Young Nak completed its church building, North Korea invaded. Numbers of the poor and weak multiplied as both sides committed atrocities. One church leader was executed at Young Nak's gate for denying entry to the invading forces that wanted to use the building as an armory. Reports circulated of 3,000 Christian pastors drowned in the Han River by communists. Han fled even further as enemy troops pushed south. Within months nearly the entire peninsula was razed. Han responded with a rhetorical fusillade, preaching that "the first enemy of a free democratic state is communism." He also organized resistance, throwing the full force of his religious and humanitarian networks behind the United Nations and South Korean armies. "My dear young patriotic soldiers!" he said, addressing a battalion of demoralized fighters who had gathered at Anyang Elementary School to regroup. "As I see your bright eyes, even in this gloomy situation, I feel inspired again. As you have reassembled to fight the North Korean aggressors, I am reassured that God is with us." Young adults from Young Nak formed a militia called the Seobuk Young Men's Association that fought in Seoul and on Jeju Island. Han also organized the Christian Volunteer Soldiers, a battalion of 3,000 sent to the front. Nearly all of them were killed in battle. Han felt a deep conviction that Christians should undergird "a political, economic, cultural, moral purifying movement and revival movement" in Korea. This multifaceted approach, according to observers, seemed to work. "So many found Christ," wrote one American admirer, "that Communism all but disappeared in several areas."[34]

Han's humanitarianism accelerated in the months after the invasion. Just one day after the war began, he launched the Korean Christian National Relief Society (KCNRS). He also led the Christian Union Emergency Committee for War. In these capacities as a respected churchman and patriot, he exploited his ties to the West. He negotiated with General Douglas MacArthur for tents from the U.S. Army and distributed them in refugee camps. Wearing an army uniform, he arrived at Incheon on September 28, 1950, on an American battleship as forces began to retake the Korean peninsula. He then accompanied South Korean, American, and United Nations forces as far north as Pyongyang, only to be turned back to the South when the Chinese invaded in January 1951. In the midst of this second crisis, he recruited the U.S. Air Force to transfer sixty Korean orphans from Borinwon to Jeju Island. Utilizing his long-standing ties with American evangelical networks, Han visited the United States on behalf of the KCNRS. He met Billy Graham, who took offerings "for the needy in the war-torn country." That Han served as a South Korean delegate to the United Nations in March 1951 only underscores his status as a consummate broker.[35]

By the end of the Korean War, Han had become a bureaucratic force of nature. He had collaborated closely with military forces, recruited doctors to serve in the refugee camps, managed orphanages, built twenty-five more Tabitha Widows Homes throughout Korea, and helped lead over one hundred other humanitarian organizations. Observers, trying to explain his organizational genius, noted that he was a quiet, unassuming leader whose subtle charisma gave his colleagues "inspiration and encouragement" to follow his lead. Others called Han a master mediator who could bring about consensus through gentle persuasion. He was also brutally efficient. One observer quipped that he operated like a rational businessman "even though he claimed to just be an old servant of God." Han's compelling persona and calculating mind made him a master builder of institutions.[36]

Bob Pierce's "rescue" of Korean Christians—and the West's portrayal of his relationship with Pastor Han, the interpreter—looks very different facing East rather than West. Before Pierce ever set foot in Asia, the foundation had already been laid for the construction of World Vision. Han, ten years older than Pierce, fluent in English, and boasting global contacts, was a distinguished Korean leader who had already established dozens of humanitarian projects. When Pierce appeared in Seoul in April of 1950, Han took notice of the energetic itinerant evangelist with a concern for personal salvation, an animus against communism, and a budding commitment to feeding starving children. Han, in fact, discovered Pierce as much as Pierce discovered Han. Quickly discerning that Pierce could contribute to the humanitarian projects he had founded, Han, at the advice of another missionary, hosted the American the very night he arrived in Seoul. Pierce preached to 1,500 congregants "huddled together in one great mosaic of human flesh" at Young Nak, and Han followed up on this new friendship almost immediately by inviting Pierce to preach at a large open-air revival at the Namdaemun plaza (Figure 2.4). When war broke out just weeks later, Han kept Pierce, who had since returned to the United States, apprised of conditions. When they reunited that fall in Pusan to hold a series of pastors' conferences, Pierce was the main speaker and paid for the entire event. Han interpreted, as the Americans frequently noted, but this did not mean he was the subordinate. Han organized everything.[37]

This collaborative arrangement became the pattern for the two humanitarians. Pierce did fundraising and publicity while Han actually ran what was becoming World Vision. Some of those had been operational even before Pierce came on the scene. Others, like Tabitha Mojawon, a center for war widows, were launched

Figure 2.4. By 1956, when Han was interpreting for Pierce at this mass evangelistic rally in Seoul, the Korean pastor's significance already was being dwarfed by the American's outsized personality. Courtesy of the Kyung-Chik Han Foundation, Seoul, Korea.

when Pierce began bringing money from the United States to Korea. Pierce pledged $700 for the construction of Tabitha Mojawon and contributed $10,000, a jeep, and a pipe organ for continuing construction on Young Nak Church. In December 1950 Pierce returned to Korea for a third time, bringing with him $18,000 from American and Canadian evangelicals. This money was pumped into projects already started by Han. Under Han's influence their collaboration increasingly took the form of humanitarianism, which became the heart of World Vision's activities during the destructive war. All of it was rooted in Pastor Han's work. Before World Vision in the United States, there was Young Nak Church in Seoul. Before Seoul was Sinuiju. And before Sinuiju was a Christian family just outside Pyongyang. The genealogy of World Vision is profoundly Korean.[38]

As the years passed, Han's role in World Vision's origin story diminished. A 1960 account only briefly mentioned Han as part of a Korean delegation that greeted Pierce at the Seoul airport. It credited Western groups for World Vision's orphanage work. A 1972 tribute described Han as a devout saint and "a gentle, dedicated pastor" who built several orphanages and schools for refugees, but it included no acknowledgment that World Vision came directly out of Han's activities before and during the Korean War. In 1983 Franklin Graham repeated the long-standing line that "a fine interpreter, Dr. Hahn [sic]" trans-lated Pierce's message "into understandable Korean." Most narratives left out Han entirely. One typical version, which did acknowledge that Pierce "became involved with the Tabitha Widows' Home, sponsored by the Yung [sic] Nak Presbyterian Church," nonetheless declared, "And behind every bit of it was the compassion, the energy, and the vision of one man; in fact, to most people World Vision *was* Bob Pierce." Despite Han's continued involvement in both World Vision International and World Vision Korea, references to his legacy were overwhelmed by the larger-than-life Pierce in the West's triumphalist nar-rative of evangelical social action.[39]

It does not appear that Pierce himself meant to obscure Han's contributions. Historian David King notes that Pierce "had always promoted indige-nous pastors alongside missionaries as heroes who sacrificed for the gospel." Historian William Yoo writes that Pierce believed Han to be a "Korean saint, praising his preaching, piety, and humanitarian work among war refugees." World Vision's earliest literature offered descriptions of—and even glowing tributes to—Han. In his first memoir, *The Untold Korea Story*, Pierce effusively praised Han's courage, piety, and prowess in serving his people. "Out of the chaos of the past," wrote Pierce, "this man of God built a future for his people." Nor did Han seem to resent Pierce's celebrity. In 1978 Han flew from Seoul to Los Angeles in order to preach at his former colleague's funeral, where he said, "The people of Korea can never forget him, for he was the best-known preacher of the gospel and welfare worker from abroad during the Korean War. . . . God be praised for him." But Han's qualifying phrase, "from abroad," also testifies to the Korean view that Pierce was never the sole founder of World Vision. In fact, Korean sources have consistently portrayed the founding of World Vision as collaborative enterprise in which Pierce and Han were cofounders. Pierce, former World Vision Korea president Jong-Sam Park told me, "was a master performer with a script. Koreans did 90 percent of it." World Vision may have been incorporated in the state of Washington, but a battered North Korean pastor actually built it in the slums of Seoul.[40]

In the early 1950s Han and Pierce stood together as exemplars of transnational evangelical social justice. Significantly, they did so in a manner that reinforced Christian Americanism. To be sure, Han acknowledged problems with capitalism, and in a 1954 sermon entitled "Christianity and Freedom," he promoted the kind of "welfare state provisions that can be seen in developed Christian nations." But as the Cold War heated up, Han preached evangelical nationalism as God's alternative to left-wing Marxism. He waxed eloquent about the divine blessing of the United States, which he called "the most blessed and peaceful nation in the world." If Korea too could establish a "Christian state," it could help lead a "global wave of new Christian democratic parties." Proclaiming "Let us rise up and act!" in a church filled with refugees from a North Korea victimized by Japanese imperialists and Chinese Marxists, Han offered Americans soul-stirring confirmation of their political righteousness.[41]

The limits of Christian nationalism were clear even in Korea. Han's fierce anticommunism—and his conviction that personal conversion could transform the social order—sometimes propped up authoritarian government. During the war, his Seobuk Young Men's Association, working with the U.S. military government, participated in the massacre of communists and innocent civilians (perhaps as many as 80,000) on Jeju Island. After the war, one critic observed, "He was concerned less about dictators' anti-democratic tendencies than about students' demonstrations and laborers' strikes." Han did not publicly oppose Chung-Hee Park's 1961 coup d'etat, or the series of dictatorships under Park and Doo-Hwan Chun that followed. Youth within Young Nak Church, dismayed by the reticence of their "silent shepherd," urged Han to become "a prophet who is possessed of courage and a razorsharp tongue," but he justified his silence because these authoritarian leaders protected Korea from communist nations. Han's interest in social order, implemented through corporate beneficence and a strong identification with the military, thus served to buttress the American empire. Important sectors of Korean evangelicalism during the Cold War featured an Asian variant of Christian Americanism, one that included a gospel of personal salvation, insatiable consumerism, and redemptive violence. Indeed,

Christian nationalism continues to pervade many global communities, some-times with an intensity that surpasses churches in the United States. A 2010 survey of evangelicals gathered at Cape Town, South Africa, for example, showed that in the United States only 21 percent favored making the Bible "the official law of the land in their country." Fifty-eight percent of leaders from the Global South, however, agreed with this idea. In most of the world, walls of sep-aration between church and state were never built in the first place.[42]

But American evangelicals have also imported from the Majority World. As emboldened missionaries pushed their way into the world, they encountered pushback. Pastor Han, for all his abetting of Christian Americanism, mentored Pierce and his colleagues on methods of humanitarian work and the language of social justice. Over the next several decades, many other global Christians would seek to instruct American evangelicals on a host of issues. In the 1950s and 1960s Christians from India and many African nations condemned racial segregation in the United States. In the early 1970s Latin Americans criticized American im-perialism at a global gathering on evangelism led by Billy Graham. In the late 1970s Majority World Christians encouraged World Vision to internationalize its organizational structure, an act that radically transformed its methods of pov-erty relief. These intense challenges reshaped sectors of American evangelicalism in the twilight of the twentieth century.

Notes

1. Richard Gehman, Let My Heart Be Broken (New York: McGraw-Hill, 1960).

2. Billy Graham, I Saw Your Sons at War: The Korean Diary of Billy Graham (Minneapolis: BGEA, 1953), 50, 54, 59; "Millions at Home Praying for You, Billy Graham Tells GIs in Korea," Hot Springs New Era, December 25, 1952; "Billy Graham at Korea Front for Christmas Eve Services," Milwaukee Sentinel, December 24, 1952, copies in "Christmas in Korea—1952, Clippings," Scrapbook 168, Records of the BGEA Newspaper and Magazine Clippings, Billy Graham Center Archives, Wheaton College, Wheaton, Ill.

3. Graham, Sons at War, 21–24; "Billy Graham in Korea Calls on Men in Hospitals," New York Times, December 16, 1952; "Billy Graham Pleased," Oregon Journal; "Pusan Buildings Catch Fire as Billy Graham Preaches," Albuquerque Tribune, December 20, 1952, copies in Folder "Christmas in Korea—1952, Clippings."

4. Graham, Sons at War, 37, 62; "Koreans Brave Cold to Hear Billy Graham," Seattle Times, December 20, 1952; "Pusan Buildings Catch Fire," Albuquerque Tribune; "Billy Graham Visits Hospital Ship, Prays for Wounded GI," Nashville Banner, December 22, 1952; Cullum Greene, "Only Prayer Can Win War, Graham Asserts at Dallas," Ft. Worth Star-Telegram, January 10, 1953, copies in "Christmas in Korea—1952, Clippings."

56 FACING WEST

5. "Billy Graham Flies Back Home, Saw No Sign of Spree in Korea," *Little Rock Gazette*,
January 10, 1953; Greene, "Only Prayer Can Win War"; "Evangelist Billy Graham
Writes Local Couple of Korea Conditions," *Phoenix Republican*, December 30, 1952,
copies in "Christmas in Korea—1952, Clippings." For stories of communist atrocities,
see Graham, *Sons at War*, 39.

6. Graham, *Sons at War*, 46; "Graham Cancels World Tour," *Kankakee Journal*,
December 28, 1952; Greene, "Only Prayer Can Win War," *Ft. Worth Star-Telegram*.
On troop morality, see "Billy Graham Flies Back Home," *Little Rock Gazette*. On
America as the hope of the world, see "Billy Graham Enplanes for Korea after Hawaii
Sermon," *Greenville News*, December 9, 1952; "Evangelist Billy Graham Writes Local
Couple," *Phoenix Republican*. On Graham's admiration for Eisenhower, see Graham,
Sons at War, 43.

7. For "compassionate army," see "Graham Aids G.I.'s," *Hampshire Gazette*, December 31,
1952. On visiting Tabitha House and other relief initiatives, see "Billy Graham Is Busy
in Korea," *Ada News*, December 18, 1952, 17; Graham, *Sons at War*, 29, 31, 35. On
the collaboration of Pierce and Han, see author interview with Jong-Sam Park, Seoul,
Korea, May 20, 2014; author interview with Hoon Song, Seoul, Korea, May 21, 2014.

8. On MacArthur and missionaries in Japan, see Sarah Miller Davenport, "'Their
Blood Shall Not Be in Vain': American Evangelical Missionaries and the Search for
God and Country in Post-World War II Asia," *Journal of American History* 99, No.
4 (2013): 1123–24. Jones quoted in Stephen Graham, *Ordinary Man, Extraordinary
Mission: The Life and Work of E. Stanley Jones* (Nashville, Tenn.: Abingdon Press,
2005), 334–37; Lawrence S. Wittner, "MacArthur and the Missionaries: God and
Man in Occupied Japan," *Pacific Historical Review* 40, No. 1 (February 1971): 77–98,
especially 80–89; Douglas MacArthur, "Patriotism and Faith," *United Evangelical
Action*, July 1, 1952, 3; "Thank You General MacArthur," *United Evangelical Action*,
February 15, 1949, 21. On other help given to missionaries in Asia by the military, see
Jared Barker, *Assignment in the Philippines* (Chicago: Moody Press, 1984), 92.

9. On missionary successes in China, see "Chiang Kai-Shek Invites Missionaries
to Lay Spiritual Bases of New China," *United Evangelical Action*, October 1,
1944, 11; Edwin Gaustad and Leigh Schmidt, *The Religious History of America*
(New York: HarperCollins, 2002), 267; Steven P. Miller, *Billy Graham and the Rise
of the Republican South* (Philadelphia: University of Pennsylvania Press, 2009), 23.
On China in the American evangelical imagination, see Miles Mullin, "Postwar
Evangelical Social Concern: Evangelical Identity and the Modes and Limits of Social
Engagement, 1945–1960" (PhD diss., Vanderbilt University, 2009), 335.

10. On the Stams, see Theodore W. Engstrom, "John and Betty Stam: Martyrs," *Moody
Monthly*, December 1943, 190; Lee S. Huizenga, *John and Betty Stam: Martyrs*
(Grand Rapids: Zondervan, 1935); Mary Geraldine Taylor, *The Triumph of John
and Betty Stam* (Philadelphia: China Inland Mission, 1935). For "running dogs of
imperialism," see Tu Yichao, "Panda Huggers and Dragon Slayers: Billy Graham,
American Evangelicals, and Sino-American Relations," 2013 BGCA Research
Lecture, Wheaton, Ill., September 25, 2013; Elmer Kilbourne, *Missionary Maverick*
(Greenwood, Ind.: OMS International, 2009), 86. On Jones's trip to China, see Jones,

"What I Saw in China," in Box 21, Folder 12, Asbury Theological Seminary Special Collections; Graham, *Ordinary Man*, 340; Jones to supporters in China, May 2, 1949, in Box 4, Folder 7, E. Stanley Jones Collection, ATSSC. On CIM persecution, see Donald E. Hoke, "The China Story," *Christian Life*, February 1951, 9. On Bill Wallace, see Mullin, "Postwar Evangelical Social Concern," 356; Jesse Fletcher, *Bill Wallace of China* (Nashville, Tenn.: Broadman Press, 1963). For more atrocities, see Mullin, "Postwar Evangelical Social Concern," 304–307. On Morken, see Hefley, *God Goes to High School* (Waco, Tex.: Word Books, 1970), 63.

11. For "real lack of spiritual insight," see Marilee Pierce Dunker, *Man of Vision, Woman of Prayer* (Nashville, Tenn.: Thomas Nelson, 1980), 73–74. On the Chiangs' spirituality, see *Generalissimo and Madame Chiang Kai-Shek: Christian Liberators of China* (Grand Rapids, Mich.: Zondervan, 1943); Mullin, "Postwar Evangelical Social Concern," 343, 349; Bob Pierce, *The Untold Korea Story* (Grand Rapids, Mich.: Zondervan, 1951), 78; Franklin Graham and Jeanette Lockerbie, *Bob Pierce: This One Thing I Do* (Waco, Tex.: Word Books, 1983), 140–41, 150–51; Kilbourne, *Missionary Maverick*, 145. For "more dedicated to Christ," see David Aikman, *Billy Graham: His Life and Influence* (Nashville, Tenn.: Thomas Nelson, 2007), 101–102. On conversions in Formosa, see Hefley, *God Goes to High School*, 63.

12. On food distribution, see Axel Schaeffer, "Evangelicals and Foreign Policy," lecture at Southampton University, United Kingdom, May 2014. For "ripples of goodwill," see Aikman, *Billy Graham*, 101. On Graham's trip to South Korea, see Graham, *Sons at War*, 19–24. On similar evangelical–military collaboration in Korea, see Elmer Kilbourne, *Missionary Maverick* (Greenwood, Ind.: OMS International, 2009), 109; "Korean Army Chief of Staff Here on Tour," *Los Angeles Times*, March 30, 1958, A1. On missionary-military collaboration more broadly, see Matthew Sutton, *Double Crossed: The Missionaries Who Spied for the United States During the Second World War* (New York: Basic Books, 2019).

13. On Broger, see Jeff Sharlet, *The Family: The Secret Fundamentalism at the Heart of America's Power* (New York: HarperCollins, 2008), 202–204; Timothy Stoneman, "Global Moderns," lecture at Southampton University, United Kingdom, May 2014; Randall Balmer, *The Encyclopedia of Evangelicalism* (Waco, Tex.: Baylor University Press, 2004), 103. On Broger and Chiang, see Mullin, "Postwar Evangelical Social Concern," 350–51.

14. *Militant Liberty: A Program of Evaluation and Assessment of Freedom* (Washington, D.C.: United States Department of Defense, 1955), 1.

15. Sharlet, *The Family*, 202–204; Anne Loveland, *American Evangelicals and the U.S. Military, 1942–1993* (Baton Rouge: Louisiana State University Press, 1996).

16. On Pierce's background and evangelistic success, see Richard Gehman, *Let My Heart Be Broken* (New York: McGraw-Hill, 1960), 180–84; David King, "Seeking a Global Vision: The Evolution of World Vision and American Evangelicalism" (PhD diss., Emory University, 2012), 21, 94. On Pierce's charisma, see Norman Rohrer, *Open Arms* (Wheaton, Ill.: Tyndale House, 1987), 178.

17. On Pierce's visit to China, see *One Thing*, 58–66. On the advances and brutality of Mao's army, see John Robert Hamilton, "An Historical Study of Bob Pierce and World

Vision's Development of the Evangelical Social Action Film" (PhD diss., University of Southern California, 1980), 21–22; Lee Grant, "He Only Wants to Save the World," *Los Angeles Times*, January 22, 1975; King, "Seeking a Global Vision," 46.

18. Pierce, *Untold Korea Story*, 5–6, 70, 79.

19. For "planned to buy a Bel Air Chevy" and the organization of World Vision, see Rohrer, *Open Arms*, 54–57. For the Pierce and World Vision timeline, see King, "Seeking a Global Vision," 49. On Pierce's continued anticommunism within YFC, see "One Ideology Will Win, Says Evangelist Graham," *Los Angeles Times*, February 16, 1951, 17.

20. For "the glorious light of the Gospel," see *Untold Korea Story*, 5, 32–36. For "canvassed the entire town," see Kilbourne, *Missionary Maverick*, 93. Rhee quoted in King, "Seeking a Global Vision," 59. On Rhee's spirituality and connection with evangelical revivalism, see Pierce, *One Thing*, 145–47.

21. *Dead Men on Furlough* (1954), seen at http://vimeo.com/37189667. For more on *Dead Men*, see Hamilton, "Evangelical Social Action Film," 71–84; "Communism in Korea Portrayed by Film," *Torrance Press*, November 22, 1954, 11. On Pierce as a war correspondent, see Gehman, *Let My Heart*, 173.

22. On the American use of Korean persecution narratives, see Gehman, *Let My Heart*, 71–74, 103, 115. On Korean prayer practices, see Gehman, *Let My Heart* 35; Pierce, *Untold Story*, 7, 10. On Korean martyrdom, see *One Thing*, 16–19, 41, 45, 71. For "a good many evangelical Christians," see Pierce, *Untold Korea Story*, 5.

23. *The Red Plague*, screened by author at World Vision International headquarters, Monrovia, Cal., June 12, 2013.

24. For "deadly red plague," see *World Vision Magazine*, June 1957, 2. For "Communist jet bombers," see *World Vision Magazine*, August–September 1957, 2. On the Seoul Crusade, see "We Are Humbly Grateful to God," *World Vision Magazine*, December 1957, 6–7. On Pierce's Asian travels, see Gehman, *Let My Heart*, ix, 172. For "strategic points today," see Pierce, *Untold Korea Story*, 78.

25. On World Vision's founding myth, see King, "Seeking a Global Vision," 42–44.

26. For "America's missionary ambassador," see Graham, *Sons at War*, 10. On Pierce's transdenominationalism, see Gehman, *Let My Heart*, 37, 82. For "this gifted man of God," see Kilbourne, *Missionary Maverick*, 134. On World Vision's evangelical connections, see Rohrer, *Open Arms*, 76.

27. On World Vision's sponsorship program, see King, "Seeking a Global Vision," 59–60, 64–67. For "America's missionary ambassador," see Graham, *Sons at War*, 10. For "my orphanages," see Kilbourne, *Missionary Maverick*, 134. On rapid growth, see Rohrer, *Open Arms*, 79–80; King, "Seeking a Global Vision," 1.

28. On the delegation's entry into Seoul, see Graham, *Sons at War*, 37. For "a majestic figure," see Joon Gon Kim, quoted in Seongchan Song, "Rev. Kyung-Chik Han's 50 Year Ministry," *Kyung Chik Han Collection/Biographies* (Seoul: Kyung Chik Han Foundation, 2010), 2: 26. Han was initially cited in World Vision literature, but that largely faded.

29. Soong-Hong Han, "Kyung-Chik Han: A Man Taking after Jesus," 291–302, in *KCHC/Biographies* 2; Sung-Deuk Oak, *The Making of Korean Christianity: Protestant*

Encounters with Korean Religions, 1879–1915 (Waco, Tex.: Baylor University Press, 2013). On the revival, see William Yoo, *American Missionaries, Korean Protestants, and the Changing Shape of World Christianity, 1884–1965* (New York: Routledge, 2017), 99, 109.

30. On Han's bearing, see Won-Sul Lee, "Just Three More Years to Live!" 90, in *KCHC/Biographies 2*. On Han's call to ministry, see Yoo, *American Missionaries, Korean Protestants,* 181. On Han's theological positioning, see Lee, "Just Three More Years," 151, in *KCHC/Biographies* 2; Unyong Kim, "The Preaching World of Kyung-Chik Han, a Luminary of the Pulpit," 488, in *KCHC/Theses 1*; Manyeol Lee, "Han's Place in Korean Church History," 44–52, in *KCHC/Theses 1*. On Han's interaction with the settlement movement, see Yun-Gu Lee, "The Influence of Rev. Kyung-Chik Han on Korean Society," 95, in *KCHC/Theses 2*. On Han's preaching style, see Eun-seop Kim, "Introduction of A Sermon Series of Rev. Kyung-Chik Han," 7, in *KCHC/Sermons 1*; "The Preaching World," 494, in *KCHC/Theses 1*.

31. On Han's Korean garb and intense patriotism, see Myung-Woo Park, "A Study on the Mission Thought of Rev. Kyung-Chik Han," 310, in *KCHC/Theses 2*. On Han's torture, surveillance, and his resentment toward the Japanese, see Lee, "Just Three More Years," 157, in *KCHC/Biographies 2*; Eun-seop Kim, "Kyung-Chik: His Spirituality and Its Effect," 535–36, in *KCHC/Theses 2*; Soong-Hong Han, "Kyung-Chik Han: A Man Taking after Jesus," 42, 343, in *KCHC/Biographies 2*. On Han's bowing before a Shinto temple, see Han, "My Gratitude," 240–46, in *KCHC/Biographies 1*. On Han's humanitarianism in Sinuiju, see Han, "My Gratitude," 224–34, in *KCHC/Biographies 1*; Lee, "Just Three More Years," 155, in *KCHC/Biographies 2*.

32. On Han's exhilaration at the Japanese defeat, see Han, "My Gratitude," 277, in *KCHC/Biographies 1*. On his oversight of the police force and the SDP, see Han, "My Gratitude," 278–90, in *KCHC/Biographies 1*. On communist attacks on the SDP and Christians, see Lee, "Just Three More Years," 169, 191–92, in *KCHC/Biographies 2*. On Han's flight to Seoul, see Soong-Hong Han, "A Man Taking after Jesus," 393–94, in *KCHC/Biographies 2*; Pierce, *Untold Korea Story*, 47.

33. On Han's work among refugees in 1945, see Pierce, *Untold Korea Story*, 48. For "A Gospel of the Propertyless," see Gol Rim, "Kyung-Chik Han's Faith Theory of Church," 274, in *KCHC/Theses 1*. On the growth of Young Nak, see Jang-Choon Yoo, "Social Service of Rev. Han," 187, in *KCHC/Theses 2*. On the construction of Young Nak, see Harold Voelkel, "Kyung Chik Han," 18, in *KCHC/Biographies 2*. On Han's advocacy on behalf of North Korean refugees, see "Rev. Kyung-Chik Han's Place in Korean Church History," 93, in *KCHC/Theses 1*. For "help the poor," see Byeonghui Kim, "Dialogue with Rev. Kyung-Chik Han," 443, in *KCHC/Biographies 1*; Han, "The Spirit of Mutual Help," 411–19, in *KCHC/Sermons 2*.

34. On Communist atrocities, see Kilbourne, *Missionary Maverick*, 107; Lee, "Just Three More Years," 195, in *KCHC/Biographies 2*. For "first enemy," see quote in Seungjun Lee, "Rev. Kyung-Chik Han and the Korean War," 225, in *KCHC/Theses 1*. For Han's famous 1947 "Christianity and Communism" sermon, see pages 421–37 in *KCHC/Sermons 1*. For "dear young patriotic soldiers," see Lee, "Just Three More Years," 190, in *KCHC/Biographies 2*. On the Seobuk militia, see Soong-Hong Han, "Kyung

Chik-Han: A Man Taking after Jesus," 414, in *KCHC/Biographies 2*; Lee, "Just Three More Years," 177–78. On the Christian Volunteer Soldiers, see Jang-Choon Yoo, "Social Service of Rev. Han," 226, in *KCHC/Theses 2*. For "purifying movement," see "Kyung-Chik Han: A Man Taking after Jesus," 489, in *KCHC/Biographies 2*. For "so many found Christ," see Kilbourne, *Missionary Maverick*, 92. For other examples of Han as an anticommunist voice for the West, see "Russians Refuse to Sell Them Rice," *Washington Post*, March 15, 1946, 2; Fulton Oursler, "In Death's Midst," *Daily Boston Globe*, September 28, 1952, A2; "Korean Clergyman Terms G.I.s Lonely," *New York Herald Tribune*, March 3, 1951, 10.

35. On the KCNRS, see Soong-Hong Han, "A Man Taking After Jesus," 418–19, in *KCHC/Biographies 2*; Seungjun Lee, "Rev. Kyung-Chik Han and the Korean War," 206–207, in *KCHC/Theses 1*. On Han's negotiations with the United Nations, General MacArthur, and the U.S. Air Force, see "Rev. Kyung-Chik Han's Life and Thought," 23, in *KCHC/Theses 1*; Soong-Hong Han, "A Man Taking after Jesus," 428–30, in *KCHC/Biographies 2*. On Han's connections with American evangelicals, including Bill Bright, E. Stanley Jones, Carl Henry, Billy Graham, see Byeonghun Gang, "That Is the Beginning of Change," 180, in *KCHC/Biographies 3*.

36. The following list is just a sampling of the organizations Han established or helped run: Borinwon in Sinuiju (1939), Korean National Council of Churches (1946), Borinwon in Seoul (1947), Daegwang School (1947), Christian Deliverance Association (1950), Korean Christian National Salvation Association (1950), Christian Delegation's Visitation to Pyongyang (1950), Christian Children's Fund (1950), Daegwang Senior High School, Boseong Senior High School (1950), Busan Youngnak Church (1951), Busan Tabitha Home for Mothers and Children (1951), Tabitha Mojawon (1951), Youngnak Kyunrowon (1952), Jeju Youngnak Church (1952), Youngnak Junior and Senior High School (1952), Seonmyeonghoe (1953), Youngnak Mojawon (1954), Youngnak Mojawon-Widow's Home (1954), Soongsil School (1954), Christian Association (1955), General Assembly of Presbyterian Church in Korea (1955), Soongsil College (dean for four years in the 1950s), Korea Campus Crusade for Christ (1958), Youngnak Women's Seminary, Soongeui School, Youngnak School (1959), Seoul Women's University (1962), Soongeui Women's College (1963), Holt Christian Adoption Program (1967), and the Asian Center for Theological Studies and Mission (1968). In all, he was instrumental in launching and developing over 200 churches, industrial missions, military ministries, and schools. See especially "Social Service of Rev. Han," 210s, in *KCHC/Theses 2*; "Kyung-Chik Han's Christian Ideology of Founding a Nation," 193–95, in *KCHC/Theses 1*.

On Han's charisma and use of persuasion and consensus, see Changgeun Choi, "Shouldn't We Make Everybody Happy?" 173–74, in *KCHC/Biographies 3*; "Kyung-Chik Han's Faith Theory of Church," 305, in *KCHC/Theses 1*; Seongkook Kim, "The Symbolic Leadership of Rev. Kyung-Chik Han, the 'Eternal Puritan,'" 511, in *KCHC/Theses 1*. On his preoccupation with efficiency, see Jaegyeong Oh, "You Should Say 'Yes' and 'No' and the Right Times," 51, in *KCHC/Biographies 3*; Wonseol Lee, "Leaders Should Be Good Shepherds," 235, in *KCHC/Biographies 3*. For "old servant of God," see Dongsu Kim, "Lying Down Is Also a Talent," 203, in *KCHC/Biographies 3*.

37. On Han's organizing of proto-World Vision activities, see Soong-Hong Han, "A Man Taking after Jesus," 425–28, in *KCHC/Biographies 2*. On Han's intensive networking with contacts in the United States when the Korean War broke out, see Jang-Choon Yoo, "Social Service of Rev. Han Who Served Korean Society," 227, in *KCHC/Theses 2*. For "huddled together," see Pierce, *Untold Korea Story*, 26. On the initial invitations to Pierce by Han and Elmer Kilbourne, see Yoo, "Social Service of Rev. Han," 190–91, in *KCHC/Theses 2*; Pierce, *Untold Korea Story*, 26–27.

38. For Han's intense concern for individual conversion and salvation, see "Rev. Kyung-Chik Han's Perspective on Mission," 265, in *KCHC/Theses 2*; 264, 270; 9–32. On Han's extensive contacts in the United States see *KCHC/Theses 2*, 227. On Pierce's financial contributions, see Pierce, *Untold Korea Story*, 79; Yun-Gu Lee, "The Influence of Rev. Kyung-Chik Han on Korean Society," 98, in *KCHC/Theses 2*; Yoo, "Social Service," 192–94, in *KCHC/Theses 2*.

39. On Han as part of a delegation, see Gehman, *Let My Heart*, 28, 36–37. For "gentle, dedicated pastor," see "A New Ministry for Dr. Han," *World Vision*, December 1972, 19. For "fine interpreter," see Graham, *This One Thing*, 145–46, 178–79. For "behind every bit of it," see Dunker, *Man of Vision*, 108. In the 2010s, there has been a slight recovery of Han's memory. See "Kevin Jenkins Joins 60th Anniversary Celebrations in South Korea," WVI website, October 13, 2010; Marilee Pierce Dunker, "How Firm a Foundation," *World Vision*, October 2015.

40. For "always promoted indigenous pastors," see King, "Seeking a Global Vision," 96. For "Korean saint," see Yoo, *American Missionaries, Korean Protestants*, 182. On Pierce's tribute to Han, see Pierce, *Untold Korea Story*, 9–19, 45–49. For "from abroad," see Graham, *This One Thing*, 213. On Han and Pierce as cofounders of World Vision, see Sundo Kim, "A Great Shepherd," 134, in KCHC/Biographies 3; Hyeongseok Kim, "Thy Will Be Done," 206, in *KCHC/Biographies 3*; "The Memorial Collection," 360, in *KCHC/Biographies 3*; Unyong Kim, "The Preaching World of Kyung-Chik Han," 470, in *KCHC/Theses 1*; Kwangsoon Lee, "Han's Perspective on Mission," 289, in *KCHC/Theses 2*. On Han as the founder of World Vision, see Yoo, "Social Service of Rev. Han," 191–92, *KCHC/Theses 2*; Sundo Kim, "Great Shepherd," 134, in *KCHC/Biographies 3*. On Han's significant role at Pierce's funeral, see Yun-Gu Lee, "Influence of Han on Korean Society," 108, in *KCHC/Theses 2*. On Han's continued involvement in World Vision, see Rohrer, *Open Arms*, 232; "World Vision Team Heads for Far East," *Washington Post*, July 11, 1959, D7; "Seoul Pastor Arrives," *New York Herald Tribune*, May 22, 1953, 7. For "master performer," see author interview with Jong-Sam Park, Seoul, Korea, May 20, 2014.

41. For Han's 1946 sermon, see "Christianity and the Foundation of the Nation," 408–20, in *KCHC/Sermons 1*. Also see Han, "Christianity and Freedom," 405, in *KCHC/Sermons 1*; Han, "Christianity and Communism," 421, in *KCHC/Sermons 1*. On American evangelical uses of Han for anticommunist ends, see Carl F. Henry and Kyung-Chik Han, "The Communist Terror: Plight of the Korean Christians," *Christianity Today*, September 25, 1961, 35; Yoo, *American Missionaries, Korean Protestants*, 199.

42. On Han's conviction that conversion results in social transformation, see Jungsik Cha, "Kyung-Chik Han and the New Testament Hermeneutics in His Sermons," 373, in

KCHC/Theses 1. For "dictators' anti-democratic tendencies," see Bong-Ho Son, "Rev. Kyung-Chik Han as an Ethical Exemplar of the Korean Christian Church," 151–55, in *KCHC/Theses 1*. On Park's coup, see Cha, "New Testament Hermeneutics," 398–99, in *KCHC/Theses 1*; Yoo, "Social Service of Rev. Han," 229–31, in *KCHC/Theses 2*. For "prophet possessed of courage," see Unyong Kim, "Preaching World of Kyung-Chik Han," 493, in *KCHC/Theses 1*. On the Bible as the "law of the land," see "Global Survey of Evangelical Protestant Leaders," Pew Research Center, Washington, D.C., June 22, 2011, 82.

PART II
GLOBAL ENCOUNTERS

3

Sat Tal 1958

Cold War and Caste

I have changed a great deal. No one can be exposed to the East and not be changed by it.
— E. Stanley Jones at Taylor College in Upland, Indiana[1]

Tension suffused Hughes Chapel in 1958 as alumnus and missionary E. Stanley Jones addressed a thousand students and faculty members. His indelicate sermon on racial integration shocked many on Asbury College's lily-white campus. In starkly corporeal terms, Jones described holding hands with his black brethren—and of lifting their hands to his lips—while praying together. He pronounced civil rights "a God-touched movement." He thundered against segregationists, arguing that their resistance was hurting the cause of Christ and democracy.

Campus itself, an evangelical holiness enclave in the rolling hills of the Kentucky Bluegrass, was split on the issue of integration. Segregationists made sure there were no African Americans at Asbury, even eight years after a state law that had prohibited integration in higher education was lifted. But while the college remained recalcitrant, it was not, in Jones's estimation, marred by a "cantankerous conservatism." He saw the college's heritage, which emphasized the revivalism of Francis Asbury and John and Charles Wesley, as bending toward racial egalitarianism. In fact, sentiment in favor of integration was blossoming on campus in the late 1950s as the civil rights movement itself came into full bloom. Jones reported that at least 85 percent of alumni, students, and faculty wanted the campus integrated. Still, it remained segregated because the college's president refused to challenge a coterie of trustees from the Deep South. Jones, called the greatest missionary of the twentieth century by *Time* magazine, was also a trustee. As he railed against racism on this crisp October morning, he never mentioned his colleagues by name. But his tempest was a direct challenge to Asbury's establishment, and everyone in the chapel knew it.[2]

Like evangelicals in postwar Chicago and Cold War Seoul, Jones invoked Scripture and American exceptionalism. He quoted the Apostle Paul's exhortation that there is no difference between Greek and Jew. Borrowing themes

Facing West. David R. Swartz, Oxford University Press (2020). © Oxford University Press.
DOI: 10.1093/oso/9780190250805.001.0001

from Gunnar Myrdal's landmark book on racism, *An American Dilemma* (1944), Jones identified disjuncture between American rhetoric and racial practices. He cited the Pledge of Allegiance's language of "liberty and justice for *all*," suggesting that the innate American ideal of freedom would overcome hypocrisy. "The best thing that ever happened in the Southland," he continued, was the Supreme Court decision four years earlier in *Brown v. Board of Education*. "People fight it. People hate it. People try to circumvent it. I give it ten years. In ten years it will all be over," he exulted. "Our democracy is sounder, and our consciences are clearer." Liberty and racial equality would prevail.[3]

At the same time, Jones's speech defied the assumption that the American civil rights movement was entirely a homegrown affair. In fact, the global orientation of the address was striking. Drawing from decades of missionary work in Asia, Jones positioned civil rights in the context of the Cold War and decolonization. He instructed Asbury students not to give rhetorical ammunition to the communists. A global revolution, he said, was taking place in reaction to imperialism and attitudes of racial supremacy. After describing protests in Asia and Africa, Jones explained that "what's happening here is an eddy in the scheme of what's happening in the world." He told stories of Indian interracial, nonviolent noncooperation in which Gandhi had worn down the enemy with goodwill. "It's the rise of man!" he exclaimed. "The old imperialism is gone, is dead, or dying!" As Jones wound down the sermon, which marked the conclusion of a weeklong revival, his pace slowed and volume softened. "Mind you, I've never seen a finer student body—potentially—than you," he said. But to "love with the love of God" and to change the world, "we need something to break down all our prejudices and all our fears and give ourselves to Jesus Christ." Wanting this moment to be decisive, Jones issued a call to personal transformation. "I want you to settle it tonight," he urged in classic evangelistic fashion. "If you're not sure of your salvation, come." He called others to dedicate themselves to full-time Christian service. In a scene that Jones called "breath-taking," over 500 students came forward to kneel at the altar.[4]

Jones's integration of revival language and social concern was no mere rhetorical flourish. His dual messages—which bridged both American and global frontiers and personal and social realms—had been rigorously cultivated. For nearly thirty years, Jones had been living at the Sat Tal Ashram, located in the foothills of the Himalayas in India. When Asbury students visited Jones there in 1931, they discovered a Christian community that looked and felt very different from American evangelicalism. Seeking to reproduce Christian faith in indigenous form, the ashram's members lived together, prayed together, discussed spirituality, and practiced simple living. In the context of the Indian caste system, which Jones called "India's curse," Sat Tal sought to establish "a miniature kingdom of God." This egalitarian, caste-defying ashram stood in stark contrast to Asbury's segregated campus in 1958. "The American caste system and American materialism," he told audiences as he toured the United States, "are the greatest hindrances to the acceptance of Christ by the East."[5]

While most white evangelicals opposed the civil rights movement—or turned away in conspicuous inaction—Jones's story shows how global encounters sometimes reoriented racial perspectives. America had no business proclaiming national triumph, some preached, when it was misbehaving at home. Pointing to racial segregation in the American South, missionaries and their potential converts noted the limits of American democracy and religion. Jones represents the strong reflexive motion from East to West carried by American missionaries. His critiques of American racism, birthed from observations of the Indian caste system, his friendship with Mahatma Gandhi, and life at his beloved Sat Tal Ashram, enjoyed a wide reach that extended beyond Asbury to broader evangelical and mainline audiences throughout the United States. Jones argued that segregation hindered both missions and American diplomacy as the United States sought to position itself as an alternative to Nazism, fascism, and Marxism. Through the 1950s Jones combined global experiences and faith-saturated appeals for racial integration as he preached to American Christian cold warriors.[6]

I. Christ of the Indian Road

In 1907 twenty-three-year-old E. Stanley Jones left for India with forty pounds in British gold, a one-way ticket to Bombay, a Hindustani grammar, and a handshake. As he boarded the *Teutonic* steamship in New York City, he also carried an evangelical zeal to spread the gospel. Jones had recently participated in a three-day revival at Asbury College. In fact, the revival had begun in his dorm room. Kneeling in prayer with several classmates, Jones was swept off his feet by a visitation of the divine. "We were all filled," he described, "flooded by the Spirit." As revival spread that evening, "all life was alive with God." By the next morning, every classroom on campus was filled with students "seeking and finding and witnessing." Classes were cancelled, and Jones described the scene as a cyclone, in the center of which he experienced a "holy calm." By the end of the revival, he had pledged himself to missionary work, a sobering commitment. "In those days," Jones later recalled, "to volunteer for Africa was like signing your death warrant. It was put up as a very grim proposition."[7]

It was difficult indeed. His mission agency sent him even further than Africa, in fact all the way to India, where the young Jones observed unfamiliar languages, exotic religions like "Hindooism," and strange animals like scorpions and black-faced baboons. But if Indian culture seemed exotic, the caste system he encountered did not. As a child in Baltimore and as a student in central Kentucky, each located south of the Mason-Dixon line, he had already lived amid stark racial separation. On one hand, Jones and other missionaries sought to exploit the caste system to gain converts. Using the strategy of "mass movement evangelism," missionaries like Jones engaged with oppressed castes and then tried to convert them en masse. "Let one great word throb . . . SOULS. . . . We left America for souls," exclaimed Jones. "Are we now content to live without them?" On the other hand, Jones was troubled by his powerlessness in addressing the fragmented state of Indian society. As pastor of an English-speaking church made up of Anglo-Indians, English, Americans, and English-speaking Indians, he sensed that he was working "on the dying edges of an imperialistic, privileged, receding group." Conversion did little to support the Indian movement for self-government. "The whole atmosphere," he later remembered, "seemed charged with criticism, suspicion, resentment. I scarcely ever looked into a native newspaper that the acid did not eat into my soul." Many Indians sharply questioned Jones's forthright pursuit of conversion. It concerned the young missionary that "the pundits came prepared—long lists of questions culled from the skeptical literature of the ages, facts from history, ugly stories of hypocrisy and rapacity of the so-called Christian nations." Jones's early years in India, then, were characterized by tension, anxiety, and struggle. Moreover, he exhausted himself with hard work. He described himself as "a house builder & contractor and labor extractor and a beater down of savages and setter of prices and settler of disputes & punisher of boys and preacher of the gospel and comforter to the persecuted few Christians and so on ad tireddom." He had arrived in India with a faith that was "neat and tied up with a blue ribbon," but he soon began to suffer from nervous collapses. The broken missionary limped home to America in 1916, well ahead of his scheduled furlough.[8]

When Jones returned to India the following year, he sought to practice a more culturally sensitive missiology. He still yearned to convert the "heathen"— writing often in the 1920s about "soul-winning"—but his theology extended beyond a sole focus on conversion and established methods of missionary work. Along with fellow Asbury graduate J. Waskom Pickett, who wrote extensive analyses of church growth and cultural contextualization in India, Jones expressed a willingness to "scratch or nick" his theological and cultural assumptions. There was ample opportunity. Low-caste Dalits, for example, upon learning how race prejudice was embedded in the American founding, expressed their revulsion toward American theology and history. "The Mayflower that carried the Pilgrim Fathers to religious liberty in America went on her next trip for a load of slaves," Jones later recounted. "Is it to be wondered that race and colour prejudice still exists in the West in spite of Christianity? It came in with it. The East feels that these things are still there." Jones argued that India saw Christ as a compelling figure but hesitated to follow because missionaries presented Christ as an extender of Western civilization. To the contrary, preached Jones, "Christ must be in an Indian setting. It must be the Christ of the Indian Road."[9]

The writings of contemporaneous missionary James M. Thoburn highlight the truly remarkable nature of Jones's assertion. In his 1906 book *The Christian Conquest of India*, the Methodist Thoburn wrote, "Side by side these two great sections of the English speaking race are moving forward through Christian and missionary agencies to bring the millions of India to share in the same liberty, enlightenment, and civilizations to which the religion of Christ has led the Aryans of the West." By contrast, Jones sought to sensitize lay Christian Americans to their reputation as "international meddlers, creed mongers to the East, feverish ecclesiastics" all seeking to "satisfy a racial superiority complex." A vital relationship to Jesus Christ, not the cultural trappings of the West, was at the heart of Christian faith. It was the missionary's job, wrote Jones, to "disentangle Christ from the accretions which the centuries had gathered around him." This argument was powerfully articulated in *Christ of the Indian Road* (1925), a runaway bestseller that brought Jones fame in his homeland and represented a powerful new movement toward the contextualization of the gospel. It reflected the commitments of the mainline missionary enterprise of the 1920s—and anticipated the move in the 1950s and beyond toward contextualization among evangelicals like Donald McGavran, Eugene Nida, and others affiliated with Wycliffe Bible Translators, the Summer Institute of Linguistics, and the Lausanne Congress.[10]

The new strategy took many forms in the 1920s. The first was cultural literacy. Jones, who wanted "the East to keep its own soul," read the *Bhagavad-Gita* and organized roundtable conferences about faith in Hindu temples, theosophical society halls, and other places where non-Christians might feel comfortable discussing religion. Jones, who articulated a desire for authentic conversation, refused to sit at the head of the table and refrained from praying without permission. These techniques were remarkably effective. He gained a large following in India and, according to historian Daniel Immerwahr, was "extraordinarily successful in influencing opinion." His dictum—that missionaries "must become more Christian and more Indian"—proved appealing in the twilight of the age of imperialism.[11]

The second major effort toward contextualization was the pursuit of justice. A strong critic of British imperialism, Jones favored Indian independence. "Our message," he wrote in 1917 to fellow Methodists in a magazine called *Indian Witness*, "must be more closely associated than ever before with the legitimate national aspirations of India." To a leading Indian nationalist who pointed out that "everyone who becomes a Christian is lost to our national cause," Jones responded, "Christianity must work with the national grain, not against it. Christ must not seem a Western Partisan of White Rule, but a Brother of Men." Some American missionaries, preoccupied with Indian nationalism, minimized caste as a justice issue. But Jones remained sympathetic to both the nationalist cause and the plight of the untouchables. He described caste as India's "curse" and suggested that the practice directly violated the "kingdom of God." Appalled by the situation in Palghat, a town in southern India located at the center of orthodox Brahmanism, Jones commented, "They will not allow the low castes to go through their villages. Pigs and dogs may. The low caste may not!" Even worse, Christians, most notably Syrian believers in southern India, continued to ostracize outcastes. By the 1930s Jones had become an outspoken activist, urging all Christians to "take the outcastes into their churches." Following Jesus, he said, demanded social concern, which meant reaching out to untouchables with "the warm touch of the personal Christ to make it tingle with life and radiance."[12]

These three impulses—cultural sensitivity, nationalism, and egalitarianism—were reflected and reinforced by Jones's participation in Hindu ashrams (Figure 3.1). He began, ironically enough, by joining high-born Indians whose

Figure 3.1. Missionary E. Stanley Jones at an ashram in the 1930s. Courtesy of Asbury Theological Seminary Special Collections, Wilmore, Ky.

participation in spiritual retreat was meant to separate themselves from the masses. Jones nonetheless accepted their invitation, hoping to learn more about India's religious culture. He soon found some egalitarian ashrams more to his liking. At Travancore, a territory at the southernmost tip of the subcontinent where caste was very strongly entrenched, Jones sat down to a subversive inter-caste dinner with high-caste Hindus, outcastes, Indian Christians, Muslims, and Westerners. Jones himself sat between a "Mohammedan" and an outcaste whose face bore "the marks of centuries of oppression." Moved by the event, Jones rendered it in verse: "I took my lamp and went and sat / Where men of another creed and custom / Dwelt together in bonds of common search." After meeting Gandhi at the Sabarmati Ashram, Jones rhapsodized about the ashram's beautiful soul to supporters in America, writing, "The spirit of the ashram is so beautiful and so self-sacrificial, Gandhi combines strength and humility, unselfishness and service." Yet Jones confided that this great man who "has been deeply influenced by the teaching of Christ" has "never seen Him."[13]

This deep ambivalence about Hindu ashrams inspired Jones to found a Christian alternative. The Sat Tal Ashram, founded in 1930, was intended to be "truly Christian and truly Indian." The thirty-five or so ashramites were housed in fourteen cottages on a beautiful 400-acre estate in the Lake District, which featured deep valleys studded with emerald lakes. At 4,500 feet above sea level, it was an Edenic setting nestled in a forest with verdant foliage and pine trees, abundant wildlife, and the Himalayas rising in the distance. Life at Sat Tal followed a disciplined schedule that stressed the holistic nature of the ashram, which sought to develop the body, mind, and soul. The soul was nurtured by private devotional times, Bible teachings, communal worship, and a large painting of Christ with an inscription that read, "Christ is the Guru of this Ashram." The mind was sharpened by rigorous lectures and panel discussions on world religions and ethics. The body was strengthened through recreational exercise and grounds maintenance.[14]

Jones explicitly modeled Sat Tal on traditional ashrams. Defending this strategy to supporters in America, he pointed out that "our gospel is universal in its very nature, but the forms in which it is expressed in the West are not necessarily universal. We have therefore endeavoured to find an expression of Christianity that would be more in line with Indian genius and life." Ashramites wore Indian clothing made of homespun *khaddar*, a symbol of the nationalist movement. Jones himself wore a *dhoti*, a sarong-like wrapping. Participants trod barefoot in the chapel and dining hall. Meals consisted almost entirely of Indian food—and nearly no meat, to avoid offending Hindus.[15]

Sat Tal was also intensely egalitarian. In fact, the ashram, in its defiance of caste, took such an idealized form that some Indian participants had difficulty adjusting to the radical flattening of status. The day began with prayers and sharing in a ritual called "Morning of the Open Heart" in which participants repented of their complicity in perpetuating racial and class barriers. They confessed personal feelings of fear, resentment, self-centeredness, and anything that interfered with "real community." Even physical space reinforced the notion of brotherhood. Ashramites sat in a circle on the floor while studying the Bible together. They shared work. Leaders and newcomers, young and old alike picked up trash, chopped wood, and prepared meals. Inscriptions on ashram walls read, "East and West are alternate beats of the same heart"; "Here everybody loves everybody"; and "Leave behind all race and class distinctions, all ye that enter here." In keeping with the egalitarian ideal, Sat Tal forbade titles. Participants became Brother Gopal, Brother Biswas, and Brother Stanley. The leveling of gender, ethnicity, economy, and nationality—meant to reflect a romanticized precolonial India—was intended also to be "a foretaste of the Christian India that is to be."[16]

Participants described their ashram experience as transformative. One called the fellowship "very deep and beautiful," another as being of the "tenderest and deepest kind." In 1931, Jones himself wrote, "It has been a great summer, one of the very best of my life. The intimate fellowships, the hours of communion, the struggle for souls that needed light, the clearing of truth in the mind, the exquisite presence of the living Christ, the enriching of the whole of life." He marveled at the heterogeneous composition of the gathering, which included religious seekers with Muslim and Hindu backgrounds and Christians from all over the world. To Jones, it prefigured the coming kingdom of God. Sat Tal's promotional literature proclaimed, "We will be the World of the Kingdom of God become flesh in a group, the Kingdom in miniature." Jones meant these words to stand in stark contrast to the religious turmoil and agitation under British rule. "While India has seethed with clash and strife," wrote Jones, "our Ashram has been a haven of brotherhood."[17]

The rise of the Soviet Union in the 1920s and 1930s also shaped Jones's views on caste and race. Compared with most American Protestant conservatives and liberals, who took up hawkish positions, Jones was rather more equivocal. He appreciated the Marxist stress on interracialism and internationalism. In these ways, he said, the principles of Marxism and the Kingdom of God coincided. But in the end, Jones felt, Marxism failed to birth a truly communitarian vision. On a trip to the Soviet Union in 1934, Jones observed firsthand its failures, which included "poverty, the lack of liberty, and the drive against religion." These sobering observations strengthened his anticommunist resolve, and a year later Jones publicly repudiated Stalin's brutalities in a book entitled *Christ's Alternative to Communism*. The book circulated widely in China, Burma, India, and Korea, and when communists made incursions into the northern regions of Burma in the late 1940s, they found copies of *Christ's Alternative* among the resistance. In China, where communists threatened arrests of those caught with

Jones's book, he worked closely with the nationalist general Chiang Kai-shek and conducted an evangelistic tour through Shanghai, Chengdu, Amoy, and Canton just ahead of Mao's advance in 1949. On his return flight to India, Jones wrote letters to Chinese Christians and exulted that several thousand had made "a first-time decision" for Christ. He praised them for the "calm and steadiness of soul as you were about to pass under Communist control." Like Bob Pierce and other evangelicals, Jones saw himself on the front lines of the battle against communism.[18]

Jones found the battle especially intense in his adopted country. India was aligned with neither the Soviets nor the Americans, but U.S. ambassador Chester Bowles and consular officers feared that it would ally with Moscow. This certainly seemed plausible to Jones, who encountered communists everywhere he turned. At the Sat Tal ashram in 1952, twenty out of the one hundred participants were or had been communists. Later that year, in front of an audience of 30,000 people in Travancore on the southern tip of India, Jones desperately sought to sway Indians away from communism. Many, he said, "found Christ as their personal Savior." At a follow-up conference two years later, Jones observed marked improvement. Residents of Travancore, he suggested, had discovered that "they could not have two totalitarianisms in their lives, and they decided to be Christian." Jones later claimed, "I can say without boasting, simply recording, that I have perhaps won more people from Communism to the Christian faith than any living man, certainly more than all my critics put together."[19]

Jones's critiques, however, extended well beyond Marxism. "After living abroad," he wrote in Christ of the Indian Road, "you see your country in the total setting of the world." If Jones's trips to China and the Soviet Union sensitized him to the limits of Marxism, his global immersion also alerted him to American atrocities. Jones reported, "Eastern travelers in America, picking and choosing their facts, can make out a very dark picture of our civilization—the slums of our cities, the lynchings, divorce statistics, crime statistics unparalleled in other cities of the world, and so on." According to scholar Gerald Horne, Indian communists, bidding for supremacy in key districts, "repeatedly zeroed in on Jim Crow." Ambassador Bowles reported, "I have met up with many questions on racial tolerance in the United States. In fact, it is a sure-fire question every time I speak." For ambassadors and missionaries alike, stepping out of the American environment exposed them to problems at home.[20]

Segregation was bad not only for the oppressed, Jones argued, but also for the oppressor. "A rattlesnake, if cornered, will become so angry it will bite itself," he explained in a memorable aphorism. "That is exactly what the harboring of hate and resentment against others is—a biting of oneself. We think we are harming others in holding these spites and hates, but the deeper harm is to ourselves." This festering hate, Jones told listeners of an NBC radio broadcast upon his return to the United States, was bilious to the American soul and wholly unattractive to those outside America. "When I landed on the shores of my native land on September 7th, had I obeyed my impulses I should have taken the first boat back to India. . . . I must confess I came to America with deep questionings and concern. From a distance your civilization seemed superficial and your Christianity inadequate."[21]

Jones, the seasoned missionary, was very different from Jones, the young Asbury graduate. He remained fundamentally grounded in the experiential piety of historic Methodism—Wesleyan scholar Bill Kostlevy called him "an unreconstructed holiness evangelist"—but his experience in India had transformed him away from dogmatic apologetics toward a profound concern for social issues. For Jones, who placed the Sermon on the Mount at the moral center of his faith, the sins of racism and imperialism were the height of hypocrisy and had set back the cause of missionary work. In the 1940s an incensed Jones responded to a critic, "The attitude which you symbolize is pushing the colored majority of the world straight into an alliance against the white minority of the world." He continued, "If I should be kept back from India permanently, which God forbid, then I should consider seriously giving the balance of my working days to help the Negroes of America to an equal status in our democracy and to their fullest development as a people. For the color question has become a world question." In the 1910s Jones had been sent from the shores of America to spread the gospel. By the 1940s he was returning to evangelize his own country.[22]

II. Christ of the American Road

The end of World War II found Jones marooned in the United States. Wartime restrictions had prohibited travel to India until 1945. Then, in retaliation for his anticolonial sympathies, British authorities refused Jones entry into India until 1947. Thereafter, until his death in the early 1970s, Jones spent at least half of each year in the United States, feeling that God had called him to pursue social reform in his homeland. Racial integration became his overriding political concern. An inveterate optimist, Jones invoked the rapid fall of the Indian caste system, preaching that black–white segregation "is doomed." Inspired by Indian precedents, he launched an evangelical civil rights campaign.[23]

Jones enjoyed celebrity status during his years at home in the 1940s. *Christ of the Indian Road* had gripped a large readership in the United States, and his speeches in large cities often drew more than 5,000 people. Though not a polished public speaker—one observer complained that he tripped over his words and that "his vocal equipment is susceptible of vast improvement"—Jones possessed a certain magnetism that resonated in strikingly diverse contexts. In holiness circles, where Jones was popular for his missionary zeal, his raw preaching style reminded listeners of nineteenth-century camp meetings. A witness of Jones's 1924 commencement address at Asbury described his "earnest face, those piercing eyes, that strong-set jaw." He also penetrated more cosmopolitan worlds. The mainline literati lauded him as seer for his "crystalline sincerity and simplicity." Jones joined a speaker circuit that drew huge crowds in Chicago, Detroit, and New York to hear intellectual and political luminaries of the era including theologian Reinhold Niebuhr, pastor Harry Emerson Fosdick, civil rights activist Benjamin Mays, social reformer Jane Addams, politician William Jennings Bryan, and diplomat Ralph Bunche. Crowds at the Chicago Sunday Evening Club were attracted to his geniality. Jaded journalists came under the spell of a "terseness of style, a vigor of thought, a flavor of humor, and a razor-edged irony." Christians from both ends of the Protestant theological spectrum were riveted by his moral authority, which according to one admirer, "throbbed with the zeal of one who has devoted himself mind and soul to an absorbing mission."[24]

For Jones and his audiences alike, wartime heightened a passion for racial equality. The considerable irony of a racially segregated America fighting Nazism was not lost on many Americans. Activists such as Walter White, a veteran of both the Pacific and European theatres and then NAACP director in the postwar years, worked hard to conflate southern racism, Aryan supremacy, and Japanese nationalism. It was not difficult to do so, as tens of thousands of African Americans in the India-Burma theater suffered persistent indignities—separate water fountains and seating—while fighting for global freedom. In his 1945 book, *A Rising Wind*, White explained, "World War II has immeasurably magnified the Negro's awareness of the disparity between profession and practice of democracy." The rhetoric about protecting global democracy against Hitler and Hirohito fell flat as African Americans were denied the privileges of democracy at home and abroad.[25]

Though not on the receiving end of discrimination, Jones too was jolted by the persistence and ferocity of racism. As he repeatedly explained in speeches, segregation offended his fundamental conception of what it meant to be American and Christian. "Two forces, democracy and Christianity, belonging together," he said, "are in the process of being separated." As Jones put it in *Christ of the American Road* (1944)—which also cited Japanese internment and limitations on women and the labor movement as examples of "democratic hesitations"—racial segregation pointed to "a false America, a traitorous America, and a greater danger to our democracy than Hitlerism." His negativity stemmed in large part from his observation that racial conditions had not improved since his childhood in Baltimore and college years in Kentucky. American democracy did not compare favorably even to India's fledgling democracy. In a 1947 article entitled "India's Caste System and Ours," Jones put it starkly: "The caste systems of India and America are fundamentally alike—they are both founded on blood." But if caste distinctions were fading quickly in India, they were "still operative in vast portions of America. . . . The center has not given way." The ultimate irony, observed Jones, was that America and South Africa, the last remaining strongholds of caste, "both claim to be democracies, and both of them profess the Christian religion."[26]

In the battle for the global soul between atheistic Marxism and Christian democracy, such hypocrisies mattered. Citizens of nonaligned India, explained Jones, were hyperaware of American racism, and Jones used this observation in his civil rights activism. In an "Appeal to the People of Alabama" written from Sat Tal, Jones described a photo printed on the front page of a leading Indian newspaper. It pictured a white southern official with his foot on the head of a prostrate black man. "I am seated in the midst of a very sensitive East," Jones wrote. "Everything that happens in any part of the world is being felt and felt deeply here in India. You are representing the American nation before Eastern peoples. And the race riots give a push to hesitant peoples—a push toward the arms of the Communists." As white retrenchment peaked in the 1950s, Jones said, "In our Christian group here in the Himalayas we are praying for Alabama. The eyes of the world are upon you." He told huge audiences across the United States about holding similar evangelistic meetings in India. Some of these revivals were apparent failures, and the reason that Indians would not "accept Christ" was because of American Christian hypocrisy. They bombarded Jones with questions: "Don't you lynch Negroes in America?" and "What do you think about the KKK?" Segregation was no longer a local issue. It was a national and global issue because "the nation gets the blame for the injustices done to the Negro in any local situation. The enemies of democracy pick up every local wrong done anywhere in America and use it against America." Jones, like many other important internationalists in this era, emphasized that American racial segregation was a public relations nightmare abroad. It could push nonaligned nations in the wrong direction.[27]

Long before most white Protestant evangelists, Jones insisted on interracial seating at his evangelistic meetings. If custom or city law mandated that blacks sit in the balcony, he typically instructed groups of whites on the main floor to move to the balcony themselves. In 1941, for example, black and white ministers from Macon, Georgia, invited Jones to spearhead a movement of interracial action. At churches and in a chapel address at Mercer University, he preached to integrated crowds. In these sermons he continued to globally frame local conditions, preaching that if America gave "equality of opportunity to everyone within our own borders, it could become the mediator of a new world order based on the central idea of democracy." These revivals, which sometimes drew crowds of over

25,000, exposed southerners to a potent blend of piety, racial egalitarianism, and internationalism. Jones earned the hostility of many whites, but blacks would remember his interracial revivals decades later.[28]

Ashrams offered a smaller, but no less intense, method of challenging Jim Crow. Beginning in the 1940s, Jones led hundreds of these intensive spiritual retreats throughout the United States. These ashrams were intended to be egalitarian microcommunities in which the wealthy and poor and black and white practiced a churchly version of the "beloved community" ideal of the civil rights movement. Like Sat Tal, participants in American ashrams avoided the use of titles, called each other by first names, and pledged to "break down barriers of race and class." As the ashram movement grew in the 1950s, Jones drew Christians from a broad spectrum of denominational and political persuasions: from the radical Dave Dellinger of the Chicago Seven, who helped start an ashram in Newark, to Lutherans, Catholics, Anabaptists, and conservative evangelicals affiliated with the Church of the Nazarene.[29]

One 1951 meeting of 208 men and women in Green Lake, Wisconsin, offers a glimpse of the remarkably egalitarian nature of these ashrams. Jones, described by a visiting *Collier's* reporter as a "snowy-haired" man with gray luminous eyes, opened the meeting by introducing himself as "Brother Stanley." He told participants that "barriers of class and cash dissolve completely. An executive bunks with a laborer, a society hostess with a shopgirl." As participants celebrated the Eucharist together, Jones intoned, "If you belong to Christ, and I belong to Christ, then, unbreakably, we belong to each other." Each—including Jones, who usually picked up trash from the ground—was assigned tasks of manual labor. The most revolutionary aspect for most, even those from the North, was racial integration. For the next four days black and white ashramites ate together, played together, prayed together, and roomed together. "We no longer see a person of a certain race," said Jones. "We simply see a person for whom Christ died." A black man announced, "This has been the first week of my life in an unsegregated world." This racial egalitarianism was even more conspicuous in the South, where gatherings sometimes had to be canceled because of hostility from local authorities. Still, the ashram movement grew rapidly. In the summer of 1963 alone, 4,000 people attended eighteen ashrams held in the United States and Canada. There were an additional twenty-five overseas.[30]

Jones amplified ground-level activism with a wide spectrum of alliances. He served on an advisory committee for the Congress of Racial Equality (CORE), which organized the Freedom Rides of the early 1960s. He constantly lobbied presidents and members of Congress. He was a featured speaker at hundreds of Kiwanis, Lions, and Rotary Club events around the country. In each of these contexts, Jones made specific calls for federal intervention and interracial committees. At a Rotary Club meeting near Philadelphia, for example, Jones argued that within a decade "the Southland's struggle with desegregation will be all over. . . . Our democracy will be sounder. The diehards will die hard and we will thank God." By the 1960s the irrepressible Jones had become somewhat notorious for his forthright defiance of racial codes in the South.[31]

It was Jones's connection with Martin Luther King, Jr., however, that stands as the missionary's most intriguing contribution to the civil rights movement. King first encountered Jones's writings in the early 1950s in the library stacks at Methodist Divinity School at Boston University. There, perusing Jones's *Mahatma Gandhi: An Interpretation* (1948) (Figure 3.2), King read about the missionary's friendship with Gandhi, which began in the early 1920s. The paean, written less than a year after Gandhi's tragic death (which Jones narrowly missed witnessing), positioned Gandhi as a prophetic voice for justice and peace. Jones wrote that this "little man, who fought a system in the framework of which I stand, has taught me more of the spirit of Christ than perhaps any other man in East or West."[32]

Figure 3.2. Boosters of Jones claimed that his biography of Gandhi introduced Martin Luther King, Jr., to nonviolent methods of civil rights protest.

Reading Jones's description of *satyagraha*, the strategy of nonviolent resistance deployed by Gandhi, helped ignite a new method of social change in King. When he was still a young, obscure minister in the years prior to the Montgomery Bus Boycott, King resolved to resist Southern segregation nonviolently. If King often recounted his nonviolent conversion to white religious audiences, Jones repeated it incessantly. One variation, told by Jones to a *Time* magazine reporter, went like this:

> When I saw Dr. Martin Luther King for the first time he greeted me with this: "It was your book on Mahatma Gandhi which gave me my first inkling of the method and spirit of non-violence. This is the method, I said to myself, to apply to the freedom of the Negro in America. I will use this method of non-violence instead of the method of violence. So it was your book that started us on this path of matching soul force against physical force. We will match our capacity to suffer against the other man's capacity to inflict the suffering. And we will wear down opposition by good-will." This made me responsible, in a way, for what is happening in our Southland. I could retreat into the anonymous, and let others take the consequential suffering. I cannot do it and live with myself and with God. So I take the responsibility for having introduced the idea to Dr. King while he introduced the method and the movement. I can only express my gratitude that I have had some small part in turning this inevitable movement from violence to non-violence.[33]

Recent scholarship on the nonviolent roots of the civil rights movement tempers Jones's claim. Scholar Sudarshan Kapur shows that links between Gandhi and W. E. B. DuBois and Marcus Garvey were in place as early as the 1910s and 1920s. And surveys of black newspapers such as *The Crisis* and the *Chicago Defender* in those decades show extensive indebtedness to Indian sources. Hindu reformer Lala Lajpat Rai and other émigrés, who experienced virulent anti-Indian racism in the United States, were fascinated by the African-American experience and introduced black leaders to Gandhian methods in the 1920s. Numerous civil rights figures reversed the path, taking what became a well-worn trek to India to meet Gandhi himself. Howard University's Howard Thurman, Benjamin Mays, and Mordecai Johnson all traveled to India in the late 1930s to investigate whether Gandhi's methods, which were beginning to free colonial India, might also be able to free American blacks. And there were, besides Jones, other white men who influenced King's nonviolence, including A. J. Muste, author of *Non-Violence in an Aggressive World* (1940); Richard Gregg, a friend of Gandhi who wrote *The Power of Nonviolence* (1935); and organizers of the Highlander Folk

Schools. In short, there were many sources of King's nonviolent strategy. King's agreeable posture toward supporters—motivated in part by the need to nurture a broad constituency—encouraged Jones and his supporters to exaggerate his influence.[34]

Despite these precedents, Jones deserves a prominent position on the roster of civil rights leaders. Along with James Farmer, Bayard Rustin, and Pauline Myers, Jones headlined a key meeting in the March on Washington Movement (MOWM), which protested segregation in the war industries (and which would eventually become the model for the 1963 March on Washington). On July 4, 1943, at an event called "We Are Americans Too," Jones delivered a public address entitled "Defeat Hitler, Hirohito and Mussolini by Enforcing the Constitution and Abolishing Jim Crow." In front of a "wildly enthusiastic" crowd of 5,000 at DuSable High School in Chicago, Jones noted the hypocrisy of racial supremacy and American freedom. The significance of the event, however, lay in the planners' deliberations over methods of social change. In private strategy sessions, one hundred leading black activists and Jones, who was the only white person present, debated the utility of civil disobedience. Some felt that civil disobedience was too radical, but Jones and Pauline Myers emerged as key voices in favor of substantial resistance. In an address entitled "Non-violent Direct Action—What It Is and How It Can Be Applied to Racial Problems in America," delivered at a closed meeting of delegates, Jones urged "the necessity of disobeying unjust laws" but doing so with discipline and in the spirit of love. Practitioners of this method, he urged, must say, "I don't hate you, but I won't obey you. This law or order is wrong and unjust. Do what you may, I won't strike back and I won't obey." In the end, delegates voted to target Washington, Richmond, and Chicago with "trained disciplined volunteers who would disobey the Jim Crow laws and then take the consequences." This was a controversial decision. In fact, mainstream organizations like the NAACP immediately distanced themselves from the MOWM because of its more militant call for civil disobedience.[35]

King's reading of Jones, half a decade later, occurred at a similarly critical moment. As civil disobedience rose in favor in the late 1940s, the nonviolent impulse began to recede. In fact, by the early 1950s Farmer and other CORE activists had nearly given up on the prospect of a Gandhian civil rights movement. King, however, resuscitated it during the 1955 Montgomery Bus Boycott, a one-day boycott that grew to a one-year campaign under the leadership of the young minister. During that year King renounced self-defense and gave up his own gun. He gave speeches making clear that Christ's "sublime teachings on love" in the Sermon on the Mount could serve as a strategy for collective resistance. "As the days unfolded," King wrote in his memoir, "I came to see the power of nonviolence more and more. Living through the actual experience of protest, nonviolence

became more than a method to which I gave intellectual assent; it became a commitment to a way of life . . . Christ furnished the spirit and motivation, while
Gandhi furnished the method." Two years later, King delivered an address entitled "Some Things We Must Do" at the second Annual Institute on Nonviolence
in Montgomery. Urging the black community to "plunge deeper into the whole
philosophy of nonviolence," King concluded with a rhetorical flourish:

> Bomb our homes and go by our churches early in the morning and bomb them
> if you please, and we will still love you. But we will wear you down by our ca-
> pacity to suffer. And in winning the victory, we will not only win our freedom,
> we will so appeal to your heart and your conscience, that we will win you in the
> process. Our victory will be a double victory. We will win our freedom, and we
> will win the individuals who have been the perpetrators of the evil system that
> existed so long.[36]

Significantly, King took these words nearly verbatim from Jones's book. Given
the growing relationship between the two religious leaders, this was no coinci-
dence. On several occasions they prayed together and discussed their mutual
desire to maintain the nonviolent character of the movement. Thereafter, King
borrowed extensively from Jones's writings. King's address at the Institute on
Nonviolence included the same words he had underlined on pages 88 and 89 of
his personal copy of Jones's *Mahatma Gandhi*. The copy itself, which contains
many more annotations, is now a historical artifact on display at the King
Center in Atlanta. One handwritten note, from a chapter entitled "The Center
of Gandhi's Contribution—Satyagraha," reads "p.98 very imp." Next to a passage that reads, "Non-violence is not for the weak, but for the strong—only the
strong," another note exclaims, "This is it!" It is likely that these annotations were
made in Georgia's maximum-security prison in 1960. On October 26, as King sat
in Reidsville State Prison after being arrested at an Atlanta sit-in, he wrote a letter
to his wife Coretta asking for his copy of Jones's book. Oral tradition at Asbury
even suggests that *Mahatma Gandhi* was on King's nightstand at the Lorraine
Hotel in Memphis the night before he was shot to death. Considering King's in-
timacy with the book—and the many other passages from Jones that appeared
in King's books, public addresses, and sermons—Fellowship of Reconciliation
representative Richard L. Deats's comment that "Jones's writings on Gandhi
were one of the important factors in turning Martin Luther King Jr. to the way
to active non-violence" seems entirely plausible. Along with Rustin, Randolph,
and others, Jones connected King to Gandhi, solidifying the nonviolent gospel
of the civil rights movement. Christ had traveled the long road from India to
America.[37]

III. Christ of the Evangelical Road

Jones's transnational insights on race did not enjoy universal appeal. His pursuit of integrated ashrams, interracial revivals, and relationships with civil rights figures drew the ire of many white Southerners and antimainline fundamentalists. Some ministerial associations refused to participate in his evangelistic meetings. In an article entitled "Methodism's Pink Fringe," *Reader's Digest* portrayed Jones as a communist sympathizer. A pastor in Texas, describing himself as "desperately sincere and in deep distress," worried that the missionary "tends dangerously toward Communism, Socialism and especially social equality between all races. . . . It is my humble judgment that the Socialists and Communists are using the negro as a blind, as a means of advancing their cause in the south and E. Stanley Jones is one of the chief aids to this cause now." Jones, infuriated by the attack, waited two weeks "until I could be sure I could give a Christian reply." He finally answered, "It seems strange that I who have fought the battles of Christianity and democracy against communism in the East, through these years, come back to my homeland to be knifed in the back by twisted, ill-informed criticism."[38]

That Jones was the target of criticisms by fundamentalists, however, suggests his remarkable impact, in both range and intensity, on American religious culture. He reached millions through his writing and hundreds of thousands through his speaking. Notably, Jones's broad appeal was rooted in an earlier era. Coming of age prior to the modernist–fundamentalist split in the Methodist Episcopal Church, he never felt comfortable circulating only in one orbit. Like many mainliners, Jones pushed evangelicals toward racial justice, and he published extensively in liberal publications like *Christian Century* and *World Outlook*, a missionary journal of the United Methodist Church. He also reflected other mid-century liberal theological sensibilities. He spoke in the language of the social gospel and the Kingdom of God, discussed the possibilities of pacifism, and held up Jesus as an ethical model for human behavior. The realist theologian Reinhold Niebuhr called Jones a "romantic and sentimental Christian" and described his book *Christ's Alternative to Communism* as "the most perfect swan song of liberal politics."[39]

Yet Jones remained solidly evangelical. He might have adopted the methods of the Hindu ashram, but he insisted that Christ was the true guru. If, like progressives, he recognized social sins and structural solutions, like evangelicals he emphasized personal relationships with God and fellow humans. He instructed white Americans to invite blacks into their homes as statements of racial justice and to invite the unsaved to be "born again" and to follow "the way of salvation." He practiced revivalistic techniques of evangelism, sought to reenergize missions in the Protestant mainline, and tried unrelentingly over several decades to convert Gandhi. His personal correspondence featured language like "personal surrender to God" and "decisions" for Christ, and he consistently self-identified as an evangelical. Jones viewed himself as a colleague of evangelist Billy Graham, and Graham reciprocated by lauding Jones's missionary work for a full ten minutes during the first Sunday meeting of the 1963 Los Angeles Crusade. The roster of other relationships is also telling. When in Washington, Jones regularly stayed with Abraham Vereide, the founder of the prayer breakfast movement. In India he interacted with World Vision founder Bob Pierce and vice president Samuel Kamaleson. Even some fundamentalists, like Maryland Bible Institute President Ronald Hoelz, who decried Jones's social and political views, acknowledged the missionary's evangelical theology. "The message that you proclaim," admitted Hoelz to Jones, "was fundamental in its content and preached the born-again experience."[40]

He was most warmly received in his native Wesleyan circles. Archival records show speaking engagements at dozens of Wesleyan-holiness colleges—including Kansas Wesleyan University, Olivet Nazarene College, Anderson University, Taylor University, Eastern Nazarene College, Greenville College, and Houghton College—and at congregations affiliated with the United Methodists, Free Methodists, Evangelical United Brethren, Nazarene, Church of God, Salvation Army, and National Holiness Association. Jones cultivated especially close ties with his alma mater. He returned from Sat Tal to Asbury dozens of times from the 1920s to the 1960s to deliver commencement addresses, stage revivals, participate in ashrams, and collaborate with Asbury Seminary professors J. T. Seamands and Thomas Carruth, who oversaw the American ashram movement. "Eternity alone," wrote Asbury Seminary's president after a visit in the early 1960s, "will reveal the results of your ministry here." Jones claimed Asbury, and most of Asbury claimed him.[41]

The resonance, in fact, was remarkable given Jones's trenchant critique of American injustices and Asbury's role in them. In 1942, when the college proclaimed an "E. Stanley Jones Day," he preached a series of sermons entitled "Christ of the Asbury Road." The series touched on all of Jones's favorite topics: global Christianity, social justice, personal spirituality, and racial integration. "May I tell you what I should like to see added to this interpretation of the Christ of the Asbury Road?" Jones rhetorically asked. "You have limited it to a very definitely personal application. It lacks a great social application. I know some people have nervous chills going up and down their backs when I talk like that. I'm going to talk about it anyhow." He continued, "I am not interested in an individual gospel or a social gospel. An individual gospel without a social gospel is a soul without a body. A social gospel without an individual gospel is a body without a soul. One is a ghost and the other a corpse. I don't want one of them. I want both." What made this critique tolerable and intelligible was its origin. Conceived in India, articulated in *Christ of the Indian Road*, and nurtured at Sat Tal, Jones's story followed sacralized missionary pathways. Preached to an Asbury audience preoccupied with evangelistic mission amid the heightened tension of decolonization and encroaching Marxism, "Christ of the Asbury Road" packed a strong punch.[42]

Jones's transnational racial advocacy during the Cold War represented a much broader phenomenon. Billy Graham was its most famous exemplar. In the evangelist's early years of crusading, which were conducted exclusively in the United States, Graham demonstrated considerable ambivalence toward the civil rights movement. In 1953 he took down a rope divider in Chattanooga that separated blacks and whites, but he also urged Martin Luther King, Jr., to "slow things down" as civil rights activism heated up in the late 1950s. "He had been prevaricating in the first half of the 1950s," wrote journalist David Aikman, "frequently expressing personal opposition to racism in America, but often failing to challenge head-on the institutions in the South that practiced segregation." During the 1957 New York crusade, however, Graham invited Martin Luther King, Jr., on the stage to offer the opening prayer. This effectively threw Graham's moral authority behind the civil rights cause.[43]

The difference between 1953 and 1957, in large part, was exposure to global contexts. In the mid-1950s, Graham began holding evangelistic crusades internationally. He did not soften his Cold Warrior views or his evangelistic resolve. Indeed, these commitments intensified Graham's sense that racial segregation was harmful. Historian Steven Miller writes that as the evangelist "began to travel through the non-white majority of the world, Graham came to see his nation's poor reputation in the area of racial relations as a potential propaganda tool for international communism and his numerous critics alike." Integrating racially, Graham came to believe, would move the world in a more Christian and democratic direction. In 1957 he wrote in the black magazine *Ebony* that the United States found itself "in a fish bowl with the whole world looking in." He continued, "Our racial tensions are causing some of the people of the world to turn away from us." Despite persistent connections with Southern recalcitrants who tied civil rights to communist sympathy, Graham's growing internationalism by the late 1950s sparked "a clear, if adaptable, declaration of racial moderation." This was a noteworthy transformation for a Southern evangelist who, as a youth, had adopted the attitudes of the rural South without much reflection. A 1960s tour of nine African nations, where he encountered more consternation over American segregation, only increased his public support for civil rights.[44]

Similar forces also shaped Graham's own denomination, the Southern Baptist Convention. This conservative Protestant denomination, the largest in the country, was highly segregated, like most religious bodies in the 1950s. But as Southern Baptist missions in Africa exploded in the postwar era, increasing ten times in size as it expanded from Nigeria throughout sub-Saharan Africa, global sources pushed persistently for integration. News of white American racism dogged Southern Baptist missionaries at every turn. This accelerated efforts to end Jim Crow at home. Antisegregation sentiments poured out from the Foreign Mission Board, the Woman's Missionary Union, and periodicals like *World Comrades*, a magazine for children. The activism came to a head in the early 1960s and was a primary catalyst in desegregating dozens of Southern Baptist colleges. Foy Valentine of the Southern Baptist Christian Life Commission, who described "the immensely absurd spectacle of loving the souls of Negroes in Africa and hating their guts in Nashville," declared in 1954 that "the ultimate failure or success of the modern missionary movement may well depend on what today's Christians do with the race problem." Stiff resistance persisted, but the moral and spiritual authority of missionaries pushed Southern Baptists ever closer to desegregation.[45]

Global pressure pervaded many other evangelical settings. At Calvin College, a missionary to Nigeria told students that Africans were closely watching the 1964 presidential election. That Barry Goldwater might win, despite his retrograde views on civil rights, "shocks them," the missionary reported. Africans receive the gospel more agreeably, he explained, when the United States promotes civil rights. A Fuller Theological Seminary student wrote that the race question "reaches also around the world, where other nations look and ask, 'Is that Christianity?'" In Korea, Kyung Chik-Han described a trip through the segregated South where he observed the exclusion of blacks from restaurants, theaters, and churches. "Such news," he preached, "worked as an impediment in spreading the gospel among blacks in Africa." In 1961 Don Rutledge, a Tennessean who grew up hearing missionary stories, published his award-winning photographs in John Howard Griffin's book *Black Like Me*. The book, which chronicled the experience of Griffin's journey across the South as a black man (he had dyed his white skin black as an experiment), focused unrelentingly on the depravities of Southern racist culture. Like so many other texts, *Black Like Me* framed conditions globally. A segregationist America loomed alongside Nazi Germany, fascist Italy, imperialistic Japan, and an authoritarian Soviet Union. Griffin wrote, "The South's racial situation was a blot on the whole country, and especially reflected against us overseas."[46]

The American civil rights movement, then, did not find sustenance only in America. Political and academic leaders situated racism in the context of World War II and the Cold War. So did missionaries, who worried that the nation's hypocrisy would drive potential converts away from Christianity and democracy. Evangelicals, increasingly invested in the public life of the nation, helped propel these efforts. Sent out to fight for freedom in Japan, Italy, Southeast Asia, and Africa, they brought the battle home to their own churches. Becoming agents of their targets, E. Stanley Jones and many others inverted the missionary enterprise.

When Jones returned from Sat Tal in 1958 to challenge his alma mater on seg-regation, he did so as one of the most accomplished Americans of the twentieth century. He had held integrated meetings in the South long before civil rights were a national concern. Twice nominated for the Nobel Peace Prize, he had helped rejuvenate an ethic of nonviolent resistance among American Christians. Because of his relationships with Gandhi and King, the FBI maintained a file that grew to 117 pages. He had delivered over 60,000 public addresses (including 736 in one six-month stretch) and written 27 books that had sold 3.5 million copies. He remained vigorous in his "retirement." A *Time* magazine article reported that at the age of seventy-nine, Jones could do thirty fast pushups without breathing hard. "I can do as much now as I could 40 years ago," he told the reporter, who noted that Jones "has spent a lifetime trying to reconcile East and West, white man and black, the world and Jesus Christ."[47]

Jones was also a beloved son of the still-segregated Asbury College. As a long-time member of the Board of Trustees, his opinions mattered. Jones arrived to campus from revival meetings in Africa. Predicting imminent Ghanaian inde-pendence, Jones explained that liberty would "permeate and stir clear through Africa. You cannot suppress the demand for human freedom." Connecting decol-onization to the American civil rights movement, Jones told students and faculty in Hughes Chapel to "embrace the social revolution." But the cosmopolitan Jones bumped up against a persistent Southern parochialism. Colleagues on the board opposed to integration and concerned about the loss of donors and students from the South blocked his efforts. In protest, Jones quit the Board. "This is a real blow to the spiritual life of the institution and an equally real blow to the spiritual influ-ence of the College as a great missionary institution," his resignation letter read. "I am at a loss to see how missionaries can go to the colored races from Asbury College and represent an institution that segregates colored people."[48]

Jones's protest worked. The resignation—combined with the broader cultural shift and a constituency that overwhelmingly wanted an integrated campus—accomplished its intended purpose. Students, faculty, and alumni rallied to the cause. An alumni survey solicited by the Board of Trustees obtained the following comments: "How can Asbury send missionaries to Africa and still keep negroes out of its school? Its missionary witness is blighted unless it admits negroes." "As a missionary here in Korea, this fact has been embarrassing." "Why is Asbury still preaching brotherly love if the Administration and Trustees do not practice it?" Faced with considerable ferment, a coterie of trustees with missionary experience guided the Board through a process that culminated in a new policy of integration.

Because of concern over interracial marriage (just 60 percent of those surveyed agreed that blacks should have "unlimited social privileges"), only married blacks were admitted at first. By 1962, however, all restrictions had been lifted. Given some of the global sources of Asbury's integration, it was no surprise that the first three black students had overseas connections. The college admitted two Africans, and the first African-American student, Ed Williams of Memphis, was recruited to Asbury by missionaries in Turkey while Williams was in the Air Force.[49]

This civil rights success, however, hid an underbelly. As the administration's resistance to "unlimited social privileges" suggested, campus still did not fully reflect Jones's hope for a "Christ of the Asbury Road." Racial minorities were slow to come to the formerly segregated college. The few who did enroll quickly discovered that explicit racism had not disappeared from campus. They also found that most students and faculty did not comprehend how economic and social systems could perpetuate racial inequality. The limits of integration were felt elsewhere too. In 1962, the same year Asbury fully integrated, James Meredith's enrollment at the University of Mississippi provoked a full-scale riot. As global critics knew well, calls for social holiness often went unheeded.

The Cold War paradigm, which animated Jones's work for racial integration, also circumscribed evangelical activism. The narrative of a pure America, set against a Marxist evil, remained as flawed as the Whiggish assumptions that undergirded it. Jones's manifest optimism about the nation betrayed a Christian Americanism that spoke of colorblindness, yet privileged white men. Like many liberals at mid-century (and like many conservatives in the decades that followed), Jones often declared that he could not see race, that he just saw an American or a Christian. In one famous episode, often recounted by white churchgoers, Jones met the black scientist George Washington Carver. The two men joined hands in prayer, and as Jones described it, Carver "lifted the back of his hand to my lips, and he lifted the back of my hand to his lips in recognition and gratitude that we both belonged to a kingdom in which there is no room for trivia like race and class. . . . We both stood in the kingdom that was race-blind and colorblind." Jones's colorblind vision may have been radical in the context of the South in the 1940s, but the civil rights movement, having secured legal rights in the decades that followed, went beyond de jure equality to celebrate racial difference—and to show how mantras of colorblindness often blind whites to structural inequalities.[50]

The chastening of America would continue from many quarters of the Majority World through the 1960s and 1970s—most visibly in 1974 in Lausanne, Switzerland, where the most important evangelical gathering of the postwar era took place. On the same issues of poverty, race, and diplomacy, global critics would echo Jones's plea in *Christ of the American Road*: "The world has given us the cue: *Be different!*"[51]

Notes

1. Quoted in "Two Missionary Types," *Christian Advocate*, April 27, 1933, 388, in Box 40, Folder 9, in Papers of E. Stanley Jones, Asbury Theological Seminary Special Collections, Wilmore, Ky.

2. For "cantankerous conservatism," see Jones, *A Song of Ascents: A Spiritual Autobiography* (Nashville, Tenn.: Abingdon Press, 1958), 67. On integration at Asbury, see Joseph A. Thacker, *Asbury College: Vision and Miracle* (Nappanee, Ind.: Evangel Press, 1990), 202–203.

3. E. Stanley Jones, "Integration," Chapel address at Asbury College, Wiltmore, Ky., October 16, 1958; Gunnar Myrdal, *An American Dilemma: The Negro Problem and Modern Democracy* (New York: Harper & Brothers, 1944).

4. For "breath-taking," see Jones circular letter, January 28, 1959, in Box 10, Folder 9, in Papers of E. Stanley Jones, ATSSC. This narrative of desegregation at Asbury echoes a growing literature on the global context of the American civil rights movement. See Gerald Horne, *End of Empires*; Tim Borstelmann, *The Cold War and the Color Line: American Race Relations in the Global Arena* (Cambridge, Mass.: Harvard University Press, 2001); Mary Dudziak, *Cold War Civil Rights: Race and the Image of American Democracy* (Princeton, N.J.: Princeton University Press, 2000).

5. On Asbury students' visit to Sat Tal Ashram, see Stephen A. Graham, *Ordinary Man, Extraordinary Mission: The Life and Work of E. Stanley Jones* (Nashville, Ky.: Abingdon Press, 2005), 212–13. On "India's curse," see "India's Conscience Awakened over Untouchables," *The Journal*, March 8, 1934. On the "American caste system," see "Stanley Jones Startles South," *Christian Century*, April 12, 1933, 510. Clippings of both articles are in Box 40, Folder 2, Papers of E. Stanley Jones, ATSSC.

6. On evangelical complicity in racism, see Mark Mulder, *Shades of White Flight: Evangelical Congregations and Urban Departure* (New Brunswick, N.J.: Rutgers University Press, 2015); Jemar Tisby, *The Color of Compromise* (Grand Rapids, Mich.: Zondervan, 2019).

7. Jones, *Song of Ascents*, 68–75; Thacker, *Asbury College*, 52.

8. On Jones's childhood and segregation in Baltimore, see Jones, *Song of Ascents*, 256; Graham, *Ordinary Man*, 41. On mass movements, see Pickett, *Christian Mass Movements in India: A Study with Recommendations* (New York: Abingdon Press, 1933). For "SOULS," see Jones, "The Revival Month—Some Thoughts," *Indian Witness*, February 1915. For "ad tireddom," quoted in Graham, see Graham, *Ordinary Man*, 106. For Jones's memories of his first years in India, see Jones, *Song of Ascents*, 79–87. On Jones's nervous collapses, see Jones, *Song of Ascents*, 85.

9. For examples of "soul-winning," see Jones, *Indian Road*, 84, 105. For "scratch or nick," see Gray, "The Four Great Immortalities of Christianity," *American Magazine*, July 1929. For more on Jones and Pickett's changing missiology, see "The Missionary Crisis," *Christian Century*, November 1, 1933, 1358–59; David Bundy, "Song of Ascents: Autobiographical Reflection and the Development of the Mission Theory of E. Stanley Jones," *Missiology* 27 (October 1999): 468. On the Mayflower, see Jones, *Christ of the Indian Road* (New York: Abingdon Press, 1925), 21–22.

10. For "Aryans of the West," see James M. Thoburn, *The Christian Conquest of India* (Philadelphia: Young's People's Missionary Association, 1906), 53–54. For "Indian setting," see Jones, *Indian Road*, 26. For "international meddlers," see Jones, *Indian Road*, 42. For "disentangle Christ," see Jones, *Christ of the Mount: A Working Philosophy of Life* (New York: Abingdon Press, 1931), 11. On Jones's sudden celebrity, see Graham, *Ordinary Man*, 167–72. On Jones and mainline contextualization, see David Hollinger, *Protestants Abroad: How Missionaries Tried to Save the World but Changed America* (Princeton, N.J.: Princeton University Press, 2017), 59–93.

11. On Jones's influence, see Daniel Immerwahr, "Caste or Colony? Indianizing Race in the United States," *Modern Intellectual History* 4, No. 2 (2007): 290–91. For "more Christian and more Indian," see Timothy Yates, *Christian Mission in the Twentieth Century* (Cambridge: Cambridge University Press, 1994), 114. On Jones's methods, see Jones, *Indian Road*, 104, 118. For "its own soul," see Jones, *Indian Road*, 46.

12. For "national aspirations," see Jones, quoted in Graham, *Ordinary Man*, 69. For "Western Partisan of White Rule," see Jones, *Indian Road*, 34. For India's "curse," see "India's Conscience Awakened over Untouchables," *The Journal*, March 8, 1934, in Box 40, Folder 2, Papers of E. Stanley Jones, ATSSC. On Jones in Palghat, see Jones circular letter, December 28, 1931, in Box 10, Folder 7, Papers of E. Stanley Jones, ATSSC. On caste and Syrian Christians in India, see Jones circular letter, March 29, 1932, in Box 10, Folder 7, Papers of E. Stanley Jones, ATSSC. For "life and radiance," see Jones, *Indian Road*, 187.

13. Barbara Brady, "Just Plain Missionary," *Sunday Digest*, October 9, 1955, in Box 44, Folder 7, Papers of E. Stanley Jones, ATSSC. On the ashram at Travancore, see Jones, *Indian Road*, 243–44. For Jones's poem "I Took My Lamp" and its background, see Jones, *Indian Road*, 164; Richard W. Taylor, "The Legacy of E. Stanley Jones," *International Bulletin of Missionary Research* 6, No. 3 (July 1982): 102, in Box "600 Faculty/Staff: E. Stanley Jones Biographical," Asbury University Archives, Wilmore, Ky. For Jones on Gandhi, see Jones circular letter, October 1, 1926, in Box 10, Folder 6, Jones Papers, ATSSC.

14. For "truly Christian and truly Indian," see Jones quoted in Taylor, "The Legacy of E. Stanley Jones," *IBMR*, 102. The description of Sat Tal comes from Dorothy Speer, "The Ashram at Sat Tal," *Woman's Missionary Friend*, November 1934, 367–68; "Indian Witness," June 6, 1963, in Box 40, Folder 2, Papers of E. Stanley Jones, ATSSC.

15. For "Indian genius and life," see Jones circular letter, July 3, 1930, in Box 10, Folder 7, Papers of E. Stanley Jones, ATSSC. On meals at Sat Tal, see Jones circular letter, July 3, 1930, in Box 10, Folder 7. On clothing at Sat Tal, see Taylor, "The Legacy of E. Stanley Jones," *IBMR*, 102; Vivian Weeks Dudley, "Indian Night: A Story of the E. Stanley Jones Ashram," *World Outlook*, February 1939, 52–55, 39, in Box 44, Folder 3.

16. For "Morning of the Open Heart," see "What Is an Ashram," in Box 17, Folder 4, Papers of E. Stanley Jones, ATSSC. For ashram inscriptions, see "Statements Appearing on the Walls at the Sat-Tal Ashram in India," in Box 17, Folder 4. On work practices, see "Beautiful Sat Tal," in Box 17, Folder 4. For "foretaste," see "And What Is an Ashram?" in Box 44, Folder 54.

90   FACING WEST

17. For "great summer," see Jones circular letter, June 30, 1931, in Box 10, Folder 7, Papers of E. Stanley Jones, ATSSC. For "kingdom in miniature," see "What Is an Ashram," in Box 17, Folder 4. For "haven of brotherhood," see "The Ashrama," 1934, in Box 17, Folder 4. For other reflections on Sat Tal, see Jones circular letter, July 3, 1930, in Box 10, Folder 7; Dorothy Speer, "The Ashram at Sat Tal," *Woman's Missionary Friend*, November 1934, 367–68, in Box 17, Folder 4.

18. On Jones's trip to the Soviet Union, see Bishop Wade, "Stanley Jones' visit to Russia— Meeting in the Catacombs" with religious leaders in Moscow, April 10, 1934, in Box 44, Folder 36, Papers of E. Stanley Jones, ATSSC; Jones circular letter, July 5, 1934; "Christ's Alternative to Communism," in Box 1, Folder 3. On Jones's trip to China, see Jones, "What I Saw in China," in Box 21, Folder 12; Graham, *Ordinary Man*, 340.

19. On the strength of communism in India, see Gerald Horne, *The End of Empires: African Americans and India* (Philadelphia: Temple University Press, 2008), 189. On Jones's anticommunist work at the Sat Tal Ashram and in Kerala, see Jones circular letters, June 18, 1952, and June 26, 1954, in Box 10, Folder 9; "Anonymous Letter," in Box 19, Folder 53, Papers of E. Stanley Jones, ATSSC.

20. For "total setting of the world," see E. Stanley Jones, *Christ of the American Road* (Nashville, Tenn.: Abingdon-Cokesbury Press, 1944), 9. For "Eastern travelers," see Jones, *Indian Road*, 6. For Bowles and "repeatedly zeroed in on Jim Crow," see Horne, *End of Empires*, 198.

21. For Jones's rattlesnake analogy, see "What Have the Churches to Offer," in Box 21, Folder 10, Papers of E. Stanley Jones, ATSSC. Also see Jones, "History in the Making in Isndia" (1946), in Box 19, Folder 2. For "native land," see NBC radio broadcast transcription, in Box 33, Folder 21.

22. For a description of Jones as rooted in the "experiential piety of historic Methodism," see William Kostlevy's 2001 biographical sketch in "E. Stanley Jones ARC 2000—007 Finding Aid," 2012, ATSSC. For a fuller description of Jones's theological and ecclesiastical location, see Kostlevy, *Holy Jumpers: Evangelicals and Radicals in Progressive Era America* (New York: Oxford University Press, 2010), 15–16. For "colored majority," see James K. Mathews, "Accomplishments of Stanley Jones by God's grace and help," circa 1973, in Box 1, Folder 3, Papers of E. Stanley Jones, ATSSC. For Jones's exchange with the Texas pastor, see the Methodist Archives, quoted in Graham, *Ordinary Man*, 282–83.

23. On Jones not returning to India, see "Stanley Jones Barred from Return to India," April 25, 1945, in Box 40, Folder 2, Papers of E. Stanley Jones, ATSSC; Jones, "Why I Do Not Return to India at Present," in Box 4, Folder 1. For "is doomed," see Jones, "After India's Independence—What?" in Box 18, Folder 3.

24. On Jones's personality and speaking style, see Edward Shillito, "An Apostle of India: An Interview with Dr. Stanley Jones," 574, in Box 40, Folder 2, Papers of E. Stanley Jones, ATSSC; "It," *Christian Advocate*, January 17, 1929, in Box 40, Folder 4; "Dr. Stanley Jones in London," *Christian Advocate*, May 16, 1929, in Box 40, Folder 4; Paul S. Rees, "E. Stanley Jones: Christ-Intoxicated," in Box "600, Faculty / Staff: E. Stanley Jones Biographical," AUA; "Jones Devotes Life to Fight on Race Hate,"

Indianapolis Recorder, February 13, 1943, 1. For "crystalline sincerity," see "Noted Missionary in City Tomorrow," in Box 13, Folder 1, Papers of E. Stanley Jones, ATSSC.

25. Andrew Manis, *Macon Black and White: An Unutterable Separation in the American Century* (Macon, Ga.: Mercer University Press, 2004), 139–40; Horne, *End of Empires*, 158, 163–65; Walter White, *A Rising Wind* (Garden City, N.J.: Doubleday, 1945).

26. For "false America," see Jones, *American Road*, 75–79, 95–98. Also see Jones, "India's Caste System and Ours," *Christian Century*, August 20, 1947, 995–96; "Stanley Jones Startles South," *Christian Century*, April 12, 1933.

27. For Jones's letter from Sat Tal, see "An Appeal to the People of Alabama," in Box 24, Folder 2, Papers of E. Stanley Jones, ATSSC. For "embarrassing our witness," see Jones, *Indian Road*, 132–34. For "hesitant people," see "E. Stanley Jones Issues Appeal," in Box 40, Folder 8. On segregation as a national issue, see Jones, *American Road*, 179.

28. On Jones's efforts in Macon—and the firestorm that Jones's presence sparked—see Andrew Manis, *Macon Black and White*, 137–38. For more on Jones's interracial revivals, see W. G. Cram, "Stanley Jones in the South," *World Outlook*, June 1933, 4–6, in Box 44, Folder 35, Papers of E. Stanley Jones, ATSSC; Jones, *American Road*, 172; J. Maurice Trimmer, "Stanley Jones Discusses Race and Imperialism," in Folder 4, Box 40. For memories of Jones's interracial revivals, see William Chafe interview of Mary Taft Smith, July 11, 1973, in University of North Carolina-Greensboro Archives.

29. "Suggestions for 'Little Ashrams,'" in Box 14, Folder 15; E. Stanley Jones, "How to Set Up and Run a Little Ashram," in Box 14, Folder 15; "The United American Christian Ashrams—1958," in Box 47, Folder 20, Papers of E. Stanley Jones, ATSSC. On Dellinger, see Joseph Kip Kosek, *Acts of Conscience: Christian Nonviolence and Modern American Democracy* (New York: Columbia University Press, 2009), 186. On the transdenominational nature of the ashrams, see "Ashram Report," September 1961, in Box 16, Folder 23.

30. Howard Whitman, "One Week with God," *Collier's*, September 1951, 24, copy in Box 44, Folder 18; Barbara Brady, "Just Plain Missionary," *Sunday Digest*, October 9, 1955, in Box 44, Folder 7, Papers of E. Stanley Jones, ATSSC; William E. Berg, "My Spiritual Journey with Brother Stanley," in Box "600 Faculty/Staff: E. Stanley Jones Biographical," AUA. On the ashram movement's interracialism, see W. W. Richardson to Brother Bill and Brother J. T. Seamands, April 21, 1964, in Box 7, Folder 1, Papers of E. Stanley Jones, ATSSC. On the North Carolina ashram, see Anna B. Mow, "I Remember!" *Transformation*, Winter 1983, 13. For numbers on ashrams in 1963, see Box 47, Folder 22. On the popularity and growth of Jones's ashrams, see Preston King Sheldon, "Retreats Slated by Church Group: 25 Christian Leaders to Join with Methodist Missionary in Conducting Assemblies," *New York Times*, June 19, 1954, 16.

31. On Jones and CORE, see James Farmer to John F. Kennedy, April 26, 1961, in Martin Luther King, Jr. Papers Project. For an example of Jones's congressional and presidential lobbying efforts, see Jones to Eisenhower, December 26, 1956, in Box 5, Folder 5, Jones Papers, ATSSC. For an example of Jones's call for interracial committees

and federal intervention, see Jones, "Christianity and Race," *World Outlook*, April 1943, 37–39.

32. Jones, *Mahatma Gandhi: An Interpretation* (New York: Abingdon-Cokesbury Press, 1947). For "little man," see the 1983 edition of *Gandhi: Portrayal of a Friend* (Nashville, Tenn.: Abingdon Press, 1983), 8. On Jones's early encounters with Gandhi, see Jones, *Indian Road*, 86–101; Jones, *Christ at the Round Table* (New York: Abingdon Press, 1928). The Gandhi biography never sold as many copies as *Indian Road*, but it did garner significant publicity with hundreds of reviews in the nation's major newspapers. For sales numbers and reviews of *Mahatma Gandhi*, see Box 38, Folder 23, Papers of E. Stanley Jones, ATSSC.

33. Jones to editor of *Time* magazine, in Box 21, Folder 43, Papers of E. Stanley Jones, ATSSC. For similar accounts, see Jones, "My Convictions at Eighty" (c. 1964), in Box 19, Folder 50; Jones, *Song of Ascents*, 259–60.

34. Sudarshan Kapur, *Raising Up a Prophet: The African-American Encounter with Gandhi* (Boston: Beacon Press, 1992), 2–3, 6, 14–16. On Rai's shock at the "treatment of the Negro," see Horne, *End of Empires*, 47, 116–19. For black pilgrimages to India, see Immerwahr, "Caste or Colony," 293–94; Horne, *End of Empires*, 93–113; Miller, *Voice of Deliverance*, 94–98; Horne, *End of Empires*, 93–113. On the black–Indian exchange, see Horne, *End of Empires*, 93–113. For white American intermediaries, see Sean Chabot, *The Transnational Roots of the Civil Rights Movement: African American Explorations of the Gandhian Repertoire* (Lanham, Md.: Lexington Books, 2012), 68, 72, 87, 114. For the story of King approaching Jones's daughter Eunice at a convocation just before King left for Sweden to receive the 1964 Nobel Peace prize, see Jonathan Raymond, "Unfolding the Story," *E. Stanley Jones Foundation Newsletter* (Fall 2013), 2–3. Raymond cites material from Jones's granddaughter Anne Mathews-Younes: "At the reception following, my mother was introduced to Dr. King and my grandfather was mentioned. Dr. King immediately became very serious and said, 'Your father was a very important person to me, for it was his book on Mahatma Gandhi that triggered my use of Gandhi's method of non-violence as a weapon for our own people's freedom in the United States.' He continued that though he had been very familiar with the writings on Gandhi and had been interested in his method of non-violence for years, it had not 'clicked' with him that it was a vehicle for 'use' in the United States. Reading my grandfather's book on Gandhi may have assisted Dr. King with the application of Gandhian principles within a Christian context." Coretta Scott King corroborated this story in 1981, describing "her husband's excitement when, after finishing my father's book, this plan of action became clear to him—that the weapon of non-violence, used with discipline, was a viable one here."

35. For MOWM, see *Calling! Calling! All! Negroes! We Are Americans Too! Conference* (Chicago: March on Washington Movement, 1943), copy available in the Historical Society Library Pamphlet Collection, University of Wisconsin; Kapur, *Raising Up a Prophet*, 114–15; Graham, *Ordinary Man*, 283; Timothy B. Tyson, *Radio Free Dixie: Robert F. Williams and the Roots of Black Power* (Chapel Hill: University of North Carolina Press, 1999), 28; *Chicago Daily Tribune*, July 5, 1943; *Philadelphia Tribune*, July 10, 1943; "Puts Race Riot Blame on New Deal Policies," *Chicago Daily*

Tribune, July 5, 1943, 22. Also see E. Stanley Jones, "Is Civil Disobedience the Answer to Jim Crow?" *Non-violent Action Newsbulletin,* No. 2, 1943, 21; A. Philip Randolph to E. Stanley Jones, May 25, 1945; Charles Wesley Burton to A. Philip Randolph, April 21, 1943, in Box 25, Reel #20; John Bracey and August Meier, eds., *The Papers of A. Philip Randolph* (Bethesda, Md.: University Publications of America, 1990).

36. King, "Pilgrimage to Nonviolence." *Christian Century,* April 13, 1960, 439–41. For King's renunciation of self-defense, see Chabot, *Transnational Roots,* 163. For King and Montgomery, see Chabot, *Transnational Roots,* 129–37. For King in Atlanta, see King to Coretta Scott King, October 26, 1960, in *The Papers of Martin Luther King, Jr.: Threshold of a New Decade, January 1959 – December 1960, Vol. 5,* ed. Clayborne Carson (Berkeley: University of California Press, 2005), 532.

37. For meetings between Jones and King, see Jones, "What Have the Church to Offer in Answer to the Black Manifesto?" in Box 21, Folder 10, Papers of E. Stanley Jones ATSSC; "In an interview with Dr. Martin Luther King (October 26, 1966)," in Box 14, Folder 11. On Jones as the source of King's language, see Clayborne Carson, ed., *The Papers of Martin Luther King, Jr.: Volume 4: Symbol of the Movement, January 1957– December 1958* (Berkeley: University of California Press, 2000), 342. For several of the many other instances of King using Jones's language, see King, *Strength to Love* (New York: Harper & Row, 1963), 40; King, *Stride toward Freedom* (New York: Harper & Row, 1958), 217; Miller, *Voice of Deliverance,* 88–90; Clayborne Carson, ed., *The Papers of Martin Luther King, Jr.: Volume 6: Advocate of the Social Gospel, September 1948 – March 1963* (Berkeley: University of California Press, 2007), 172, 250, 251, 373, 460. For the description of King's annotated notes of the Jones's Gandhi biography, see Graham, *Ordinary Man,* 423. For assessments of Jones's influence on King, see Richard L. Deats, "E. Stanley Jones—A Tribute," Fellowship, February 1973, in Box 1, Folder 26; Miller, *Voice of Deliverance,* 95–98.

38. On Jones as a communist sympathizer, see Stanley High, "Methodism's Pink Fringe," *Reader's Digest,* February 1950, 134–38. For the Texan Methodist attack, see Graham, *Ordinary Man,* 282; E. Stanley Jones, "A Reply to John T. Flynn's Attack," in Box 13, Folder 10, Papers of E. Stanley Jones, ATSSC; "My Reply to an Anonymous Sheet Circulated in Montgomery, Alabama," in Box 19, Folder 53.

39. Kostlevy, "E. Stanley Jones ARC 2000-007 Finding Aid." Niebuhr quoted in Graham, *Ordinary Man,* 396.

40. On reenergizing missions in the mainline, see Jones, "The Missionary Crisis," *Christian Century,* November 1, 1933, 1358–59. For "way of salvation," see Florence E. Clippinger to E. Stanley Jones, January 23, 1944, in Box 35, Folder 38, Papers of E. Stanley Jones, ATSSC. For Jones and Graham, see undated, unattributed biographical sketch of Jones, in Box 1, Folder 3; Box 5, Folders 5 and 6. For Vereide, see Abraham Vereide to Jones, December 7, 1964, in Box 7, Folder 2. On Jones's relationship with Kameleson, see the 1983 edition of *Gandhi: Portrayal of a Friend*; Ronald Hoelz to Jones, November 20, 1962, in Box 5, Folder 6.

41. For "personal piety and social gospel activism," see Kostlevy, "E. Stanley Jones." For correspondence with Wesleyan institutions, see Box 8, Folder 2; Box 14, Folder 3; Box 6, Folder 2; Box 7; Box 3; Box 47, Folder 21, Papers of E. Stanley Jones, ATSSC.

On Jones's commencement addresses, see Thacker, *Asbury College*, 49; Box 40, Folder 9. On his 1934 return to campus, see "E. Stanley Jones Returns to Asbury to Get New Start in World Missions," *Journal Enterprise*, January 19, 1934, in Box "600 Faculty / Staff: E. Stanley Jones Biographical," AUA.

42. For "Christ of the Asbury Road," see Box "600 Faculty/Staff: E. Stanley Jones Literary Productions," Folder "Faculty/Staff: Dr. E. Stanley Jones Day, May 8, 1942," AUA.

43. David Aikman, *Billy Graham: His Life and Influence* (Nashville, Tenn.: Thomas Nelson, 2007), 104, 136–40.

44. For "potential propaganda tool," see Steven Miller, *Billy Graham and the Rise of the Republican South* (Philadelphia: University of Pennsylvania Press, 2011), 23. For "fish bowl," see Graham, "No Color Line in Heaven," *Ebony*, September 1957, 102. For "racial moderation," see Miller, *Billy Graham*, 24.

45. On growing missions to Africa, see Alan Scot Willis, *All According to God's Plan: Southern Baptist Missions and Race, 1945-1970* (Lexington: University of Kentucky Press, 2005), 91. On *World Comrades*, see Mark Newman, *Getting Right with God: Southern Baptists and Desegregation, 1945-1995* (Tuscaloosa: University of Alabama Press, 2001), 131. For international pressure on Southern Baptist colleges, see Newman, *Getting Right with God*, 140. For Mobley, see Willis, *God's Plan*, 81. For Valentine, see Newman, *Getting Right with God*, 143; Willis, *God's Plan*, 14, 17. For more on the strident critiques of segregation made by anticommunist missionaries to Africa, see Newman, *Getting Right with God*, 129; Willis, *God's Plan*, 67–92.

46. On Calvin College, see John LaGrand, "Christian Political Action?" *Chimes*, October 30, 1964, 3. On Fuller Seminary, see Carol Reiss, "Relationship in Action," *The Opinion*, November 1967. For "impediment in spreading the gospel," see Han, "One Race, Once Gospel, and One Task,"440, *Kyung-Chik Han Collection/Sermons 3*. On Rutledge, see John Howard Griffin, *Black Like Me* (New York: New American Library, 1960), 3, 43, 49.

47. On Jones's reputation as a civil rights leader, see Fellowship of Reconciliation Executive Secretary Richard L. Deats, "E. Stanley Jones—A Tribute," *Fellowship*, February 1973, in Box 1, Folder 26, Jones Papers, ATSSC. On Jones's accomplishments, see the *Encyclopedia of Christian Literature, Volume 2* (Lanham, Md.: Scarecrow Press, 2010), 396; "Missions: Keeping Up with E. Stanley Jones," *Time*, January 24, 1964, 34; "E. Stanley Jones' Name Cited for 1962 Peace Award," *New York Times*, January 26, 1962, 16; "E. Stanley Jones, Wrote on Religion: Methodist Missionary for 60 Years Dies at 89," *New York Times*, January 26, 1973, 38.

48. On Jones's 1958 reception at Asbury, see Box 5, Folder 7, Papers of E. Stanley Jones, ATSSC. On Jones's visit to Africa, see January 25, 1958, circular letter, quoted in Graham, *Ordinary Man*, 368–69. For "real blow," see Jones to Z. T. Johnson, February 20, 1959, in Box "600 Faculty/Staff: E. Stanley Jones Correspondence," AUA.

49. "Results of Integration Questionnaire Tabulated," *Asbury Alumnus*, December 1958, 3; Zachary Taylor Johnson, "The Story of Asbury College"; Appendix in Vol. 3, in Box "600 Faculty/Staff: E. Stanley Jones Correspondence," AUA; Thacker, *Asbury College*, 202-203. On the lifting of all restrictions, see "Asbury College Trustees Approve Full Integration," October 3, 1962, in Box 100-2, Folder 7.

50. On the limits of colorblindness and the persistent individualism of postwar evangelicals, see Michael Emerson and Christian Smith, *Divided by Faith: Evangelical Religion and the Problem of Race in America* (New York: Oxford University Press, 2000); Carolyn DuPont, *Mississippi Praying: Southern White Evangelicals and the Civil Rights Movement, 1945-1975* (New York: New York University Press, 2013); Nancy Wadsworth, *Ambivalent Miracles: Evangelicals and the Politics of Racial Healing* (Charlottesville Va.: University of Virginia Press, 2014).

51. For "be different," see Jones, *American Road,* 172.

4

Lausanne 1974

A Latin American Challenge to North American Missiology

> *Do not reduce the mission of the Church to rote repetition of unassimi-*
> *lated doctrinal formulas coined in North America or Europe.*
> —René Padilla in *Christianity Today*

On its third evening the International Congress on World Evangelization in Lausanne, Switzerland, took a dramatic turn. A group of mostly non-Western delegates calling themselves the "radical discipleship caucus" met to plot their resistance to Western dominance of the Congress. The dissatisfaction, one of the caucus members later explained, had "bubbled" up out of irritation with an establishment sensibility that did not take social justice seriously. More than two hundred people opted out of a scheduled tour of nearby Geneva to join the chaotic ad hoc meeting on Sunday night. It opened with a sixties-style folk song featuring ominous lyrics: "This is the calm before the storm." Solomon Mergie of Papua New Guinea offered a prayer, which was followed by a series of plaintive monologues from Australian prophet Athol Gill and Latin American Theological Fraternity members René Padilla and Samuel Escobar. Their extemporaneous speeches, diverse in style and frequently punctuated by laughter, grumbling, amens, and applause, were followed by hours of intense discussion.

If the accents were diverse, the message was uniform. Those gathered intended to press the larger Congress, comprised of more than 2,400 representatives from 150 nations, on the social implications of true and radical evangelization. Gill, the Baptist founder of an intentional community called House of the Gentle Bunyip, urged delegates, entombed in a concrete bunker of respectability, to break free of the modern amenities of the Palais de Beaulieu conference center. Evangelicals needed to recover Scripture's "cutting edge." God's people, Gill continued, included tax collectors, sinners, the poor, and prostitutes. Padilla, who plotted the rebels' gathering, made a case for radical biblical ethics. He asked, "Are we really a community of love, of reconciliation, that serves as a basis for resistance for the conditioning of the world with all its values, its prejudices, including racial and social prejudice? Or is the church just a reflection of the whole society?" To

Facing West. David R. Swartz, Oxford University Press (2020). © Oxford University Press.
DOI: 10.1093/oso/9780190250805.001.0001

applause, Escobar accused Westerners of merely "reproducing pagans or semi-Christians in our own likeness, instead of really evangelizing." The architects of the Congress, he said, were converting pagans into followers of Americanism, not authentic Christianity. "Nothing against Americans," one delegate said to lots of laughter. "We all love them and are grateful to them." But the message of Jesus was most certainly not "this American-culture Christianity" that planners were trying to perpetuate at Lausanne.

The caucus then challenged the proposed Lausanne Covenant. "This statement clearly doesn't come out of the life of this conference. I presume it was largely prepared before it. It's got phrases we've been hearing for donkey's years, and it doesn't speak to contemporary life," complained one critic. Another proposed writing an entirely different document that would articulate the concerns of non-Westerners. As the caucus contemplated its next move, a security guard notified the caucus that the building was closing. The gathering ended in prayer, which was cut short as doors began to shut and lock.[1]

A smaller group of six decamped to another location in order to plot their next steps. But first John Stott, the primary author of the working draft of the Lausanne Covenant, intercepted the dissenters. Stott was sympathetic to their concerns, but he worried that an alternative Covenant might cause the Congress to "end with some degree of misunderstanding, confusion, even disunity." He convinced the caucus's leaders to instead release a "report" that would be included in the official compendium of proceedings. But late that night, an intermediary was dispatched back to Stott. The leaders had not been able to convince the "rank and file" of the caucus to go along with the compromise. Instead, they planned to double down by publicly releasing the dissenting document in the morning.[2]

The impact of the Sunday night rebellion hit the Congress with full force on Monday. Copies of "A Response to Lausanne," full of stark words of resistance, circulated quickly through the Palais de Beaulieu. The polemical document described "demonic" attempts "to drive a wedge between evangelism and social action." It confessed that evangelicals were guilty of triumphalism, arrogance, and social sin. It charged that they had "neglected the cries of the underprivileged" and allowed "eagerness for quantitative growth to render us silent about the whole counsel of God." More than 500 delegates, roughly a quarter of the assembly, immediately signed it.

The scene that followed almost seemed choreographed. Samuel Escobar, already scheduled to give a plenary address to the entire assembly, delivered a trenchant critique of Western imperialism. American conservatives, he said, might justifiably critique theological rivals on the left. But they had their own blind spots. "We should also reject," Escobar explained, "the adaptation of the Gospel to the social conformism or conservatism of the middle class citizen in the powerful West." Delegates from the West and non-West alike recognized the import of the moment, which ultimately shaped the language of the document that would emerge from the conference. "With this covenant," Padilla said, "evangelicals took a stand against a mutilated gospel and a narrow view of the Christian mission." Canadian evangelist Leighton Ford, Billy Graham's brother-in-law, noted, "If there has ever been a moment in history when evangelists were in tune with the times, it surely must have been in July of 1974. Lausanne burst upon us like a bombshell. It became an awakening experience for those who attended."[3]

The global challenge was truly underway. Starting in the 1960s with disillusioned Latin Americans, dissent surged worldwide in the 1970s. The specific critiques at Lausanne, as scholars have already shown, concerned cultural insensitivity and a quietist reluctance to confront global injustices. But these Majority World critiques grew out of an even more basic concern: Western dominance. In the context of decolonization, this charge was sometimes received with openness and often with hostility. But always it sparked intense missiological debates about how to contextualize the gospel.

I. Christian Americanism at Berlin

The 1966 World Congress for Evangelism, which convened 1,200 delegates from nearly one hundred nations nearly eight years before Lausanne, promoted a traditionalist missiology. In front of hundreds of newsmen, including a reporter from the *New York Times*, two Huaorani converts from the lush jungles of Ecuador stood on the concrete Berlin stage. Komi Gikita and Kimo Yaeti were murderers who had been redeemed (Figure 4.1). As cameras flashed, the dazed men, who may have thought they were being worshipped, gave their testimony. Rachel Saint, whose brother Nate and four missionary colleagues had been speared in the Ecuadorian jungle by Gikita's father and others in the indigenous tribe, translated. Twenty-nine-year-old Yaeti, known back home as Red Squirrel, told reporters, "Before knowing about Itota (Jesus), we killed. There was much revenge and much madness." But after the killings, "we heard that the word of God is stronger than the devil. We listened. We were told that God said not to spear other people, only the wild hogs, the tapir, and the fish of the stream." He concluded, "Before I lived sinning and God has done wonderful things for us and now I live well." Of the ninety remaining members of the tribe, only five had not yet "received Christ as their personal Savior." In fact, only a year before, Yaeti had helped baptize Nate Saint's two children near the spot on a river where the massacre occurred. Now, dressed in suits and ties with their hair parted on the side, they stood as trophies of evangelical mission.[4]

Figure 4.1. Ten years after they participated in the slaying of evangelical missionaries in the Ecuadorian jungle, Komi Gikita and Kimo Yaeti, Huaorani converts to Christianity, attended the 1966 World Congress for Evangelism. Rachel Saint, the sister of martyr Nate Saint, dressed them in suits and ties and fedoras during this tour of Berlin. Courtesy of the Billy Graham Center Archives, Wheaton, Ill.

To be sure, the ten-day gathering was not entirely supportive of the status quo. Bob Pierce, by now a veteran humanitarian, noted, "We are deluding ourselves if we think that Western missionaries and the Western cultural encrustations of the Christian Church will be accepted without question in the rest of the world." William Pannell, a black Youth for Christ evangelist from Detroit, was the bluntest. In a direct challenge to the emphasis of the Berlin gathering—and the quietist approach to civil rights advocated by most delegates—he declared, "Law did for me and my people in America what empty and high powered evangelical preaching never did for 100 years." Other delegates urged missionaries to adopt the insights of social science. In fact, evangelical colleges were developing new academic programs in sociology and anthropology, and Billy Graham himself had majored in anthropology at Wheaton College in order to develop new evangelistic techniques. Key publications—including the journal *Practical Anthropology*, which was launched in 1953, and the influential book *Customs and Cultures: Anthropology for Christian Missions* (1954)—contended for a more culturally sensitive missiology.[5]

Several delegates from the non-Western world, themselves victims of Western ethnocentrism, set aside the niceties of scholarly convention. Like Pannell, they protested the absence of talk about social justice. José D. Fajardo, an evangelist from Colombia, described his irritation with missionaries who said, "Do not preach a social gospel, because that will not save or change the people." Felix Dias-Abeyesinghe of Ceylon observed, "I have seen and heard much about our Congress motto—One Gospel and One Task—but I have not heard so much about "One Race." He wanted the Congress to take a more "clear-cut racial position," noting that the "racial problem, especially as it exists in the United States, presents grave hindrances to the preaching of the gospel in Negro-dominated lands." A *Washington Post* reporter observed that Asians, Africans, and Latin Americans spoke "passionately" about Western racism. Congress organizers, she noted, "had not anticipated this bubbling up from the depths of a demand that the church speak specifically about social conditions." New ideas were percolating.[6]

At its core, though, the Berlin Congress sustained Christian Americanism. Nearly all the planners were of the Youth for Christ species of evangelical. Carl Henry planned the event, and *Christianity Today*, the magazine he edited, sponsored it. Henry was assisted by Robert Evans, a Youth for Christ missionary and an organizer of the 1945 evangelistic rally at Soldier Field. J. Howard Pew, the archconservative heir of the Sun Oil fortune and financier of *Christianity Today*, funded the event. Billy Graham, the honorary chairman and headline speaker, opened and closed the Congress with major addresses. Western delegates gave all six of the main position papers and led seventeen of the twenty-four Bible studies. These men maintained the Congress's conservative ethos largely through delegate selection. Issuing invitations to individuals, not to organizations, gave planners more control. Rumors even circulated that official statements of the Congress had been predetermined and that 1,000 persons had been "uninvited" because they were not sufficiently orthodox in their missionary methodologies. Officials denied these accusations, but they were unquestionably eager to distinguish the gathering from prominent white Western liberal voices of the World Council of Churches. The presence of many Majority World delegates—just over half were from outside North America—reminded Westerners of the burgeoning international flavor of evangelicalism, but they were chosen for their conventional views on missions and generally toed the line. World Vision cofounder Kyung-Chik Han, who spoke at length in a major evening address about salvation, conversion, and growing churches, effusively thanked Western missionaries for bringing the gospel to Korea. But Han was not necessarily representative of many in the Majority World who were also concerned about wealth inequality and neoimperialism. In short, the Congress was a global gathering, but it was dominated by the concerns of white, conservative, middle-aged, English-speaking American men.[7]

The Cold War reinforced the Christian American character of the event. West Berlin, an enclave surrounded by Communist-controlled East Germany, remained partitioned, having barely survived a Soviet blockade in 1949. The Congress organizers had scheduled a pilgrimage to Wittenberg in honor of the approaching 450th anniversary of Luther's "95 Theses," but it was located across the border, and East German officials denied their travel permits. So instead, the 1,200 delegates gathered for a "Reformation Rally" at Wittenberg Square in Berlin, then marched to the nearby bombed-out Kaiser Wilhelm Memorial Church, where they joined some 18,000 West Berliners. As the delegates huddled in a cold rain under overcoats lent to them by German Christians, Billy Graham, whose nickname during the Congress was "God's Machine Gun," delivered a forceful sermon.[8]

The Congress's architecture reinforced this Cold War performance. Delegate sessions were held in the ultramodern Kongresshalle, located not far from the Berlin Wall and its barbed-wire fences, concrete and steel barriers, searchlights, and guards in towers with submachine guns. Designed by American architect Hugh Stubbins and lobbied for by Eleanor Dulles, who ran the Berlin Desk of the State Department and who was the sister of sitting CIA Director Allen Dulles and Secretary of State John Foster Dulles, the building had been a gift from the United States government. Though West Germans affectionately called it "the pregnant oyster," Stubbins said that the curved roof, elegantly supported by huge arches, resembled wings in flight. The spacious interior featured open spaces for conversation and the latest in technology: television cameras, telephone systems, and audio equipment for language interpreters. Each of these architectural features was intended to buttress the ideals of openness, freedom, communication, and the superiority of democratic capitalism. As if to proclaim these ideals to the world (or at least to nearby communists), the entire structure was perched on an artificial hill in plain view of East Berlin, which lay a mere 800 yards away. East German citizens living in the giant socialist housing project erected along Stalinallee—or wandering through the Palast der Republik, East Germany's congress hall that was a concrete hulk with a giant hammer and sickle emblazoned on the front—could gaze upon "Europe's boldest edifice." The Kongresshalle was built as a beacon of freedom for the oppressed.[9]

Proceedings inside also reflected Western ideals. As the Congress got underway, Graham, who was lodging in the Hilton Ambassador Hotel, announced plans to accept the invitation of General William Westmoreland, commander of U.S. forces, to preach the gospel to American soldiers in Vietnam. The German newspaper Die Welt noted the entrepreneurial flair of the event, calling it "strikingly American" in its methods of "Yankee efficiency." The reporter described the "attractive secretaries" rushing from office to office and the large identification badges worn by participants. The Congress gave the impression of "a general meeting of a gigantic stock company." Henry saw no rebuke in the observation, telling a *New York Times* reporter who was filing daily reports that Christians must use "methods of mass communication, modern travel, and up-to-date knowledge in spreading the Gospel." Bob Pierce and Ted Engstrom of World Vision unveiled PERT (Program Evaluation and Review Technique), a computer program developed for the aerospace industry. Pierce described it as the future engine of global evangelism. For modernist theology to be undercut, organizers felt, modern methods needed to be exploited. As historian Uta Balbier has observed, Berlin was an expression of American "soft power" in which Graham and company sought to create a moral empire based on democracy, technology, capitalism, and religion. They were exporting Christian Americanism to the world.[10]

For these evangelicals, however, authentic Christianity required spiritual conversion more than commitment to a particular politics. In fact, it was the lack of attention to traditional evangelism on the part of the World Council of Churches (WCC) that defined Berlin's animus against liberal Protestantism. Newspapers uniformly framed their stories around the Congress's attacks on the mainline. "For the liberal," Harold Ockenga was quoted as saying, "the Bible is not authoritative, not dependable, and not authentic." Ockenga could only imagine one worse rival: Roman Catholicism, whose power could never be challenged by the weak mainline. Henry piled on, complaining, "The kind of evangelism espoused by many of their leaders wouldn't be recognized as Christian by the early apostles." The rhetoric was so strident that WCC representatives protested. In response, Graham offered an olive branch a month later at a mainline conference in Miami Beach. He acknowledged that Christians can "also communicate [the Gospel] by loving our neighbor and by a compassionate social concern," as World Vision already was doing. But this was only a step toward the ultimate goal: "the winning of men to a personal relationship with Jesus Christ." In short, conversion is preeminent, and positive social change comes through the accumulation of individual conversions.[11]

The Berlin Congress reinforced traditional evangelism alongside a neocolonial Cold War politics. Faint signs of a global egalitarianism were circumscribed by a Western ethos. As one British observer put it, participants were participating in "an American sacramental occasion." Pew, Graham, and Henry brooked very little interference on the grounds that social and theological experimentation would distract from the proclamation of the gospel. In the future, however, these organizers would not be able to stifle opposition so easily.[12]

II. Dissent at Lausanne

The 1974 Congress on World Evangelization in Lausanne, Switzerland, brought together the most significant characters in twentieth-century evangelicalism (Figure 4.2). They included Billy Graham, Carl Henry, Robert Evans, and Bob Pierce. Also attending were a large number of delegates whose names— Kyung-Chik Han of Korea, Samuel Escobar of Peru, F. S. Khair-Ullah of Pakistan, B. V. Subbamma of India, and John Gatu of Kenya—were not well known by their

Figure 4.2. Lausanne I, held at the Palais de Beaulieu conference center, enjoyed wide media coverage. Courtesy of the Billy Graham Center Archives, Wheaton, Ill.

Western counterparts. Lausanne's stage would lift some of them to prominence, and their activism would begin to reshape American institutions.

Comparisons with Berlin are illuminating. The presence of Koreans and Huaorani in 1966 established that conservative evangelicalism, as one observer put it, was not a "peculiarity of Anglo-American culture." But in 1974 the presence of non-Western delegates turned into much more. They participated in mutual, if not equal, exchange. In fact, the chorus of voices from the Majority World— representing more than half of the 2,473 delegates and about one third of the plenary speaker roster—completely transformed the tenor of the event. The Lausanne Congress still preached evangelism, but with new sensibilities attached: a social consciousness and a critique of colonialism. For John Stott in particular, Lausanne marked a profound change. At Berlin, the Anglican priest and theologian, who was the most important Western voice besides Billy Graham, had joined the consensus that mission was defined solely by conversionist preaching. After Lausanne, Stott declared, "Today, however, I would express myself differently. . . . I now see more clearly that not only the consequences of the commission but the actual commission itself must be understood to include social as well as evangelistic responsibility." Otherwise, Stott concluded, "We are to be guilty of distorting the words of Jesus." Stott's transformation reflected the influence of new global voices.[13]

Latin Americans led the charge. Frustrated by Western dominance at Berlin, they were truly offended three years later by an evangelical conference in Colombia. Samuel Escobar, a delegate at both, noted that the 1969 Primer Congreso Latinoamericano de Evangelización (CLADE), though held in Bogotá, was "a meeting designed in the United States." In fact, it was one of many regional conferences around the world funded and organized by the Billy Graham Evangelistic Association—and intended to ramp up interest in the mammoth congress that would become Lausanne. C. Peter Wagner, a "church growth" expert from Fuller Theological Seminary, arrived in Bolivia with cases of his new book *Latin American Theology: Radical or Evangelical?* Distributed to all the delegates, Wagner's book suggested that churches could grow only in the setting of an evangelical capitalistic democracy. One Puerto Rican delegate, who wanted to see what could be learned from ecumenical liberals, was "offended by the purpose, the content, and the methodology of the book." An Ecuadorean delegate criticized CLADE for committing "numerolatry" and for replacing discipleship with "cheap evangelism." At Bogotá, a vocal Latin American contingent, committed both to conservative theology and to critiquing the excesses of Western capitalism, refused to conform to Cold War categories.[14]

The frustrations of Bogotá sparked an organized resistance. In 1970 twenty-four Latin American evangelicals met in Cochabamba, Bolivia, to form the *Fraternidad Teológica Latinoamericana*, known in English as the Latin American Theological Fraternity. Initially the meeting shaped up to be a typically North

American affair. The conservative National Liberty Foundation funded it, and the Evangelical Committee on Latin America, based in Wheaton, Illinois, expressed the hope that "a nucleus of conservative, evangelical theologians could be brought together to listen to the Word of God." Wagner showed up again, perhaps to keep an eye on the emerging rebels. But the group of pastors, seminary professors, evangelists, editors, and writers from nine denominations and twelve nationalities established their independence early by electing Samuel Escobar, a Peruvian expert on Brazilian educational theorist Paulo Freire, as president. Moving quickly beyond the strictly theological agenda established by the donors, they proposed to expand their topics of deliberation to include ethics, missiology, apologetics, and pastoral psychology.[15]

On one hand, Cochabamba retained explicitly evangelical themes. Delegates espoused the notion that people needed to be saved. They also criticized Latin American liberation theology for using Marxist ideology as a hermeneutical key to understanding Scripture. On the other hand, Fraternity members pushed back hard against Western imperialism, and they pushed for a more robust sense of social responsibility. The conference produced a 389-page volume with dozens of position papers, one of which was entitled "Biblical Content and Anglo-Saxon Trappings in Evangelical Theology." A much shorter one-thousand word Evangelical Declaration included the statement: "We recognize our debt to the missionaries who brought us the Gospel. At the same time we believe that a theological reflection relevant to our own peoples must take into account the dramatic reality of the Latin American scene, and make an effort to identify and remove the foreign trappings in which the message has been wrapped." Specifically, explained René Padilla to *Christianity Today*, Latin Americans should not be distracted by antiliberal apologists concerned about a "secularised Christianity." Nor should they "reduce the mission of the Church to rote repetition of unassimilated doctrinal formulas coined in North America or Europe." Rather, they should nurture indigenous networks, acknowledge God's preference for the poor, and produce theology "from the underside."[16]

American leaders watched with concern as the influence of the Fraternity grew. The products of their missionary work were still drawn to the conversionist theology of Graham, but they resisted his intense Christian Americanism. One of them was Orlando Costas, a Puerto Rican immigrant to the United States who was converted at Graham's 1957 New York crusade. As a Fraternity member and dean of the Latin American Biblical Seminary in Costa Rica, Costas helped build a coalition of critics who articulated the limits of American justice and evangelization. In 1970 Wagner, who served on Lausanne's executive committee, warned fellow North Americans, "It looks like we might be getting into a real struggle with the Costas gang. Be sure anything you write concerning them is couched with plenty of ifs and buts and possiblys so that a direct quote taken from one of your letters won't be devastating." As Wagner continued, his ambivalence showed: "Best approach to Costas & Co.: they're fine brothers in Christ and sincere in following a certain mediating line, but they are out to present only one point of view—we have another which we consider more biblical and appropriate for Latin America today." "I would say that we shouldn't fight this but rather make room in our thinking for it," he concluded. As Lausanne approached, Western organizers felt both genuine interest in and wariness about learning new missionary methods from their non-Western counterparts.[17]

The Latin Americans carved out considerably more space than Wagner anticipated. From his strategic position on the Lausanne planning committee, which demonstrated a real concern for geographical and ethnic representation, Escobar helped recruit over a thousand Majority World evangelicals. In the end, there were 660 delegates from Asia, 370 from Africa, and 219 from Latin America (compared with 1,100 from Europe and North America). In registration paperwork, these non-Western delegates articulated notably different concerns than their Western counterparts. Those from the United States wanted to discuss secularism, syncretism, the World Council of Churches, efficient methods of evangelization, and authentic partnerships. By contrast, Majority World voices stressed the power of the Holy Spirit and the need for cultural sensitivity, so as not to make Christ, wrote a Singaporean delegate, "into a foreigner." Organizers responded. Western donors fully subsidized the travel costs of non-Western delegates. Graham, pledging his financial support to the effort, declared that "there should be massive Third World input and that this continuing committee not be dominated and maneuvered by those of us from America and Europe."[18]

Despite Graham's conciliatory words, the stage was set for a showdown at the stately Palais de Beaulieu conference center on the shores of Lake Geneva. Lausanne's aesthetics—even bigger and grander than Berlin—seemed as tone-deaf as Berlin eight years earlier. Russ Reid, an evangelical marketing specialist who pioneered World Vision television infomercials and personalized computer-generated direct mailings, publicized Lausanne with a sophisticated media blitz. The Congress's logo (a stylized depiction of "74" and four fishes) was everywhere, and an enormous projection system featuring an image of Graham's face greeted delegates at the first session. In keeping with the urgency of evangelizing "the three billion living with no knowledge of Jesus," organizers kept things moving efficiently. Standing in the lobby was a huge "population clock" ticking off the number of non-Christians being born every minute. (The number reached two million by the end of the Congress.) The so-called "church growth experts," C. Peter Wagner, Donald McGavran, and Ralph Winter, introduced a *Handbook of Unreached Peoples* that used words like "E-3 evangelism." In one speech McGavran declared that social action "must neither be called evangelism nor substituted for it." Many delegates from the Majority World rolled their eyes at the Madison Avenue spectacle, which seemed predictably "materialistic, banal, and flat." McGavran's words, which seemed to fly in the face of Congress's intent to consider "the whole mission of the Church," were even more poorly received. Critics readied themselves to confront these "evangelical tycoons," as Escobar called them.[19]

Finally, if reluctantly, granted a platform on the third day of the ten-day Congress, Latin Americans led the rebellion. Fortified by prayers from home (in Buenos Aires, Catharine Feser Padilla gathered her children around a globe and told them, "Today, when he gives his talk here, in Lausanne, Switzerland, Papi will say some things that not everyone is going to want to hear. Let's pray for him and for the people listening to him"), René Padilla delivered the first of the contentious addresses. An Ecuadorian who had attended Wheaton College, studied with noted New Testament scholar F. F. Bruce at the University of Manchester, and traveled widely in the United States, Padilla directly confronted the technocratic Church Growth group. He condemned the "American culture-Christianity" that had turned the gospel into "a cheap product." Missionaries from the United States, he continued, were captive to a "fierce pragmatism" that "in the political sphere has produced Watergate." They were exporting, Padilla said, an obsession with efficiency and the "systematization of methods and resources to obtain pre-established results." They had identified the Gospel with worldly power, perpetuated patterns of dependence, and conflated "Americanism with the Gospel." *Time* magazine described Padilla's "most provocative" keynote address as having "assailed the sort of easy Christianity the U.S. has often exported." Delivering the speech in Spanish to accentuate resistance to colonialism and to "teach Western delegates the experience of listening to a translator," Padilla earned one of three standing ovations at the Congress. It also received the longest and most sustained applause to that point, which stopped only when song leader Cliff Barrows began to lead a hymn. More than a few international delegates saw "deep political overtones" in the ovation's premature end. More than a few Western organizers saw Padilla as the *enfant terrible* of the Congress.[20]

Fraternity colleague Orlando Costas offered the second major dissent. He directly challenged a speech by G. W. Peters, a professor at the fundamentalist Dallas Theological Seminary, which had advocated a wide spectrum of evangelisms: confrontation evangelism, friendship evangelism, camp evangelism, dinner evangelism, and mass media evangelism. Too often, Costas contended, these activities became "a commercial, manipulative whitewash." Borrowing from Paulo Freire's *Pedagogy of the Oppressed* (1968), Costas encouraged Latin Americans to interrogate their cultural and social contexts and to recognize that "American evangelical missionary support is tainted by links to imperialistic culture and vested economic interests." In the wake of Lausanne, Costas would decry the use of the term "third world." He preferred the term "two-thirds world," explaining that Latin America was not third rate. Indeed, it was part of a global sector that comprised the bulk of the world's population.[21]

Escobar then delivered the coup de grâce. He already had engineered the new emphasis on social concerns as a member of the program planning committee and then stirred up intense debate by precirculating a provocative paper that had received over 1,200 responses before the Congress even began. On Monday morning, inspired by the radical discipleship caucus the night before, he challenged Graham directly. In his speech, Escobar rejected Graham's earlier worry that an emphasis on social issues "would lead to the abandonment of the gospel" (Figure 4.3). He declared emphatically, "I would like to affirm that *I do not believe in that statement*." Rediscovering the social dimensions of the gospel could help remove suspicion that evangelization was merely "an imperialist plot, a Western way of manipulating people." Escobar elaborated, "Christians in the Third World who contemplate the so-called West, expect from their brethren a word of identification with demands for justice in international trade, for a modification of the patterns of affluence and waste that are made possible because of unjust and exploitative trade systems, for a criticism of corruption in the arms race and in the almost omnipotent maneuverings of international intelligence agencies." Evangelists who concentrate solely on souls, he concluded, resemble

Figure 4.3. Samuel Escobar of the Latin American Theological Fraternity rejected Billy Graham's worry that an emphasis on social issues at Lausanne would lead to the gospel being abandoned. Courtesy of Samuel Escobar.

the conquistadors who carried both the sword and the cross, baptizing Indians before executing them. Escobar beseeched delegates not to separate the gospel from social justice.[22]

The concerns of these Latin Americans resonated broadly. According to a British delegate, the speeches were "much more deeply felt than many Western evangelical Christian leaders here could have expected." Padilla himself, greeted by a deluge of hugs and congratulations after his speech, was "surprised at the number of Asians and Africans and Latin Americans who felt represented by what I said." In one of hundreds of small groups that convened in the wake of these speeches, K. N. Nambudripad of India described how Western apparel and language hindered the spread of the Gospel among Hindus. Indian physician B. V. Subbamma lauded the cultural sensitivity of E. Stanley Jones's Christian ashrams. In the lively discussion that followed, the group came to a consensus that "as soon as possible the Indian church should be indigenized. . . . We would welcome missionaries but only as colleagues and workers, not as leaders or controllers." In another small group, F. S. Khair-Ullah of Pakistan urged empathetic study of Islam, informed dialogue, and honesty "in recognizing the best that is in Islam." In yet another small group, Okgill Kim of South Korea reminded Western representatives that "the ideology of the Third World is neither democracy nor Communism but nationalism. The peoples in the Third World are all alert to discover national identity which has been lost through the Western economic, political, and cultural invasions." In sum, many non-Western delegates urged sensitivity to local ethnic traditions and an end to Western Christian triumphalism. A few, wanting to encourage the integrity of national churches, even flirted with the notion of a moratorium on Western missionaries.[23]

The activism provoked a backlash. Some organizers, with crossed arms and stone faces, were "so mad," Padilla later recalled, that they refused to acknowledge or speak to him after his address. He had portrayed, said one Western delegate, "so patently a caricature as to create static that cannot but block . . . many insights which people attending the conference will need." Church growth leaders sought to minimize the fallout and to shape the historical memory of Lausanne. In a widely read *Christianity Today* article, Wagner wrote that a faction that appeared to ignore the gravity of individual moral sins had tried unsuccessfully to "torpedo" the Congress with an "attempt to confuse evangelism with social action." He also asserted that the Fraternity enjoyed more support "from Anglo-Saxons than they did from their Latin American peers." In fact, the writer claimed, Escobar had been "promptly rebuked by a dozen leaders" from Latin America. Escobar contested the report, saying that there was "no rebuke" and that Wagner's essay was "a totally biased" account that betrayed a "concerted effort on the part of the conservative elements that are in charge of *Christianity Today* to change the meaning and the directions of Lausanne." Carl

Henry, unhappy with the "self-proclaimed champions of 'radical discipleship,'" fumed that instead of "doing their own thing," they should have "been a little more social."[24]

But even establishment evangelicals had imbibed some measure of the spirit of decolonization. Billy Graham himself, who had been a harbinger of Christian Americanism in the 1940s and 1950s, set a chastened tone in his opening address. He confessed that identifying "the Gospel with any one particular system or culture . . . has been my own danger." Then to warm applause, he declared, "When I go to preach the gospel, I go as an ambassador for the Kingdom of God—not America." After Padilla's address, Graham pronounced it "one of the most brilliant contributions for the analysis of the evangelistic task today." As the Congress rolled on, many more confessed to Western materialism, poverty, racial problems, and pollution. Harold Lindsell mourned "man's unceasing quest for ecological suicide," and church growth theoretician Ralph Winter declared that Jesus "did not die to preserve our Western way of life." To be sure, there was recrimination and much debate about how to contextualize the gospel, but there was consensus that contextualization itself was good.[25]

The Lausanne Covenant, which underwent telling revisions in the wake of Latin American dissent, enshrined these new sensibilities (Figure 4.4). While the rebels were not completely successful in overturning conventional definitions of evangelism—when Escobar objected to Stott's insertion of the phrase "evangelism is primary," the language stood anyway—the trajectory was undeniable. Several hundred amendments were proposed during the Congress, and the final document, said Stott, bore "no resemblance" to the original. For perhaps the first time, conservative American evangelicals denounced the totalitarianism of the Right as well as the Left. The first draft included one sentence on social justice; the second draft promoted simple living, international sensitivity, and social justice in a section that was larger than any other in the Covenant. The revisions did not come easy. Australian Jack Dain recalled the drafting committee's labors: "No one will ever know except the members the agonies through which we all passed. . . . I can only marvel after grappling for hours with these matters we did come to a common mind." The end result, driven largely by the radical discipleship caucus, was a document that cautiously acknowledged global alienation, oppression, discrimination, and injustice. Much had changed in the eight years since Berlin.[26]

Lausanne stirred hopes among Majority World delegates. Orlando Costas, who said he "came with deep fears, conscious of the potential dangers imbedded in a world gathering dominated by Western leadership and money," left optimistic about the "many creative possibilities [that had] appeared on the horizon." Escobar, thrilled by several dynamic addresses from Westerners on the topic,

Figure 4.4. Jack Dain and Billy Graham signing the Lausanne Covenant. Despite—or perhaps because of—the intervention of Latin American activists, I could find no photographs of Samuel Escobar, René Padilla, or Orlando Costas in the Lausanne archival collection. Courtesy of the Billy Graham Center Archives, Wheaton, Ill.

noted the pervasive talk about "evangelistic partnership" and the "disappearance of the dominant role of western missions." In a post-Lausanne letter to Padilla, the head of the International Fellowship of Evangelical Students, Chua Wee Hian of Singapore, wrote, "Pax Americana has reached its zenith and is now in a state of rapid decline. The bubbles of triumphalism of North American 'success Christianity' have been pricked and deflated at Lausanne. We hope that there will be genuine repentance. I personally think there will be a new and better understanding between us and our American brethren in the post-Vietnam and post-Watergate era."

The reverberations of Lausanne continued for years. The electrifying Kenyan preacher Gottfried Osei-Mensah was named as the first Executive Secretary of the Lausanne Committee. The Latin American Theological Fraternity remained very active, extending its prophetic witness on imperialism and social injustice. The Fraternity's publications, published in English in addition to Spanish and Portuguese, spread Latin American evangelical social thought across the globe. It truly appeared as if Lausanne, unquestionably one of the most significant religious events of the twentieth century, was overcoming Western dominance. The American missions monologue was over.[27]

III. Contextualizing the Gospel

The Majority World, in fact, increasingly colonized North America. Using networks built at Lausanne, Fraternity members circulated widely within white evangelicalism. Escobar, following his Lausanne moment, remained very popular in InterVarsity circles and served as president of InterVarsity in Canada during the mid-1970s. Costas wrote a book entitled *The Church and Its Mission: A Shattering Critique from the Third World* (1974) and taught missiology at several prominent seminaries in North America, including Fuller, Gordon-Conwell, Andover Newton, and Eastern Baptist. They and hundreds of others added to a growing literature on contextualization. Mainline missionaries had debated methods of indigenization and multiculturalism as early as the 1920s and 1930s, and Taiwanese theologian Shoki Coe coined the term "contextualization" in the early 1970s, but Lausanne truly launched the contextualization movement in evangelical circles. At its core, contextualization meant to spread the gospel in ways that were sensitive to local conditions. The new missiological direction confessed a colonial past, acknowledged persistent imperialism even in the midst of decolonization, and urged the adoption of indigenous languages and non-Western theologies.[28]

While expressing appreciation for the gift of the Gospel, Majority World evangelicals condemned the imperialistic aims of the West and decried the devastation brought by Western armies and corporations. As debate over the future of the Panama Canal raged in the mid-1970s, for example, members of the International Fellowship of Evangelical Students in Costa Rica wrote:

> You condemn the relics of colonialism in Rhodesia and South Africa. Why are you so slow to see the 'beam in your own eye?' During the construction of the canal more than 25,000 poor laborers from the Third World laid down their lives on the altar of the First World economic development—yet your politicians have the gall to boast "we built it!"

Orlando Costas described his homeland of Puerto Rico as a "sugar-colony" whose overseers "worried little for the pathetic social and economical situation of its people." Worst of all, Protestant missionaries "served as ideological instruments of the colonial power." American missionaries, when confronted by local resistance, often confessed to imperial sins: atrocities in the American West, military intervention in Latin America, and support for authoritarian "rightist regimes" in Asia and Latin America. Miriam Adeney, a missionary to the Philippines, wrote in a 1974 *Christianity Today* article that Western moral superiority "was hardly apparent to Africans in the holds of slave ships . . . or to the Tasmanians, against whom the whites enjoyed regular open hunting season."[29]

International evangelicals suggested that instead of ignoring—even annihilating—local economies and symbols, Americans work harder at making the Gospel intelligible outside the West. Adeney wrote that "every culture is the lifeway of people made in the image of God, regardless of their standard of living." Missionaries should seek out "solid contextual information about how our brothers live." In Asia, missionaries pondered group conversions, a difficult concept for individualistic Americans to fathom. B. V. Subbamma, a Fuller Seminary graduate who practiced vegetarianism and participated in Indian ashrams, argued that "each ethnic unit in each land" should "follow its own culture." "Either you baptise us all," she declared, "or none." In Africa, missionaries wondered what to do with polygamists who became Christians. Ghanaian Kwame Bediako, an important African theologian, criticized the "civilizing" programs of Western missionaries. Instead, they should describe Jesus to the clan as the Great Ancestor. In this way, Africans could be assured that they can be "authentic Africans and true Christians." Decentralization and local autonomy became the watchwords of evangelical missiology in the 1970s.[30]

Bible translation offered the most convincing evidence for the efficacy of contextualization. Lamin Sanneh's extensive work on translation shows that missionaries were in fact "unwitting allies of mother-tongue speakers and reluctant opponents of colonial domination." As noncatechized indigenous peoples under colonization began reading freshly translated texts, Christianity began to look less like "colonialism at prayer." Instead of reproducing Western theology, translations into the vernacular produced cultural reawakening, the preservation of indigenous language, and a breathtaking interpretive heterogeneity. In fact, some American missiologists began to argue that the orality of African culture resembled that of biblical Palestine and was better positioned to interpret ancient texts than their own rationalist culture.[31]

The pressing task of global theological production and exchange loomed large in the missiological imagination. In 1976 John Mbiti asked, "We have eaten theology with you; we have drunk theology with you; we have dreamed theology with you. But it has been all one-sided; it has all been, in a sense, your theology. . . . Would you like to know us theologically?" Sites for such exchanges burgeoned in the late 1970s and 1980s. They included the Asian Theological Conference of Third World Theologians, the International Fellowship of Evangelical Mission Theologians (INFEMIT), the Latin American Theological Fraternity, and the Pan African Christian Leadership Assembly. Majority World scholarship was published in the *Asia Journal of Theology*, *Journal of Theology for Southern Africa*, the *Journal of Latin American Theology*, and *Studies in World Christianity*. The World Evangelical Fellowship (WEF), which represented one hundred national assemblies and more than 150 million people, launched the Theological Assistance Programme, which was administered by Bruce Nichols of New Zealand and then overseen by Saphir Athyal of India and Eui-Hwan Kim of Korea. In 1982, Tokunboh Adeyemo, general secretary of the Association of Evangelicals of Africa and Madagascar, became chair of the WEF executive council. He initiated strong efforts to hold general assemblies in non-Western countries. The non-Western shift continued in 1986 as headquarters moved to Singapore, which WEF leaders called "a major crossroads of the non-Western world." In the 1990s Filipino Jun Vencer became its first Majority World director. The internationalization of WEF helped revitalize an organization burdened by a too-close association with the West.[32]

The global turn marked a departure from the Western theological baseline. The new methodology focused more on intersubjectivity and less on objectivity. More missionaries and indigenous people began to interpret texts communally, not individually. They practiced theology not from a position of power, but from below. Hispanic theologians, noted church historian Justo Gonzalez, "interpret from a place of marginality, poverty, mestizaje/mulatez exile and solidarity." This perspective yielded a striking critique of Western triumphalism. Palestinian theologian Yohanna Katanacho wrote about how an American "theology of land" contributed to "the marginalization and oppression of his people." By contrast, strong strains of Majority World theology stressed freedom, liberation, and biblical justice. The resemblance to liberation theology scared some Westerners. But those who saw the language of justice as a liberal project were often then bewildered by the literalistic, conservative theology espoused by many from the Majority World. "I don't understand you," declared a British observer. "One minute you are talking about social issues, and the next about moral issues! What are you evangelicals—left-wing or right-wing?" Idiosyncratic as it appeared, the gospel as interpreted from the margins, according to Gottfried Osei-Mensah, was unearthing "an 'Eastern' Jesus that was more than able to meet their needs." According to the Nairobi pastor, the "apostles of Christ" at Lausanne had "voted out cultural imperialism and instituted instead the concessions of responsible fellowship in Christ."[33]

The Eastern Jesus did more than meet needs. He enjoyed spectacular success. As the theory of contextualization suggested, missionary work was most successful when it was sensitive to local conditions and when the gospel was communicated in the vernacular by natives. In fact, the most successful missionary ventures—the conversion of the Yoruba in Nigeria and the astonishingly rapid rise of the Korea church as a global Christian power—were not launched by Americans. These examples, writes historian Mark Noll, showed that "the primary agency in recent movements of Christianization has been not the missionaries but the new converts themselves." The chronology is significant. If Christianization had been Western driven, the numbers of believers would have contracted during decolonization in the mid-twentieth century. Instead,

Christian growth exploded. "Judging from where churches were growing rapidly," writes sociologist of religion David Stoll, "it seemed as if the recipe for success was for missionaries to leave." Or get expelled. The expulsion of missionaries by Mao, said some observers, paved the way for a self-led, local faith in China. When Marxists could no longer claim that Christianity was inherently imperial and Western, the faith spread like wildfire. To be sure, Western religious presence did not disappear when colonialism receded. But missionaries grew more ambivalent about their own capacity to adequately contextualize the gospel.[34]

The heightened emphasis on contextualization transformed evangelical missiology. A flood of books and conferences in the United States buttressed strong intercultural programs at seminaries such as Trinity Evangelical Divinity School and Asbury Theological Seminary. In 1977 veteran missionary Dean Gilliland joined Fuller Seminary's School of Intercultural Studies, using his twenty-two years of experience in Nigeria to teach potential missionaries the theoretical basis for "the groundbreaking practice of intentionally presenting the gospel in terms that are accessible to the local community." The Billy Graham Evangelistic Association, while still using the world's most famous evangelist, began to use native evangelists like Akbar Abdul-Haqq in its crusades. Between 1984 and 2000, *Transformation* magazine—edited by Tokunboh Adeyemo and Vinay Samuel—published eighty-five articles from Asia, fifty-three from Africa, forty-six from Latin America, five from the Middle East, fourteen from Australia, eighty-seven from Europe, and 120 from North America. Western contributions still outstripped non-Western offerings, but the non-Western presence was rising. The postcolonial turn to contextualization, a key legacy of Lausanne, was reshaping the West.[35]

IV. Retrenchment

There were limits to the transforming power of the Majority World. The very public challenge by Escobar and other Latin American provocateurs may have moved the needle on contextualization and social justice, but not all global Christians, especially those trained at American fundamentalist seminaries, were so quick to push against American imperialism. Far from being champions of progressive politics, some maintained a singular focus on individual conversion. In fact, several of the sharpest critiques of Padilla and Escobar came from conservative and traditionalist delegates from Africa and Asia. Dozens of non-Western speakers emphasized the exclusivity of the Christian faith even more strongly than those from the United States. They denounced universalism and called for the evangelization of Hindus, Muslims, Catholics, animists, and hippies. Luis Palau of Argentina, sidestepping calls for social justice, declared that "some 145,000 people around the world die daily and go to eternity." In this and other public presentations at Lausanne, many international delegates emphasized the urgency of preaching a spiritual gospel to "unreached people groups." Inspired by the church growth sensibility of McGavran and Wagner at Lausanne, they reinforced traditional white American evangelical convictions.[36]

A rising movement of charismatic delegates bypassed the prevailing public debate entirely. Juan Carlos Ortiz and other Pentecostals emphasized that the best methodology for missions was provided by the Holy Spirit. "Personal Information" cards filled out by delegates during the Lausanne registration were suggestive, revealing a stark contrast between West and East. While Western delegates typically sought discussion about the statistically driven theory of church growth, non-Western delegates called moderately for more social justice, strongly for an end to Western dominance, and overwhelmingly for a "supernatural demonstration of God's power" and an "outpouring of the Holy Spirit." Many of these delegates, however, did not receive speaking invitations at Lausanne, so this Pentecostal emphasis only bubbled below the surface. Had North American gatekeepers not screened so carefully, it is possible that Lausanne would have been overwhelmed by charismatic Pentecostals associated with the "health and wealth" prosperity movement beginning to grow in Latin America and Africa.[37]

The screening of certain Majority World voices continued. Lausanne's most prominent nonconformists—Padilla and Escobar—were not invited to join the continuation committee that met in Mexico City six months later. Roughly half of the invited international delegates were unable to come to the meetings at the Hotel Del Prado. Even still, it appeared that Western imperialism had been stanched. The committee elected a non-Western general secretary, and in an opening speech, Billy Graham, who was bankrolling the gathering, pledged to help develop an "evangelicalism that is not controlled by the First World." *Time* magazine quoted him as saying, "Jesus Christ was not a Westerner." But the apparent consensus at Lausanne about social action did not hold in Mexico City. After quoting from a letter from the Majority World that pled for the new "world organization" to "serve men, aid development, attack imperialism, fight the population explosion, liberate the oppressed, and do God's work in the world and from an evangelical stance," Graham backed off. "I do not oppose any of this . . . but I do feel that the Continuation Committee would be off the mandate given us at Lausanne if we got involved in all of this." It was the critics' turn to feel hijacked.[38]

John Stott, the British churchman who advocated for the broad definition of missions at Lausanne, came through again. Having just arrived in Mexico City from India, Stott stewed after Graham's evening speech. In the debate that ensued the next morning, Stott objected to Graham's plea to "not get bogged down in peripheral matters." Stott insisted that the committee explore "the entire range of concerns" as articulated in the Lausanne Covenant. He ended his rebuttal with a strong plea to elevate the social concerns of the gospel. "If we go back now, and concentrate exclusively on evangelism," he declared, "it will not be an implementation of the Covenant but a betrayal of it." Such a repudiation, he knew, would alienate rising global leaders who had populated the radical discipleship caucus. "If we didn't find room for their concerns," he later recalled, "Lausanne was doomed." Stott and several other Western advocates vowed to resign if the committee went down the narrow path desired by Graham.

The stunned gathering fell into silence, which receded as angry Americans launched a counterattack. As Stott put it in his diary, "Well, then the fat was in the fire!" Graham's supporters, who interpreted Stott's threat as "an illicit form of blackmail," were aghast, for the Lausanne movement would likely founder if Stott resigned. Debate raged for several tense days, and the impasse ended only when the committee locked adversaries Stott and C. Peter Wagner in a room to work on a compromise. The next morning, when it seemed as if the radical discipleship caucus's perspective might be lost, a sleepless Graham yielded. He spoke warmly of Stott's friendship, agreed to support the inclusion of stronger language on social justice for "the sake of Christian unity," and pledged his continued financial support. Some rejoiced over Graham's "magnanimous expression of tenderness and understanding." But many found the consensus language—"Evangelism is primary and our chief burden must be the unevangelized millions"—less than satisfying. By contrast, a relieved Wagner, worried about Lausanne becoming "a new WCC," wrote in his conference notes that "This was a close call!" Lausanne, it was clear, had not been an unalloyed victory for the cause of social concern.[39]

In the end, the Mexico City compromise exacerbated differences. On one side were Wagner, *Christianity Today* editor Harold Lindsell, and an American power structure. On the other side were Stott, Padilla, the Latin American Theological Fraternity, and large numbers of radical missionaries and global evangelicals who questioned whether Graham's social concern was authentic. "In many instances," wrote Ralph Covell, a former missionary to Taiwan and China, "I get the distinct feeling that lip service is being paid to the matter of social responsibility and that in reality, there is no deep concern." As the 1970s wore on, Graham, according to historian Brian Stanley, only halfheartedly participated in the Lausanne movement. Many within the Billy Graham Evangelistic Association saw Lausanne as a liberal rival that could mar Graham's evangelistic legacy, and it gradually redirected funds to active evangelists in its ranks.[40]

For the next decade, the low-grade rift festered, sometimes erupting dramatically. At a 1977 "Colloquium on the Homogenous Unit Principle" at Fuller Seminary, Padilla again clashed with McGavran and Wagner. A disgusted Stott wrote in his diary that when Padilla got up to speak, they "put down their pads and pens, folded their arms, sat back and appeared to pull down the shutter of their minds." At a 1980 conference in Pattaya, Thailand, global evangelicals yet again found familiar irritations. They worshiped exclusively with Western music in a high-end resort town noted for being "one of Southeast Asia's most lively adult playgrounds." They listened to a predominantly American set of speakers from large establishment agencies. Once again, a dissenting faction released a "Statement of Concerns" objecting to how planners had skirted "the social, political and economic issues in many parts of the world that are a great stumbling block to the proclamation of the Gospel." A full one-third of delegates signed the document, but the result was largely the same. Lausanne's leaders reassured the faction that they would "gladly reaffirm" the commitment to social justice found in the original Lausanne Covenant, but they were unwilling to be any more specific.[41]

In response, Majority World agitators reconfigured their religious networks. Many continued to participate in the Lausanne movement, but they also began meeting on their own. In 1979 in Lima, Peru, attendees of CLADE II used the motto "Let Latin America Hear His Voice," clearly taking Lausanne as its frame of reference, but implying that the movement had never fully included their region. Padilla explained that CLADE II "sought to relate its message to the concrete reality of poverty and oppression, moral corruption and abuse of power in this area of the world." In 1982 at the first "Conference of Evangelical Mission Theologians for the Two-Thirds World" in Bangkok, twenty-five theologians from Asia, Africa, and Latin America met to discuss "evangelical Christologies from the contexts of poverty, powerlessness, and religious pluralism." A year later they were hosted by the Fraternity in Cuernavaca, Mexico, to discuss spirituality and the Holy Spirit. In 1987 the African Theological Fraternity hosted a conference in Kabare, Kenya, on "The Living God in Contemporary Life." In Seoul, Koreans hosted a "Third World Theologians Consultation" that emphasized "democratization, the socialization of power, and the just distribution of wealth." This coalition continued to engage the West, just more selectively. Avoiding sites where church growth strategists circulated, they began to collaborate with Westerners at the margins of Lausanne on projects such as the new *Transformation* magazine, Regnum Books, and the Oxford Centre for Mission Studies. These were places where Majority World evangelicals could shape missiology away from the shadow of Wagner and Graham.[42]

Within the Lausanne movement it always had taken the strong advocacy of Westerners to give the Majority World a voice. Western discourse, grounded in the written word, ecclesiastical hierarchies, and organizational charts, often did not accommodate non-Western styles. Chua Wee Hian explained that "letter-writing is not one of the fortes of many of us from Asia, Africa and Latin America. We thrive on face-to-face encounters." The intervention of prominent Westerners helped. Gottfried Osei-Mensah, for example, was elected executive secretary of Lausanne only after Graham pushed hard. Australian Anglican bishop Jack Dain, Charles Troutman of Latin America Mission, Paul Rees of the National Association of Evangelicals, C. Stacey Woods of InterVarsity, Hans Bürki of the International Fellowship of Evangelical Students, and Stanley Mooneyham of World Vision were other notable Western promoters of non-Western leadership.[43]

John Stott, beloved by Majority World Christians and profoundly shaped by them, was their most critical advocate. A trusted conservative who had been ordained in London's St. Paul's Cathedral, Stott was known as the "evangelical pope." But relentless globetrotting turned him into a social and economic progressive and a confidant to emerging church leaders in Africa and Asia. In 1974 Stott kept the radical discipleship group in the spotlight and incorporated their concerns into the Lausanne Covenant, working through the night as new ideas came from the Majority World delegates. He then presented the document and, according to one delegate, "expounded it in a way which brought to life the passion beneath the cold print." Importantly, he actually signed their document and kept the pressure on for years after. After Mexico City Stott spoke "almost gleefully," says his biographer Alister Chapman, of "opposing the Americans." By correspondence, he shamed C. Peter Wagner for "sniping . . . at brothers five thousand miles away" and not "accurately representing what we have written and said." Stott wrote that the radical discipleship group should not have to "swallow indiscriminately everything you and your colleagues say!" Stott was their interpreter and champion.[44]

Geography mattered. From the perspective of the West, still operating with a latent Christian Americanism, Billy Graham was the linchpin of Lausanne. From the perspective of the East, Stott was the glue that held it all together. Indeed, Stott appealed to just about everyone. Beyond his personal qualities, the Anglican cleric benefited from a residual Anglophilia in the United States. Americans, bingeing on the writings of C. S. Lewis and Stott's best-selling theological books, were at least modestly receptive to Stott's critiques. He appealed to the Majority World for different reasons. Britain, which had suffered great losses through decolonization, seemed like less of a threat than the surging United States. According to Chapman, Stott was "an ideal broker between evangelicals from the United States and those from the Third World." He kept a diverse global community in conversation with itself. "If it hadn't been for John Stott and Lausanne, I wouldn't be an evangelical today," explained more than one unsettled Latin American. Even in a postcolonial era, it took a product of Western imperialism to smooth the way for non-Western voices.[45]

Nevertheless, the transformation in the decades following the Berlin and Lausanne gatherings was remarkable. A 1989 congress in the Philippines—dubbed Lausanne II—offers a helpful contrast. There were still complaints about American dominance, evocatively described as "too much vanilla in Manila."

Ruth Padilla DeBorst, René Padilla's daughter and a formidable theologian in her own right, complained that "Manila was just the triumph of managerial perspective—the unreached peoples, church growth, and all of that." She was right, but much had changed. Many of the familiar players—like Billy Graham, who did not attend due to exhaustion—were tired, ill, or dead. In their place was a colorful roster of speakers whose sermons demonstrated a broader range of social concerns.[46]

Amid the backdrop of densely populated, poverty-afflicted Manila, Filipinos hosted an even more diverse gathering than Lausanne I fifteen years before (Figure 4.5). Among the 4,300 delegates from 173 countries, 22 percent were women. They were also much younger, 50 percent under the age of forty-five. A larger percentage of speakers hailed from the Majority World. Delegates were led in worship by diverse musicians: a guitarist from Nagaland, India; a flautist from Venezuela; a vocalist from Egypt; a Ghanaian drummer; a female vocalist from Nicaragua—all led by Ken Medema, a blind American. Corazon Aquino, president of the Philippines, opened with a strong call for the Congress to attend to justice imperatives and physical needs in the Third World. The gathering was also structured in ways that allowed for more dialogue. Delegates participated in and led many small group discussions. Some took tours of Manila, including Smokey Mountain, a rubbish hill where thousands of poor people lived, to learn about the challenges of urban evangelism and justice.[47]

In addition to pride of place, the Majority World insistently articulated a holistic vision of mission. Old luminaries like Samuel Escobar and René Padilla, who

Figure 4.5. By Lausanne II, held in Manila fifteen years later in 1989, nonwhite participants were more visible and vocal at press conferences and on stage. Courtesy of the Billy Graham Center Archives, Wheaton, Ill.

by then had edited over 200 books, returned as featured speakers. Their longtime booster John Stott declared that evangelism was "no longer a one-way traffic, out from Western Christendom." A younger generation also pressed. Caesar Molebatsi, a black South African youth worker, delivered a powerful presentation against apartheid entitled "Reaching the Oppressed." Valdir Steuernagel, a young evangelical liberation theologian from Brazil, censured the "North American cultural imperialism of the conference." Vinay Samuel of Bangalore, India, urged Westerners to facilitate access to capital to release poor people from the bondage of crippling debt. The language of the Manila Manifesto, containing long sections on poverty, was striking compared with Berlin and Lausanne I. Some even criticized it as relying "too heavily on the language of liberation theology." Veterans of the radical discipleship caucus expressed deep frustration that old battles still had to be fought. But many of their concerns were being institutionalized. Ron Sider, a leading luminary of the American evangelical left, declared, "What especially impressed—and delighted—me was the extent to which . . . holistic concern for both evangelism and social action has now become the prevailing perspective of mainstream evangelicalism worldwide." Linguistically, theologically, and geographically, Lausanne II was a fitting sequel.[48]

The influence of these global missiologists varied. They reinforced a growing discontent with wealth inequality and Western triumphalism among American progressives associated with Evangelicals for Social Action, Sojourners, the Association for Public Justice, and growing numbers of urban activists. They inspired African Americans and Hispanics in North America to claim "third-world status" and solidarity with the Majority World. They fueled a noteworthy simple living movement that drove the shockingly high sales of Ron Sider's *Rich Christians in an Age of Hunger* (1977). They also got considerable pushback from right-wing critics such as David Chilton, who wrote *Productive Christians in an Age of Guilt Manipulators* (1982). Peter Beyerhaus, a longtime participant in the Lausanne movement, accused the global dissenters of "importing ecumenical ideology in the belly of the Trojan horse!" Even if not everyone was transformed by the global reflex, it unquestionably provoked a substantive debate.[49]

The Lausanne movement, however, made its biggest impact on a swath of conservative Protestants who fit neither with the evangelical left nor the religious right. Like Billy Graham, who in the 1980s backed away decisively from his old tropes of American exceptionalism and devoted more time to nuclear disarmament, international peace efforts, and rapprochement with the Soviet Union, these mainstream evangelicals also became more cosmopolitan and adopted a new ethos of cultural sensivity and contextualization. In 1981 Wagner, the radicals' most vigorous interlocutor, said he felt "like a candidate for the 'how my mind has changed' series." In contrast to his views at Lausanne I, he now said that "matters having to do with the poor and oppressed, with justice and peace, with brotherhood and liberation, with wealth and lifestyle, with discipleship and the kingdom of God are all part of the concerns of biblical Christians, church growth advocates included." Wagner cited interactions with global evangelicals as the reason for his new perspective.[50]

While not every American could narrate such a dramatic conversion, Lausanne had, in fact, made a difference. It provided space for Western theologians to circulate in the East and for Majority World Christians to circulate in the West. In doing so, it sparked a transformative conversation about the nature of missionary work, imperialism, and social responsibility. Just beginning to understand the magnitude of global Christianity, American evangelicals in the 1970s were living in a brave new postcolonial world. The Majority World had put them on notice that missiology would no longer develop in North American isolation.

Notes

1. Tapes 180–84 of the "radical discipleship" gathering, July 21, 1974, in International Congress on World Evangelization Collection, BGCA; Tape 3, interviews with René Padilla, March 12, 1987, in Oral History Collection 361, BGCA. On Padilla's key role in the caucus, see David Kirkpatrick, *A Gospel for the Poor: Global Social Christianity and the Latin American Evangelical Left* (Philadelphia: University of Pennsylvania Press, 2019), 23–27.
2. John Stott to Paul Little, n.d., in Box 4, Folder 1, in ICWE Collection, BGCA.
3. Athol Gill, "Christian Social Responsibility," 91–92, in René Padilla, ed., *The New Face of Evangelicalism* (Downers Grove, Ill.: InterVarsity Press, 1976); "A Response to Lausanne" and Little to Stott, August 8, 1974, in Box 4, Folder 1, in ICWE Collection, BGCA. For "powerful West," see Escobar, "Evangelism and Man's Search for Freedom, Justice and Fulfillment," 317, in J. D. Douglas, ed., *Let the Earth Hear His Voice* (Minneapolis, Minn.: World Wide Publications, 1975). Ford and Padilla quoted in Padilla, ed., *Mission between the Times* (Carlisle, UK: Langham Monographs, 2010), vii–viii.
4. "Transcript of the 11/4/1966 Press Conference," in Box 1, Folder 3, ICWE Collection, BGCA; "Converted Indian Slayer at Evangelism Session," *Sunday Republican* (Springfield, Mass.), October 30, 1966, 12A. On the dazed Huaorani, see Donald MacLeod, *C. Stacey Woods and the Evangelical Rediscovery of the University* (Downers Grove, Ill.: InterVarsity Press, 2007), 185; Carl F. H. Henry, *Confessions of a Theologian* (Waco, Tex.: Word Books, 1986), 257. Casey High contends that the lasting effect of the missionary work was minimal. See Casey High, *Victims and Warriors: Violence, History, and Memory in Amazonia* (Urbana, Ill.: University of Illinois Press, 2015).

For a more sympathetic account, see Kathryn T. Long, *God in the Rainforest: A Tale of Martyrdom and Redemption in Amazonian Ecuador* (New York: Oxford University Press, 2019).

5. Bob Pierce, "Commissioned to Communicate," 20–23; William Pannell, "Spiritual Needs of the Negro," 376–80, in Carl F. H. Henry, ed., *One Race, One Gospel, One Task* (Minneapolis, Minn.: World Wide Publications, 1967). For "law did for me," see "The World Congress: Springboard for Evangelical Renewal," *Christianity Today*, November 25, 1966, 34–35. For the growing use of anthropological insights within the evangelical missions movement, see Eugene Nida, *Customs and Cultures: Anthropology for Christian Missions* (New York: Harper, 1954); Richard Pierard, "Pax Americana and the Evangelical Missionary Advance," 176; Wilbert Shenk, "North American Evangelical Missions since 1945," 320–22; Charles Van Engen, "A Broadening Vision: Forty Years of Evangelical Theology of Mission, 1946-1986," 216–17, in Joel Carpenter and Wilbert Shenk, eds., *Earthen Vessels: American Evangelicals and Foreign Missions, 1880–1920* (Grand Rapids, Mich.: Eerdmans, 1990).

6. On discussions at Berlin, see *One Race, One Gospel, One Task*, 499–501, 523. For "rejection of racism," see Katherine Clark, "Evangelism Is Denounced at Evangelism Parley," *Washington Post*, November 5, 1966, C7.

7. On Evans's role, see Arthur Johnston, *The Battle for World Evangelism* (Wheaton, Ill.: Tyndale House, 1978), 159, 174. On the role of *Christianity Today*, see Henry, *Confessions of a Theologian*, 252–53. On the lineup of speakers, see Uta Balbier, "The 1966 World Congress on Evangelism: Billy Graham, the Cold War, and Global Evangelicalism," lecture at the University of Southampton, April 24, 2014. On delegate selection, see "Billy Graham Aide Denies Claim Bids Withdrawn to Church Meet," *The Oregonian*, October 22, 1966, 15; Robert Preus, "Reflections on the World Congress on Evangelism," *Concordia Theological Monthly* 38, No. 3 (March 1967): 186–87. For "unsaved millions of the world," see Kyung-Chik Han, "By My Spirit," 114, in *One Race, One Gospel, One Task*.

8. On the East German denial of the visit to Wittenberg, see "Faith Answer, Says Graham: Speaks at Reformation Rally in Berlin," *Times-Picayune*, October 31, 1966, 2. On the Reformation procession, see "West Berliners and Evangelists Hold Parade," *Washington Post*, October 31, 1966, A16; Henry, *Confessions of a Theologian*, 256. For "God's machine gun," see "Graham Delivers Message," *Augusta Chronicle*, October 13, 1966, 1.

9. Bernrd Scherer, *The House. The Cultures. The World: Fifty Years from the Congress Hall to the House of World Cultures* (Berlin: Nicolai Verlag, 2007); Klaus Grimberg, "The Cold War in Architecture," *Atlantic Times*, September 2007; Thorsten Klapsch, *Palast der Republik* (Mannheim, Germany: Ed. Panorama, 2010).

10. On Westmoreland, see "Billy Graham Planning to Visit Vietnam Soon," *New York Times*, October 28, 1966, 16. On Graham's key role, see Henry, *Confessions of a Theologian*, 255, 259. For "strikingly American," see John Cogley, "Evangelical Parley Denounces Liberal Protestants' Doctrines," *New York Times*, October 29, 1966, 29. For "methods of mass communication," see Cogley, "Emphasis on Serious Theology Is Urged by Evangelical Leader," *New York Times*, November 3, 1966, 10. On PERT

and Berlin as an expression of "soft power," see Balbier, "The 1966 World Congress on Evangelism."

11. For Ockenga, see "Pastor Gives Role of Liberal Protestant," *Springfield Union*, October 29, 1966, 6; Timothy Yates, *Christian Mission in the Twentieth Century* (Cambridge: Cambridge University Press, 1994), 195. On the sharp evangelical-mainline divide in mission work as early as the 1940s, see David Hollinger, *Protestants Abroad* (Princeton, N.J.: Princeton University Press, 2017), 84. On the Congress's hostility toward the WCC, see Edward B. Fiske, "Billy Graham Links Concern with Social Issues to Religious Conversion," *New York Times*, December 6, 1966, 38; John Cogley, "Christians Urged to Get Closer to the Unbelievers," *New York Times*, October 28, 1966, 6. On Graham's visit to the NCC, see Louis Cassels, "Elements in Church Nearer Understanding on Evangelism," *Evening Times* (Trenton, N.J.), December 16, 1966, 24. For "winning of men" and the idea of social change as the result of evangelism, see Johnston, *Battle for World Evangelism*, 167–69.

12. For "American sacramental occasion," see Balbier, "The 1966 World Congress on Evangelism."

13. For "peculiarity of Anglo-American culture," see Brian Stanley, *The Global Diffusion of Evangelicalism: The Age of Billy Graham and John Stott* (Downers Grove, Ill.: InterVarsity Press, 2013), 70. On Stott's transformation, see Stott, *Christian Mission in the Modern World* (London: Falcon, 1975), 23.

14. For "designed in the United States," see Daniel Salinas, *Latin American Evangelical Theology in the 1970s* (Boston: Brill, 2009), 75. For "offended by the purpose," see Salinas, *Latin American Evangelical Theology*, 85. For "numerolatry," see Padilla, "A Steep Climb Ahead for Theology in Latin America," *Evangelical Missions Quarterly* 7, No. 2 (1971): 135. Also see "Evangelism in Latin America," *Christianity Today*, December 19, 1969, 22.

15. "Conservative Theologians Meet in Bolivia," *Latin American Pulse*, December 1970, 9; "Special Issue: Report on Latin American Theologians," *Latin American Pulse*, February 1971, 1–9. For more on the National Liberty Foundation and the establishment of the Fraternity, see Kirkpatrick, *Gospel for the Poor*, 88–89.

16. On the meeting in Cochabamba, see Salinas, "Beginnings," 51–58; Escobar, "La Fundación de la Fraternidad," 7–25; "Theological First for Latin Americans," *World Vision Magazine*, March 1971, 17. On the Fraternity's concerns about liberation theology, see Samuel Escobar, "Divided Protestantism Struggles with Latin American Problems," *World Vision Magazine*, November 1969; "Latin American Protestants: Which Way Will They Go?" *Christianity Today*, October 10, 1969, 14–16. For "reduce the mission," see Padilla, "Theology in the Making," *Christianity Today*, May 10, 1974, 59–60.

17. Wagner to Savage, April 14, 1970, in Box 2, Folder 7, C. Peter Wagner Collection, BGCA.

18. On geographical representation, see "Working Groups," in Box, 4, Folder 9, Wagner Collection, BGCA; Yates, *Christian Mission*, 200. On funding, see D. E. Hoke to Harry Williams, July 30, 1973, in Box 24, Folder 10, Lausanne Collection, BGCA. For "into a foreigner" and hundreds of other registrations, see James Y. K. Wong, "Personal

Information," in Box 26, Folder 3, Lausanne Collection, BGCA. For "massive Third World input," see Graham to Stanley Mooneyham, May 21, 1974, in Box 30, Folder 18, Lausanne Collection, BGCA.

19. On the marketing of Lausanne, see "Int'l Evangelism Congress Involve More Youth," *Chicago Defender*, December 1, 1973, 25. On Russ Reid, see Steve Chawkins, "Russ Reid Dies at 81; Creator of Pioneering World Vision Infomercials," *Los Angeles Times*, December 14, 2013. On the population clock, see William Martin, *A Prophet with Honor: The Billy Graham Story* (New York: Morrow, 1991), 444. For "substituted for it," see McGavran, "The Dimensions of World Evangelization," 94, in J. D. Douglas, ed., *Let the Earth Hear His Voice* (Minneapolis: World Wide Publications, 1975). For "materialistic, banal, and flat," see Salinas, *Latin American Evangelical Theology*, 39. For "evangelical tycoons," see Kirkpatrick, *Gospel for the Poor*, 19.

20. On prayers from Buenos Aires, see Kirkpatrick, *Gospel for the Poor*, 17. For the text of the address, see René Padilla, "Evangelism and the World," 116–46, in *Let the Earth Hear*. For "most provocative," see "A Challenge from Evangelicals," *Time*, August 5, 1974, 48–50. For "teach Western delegates," see Kirkpatrick, *Gospel for the Poor*, 211. For "deep political overtones," see John Capon, "Let the Earth Hear Whose Voice?" *Crusade*, September 1974, 26. For *enfant terrible*, see Daniel Salinas, "The Beginnings of the Fraternidad Teológica Latinoamericana," *Latin American Theology*, 2007, 83.

21. Orlando E. Costas, "In-Depth Evangelism in Latin America," 211–12, in *Let the Earth*. On conscientization, see Stanley, *Global Diffusion*, 167. Costas would go on to condemn U.S. "ignorance, greed, and ethnocentrism" in its control of the Panama Canal. See "An Open Letter to North American Christians," *Vanguard*, January–February 1977, 4–5.

22. Escobar, "Evangelism and Man's Search for Freedom, Justice and Fulfillment," 303–18, in *Let the Earth Hear His Voice*. On Graham's health, see William Martin, *A Prophet with Honor: The Billy Graham Story* (New York: Morrow, 1991), 450. For more on these themes, see Escobar, "The Return of Christ," 262, in René Padilla, ed., *New Face of Evangelicalism* (Downers Grove, Ill.: InterVarsity Press, 1976), 262; Escobar, *Diálogo entre Cristo y Marx y Otros Ensayos* (Lima, Peru: Publicaciones AGEUP, 1967), 13–27; Escobar, *Decadencia de la Religión* (Buenos Aires: Cuadernos de Certeza, 1972), 64–65; Escobar, "The Social Impact of the Gospel," 89, in Brian Griffiths, ed., *Is Revolution Change?* (Downers Grove, Ill.: InterVarsity Press, 1972).

23. On the reaction to Padilla's address, see Alan Nichols, "Plain Speaking on Social Issues," *New Life*, August 8, 1974; Salinas, *Latin American Evangelical Theology*, 132; interview of Padilla, March 12, 1987, in Oral History Collection 361, BGCA. For similar themes by Majority World delegates, see Okgill Kim, "Christian Higher Education and the Evangelization of the Third World," 658–61; K. N. Nambudripad, "Evangelism of the Hindus," 790–99; B. V. Subbamma, "Evangelization among Women," 765–73; F. S. Khair-Ullah, "Evangelism among Muslims," 816–27, in *Let the Earth*. On the missions moratorium, see Stanley, *Global Diffusion*, 167–69.

24. On the backlash of the North American missionary establishment, see Padilla, "Evangelism and Social Responsibility from Wheaton '66 to Wheaton '83," 29, in Padilla and Chris Sugden, eds., *How Evangelicals Endorsed Social Responsibility*

(Nottingham, UK: Grove Books, 1985); interview of Padilla, March 12, 1987, in Oral History Collection 361, BGCA; Kirkpatrick, *Gospel for the Poor*, 21. For "patently a caricature," see Padilla, *Mission between the Times*, 52. For "promptly rebuked" and "no rebuke," see "The View from Lausanne," *Christianity Today*, August 16, 1974, 36; Escobar, "No Rebuke," *Christianity Today*, September 27, 1974, 21–22. For "totally biased," see Stanley, *Global Diffusion*, 175; Salinas, *Latin American Evangelical Theology*, 154. For "torpedo" and "prevent chaos," see Wagner, "Lausanne Twelve Months Later," *Christianity Today*, July 4, 1975, 7–9. For "a little more social," see Carl Henry, "The Gospel and Society," *Christianity Today*, September 13, 1974, 67.

25. For "any one particular system," see Billy Graham, "Laustade '74 Message," 409–10; Graham, "Why Lausanne?" 30, *Let the Earth*. For "warm applause," see Martin, *Prophet with Honor*, 443. For Graham's assessment of Padilla, see Salinas, *Latin American Evangelical Theology*, 26. For "ecological suicide," see Lindsell, "The Suicide of Man," 422, in *Let the Earth*. For "Western way of life," see Winter, "The Highest Priority: Cross-Cultural Evangelism," 241, in *Let the Earth*.

26. For "no resemblance," see Dudley-Smith, *John Stott*, 212. On revisions to the Lausanne Statement, see Athol Gill, "Christian Social Responsibility," 91–92, in *The New Face of Evangelicalism*; Sharon Heaney, *Contextual Theology for Latin America: Liberation Themes in Evangelical Perspective* (Colorado Springs, Colo.: Paternoster, 2008), 58; Samuel Escobar, "Doing Theology on Christ's Road," 73–74, in Jeffrey Greenman and Gene Green, eds., *Global Theology in Evangelical Perspective* (Downers Grove, Ill.: InterVarsity Press, 2012); Padilla, *New Face of Evangelicalism*, 11. Dain quoted in John Pollock, *Billy Graham: Evangelist to the World* (San Francisco, Calif.: Harper & Row, 1979), 209.

27. For "dominant role," see Escobar, "A Sign of Hope," *Latin America Evangelist*, November-December 1974, 2–3. On Hian, see Salinas, *Latin American Evangelical Theology*, 141; McLeod, *Stacey Woods*, 223.

28. On Osei-Mensah's interactions with Americans, see "Schedule for the Visit of the Rev. Gottfried Osei-Mensah," Box 28, Folder 4, Lausanne Collection, BGCA. On the Fraternity's activism in the United States, see Costas, *The Church and Its Mission: A Shattering Critique from the Third World* (Wheaton: Ill., Tyndale House Publishers, 1974); Costas, *Christ Outside the Gate: Mission beyond Christendom* (Maryknoll, N.Y.: Orbis Books, 1982); David R. Swartz, *Moral Minority: The Evangelical Left in an Age of Conservatism* (Philadelphia: University of Pennsylvania Press, 2012), 113–34. On mainline missiology, see Hollinger, *Protestants Abroad*, 59–93. On Coe and the role of Lausanne, see Sung-Wook Hong, *Naming God in Korea: The Case of Protestant Christianity* (Oxford, UK: Regnum Books, 2008), 20.

29. On the Panama Canal, see "Letter from Central America," *Sojourners*, November 1977, 9. Costas quoted in Salinas, *Latin American Evangelical Theology*, 45. For "rightist regimes" and "hardly apparent to Africans," see Sarah Ruble, *The Gospel of Freedom and Power: Protestant Missionaries in American Culture after World War II* (Chapel Hill: University of North Carolina Press, 2012), 78.

30. For "culture is the lifeway of people," see Ruble, *Gospel of Freedom and Power*, 78. For "baptise us all," see Yates, *Christian Mission*, 55–56. For "ethnic unit," see

Subbamma, *Let the Earth*, 765–73. On polygamy, see John T. Mpaayei, "How to Evaluate Cultural Practices by Biblical Standards in Maintaining Cultural Identity in Africa," *Let the Earth*, 1229–37; Byang H. Kato, "The Gospel, Cultural Context and Religious Syncretism," 1217. On Bediako, see "Biblical Christologies in the Context of African Traditional Religions," 94–100, in Vinay Samuel and Chris Sugden, eds., *Sharing Jesus in the Two Thirds World: Evangelical Christologies from the Contexts of Poverty, Powerlessness and Religious Pluralism* (Bangalore: Partnership in Mission-Asia, 1983); David Neff, "Theologian Kwame Bediako Dies," *Christianity Today*, June 13, 2008.

31. For "unwitting allies," see Sanneh, *Translating the Message: The Missionary Impact on Culture* (Maryknoll, N.Y.: Orbis Books, 1989), 94–95. On the cultural and theological effects of translation, see Sanneh, *Whose Religion Is Christianity?: The Gospel beyond the West* (Grand Rapids, Mich.: Eerdmans, 2003), 18. On orality, see Susan VanZanten Gallagher, *Postcolonial Literature and the Biblical Call for Justice* (Jackson: University Press of Mississippi, 1994), 82.

32. For "know us theologically," see John Mbiti, "Theological Impotence and the Universality of the Church," in *Mission Trends No. 3: Third World Theologies* (Grand Rapids, Mich.: Eerdmans 1976), 16–17). On the rise of Majority World seminaries and theological publishing, see Martin, *Prophet with Honor*, 452; Ogbu Kalu, "Africa," 155–56, in *Global Evangelicalism*. On the WEF, see David Howard, *The Dream That Would Not Die: The Birth and Growth of the World Evangelical Fellowship, 1846-1986* (Exeter, UK: Paternoster Press, 1986), 147–60; Harold Fuller, *People of the Mandate: The Story of the World Evangelical Fellowship* (Grand Rapids, Mich.: Baker Books, 1996), 120. For "major crossroads," see Howard, *Dream That Would Not Die*, 219. On the move to Singapore, see Fuller, *People of the Mandate*, 36.

33. On holism and subjectivity, see David Bosch, *In Word and Deed: Evangelism and Social Responsibility* (Grand Rapids, Mich.: Eerdmans, 1986), 67. On the emphasis on communal theology and intersubjectivity, see Elsa Tamez, "Reading the Bible Under a Sky without Stars," 4, 9, in Walter Dietrich and Ulrich Luz, eds., *The Bible in a World Context: An Experiment in Contextual Hermeneutics* (Grand Rapids: Eerdmans, 2002). For "marginality," see Justo González, *Santa Biblia: The Bible through Hispanic Eyes* (Nashville, Tenn.: Abingdon, 1996). On the conservative theology of the Majority World, see Green, "Global Hermeneutics," 53, in *Global Theology*. For "left-wing or right-wing," see Fuller, *People of the Mandate*, 23. For "voted out cultural imperialism," see Osei-Mensah, "Have We Ears to Hear?" *World Evangelization*, November 1979, 3, copy in Box 26, Folder 8, Lausanne Collection, BGCA.

34. For "the new converts themselves," see Mark Noll, *The New Shape of World Christianity* (Downers Grove, Ill.: IVP Academic, 2009), 106. For "recipe for success," see Stoll, *Is Latin America?: The Politics of Evangelical Growth* (Berkeley: University of California Press, 1990), 72. On the success of indigenous Christians in China, Africa, and elsewhere, see Mark Noll, *From Every Tribe and Nation: A Historian's Discovery of the Global Christian Story* (Grand Rapids, Mich.: Baker Academic, 2014), 2, 115, 163, 168–69, 188–92. On the persistent Western presence in the Majority World,

see Robert Wuthnow, *Boundless Faith: The Global Outreach of American Churches* (Berkeley: University of California Press, 2009).

35. On the rise of intercultural and contextual studies at seminaries, see Wilbert Shenk, *History of the American Society of Missiology, 1973-2013* (Elkhart, Ind.: Institute of Mennonite Studies, 2014), 19. For a small sample of the flood of books on contextualization, see Bruce Nicholls, *Contextualization: A Theology of Gospel and Culture* (Downers Grove, Ill.: InterVarsity Press, 1979); Melba Maggay, *Communicating Cross-Culturally: Towards a New Context for Missions in the Philippines* (Quezon City, the Philippines: New Day Publishers, 1989). On Gilliland, see Janette Williams, "Fuller Professor, Pioneer in Cross-Cultural Missionary Work, Dies at 87," *Pasadena Star-News* (February 18, 2013). On the BGEA, see Stanley, *Global Diffusion*, 69. On *Transformation* journal, see Al Tizon, "Mission as Transformation in the Philippines" (PhD diss., Graduate Theological Union, 2005), 10–11.

36. For critiques of Padilla and Escobar from conservative global delegates, see J. Ramsey Michaels, "Lausanne: A Show of Strength," *Reformed Journal*, September 1974, 12. Also see Luis Palau, "Citywide Crusade Evangelization," 604; Festo Kivengere, "Testimony," 416–17; Subodh Sahu, "Evangelism in the Hard Places of the World," 468–69; K. N. Nambudripad, "Evangelism of the Hindus," 797; Keat Peng Goh, "Universalism Report," 1214, in Douglas, *Let the Earth*.

37. Juan Carlos Ortiz, "The Work of the Holy Spirit," 271, in Douglas, *Let the Earth*. For "Personal Information" cards, see Box 26, Folder 3, Lausanne Collection, BGCA.

38. On the selection of delegates, see Stanley, *Global Diffusion*, 172; Chapman, *Godly Ambition*, 142. On Graham in Mexico City, see speech transcript, January 20, 1975, and John Stott," Lausanne Continuation Committee Meets in Mexico City," *Theological News*, in Box 2, Folder 2, Wagner Collection, BGCA; "Evangelicals Unite," *Time*, February 3, 1975, 60.

39. For details of Stott's confrontation of Graham in Mexico City, see Chapman, *Godly Ambition*, 142–43; Dudley-Smith, *John Stott*, 221–23; Martin, *Prophet with Honor*, 440s–50s; Stanley, *Global Diffusion*, 173; Mark Shaw, *Global Awakening: How 20th-Century Revivals Triggered a Christian Revolution* (Downers Grove, Ill.: IVP Academic, 2010), 127–28. For Wagner's marginal notes, see "Summary of Responses as to the Purposes of the Continuation Committee," in Box 2, Folder 2, Wagner Collection, BGCA.

40. On Graham and Lausanne, see Stanley, *Global Diffusion*, 177; Chapman, *Godly Ambition*, 149; Martin, *Prophet with Honor*, 454. For "lip service," see Ralph Covell to Leighton Ford, November 25, 1980, in Box 26, Folder 13, Lausanne Collection, BGCA.

41. For "put down their pads and pens," see Dudley-Smith, *John Stott*, 224. On the influence of huge Western organizations, see Michael Griffiths, "Report on Consultation on World Evangelization at Pattaya," 27, in Box 5, Folder 1, Packet 2, John Stott Collection, BGCA. For "adult playground," see C. Peter Wagner, "Lausanne's Consultation on World Evangelization: A Personal Assessment," 1, in Box 5, Folder, 1, Packet 6, Stott Collection, BGCA. For the "Statement of Concerns," see Executive Committee Minutes, June 24, 1980, in Box 5, Folder, 1, Packet 6, Stott Collection,

BGCA. For "gladly reaffirm," see Waldron Scott, "The Significance of Pattaya," in Box 5, Folder 1, Packet 6, Stott Collection, BGCA.

42. For "Let Latin America Hear His Voice" and "concrete reality of poverty," see Padilla, *Mission between the Times* (Grand Rapids, Mich.: Eerdmans, 1985), ix, xvii. For "evangelical Christologies," see Samuel and Sugden, eds., *Sharing Jesus in the Two Thirds World, iii.* On the Fraternity's conference in Mexico, see Mark Lau Branson and C. René Padilla, eds., *Conflict and Context: Hermeneutics in the Americas* (Grand Rapids, Mich.: Eerdmans, 1986). For "democratization," see Costas, "Evangelical Theology in the Two-Thirds World," 243, in *Earthen Vessels.*

43. For "face-to-face encounters," see Chua Wee Hian to Jack Dain, February 20, 1975, in Box 26, Folder 8, Lausanne Collection, BGCA. On cross-cultural communication problems, see Stanley Mooneyham, "Presentation to Continuatino Committee— ICOWE," in Box 2, Folder 2, Wagner Collection, BGCA. On the advocacy of Jack Dain and Billy Graham, see Stanley, *Global Diffusion,* 158; Dain to Escobar, March 17, 1975, and Graham to Mooneyham, May 21, 1974, in Box 26, Folder 5, Lausanne Collection, BGCA.

44. On the strong relationship between Stott and Padilla, see Kirkpatrick, *Gospel for the Poor,* 5–6, 9, 20, 26, 29–31, 114, 144–49. For "evangelical pope," see Chapman, *Godly Ambition,* 141. On Stott's advocacy at Lausanne and beyond, see Stanley, *Global Diffusion,* 174; Dudley-Smith, *John Stott,* 213; Box 4, Folder 1, Stott Collection, BGCA; Kirkpatrick, *Gospel for the Poor,* 29–31. For "passion beneath the cold print" see Dudley-Smith, *John Stott,* 215. For "opposing the Americans," see Chapman, *Godly Ambition,* 144. For "sniping at brothers," see Stott to Wagner, December 30, 1974, in Box 2, Folder 2, Wagner Collection, BGCA.

45. On Graham's increasing disinterest in Lausanne in the 1980s, see Alister Chapman, "Evangelical International Relations in the Post-Colonial World," *Missiology* 37, No. 3 (July 2009): 363. For Stott as an "ideal broker," see Chapman, *Godly Ambition,* 148. For "wouldn't be an evangelical today," see Dudley-Smith, *John Stott,* 229.

46. For "vanilla in Manila," see "Overheard at Lausanne," *Transformation,* January 1990, 32. For "managerial perspective," see Kirkpatrick, *Gospel for the Poor,* 158. On Billy Graham's absence at Lausanne II, see "Global Camp Meeting," *Christianity Today,* August 18, 1989, 40.

47. J. D. Douglas, ed., *Proclaim Christ Until He Comes* (Minneapolis: World Wide Publications, 1990), 14–18, 41–45, 417.

48. On Padilla's publishing record, see Kirkpatrick, *Gospel for the Poor,* 153. For "one-way traffic," see Dudley-Smith, *John Stott,* 277. For "incisive critique," see Graham Kings, "Evangelicals in Search of Catholicity," 2, in Box 5, Folder 2, Packet 11, Stott Collection, BGCA. For "language of liberation theology," see "Global Camp Meeting," *Christianity Today,* 39. For "what especially impressed," see Ron Sider fundraising letter, December 5, 1989, in Folder "1989," Evangelicals for Social Action Archives, Philadelphia.

49. For the impact on the evangelical left, see Swartz, *Moral Minority,* 113–34; Ron Sider, *Rich Christians in an Age of Hunger* (Downers Grove, Ill.: InterVarsity Press, 1977); Clarence Hilliard, "Open Letter to the Committee on the Lausanne Covenant"

from Circle Church in Chicago, October 7, 1974, in Box 4, Folder 1, Packet 3, Stott Collection, BGCA. For conservative critics, see David Chilton, *Productive Christians in an Age of Guilt Manipulators* (Tyler, Tex.: Institute for Christian Economics, 1982); C. Peter Wagner, *Church Growth and the Whole Gospel* (New York: Harper & Row, 1981), 92.

50. For "like a candidate," see Wagner, *Church Growth and the Whole Gospel*, xi, 62–64.

5

Occidental Mindoro 1983

Transformational Development and the De-Americanization of World Vision

Go to the peasant people.
Live among them.
Learn from them.
Plan with them.
Build on what they have.
Teach by showing.
Learn by doing.
Not a showcase, but a pattern,
Not odds and ends, but a system,
Not relief but release.

—Jimmy Yen, founder of the International Institute of Rural Reconstruction in the Philippines[1]

Severe malnutrition persisted amid the plentiful natural resources of Occidental Mindoro. In the rural backwaters of this midsized Filipino island, illiteracy was pervasive. Few families sent their children to school. Disease, especially tuberculosis, was rampant, and sanitary latrines were rare. Farmers and fishermen had such low incomes that they could not sustain their families through the whole year. The problems, severe and interlocking, were compounded by civic inertia. In San Jose, a small town in the southwest corner of Mindoro, local political leaders failed to take much action. The few humanitarians brave enough to show up quickly left discouraged. For decades Western interventions had not worked.[2]

In the 1970s World Vision workers reached the beautiful, bleak shores of Mindoro. They fared no better. After working for nearly two years with displaced squatters in the Labangan barrio of San Jose, these American evangelicals were as dispirited as those who had come before. But then they learned of a new model for development. Launched in China before Mao's triumph and perfected in the Philippines by Y. C. James "Jimmy" Yen, the "People's School" system discarded Western models of development. Stressing indigeneity, it practiced culturally and technologically appropriate development from within. In 1978 World Vision

Facing West. David R. Swartz, Oxford University Press (2020). © Oxford University Press.
DOI: 10.1093/oso/9780190250805.001.0001

workers and civic leaders from San Jose together went to Yen's International Institute of Rural Reconstruction near Manila to be trained.

The delegation was captivated by the new methodology. They returned to Mindoro inspired to transform the island using the People's School model. Within months World Vision had surveyed the people of San Jose and, based on their own ideas, established a training program on operating efficient pig farms. It was a startling success. The training program, called "Paaralan ng Anak-Pawis," which meant "Children of the School of the Sweat," quickly expanded to include many other skills. According to reports, considerable increases in prosperity, cultural vitality, and civic pride resulted. World Vision trumpeted the success of this pilot program. By 1983, when the Mindoro project seemed to be truly thriving and multiplying throughout the region, the site had received more than one hundred visitors from around the world to observe their operations. Then, with several million dollars in funding from the United States Agency for International Development (USAID), World Vision launched three more training programs in the Philippines, two in Thailand, four in Indonesia, and a new trajectory for the organization. Indeed, the pilot project in Mindoro was ground zero in a fundamental shift within World Vision from American-led relief work to long-term sustainable development undertaken by the people themselves.

Critics had long complained that World Vision was an instrument of American foreign policy, the latest in a long line of imperial impositions. Colonized by Spain for more than three centuries, ceded to the United States for $20 million at end of the Spanish-American War in 1898, ruled by the Japanese during World War II, and then recovered by the United States, the Philippines had long been subject to foreign powers. Was World Vision simply the latest to impose its culture in the Philippines? If the answer was yes, that World Vision was an agent of Christian Americanism, it was less true in the 1970s than it had been in earlier decades. The work in Mindoro belied the American imperial project. The "School of the Sweat" was not a large spectacle, like the expensive Manila Crusade, World Vision's first foray into the Philippines, at which 5,000 of the 140,000 Filipinos who attended converted to Christianity. The 1956 crusade, said the organization's promotional literature, was "glorious in its intent, spectacular in its execution, and fruitful in its results." Nor was the Mindoro project was directed hierarchically. Previously, no beneficiary had a voice in the dispersal of money, management of orphan sponsorships, or in the direction of relief projects when the Philippines was hit by killer typhoons and severe droughts. But using Yen's notion of indigeneity, World Vision had begun to "go to the peasant people; live among them; learn from them; plan with them."[3]

This pioneering work in Mindoro brought the Lausanne movement's demand for a more culturally sensitive missiology into the humanitarian realm. In the name of Christ, according to one World Vision executive, the NGO moved from "simple child-care" toward "an integrated development" that addressed "the causes of poverty, not merely the results." There were limits to "transformational development," as the new approach came to be called, but the de-Americanization of World Vision's bureaucratic structures reshaped its methods in the late twentieth century.[4]

I. De-Americanizing World Vision

The path toward transformational development passed through the Global South. Missionaries had long encountered intractable poverty, and in response they built schools and hospitals to relieve the suffering. In the 1950s World Vision began to advance a more robust theological and social rationale for materially improving a destitute world. As Bob Pierce put it after meeting White Jade in China, "Underwear, stockings, shoes, a spaghetti-making machine, a rope-making machine? Somebody says, 'Is that missions?' Yes, that's missions. If it's something that is breaking the heart of a compassionate God, then—yes—you can call it missions." Pierce supplemented his Christian compassion with obligation to the nation. Viewing the world through American eyes, he framed intervention in Korea as that of a capitalist, democratic, Christian nation protecting the masses from atheistic communism. That posture, however, would evolve through a series of wrenching global encounters.[5]

In contrast to the triumphs of the 1940s, circumstances in the 1960s and 1970s subdued World Vision's Christian Americanism. First, World Vision experienced a chastening in Vietnam. The organization's substantial investments in Southeast Asia were lost when the United States pulled out, and the appeal of its strong anticommunism diminished after the defeat. Second, decolonization opened eyes to the dangers of imperialism. In a political and cultural climate that was, according to one internal report, "more searching, more testing, more threatening than it has ever been," the organization's work was compromised because of its overtly American identity. "We cannot assume a welcome because we come with gifts and compassion," stated the report. Third, the magnitude of the crises grew beyond the personal capacities of its president. "In the beginning there was Bob Pierce," began one insider history of World Vision. "We used to say that Bob went around the world writing checks for needy situations and then wiring home to tell people what he had done." By the late 1960s World Vision, which was near bankruptcy, had been careening from crisis to crisis for nearly two decades. Pierce's pulsating spirit—described by his lieutenant Paul Rees as "A vision of need in Asia! The passion to act in meeting that need!"—was wonderfully energizing, but the vexing problems of imperialism, Vietnam, and world hunger could not be sustained by mere passion.[6]

In this era of global disorder, World Vision decisively changed course. The board of directors unceremoniously removed the domineering, erratic Pierce as president in 1967. The new leadership, surveying its global partners in order to discern future directions, identified significant tensions. The work, directed from headquarters in Monrovia, California, to four support offices, ten field offices, and work in thirty-six nations, had become increasingly complicated and technical. Confusion over roles and coordination had led to a "strain on relationships." If some of the tension was rooted in the stress of rapid growth in a small, obscure, sectarian relief organization, much also resulted from imbalanced governance. Specifically, non-American fieldworkers complained about not having a voice. According to a 1975 evaluation, it appeared to some that the "Monrovia office sometimes takes unilateral actions on matters that involve the other countries." A growing chorus of global voices, according to former staffer Alan Whaites, began calling for more democratic structures and a "strict equality between North and South." A chastened headquarters even began to worry that national offices might secede.[7]

Stanley Mooneyham, who had directed the World Congress on Evangelism in Berlin in 1966 and then became World Vision's president in 1969, led the organization through a process of de-Americanization. Opposed to the Vietnam War and less committed to a Cold War mentality, Mooneyham hoped that the "internationalizing of missions, stripped of Western Christian imperialism, would be a magnificent demonstration of the validity of our message in the non-white world." The "new frontier," he declared at a 1973 meeting of evangelical leaders in Pattaya, Thailand, was internationalism, not the nationalisms that had resulted in two world wars. World Vision invested considerable theological reflection into the new paradigm. Mooneyham recruited Indian church leader Samuel Kamaleson to articulate a "theology of internationalization" that stressed a common humanity and the communal nature of the global church. Wanting to encourage this "international spirit beyond what can be legislated," World Vision also invested in a cultural shift. Its public relations specialists began using international symbols, and there was serious talk of moving its headquarters abroad in order to give it a "truly international image."[8]

Mooneyham was encouraged from abroad. At a 1972 meeting Kyung-Chik Han, the Korean pastor who had cofounded World Vision, recommended that "each field country should have a national board." A task force, which represented a cross section of employees, outside advisors, and representatives of the Global South, studied the feasibility of fourteen potential models of internationalization. Noting that non-American countries were providing 40 percent of the field ministry budget, the task force's report confirmed the global trajectory. It nixed the idea of an "international advisory council" as insufficient, instead favoring a full-blown restructuring. Stronger international representation would offer access to a larger personnel pool, better coordination of structures and programs, and increased cultural competency at headquarters. The report called for "decision and policy making to be representative of the constituent elements of the partnership."[9]

The international vision was institutionalized at a 1976 meeting in Honolulu. In what Mooneyham called "a grand experiment," delegates almost unanimously ratified "a supra-national organization" that allowed recipient nations from Europe, Asia, Latin America, and Africa to become full partners of World Vision International (WVI), a religious nonprofit corporation distinct from any of the national structures. Mooneyham, presiding over a ceremony that included prayer, worship, readings of Scripture, and communion, confessed that headquarters had frequently taken "unilateral action. There was not enough international contribution to thinking and strategy." He declared that this moment would "cast the die . . . for World Vision's future." He hoped that internationalization would recapture "the pulsating life" of the early years, which had been lost to an "organizational hardening of the arteries." Mooneyham meant to quiet conservative critics worried that World Vision was going secular. He was signaling that more international influence would actually enhance World Vision's evangelical spirituality.[10]

Implementation of the new structure, which went into effect on May 31, 1978, drew both praise and criticism. In 1984, six years after internationalization began, 72 percent of employees said in a survey that increased international presence at headquarters had improved communication to field countries. Ninety-six percent agreed that "our competence in carrying out development ministries has increased in the past five years." Ninety-three percent affirmed that "our decision to create an international organization was correct." But employees also decried its shortcomings. Even as national offices in Bolivia, Chile, Costa Rica, Ghana, Malawi, Mali, Peru, Somalia, Tanzania, and Zambia launched in the early 1980s, the United States, which contributed 75 percent of the funding, remained dominant. After Mooneyham was named WVI's first president, one American board member ruefully acknowledged that "children of the British Empire" comprised nearly all of the senior leadership. Moreover, in the new weighted system, the United States, with four seats on the board, retained a higher proportion of voting members than any other nation. Combined with other English-speaking nations—including Canada with two, Australia with two, and New Zealand with one—the West could still outvote the Global South, which collectively only had access to between six and eight at-large seats.[11]

This arrangement prompted more global challenges. The first iteration of internationalization, said one global critic, did not give "true partnership" to national entities. Another complained that WVI perpetuated a "rhetoric of equality" when in reality "the fields are controlled with little room for creative involvement."

There were reports of Latin Americans in the early 1980s hijacking meetings with "suits" from California. Subversive aphorisms—"the one who has the gold makes the rule"—became commonplace. Non-American Westerners, such as Canadian Bernard Barron and Australian Graeme Irvine, who led the internationalization committee, also agitated. Just as John Stott had provided aid and comfort to Majority World evangelicals at Lausanne, so too did Canadian, British, and South African leaders in World Vision. Australians were particularly important, given their very large contributions to World Vision coffers and their political orientation to the left of center. As scholar Rachel McCleary notes, they were "geographically literate, more globally knowledgeable, and aware of Asian history."[12]

The first meetings of the International Council in the 1980s revealed the high levels of inequity and dissent. "It became clear that this would not do," conceded one American board member. World Vision U.S. agreed to surrender its control of the board, and a change of the bylaws in 1986 provided for a more equal balance of representation. The adjustments received plaudits. It also transformed long-established funding streams and methodologies. As World Vision continued to de-Americanize, income from support countries increased from $20 million in 1976 to $50 million in 1984. The number of field offices jumped 74 percent, the number of field staff increased from 260 to 1,800, and the number of projects directed from field offices increased from zero to 3,300.[13]

These shifts, however, put pressure on World Vision's historic emphasis on orphan sponsorship. The stunning success of this Korean initiative—from 7,961 in 1956 to 14,000 in 1960 to 33,000 in 1970 to 97,000 in 1975 to a whopping 335,000 in 1982—had for decades pulled on the heartstrings of American donors (Figure 5.1). But workers from the Majority World were ambivalent. They criticized orphan care as a marketing gimmick that avoided the hard work of real community development. The most compelling critiques came from Korea itself. In the wake of war, fieldworkers in the mid-1950s realized that the families of children needed aid also. In some cases, families shifted resources meant for the child to other family members. In other cases, the sponsored child was the object of considerable jealousy. Moreover, feeding and educating a single child in the short-term, writes historian Michael Barnett, seemed to have "little permanent impact in an impoverished community." Kyung-Chik Han championed broader social transformation beyond short-term relief. He offered scholarships, conducted vocational training, and established a medical center. By the end of the 1970s, about 20,000 children had received help from these development projects. Han contended that "relief and charity should not stay in the area of helping people but go further to a more organized . . . dimension." This approach contrasted sharply with Pierce's emergency-driven methodology.[14]

Figure 5.1. Jimmy Yen (left) and his colleagues in the Mass Education Movement. Courtesy of the Sidney D. Gamble Photographs Collection, David M. Rubenstein Rare Book & Manuscript Library, Duke University.

Other international voices supported Han's approach to global poverty. WVI's Latin America field offices modeled their work after the Nicaraguan Evangelical Committee for Aid and Development (CEPAD), whose work at the end of the Somoza regime in the late 1970s, according to World Vision insiders, was going "beyond relief to a completely new dimension of exciting development." Significantly, a 1984 survey of field offices reflected a strong desire to move beyond "simply welfare" and the "ministry mainstay" of childcare toward a "long-range planning system" and "community development." These global voices, heard more clearly in the internationalized structure, shaped WVI's rhetoric and methods going forward. "There are two words we are probing and exploring in a new way," declared Mooneyham. "We have come face-to-face with them in the daily experience of trying to work out the most vital expressions of our twin mandates. One of these words is development. The other is internationalism." As its international field offices cheered, WVI borrowed development strategies from the World Bank, added the phrase "long-term survival and growth" to its list of "basic objectives," launched a new Relief and Development department, and prioritized "development" in its list of field projects.[15]

Rank-and-file Americans were less impressed. In 1979 WVI halted its bread-and-butter child sponsorship program. "Our scope of concern for children had to be extended beyond the child to include the family and community," wrote staffer Robert Ainsworth in 1981. Contributions, however, plummeted. Without the "emotional tug" generated by a relationship with a representative child, fundraising became far more difficult. Community development proved to be a tougher sell than activities related to disaster relief. WVI executives, desperate to recoup lost donations, resumed child sponsorship. But they also launched a campaign to help Americans understand the nature of structural inequalities and solutions. This promotional push, which was only moderately successful, resulted in child sponsorship becoming a facade for the development work that World Vision truly wanted to pursue.[16]

As this episode demonstrates, there were clear limits to de-Americanization. Internationalization occurred in fits and starts, and global evangelicals, while enjoying more of a voice, still complained of an imperial Monrovia. Nevertheless, the process launched a fundamental transformation from relief to development. Ahead of Médecins sans Frontieres, Oxfam, Food for the World, and Save the Children, World Vision was one of the first nongovernmental organizations (NGOs) to voluntarily internationalize. Conceived just after Vietnam and birthed before Reagan-era triumphalism, de-Americanization set in motion a substantial flow of influence from East to West.[17]

II. The People's School

Early attempts to implement overseas development, though, fell largely flat. Led by Cold Warrior Henry Barber, whose thirty-year military career in France, Germany, Korea, and Vietnam was followed by a second career at World Vision, these efforts depended on a modernization model of development. This approach assumed that advanced technology and abundant capital would help poor nations become, as one American worker put it, "just like the West, that is—'developed.'" The global encounter interrupted these assumptions. In one of Barber's first development projects—at Loksado, Indonesia, in 1973—the implementation of an agricultural program presented "many problems and many answers." Workers flailed when clear results failed to appear. "We didn't know a lot about development ourselves then," recalled Bryant Myers, who would later become World Vision's development guru. "It was sort of like the teacher who keeps one page ahead of the student. We introduced the subject of development, then went out with the people to turn the abstract into the concrete." Theoretically convinced about the value of development, this evangelical NGO did not know how actually to accomplish it. By the end of the decade, however, World Vision would identify a promising methodology in Asia.[18]

The story begins eight decades earlier in the twilight of the Qing dynasty. Yen Yang-ch'u, who would become one of the foremost development experts in the world, was born in 1893 to an aristocratic family in the remote Chinese province of Sichuan. Wearing a "crisp scholar's gown and glistening hair neatly bound up in a queue," Yen converted to Christianity at the age of eleven in a China Inland Mission school. The world opened for the boy. After learning English at the mission's School of Western Learning and circulating in the ecumenical Protestant world of the John Mott, Sherwood Eddy, and the YMCA, he sailed for America to attend Yale University. After graduating from the Ivy League school in 1918, he immediately left for the trenches of Europe. There he tutored hundreds of the 200,000 Chinese laborers who were digging those trenches, building roads, and hauling heavy loads of salt on the Western Front. Yen marveled at the substantial intellectual capacity and deep joy of learning of these "coolies," a term that literally meant "bitter strength." It inspired him to pursue the work of global rural reconstruction. Shaped by Confucius, Christ, and coolies, he was perfectly suited for his future role as a transpacific bridge between East and West.[19]

Yen returned to China after the Great War to establish a "social laboratory." Called the Mass Education Movement (MEM), it began in 1923 as a literacy project in Ting Hsien, a region of North China where people still lived in bamboo hovels and mud shanties without windows (Figure 5.2). They also struggled with health, employment, repressive politics, and a lack of education. Yen brought $1,000, a banner that read "An Illiterate Man Is a Blind Man," and a textbook called the *1,000 Character Primer*. Over time, however, Yen discarded Western-style education as he sought to address tangled social problems. Living with farmers in their huts, he turned fields and homes into classrooms. He utilized Chinese-style "People's Theater" to teach principles of health and to reinforce the virtues of local culture. A Western observer remarked, "At the plow, carrying water, in the kitchen . . . they fill the air with song—plantation songs of the people." It was a vision that could have been articulated by a young Mao Tse-tung. In fact, the future Supreme Leader first learned community organizing in one of Yen's schools. Mao participated in an early MEM campaign in Changsha before deciding that Yen was not radical enough and producing his own literacy primer that attacked capitalists. At the time, though, Yen's project seemed more promising than Mao's. Within five years, Yen mobilized 100,000 volunteers to teach five million illiterate workers. Predating Gandhi in India and Paulo Freire in Brazil, Yen was building a vast people's movement intended to transform China's 340 million rural peasants.[20]

Figure 5.2. World Vision stopped organizing its humanitarian efforts around orphan sponsorship in the early 1980s. After donations dropped precipitously, this fundraising strategy was quickly reinstated. Courtesy of World Vision International Archives, Monrovia, Calif.

In the 1930s Yen's movement of indigenous mass education truly blossomed. It used "People's Schools" to encourage a "four-fold" program of agricultural production, public health, political participation, and a harder-to-measure category of self-respect and dignity. Wanting to move beyond welfare and relief measures, Yen continually intoned the aphorism, "We do not offer relief to the poor, but release." The strategy, which required teachers to live with the people because it was important to understand peasants' perspectives, claimed stunning results. In Ding Xian, for example, cotton revenue increased from $12,000 in 1932 to $1.8 million in 1937. Peasants participated in local governance, and health improved. A Western visitor exulted that "the people of these villages had a different air, a poise, an expectancy that made you feel they found life worth living." The MEM spread rapidly from Ting Hsien to the central region, then toward the west, and finally to Hunan province, the strategic "rice bowl" province of China. This narrative of success proved so compelling that in the late 1930s Chiang Kai-shek named Yen as his advisor.[21]

In the 1940s Yen's fame spread beyond China. Americans were particularly captivated by the wiry humanitarian's magnetism, moral authority, and innovative ideas. In 1943 Yen was named one of ten "modern revolutionaries" during a celebration at Carnegie Hall, where he hobnobbed with Albert Einstein and John Dewey. In the wake of this triumph, he was feted by industrialists, played poker with Franklin D. Roosevelt's "kitchen cabinet," and generally, according to historian Charles Hayford, "basked in the rapt attention of the American public." Yen successfully raised money from Nelson Rockefeller, Henry Ford, J. P. Morgan, Philip Morris, the Reader's Digest Association, General Electric, and the Carnegie Foundation. In these years before Mao's victory, the heightened expectations for a democratic China propelled Yen to prominence as an international celebrity. The U.S. Congress even earmarked $30 million (ten percent of the entire package) as a special "Jimmy Yen Provision" in the China Economic Aid Act of 1948 to fund rural reconstruction in China. In the end, though, only $4 million was spent before Mao conquered mainland China in 1949.[22]

On one level, Yen seemed like an eminent international champion of Christian Americanism. He spoke with passion about how the "forces of evil and destruction are actively and aggressively at work" among Marxists in China. Allied with Walter Judd, an evangelical Republican congressman, Yen encouraged American politicians to carry Western democratic ideals abroad. And yet he pushed back in ways both subtle and explicit. During his career Yen made a point of not doing things in an "American pattern." He believed in the people's power to defeat the excesses of communism, not the military might of Chiang and Truman. "Until you have first conquered it in villages and rice fields," said Yen, "it is the poverty and hopelessness of the peasants which is giving Mao his chance." To American evangelical Cold Warriors who would adopt his methodologies decades later, it seemed at the time as though Yen had "vaguely socialist leanings."[23]

Exiled by Mao during the Communist Revolution, Yen found refuge in the Philippines. With support from politicians like President Ramon Magsaysay and local civic leaders like Juan Flavier near Manila, he founded the Philippine Rural Reconstruction Movement (PRRM). By 1952 he had established two pilot projects in more than sixty barrios near Manila. In these years of experimentation, Yen sought to adapt the Chinese model to the Filipino context. After PRRM worked with villagers in San Luis to nearly eliminate illiteracy and to experiment with new methods of land cultivation, the average annual income rose from $300 to $960. This seemed to confirm that a persistent focus on village participation, rather than a top-down imposition from the outside, could address interdependent conditions of poverty, illiteracy, disease, and civic apathy. As the movement spread to seventeen Filipino provinces by the late 1950s, the credo of the People's School—called the "Paaralan ng Anak-Pawis" in Tagalog—remained the same as in China: "Go to the peasant people. Live among them. Learn from them. Plan with them."[24]

From the Philippines, Yen's development strategy spread to the world. In addition to launching a resource for development practitioners called the *Rural Reconstruction Report* in 1965, Yen built a one-hundred-acre complex in Cavite that became the base for the International Institute of Rural Reconstruction (IIRR). The laboratory boasted a diverse landscape—rice paddies in the lowlands and upland mountains full of intercropped coconut, coffee, pineapple, papaya, and vegetables—that simulated the agricultural patterns of poverty-stricken countries around the world. Visitors, including social workers, farmers, technicians, planners, donors, and missionaries, attended lectures and participated in wide-ranging discussions about how to adapt methods to local contexts. They practiced building water-sealed toilets, helped farmers with test plots of rice, and maintained vegetable and herb gardens. They met with local politicians and the provincial governor. After sixteen workers from Colombia came for four months in the mid-1960s, Yen established the Colombia Rural Reconstruction Movement. Guatemala, Thailand, Ghana, India, and Korea followed. By 1976, when the IIRR completed its seventh graduate training course for specialists from eleven nations in Asia, Africa, and Latin America, alumni numbered in the tens of thousands. They represented some of the highest hopes in the development world. To be sure, the notion of transformational development was not new anymore; scholars and practitioners from a variety of disciplines were proposing similar strategies. IIRR, however, was one of the most visible and energetic in selling its vision.[25]

The Philippines branch of World Vision, drawn to Yen's vision, notified American headquarters about the People's School. Struggling to run 429 just-launched development initiatives in the "grueling training grounds" of Africa, Latin America, and Asia, World Vision desperately needed help. In 1978, thirty-five executives from Monrovia and national coordinators from more than a dozen nations made a pilgrimage to Cavite. They spent five weeks at IIRR studying development theory, rural industry, economic cooperatives, health and family planning, and the importance of local culture and leadership. World Vision workers were compelled by his "science" of development and the "remarkable group of specialists" he had assembled. They were also attracted to the spiritual vision of Yen, now an eighty-four-year-old "Christian humanitarian" who explained that his life's work was really God's. He described "mystical prayer experiences" as he had developed his life's work in French trenches and Chinese villages, and he continued to pray every morning, sing hymns about the cross, and read devotional literature. Yen was an ideal guru for these evangelical technocrats.[26]

The encounter with Yen in the Philippines transformed World Vision. Robert Ainsworth, the brand-new replacement for Barber, described "euphoric days that will remain in our hearts and minds for at least as long as we have the strength to visit piggeries . . . discuss irrigation problems, and plead the case for better latrines." Other executives and workers said that they finally understood theoretically what they had been blindly experiencing for several years in the field. As an organization, World Vision was so convinced by Yen's training that only one year later it published a landmark issue of its magazine. Bryant Myers, an instrumental figure in World Vision's Relief and Development department, declared that "development was to be a major direction for the next 10 years" and that the organization would henceforth commit 75 percent of its budget to development initiatives. "It's our single greatest commitment," he declared. From 1978 on, personnel showed a clear dependence on Yen's ideas, often parroting his exact words: that dependency was insidious, that methods should mesh with local culture, that workers need to mobilize the people, that projects should not impose Western technology or focus solely on economic growth, that projects should focus on "human reconstruction" and "people development," and that projects should "remake villagers, not just rebuild villages." World Vision was all in.[27]

Executives chose Occidental Mindoro as a site for experimentation. The island was relatively close to World Vision Philippines (WVP) headquarters in Manila, where Filipino staff had already begun converting the country's 29,750 child sponsorships to developmental aid projects. It was also near IIRR's headquarters, where World Vision workers returned often to continue learning Yen's principles. The new program, of course, required learning "from the people," and so in the small town of San Jose, where World Vision had already spent two years applying Western-style fixes on sixty displaced families squatting in Labangan Barrio, they paused to ask what the people in fact wanted. In April 1978, less than two months after World Vision staff attended Yen's training, workers conducted surveys throughout San Jose's thirteen village units (called barangays). Despite Mindoro's beauty, vast natural resources, forests, fishing grounds, and fertile land, the surveys revealed great needs. There were severe cases of malnutrition among the Mangyan tribe just north of San Jose. "With meager income to subsist on, and an average 10-kilometer trek to the town proper daily, most rural parents are hesitant to send their children to school," explained the survey report. The village leadership seemed helpless to do anything about the problems. Mindoro, plagued by despair but blessed with abundant resources, was a perfect test case for the People's School.[28]

Everyone—except the Mindorans themselves—agreed. After WVP successfully pitched their proposal to Monrovia as "a better strategy for effecting positive changes than the childcare concept of a 'one-to-one' welfare approach," they turned to Johnny Santos, San Jose's mayor, for help in rallying the people. He was skeptical, so Roman Garma, a Yen disciple and pioneer of the Philippine Rural Reconstruction Movement who had just been hired by WVP, convinced

Santos and local officials from the Bureau of Soils, Bureau of Plant Industry, and the Rural Health Unit, to visit IIRR. It worked. After two days of observation in Cavite and at WVP sites in Manila, the San Jose delegation returned "full of jubilation and high hopes that the People's School model could be modified and implemented to meet the people's needs." Mayor Santos immediately recruited thirty local leaders to join a Municipal Development Council. The barangay council loaned a municipal building, the Santos-Nazareno Multi Purpose Hall, free of charge to WVP for trainings. When trainees from the surrounding region arrived, they enjoyed the "generous hospitality of the town people." In fact, the townspeople "pushed ahead" with their plans for a People's School, moving faster than WVI, which was still processing WVP's proposal. When the doors opened on October 24, 1978, for the first two-week training, it was clear that Mindorans were committed. As breathless reports to American headquarters noted, this was precisely Yen's method: development pursued by the peasant people themselves.[29]

Evidence of indigeneity was plentiful. The project itself, though officially designated by WVI as the Community Leadership Training (COLT), was called "The School for the Children of the Sweat" by local Filipinos. The first course in rondalla, an ensemble of stringed, guitar-like instruments plucked with a tortoise-shell pick, served several purposes. As an activity prized in every social stratum of the Philippines, it could, as Yen hoped, "bring all factions together in a common purpose." Moreover, beginning with a Filipino cultural component ensured that COLT would not be perceived primarily as a Western import. As hoped, the course "caught the imagination of the local community." Supporters initiated an *Alay Lakan*, a "walk for the cause," to raise awareness and money for the project. This garnered 10,000 pesos to purchase instruments, which were then played by thirty-seven students chosen by local leaders from their respective barangays.[30]

Three days after the rondalla course began, a training in raising pigs began. Many other courses followed, falling into every category of Yen's four-fold program. Courses in rural drama and sports maintained cultural identity. Courses in livelihood included raising poultry, mushrooms, mango, tilapia, and cattle. Courses in self-government included leadership training and barangay development. Courses in health included paramedics, vaccination, first aid, and toilet-bowl making, which followed the legendary latrine design of Juan Flavier, a Filipino groomed by Yen to lead IIRR. Courses in Christian education, a fifth category added by World Vision, were led by local pastors. Lasting eight hours a day for up to five days in length, these indigenous courses used vernacular languages, local experts, and pedagogical techniques of demonstration and practice.[31]

World Vision hoped to rapidly expand COLT. "As the program progresses," explained Roman Garma, "World Vision expects to saturate the entire town and province." Barangay scholars, as graduates of these development courses were known, would leave San Jose to teach in their home villages. As the World Vision manual put it, each would become the "village simplifier of technology." At the end of their training, these scholars were commissioned in a solemn ceremony. With candles in their hands, they pledged their "duty bound" commitment to train five others in the craft they had just learned themselves. Lined in front of San Jose officials, Juan Flavier, WVI president Stanley Mooneyham, and a member of Australian parliament, they "looked as pleased as if they have received a PhD," said one World Vision staffer. After a celebration—in which Mayor Santos supplied two crisp, succulent pigs that had been roasted on a spit for an entire day— scholars left for their home barangay. Within the week, they began their own trainings and attended a follow-up meeting. Within a month, many reported substantial progress. The piggery graduates had trained twenty-seven more barangay scholar associates, and the rondalla graduates had started groups in twenty more barrios. Together they hosted an *Alay Kaunlaran*, a village trade fair in which the native Mindorans displayed their produce and wares. World Vision exulted in "the impact of COLT on the lives of the villagers."[32]

Crisostomo Supranes, a rice farmer, was exemplary. Before training at the People's School, he was producing only 130 *cavan* (about 12,600 pounds) of unhusked rice called *palay* from a two-hectare farm each year. During training, instructors convinced him to invest more effort and supplies. This doubled his expenses, but it also doubled his harvest to 260 *cavan*. Supranes realized an impressive net profit of 8,739 pesos, 50 percent higher than before. He went on to train eighteen barangay scholar associates, taking them to his demonstration farm to watch new techniques in action. His wife, with whom he cochaired their local Rural Reconstruction Committee (RRC), took a People's School course in nutrition and trained ninety-two barangay associates herself. A World Vision analyst, inspired by the village's improved conditions, wrote that they "have provided energetic and spirited leadership within the Barangay" and "have demonstrated the value of a 'critical mass' of trained villagers in advancing the cause of self-reliance."[33]

Supranes had modeled the potential of indigeneity. Going "to the people," as Yen had predicted, encouraged Mindoran villagers to pursue development on their own terms (Figure 5.3). Once World Vision outsiders from Monrovia and Manila set up a localized structure—based on existing trail networks in San Jose—the people took over. Led by seven-member RRCs, each barangay held assemblies where villagers verbalized needs, prioritized action steps, and raised the eight dollars it cost to send a barangay scholar to a three-day training. By the end of the project's second year, 335 scholars from thirty-eight barangays had completed the leadership-training course. They, in turn, had trained 782 barangay associates in skills learned at the People's School. By the end of the

GO TO THE PEOPLE
LIVE, LEARN, PLAN AND WORK
WITH THEM.

Figure 5.3. This illustration appeared in a 1984 World Vision report on its COLT programs in Southeast Asia. Taken directly from development expert Jimmy Yen, the words and images reflected a new commitment to indigeneity in its humanitarian work. Courtesy of World Vision International Archives, Monrovia, Calif.

third year, 2,952 villagers had been trained in a new skill. The transformation was extraordinary, reported WVP workers. RRCs were taking their work seriously, local businesses were launching, and social organizations were thriving. Most impressive were the *Botika sa Baryo* (a pharmacy), *Anak Bukid* (a village youth organization resembling a 4-H club), and a cooperative store in the public market of San Jose. Participation from below seemingly had rebuilt a fractured community.[34]

The Mindoran project captured national and international attention. Filipino government officials, who observed the trim nipa huts, the clean bodies, the growing literacy, and the revival of rondalla music, effused to a reporter from the *Manila Times Journal*, "Where disease, filth and death once prevailed, sparkling health, cleanliness and the zest for life now reign." World Vision headquarters in Monrovia, ecstatic as positive reports arrived from other sites in the Philippines, doubled down on their commitment to indigeneity and participatory development. World Vision's office in Manila hired Filipinos to fill positions at the board level and in midlevel management, and those staffers proceeded to implement "community-based holistic development projects" in 770 more communities in 1981 alone. As the successes multiplied, WVP operations in Mindoro became the site of intense observation. International visitors were told that the People's School worked because it was "of the people, by and for the people."[35]

Problems, however, lay beneath the surface. First, the "multiplication effect" often fell far short of the goal. Barangay scholars, who had been told to share their training with at least five other villagers, chafed at such specific target numbers. The system failed at even higher rates at the associate to cooperator levels, where trainings had to cross family networks and class lines. Many villagers did not want to be taught by second- and third-generation scholars, saying that their trainings were of diluted quality. Moreover, the diffusion system, despite its efforts at indigeneity, did not quite translate culturally given the diversity of Filipino society. Wealthy and poor Mindorans, analysts finally acknowledged, required different pedagogical methods. Moreover, some small farmers resisted these "science missionaries" who sought to introduce modern agricultural tools. World Vision also worried that the program, driven by a focus on "individual upliftment," did not fit the group orientation of Mindoran culture. The new methods had not gone far enough. World Vision was off to a "promising start" in implementing culturally sensitive projects, wrote one observer, but it still had "many miles to travel."[36]

Second, the People's School did not reach all Mindorans. On this Filipino island, one of the most remote and poorest in the nation, World Vision intentionally targeted all income levels, including the "poorest of the poor." But many of the most disadvantaged, who were just trying to survive, could not afford to leave their work, even for a short time. Most who did manage to attend a People's School never implemented their new knowledge. In fact, the majority of trainees in the cattle fattening course did not own cattle. Similarly, many barangay scholars of *maisagana* were tenants who did not have land or equipment or seedlings to actually cultivate their own maize. In 1982 World Vision finally began to search for capital loans, but banks hesitated to loan capital to poor farmers who might not repay the money. The few who did secure loans faced a market glut of poultry, rice, or whatever else had been produced because of a recent training. Meanwhile, the bulk of scholars from the middle and upper classes concentrated on helping their own already-resourced relatives to corner the market. In the end, the People's School, against all intentions, produced a "widening of income differences." The disillusionment was profound.[37]

Finally, the hyperlocal focus of the People's School could not address bigger crises that swamped Mindoro's barangays. In 1983, for example, the assassination of Senator Benigno Aquino and consequent political unrest sparked an economic slump. Foreign investors lost faith in the economy, the peso was devalued twice, and inflation plagued consumers and entrepreneurs alike. Natural disasters compounded the troubles. WVP's Roman Garma lamented that the Philippines suffered an average of nineteen typhoons and 300 major fires a year in addition to numerous earthquakes and thirteen active volcanoes. When government offices in Manila seemed unable to deal with these crises, World Vision was forced to return to relief work. This hamstrung efforts to generate appropriate technology and loan assistance for barangay scholars.[38]

Given these shortcomings, reviews of the People's School by outside experts were mixed. One critical 1983 USAID audit concluded that it had "little measurable impact." Two other external evaluators, however, disagreed. One called World Vision's work a model of "compassionate professionalism" at a very difficult site "served little by others." He concluded that USAID, which helped fund the project to the tune of $3 million, had "received very high return for its modest investment." The other evaluator, after visiting San Jose, praised World Vision's "organizational élan." Having spent most of its history focusing on relief work, it was "creatively ignorant" about development strategies. Though still learning, its leaders were nonetheless "asking the right questions and are open to whatever resources can be called upon to advance their mission." World Vision itself pronounced the People's School a provisional success. A WVP analyst noted increased agricultural yields, improved health, spiritual growth, more self-confidence among barangay scholars, better civic coordination, and a positive impact on 17,325 people. "As a pilot project," he concluded, "it has served its purpose."[39]

World Vision, however, nurtured greater ambitions. In 1982 the organization hired Ben Chitamber, a noted Indian sociologist from the Allahabad Agricultural Institute, to modify the People's School model based on the critiques of USAID and still-destitute Mindorans. Chitamber, whose textbook on rural sociology emphasized anthropology, culture, folkways, and rural values more than new technology, redoubled World Vision's commitment to grassroots action and cultural sensitivity. In this third phase of development—from relief to development to an even more indigenous brand of development—the People's School eliminated its rigid multiplication requirement, instead encouraging communication through informal and communal means like gatherings for drinking and card games. Chitamber also deemphasized individual productivity, which had led to rivalry and factionalism within villages. Instead, he emphasized village unity.

This new iteration of the People's School, called Development Assisting Centre (DAC), expanded to Thailand and India, then to the continents of Africa and Latin America. By the mid-1980s nearly 400,000 people in 161 project areas had been direct beneficiaries.[40]

Chitamber also leveraged his organization's size and influence. USAID evaluators had pointed out that World Vision was "big stuff in a place like the Philippines." When the national government did not follow up with promises for loans, WVP needed to "exact certain things from those with whom you are working." The report suggested that the organization demand written contracts, not just promises. In response, World Vision began to connect with Filipino elites. In 1983 WVP invited a provincial governor to lead a DAC training. By the mid-1980s WVP's board of directors included a senior economist with the Asian Development Bank, a senior chaplain with the Armed Forces of the Philippines, and the director of the Philippine Council of Evangelical Churches. Connections with Christians in high places extended the reach of World Vision's development programs and generated funds for its burgeoning loan program.[41]

In the late 1980s World Vision pursued even more expansive projects. It did not matter how skilled Mindorans were in swine production if national economic disturbances interrupted loans, supply chains, and markets in which to sell pork. World Vision conceptualized plans for large-scale development over entire municipalities and regions that would use social and political power to advocate on behalf of the poor. This impulse took two programmatic forms: Area Development Programs (ADP) and Large Scale Development (LSD). Each, modeled on the People's School, sought to integrate the insights of small-scale development with regional transformation, government action, and macrolevel actors. The 1984 Ethiopian famine jump-started these new initiatives. Beginning as the largest relief effort in World Vision history, one that ballooned the organization's budget for Ethiopia from $5 million to $70 million in less than a year, it gradually transitioned into a phase of large-scale development projects led by Ethiopians. These agricultural and health programs, according to a World Vision administrator, turned "arid valleys into green meadows and destitute peoples into confident, self-reliant communities." These projects also had the effect of transforming World Vision itself. By the mid-1980s headquarters in Monrovia had mushroomed into an eleven-acre complex adjacent to a hissing freeway. Inside several buildings, a staff of 900 workers used 450 typewriters and 650 computer terminals to process 18,000 pieces of mail each day. Bob Pierce, whose notion of long-term development was sustained spiritual conversion, would not have recognized his own organization.[42]

The new trajectory—from emergency relief to large-scale holistic development—emanated largely from the Majority World. Personnel in Manila such as Ivy Abellanosa, Adora Balancio, Minda Banua, Albert Barador,

Iryn Boco, Marina de la Cruz, Roman Garma, Daday Maligmat, Earl Patino, and Boy Tupaz, many of whom became "full-fledged development experts" for World Vision in the 1980s and 1990s, sought to encompass, as Garma put it, both the "total Development of the Total man—body, mind, and spirit" and "the structures and systems of the society." Defying those who worried that the organization might secularize as it adopted development methods, they practiced an intense spirituality that included rigorous prayer, "life verses," and Bible study during conferences and trainings. The Global South kept World Vision evangelical even as it pushed the organization away from the one-to-one welfare approach of orphan care. Indigenization in both of these respects—personal spirituality and holistic development work—insulated evangelical missionaries from the post-Protestant secularism that characterized many midcentury ecumenical missionaries. Filipino insights thus traveled from Mindoro to Manila to Monrovia—and then out again around the globe.[43]

III. Evangelical Transformational Development

World Vision's new direction did not occur in a vacuum. The commitments of Lausanne had been moving toward indigeneity, participation, and holism for at least a decade. WVP workers were also theoretically grounded in the rapidly changing discipline of development studies. Scholars such as David Korten, John Friedman, John Sommers, and Robert Chambers were questioning economic growth as the key goal or the primary engine of true development. USAID, which followed a trajectory similar to World Vision—an agency birthed in the Cold War to stop the communist threat—also contended that the Global South could benefit most from a "people-centered development" in which the poor defined their own aspirations. World Vision benefitted from the movement's deep financial coffers, and it drank deeply from this scholarly well. "We used to read the new development manuals at night," explained one early practitioner, "and then teach the villagers what we learned the next day," often using funds from USAID. Despite the conspicuous irony of this Western attempt to implement a people-centered strategy among "the people," World Vision began to conceive of itself more as a catalyst than a service provider. The broader humanitarian world encouraged this path.[44]

Evangelical humanitarians also received a theological imprimatur. At a two-week conference in the white suburban enclave of Wheaton, Illinois, 336 delegates from fifty-nine nations sought to move beyond Lausanne's tired debate over the appropriateness of social action. The self-selecting delegates at this 1983 conference, unlike the North American planners of Lausanne in 1974, were already convinced that social justice was part and parcel of mission, and they sought to develop a theology that would allow evangelicals to implement methods of development. Indeed, this gathering at Wheaton was remarkable for the way in which it brought World Vision and Lausanne's constituencies together. While encouraging economic uplift, delegates repudiated "a mechanistic pursuit of economic growth" as barren. They proclaimed a transnational "kingdom of God" in which people transformed into followers of Christ. "Transformation," they contended, was a more biblical term for promoting equity, justice, freedom, dignity, mutuality, participation, and cultural integrity. The term also enjoyed the public relations virtue of being distinguishable from Marxism, revolution, and liberation theology in the minds of the rank and file. Again, delegates from the Global South, who made up 60 percent of the gathering, played an important role in retaining an evangelical ethos while simultaneously pushing the guiding principle of "equitable partnership in which local people and Western agencies cooperate together." Keeping the pressure on white Americans, this gathering formalized several years later as the International Fellowship of Mission as Transformation (INFEMIT). Lausanne's radical discipleship wing thus continued to add theological heft to World Vision's brand of development.[45]

Bryant Myers, a veteran of World Vision, codified the emerging themes of transformational development. A polymath who taught physics and biochemistry at UCLA, dabbled in theology, and served as a delegate at Wheaton '83, Myers indicted American evangelicals for their lackluster efforts. "The poor deserved better than gifted amateurs with their hearts in the right place," he wrote. "Good intentions were no longer enough." In *Walking with the Poor: Principles and Practices of Transformational Development* (1999), which became the development bible for evangelical humanitarians, Myers wrote that poverty could not be reduced to material conditions. The spiritual and physical realms, he suggested, cannot be separated. Employing a "theology of sin," he described the deleterious effects of transnational corporations that constructed a "web of lies and deceit in big structural systems" and that "played god in the lives of the poor." The poor, internalizing a lifetime of suffering and exclusion, "believe they are truly god-forsaken." "This is spiritual and psychological poverty of the deepest kind," wrote Myers, "the root of fatalism." Transformational developers needed to "walk with the poor." Instead of blaming the victim or demanding modernization, true humanitarians should look to the poor for insight into their plight. "Indigenous people can do what I can't," observed Myers. It is a partnership, "not the 'developed' going out to fix the 'undeveloped.'" Myers's synthesis questioned the modernist assumptions of Christian Americanism.[46]

Significantly, Majority World voices had informed Myers's most cogent insights. His "development journey," Myers wrote in the preface, had begun with the "stimulating" 1978 seminar at IIRR with Yen that had launched the Mindoran experiment. It continued through the 1980s when he was a World Vision worker in Asia and Africa. Colleague Jayakumar Christian, who would become CEO of World Vision India, gave theoretical heft to Myers's ground-level encounters. Poverty, Christian had pointed out in his dissertation-turned-book *God of the Empty-Handed: Poverty, Power and the Kingdom of God* (1994), was a marring of identity caused by the "grind of being poor and also by being captive to the god-complexes of the non-poor." The solution, echoed in Myers's writing several years later, was to restore identity through participation and the implementation of indigenous knowledge. That *Walking with the Poor*'s acknowledgments section was disproportionately populated by non-Westerners underscores the profound influence of the global reflex. Asian, African, and Latin American villagers helped forge transformational development.[47]

The consensus reached by Lausanne, World Vision, Wheaton '83, and Myers radiated through American evangelicalism. Senator Mark Hatfield, a liberal Republican, joined World Vision's board of directors and applied the insights of transformational development to the issue of world hunger. Carl Henry, the editor of *Christianity Today*, traveled widely as World Vision's "theologian-at-large" preaching both justice and justification. Ron Sider and other members of the evangelical left preached the importance of both personal and structural transformation. The spectacular growth of humanitarian agencies in this era also suggested the broad appeal of such efforts. In 1978 World Vision and Food for the Hungry led ten others in founding the Association of Evangelical Development and Relief Organizations (later renamed Accord Network). By the 2000s nearly fifty member agencies had developed urban food-for-work and leadership training programs; facilitated the building of roads, hospitals, and schools; established cooperatives, credit unions, and loan programs; and funded microenterprises around the world. Transformational development sought to channel the considerable energies and naïve exuberance of evangelical compassion. It encouraged would-be humanitarians to walk with the poor, not bury them under mammoth tractor tires manufactured in Akron, Ohio. During the 1980s and 1990s, these sensibilities, which sidestepped the developing culture wars, appealed to a broad band of activists ranging from Jim Wallis on the left to Franklin Graham on the right. The discourse of transformational development dominates to this day, even among NGOs more conservative than World Vision such as Compassion International, the second largest American evangelical NGO, and Graham's Samaritan's Purse, the third largest. To be sure, methods do not always match discourse. Public advocacy that accounts for structural inequalities comprises only a fraction of Accord Network programming compared to relief work, and critics assail Operation Christmas Child as a toxic charity initiative that exports Western culture more than it alleviates poverty. But even Samaritan's Purse has quietly invested in sustainable development projects.[48]

Transformational development, then, prompted a more substantive consideration of long-term approaches to justice. These approaches were most popular in academic institutions. A Calvin College economist, for example, decried the lack of U.S. aid to the poorest of the world's nations and condemned the rise of multinational corporations and their tendency to eliminate indigenous firms in the Majority World. Others urged acts of moral suasion, boycotts, selective investment, and shareholder resolutions in order to constrain American corporations. Wheaton College's Human Needs and Global Resources program (HNGR) offered a minor degree, periodic seminars, and a mandatory nine-month overseas internship. Upon reentry into the United States, HNGR students (and those in similar programs on other campuses) offered some of evangelicalism's most trenchant critiques of American diplomacy and culture. These new sensibilities sometimes made their way to the rank and file, most notably through Doris Longacre's *More with Less Cookbook* and Ron Sider's *Rich Christians in an Age of Hunger*, which remained evangelical bestsellers into the 1980s and beyond.[49]

The second major effect of internationalization was to challenge Christian Americanism. To be sure, the religious right persisted. In 1983, as World Vision championed its People's School project in Mindoro, President Reagan delivered his "Evil Empire" speech to a meeting of the National Association of Evangelicals. Advocating a hardline approach that would "write the final pages of the history of the Soviet Union," Reagan was repeatedly interrupted by applause. Several years later Jerry Falwell, leader of the Moral Majority, threw his support behind Ferdinand Marcos. After being lavishly hosted by the Filipino strongman in Manila, Falwell told American critics to quit "bellyaching" about his corruption and brutality and instead to urge Washington to put "its money where its mouth is" to prevent a communist takeover in a vulnerable region. Moreover, Filipino fundamentalists touted strong pro-Americanism and unfettered capitalism. This narrative of a resurgent fundamentalism—of Reagan's triumphalism overwhelming Jimmy Carter's theology of limits—grabbed headlines in the 1980s and rightly remains the focus of sustained scholarly attention.[50]

But other sectors were moving in a different direction. In the mid-1980s, forty years after John Broger founded the Far East Broadcasting Company (FEBC) in Manila, evangelicals at the radio network, some of whom were closely connected to World Vision, helped lead a "People Power" movement that opposed Marcos in the mid-1980s. Billy Graham, after increased international travel in the 1970s and 1980s, pled for an end to the arms race, apartheid in South Africa, and "America's exploitation of a disproportionate share of the world's resources." According to biographer David Aikman, Graham "ceased to be a conservative Protestant patriot urging military readiness against the Soviet threat." As Reagan denounced Russia as an evil empire to Graham's constituents in America, Graham himself promoted détente in Moscow. Many, though certainly not all, followed the evangelist's lead. A *Christianity Today* poll showed that most pastors wanted disarmament and less military spending. Sizable numbers of pastors, missionaries, humanitarians, and professors insisted that God's covenants were transnational.[51]

In the wake of Vietnam, Watergate, and Lausanne, World Vision, in fact, broke decisively from American interests. It was one of the first humanitarian organizations to return to Cambodia after the Khmer Rouge forces emerged victorious. Declaring a deep Christian commitment to a traumatized and impoverished population, World Vision provided millions of dollars of humanitarian aid in this Marxist nation. It also worked with the Sandinista government in Nicaragua and in support of Palestinian human rights in Israel. By the 1980s its president was non-American, and its eighteen-member board represented twelve nationalities. Senator Hatfield encouraged Christians to lobby the government to pass the Food for Peace program, which would remove political considerations from the distribution of aid. He also introduced legislation, which became law in 1977, banning the CIA from using missionaries as agents of the state. Critiques of communism continued—as did expressions of appreciation for American freedoms—but growing numbers of leaders displayed ambivalence toward the role of the nation in the world. Indigenous transformational development, not saber-rattling, became the method by which most evangelicals associated with World Vision engaged the world.[52]

But both of these important trajectories—a new focus on transformational development and a resurgent Christian Americanism—paled in comparison with an even more consequential movement. The largest churches in the Philippines were most concerned with supernatural transformation. As World Vision pursued modest, small-scale community development in Mindoro—even as it built large-scale projects in Ethiopia—it was being dwarfed by the astounding growth of Pentecostalism.

Notes

1. Yen quoted in Norman B. Rohrer, *Open Arms* (Wheaton, Ill.: Tyndale House, 1987), 156.
2. Russell Kerr, "Community Leadership Training (COLT) Program," 1–3, in "WV History Philippines—Miscellaneous," FY81, ORG/WVI 18, World Vision International Archives, Monrovia, Cal.
3. For critiques of World Vision and Christian Americanism generally, see Erica Bornstein, *The Spirit of Development: Protestant NGOs, Morality, and Economics in Zimbabwe* (Stanford, Calif.: Stanford University Press, 2005); David Stoll, *Is Latin*

America Turning Protestant? The Politics of Evangelical Growth (Berkeley: University of California Press, 1990), 266–304; Alan Whaites, "Pursuing Partnership: World Vision and the Ideology of Development," *Development in Practice* 9, No. 4 (August 1999): 413. On the spectacular crusades in the Philippines, see Norman Rohrer, *Open Arms* (Wheaton, Ill.: Tyndale House, 1987), 164, 188, 194–95, 199–200.

4. Rohrer, *Open Arms*, 189.

5. On earlier evangelical relief efforts, see Heather Curtis, *Holy Humanitarians: American Evangelicals and Global Aid* (Cambridge, Mass.: Harvard University Press, 2018). For "you can call it missions," see Robert Pierce, *This One Thing I Do* (Waco, Tex.: Word Books, 1983), 204.

6. On the fallout of Vietnam on World Vision, see Robert Wuthnow, *Boundless Faith: The Global Outreach of American Churches* (Berkeley: University of California Press, 2010), 123. For "more threatening," see "Report of the Internationalization Study Committee," December 8, 1975, 4, in "Correspondence—VPIR," FY76-8, ADM/WVI 2, WVIA. On the problems of overt American identity, see Rachel McCleary, *Global Compassion: Private Voluntary Organizations and U.S. Foreign Policy since 1939* (New York: Oxford University Press, 2009), 114. For "In the beginning was Bob Pierce," see "Commission on Internationalization, 1978–1983," September 1984, 14, in ORG/WVI 3, WVIA. For "emergency by emergency," see "A Declaration of Internationalization," May 31, 1978, in FY78, ORG/WVI 3, WVIA. Rees quoted in Michael Barnett, *Empire of Humanity: A History of Humanitarianism* (Ithaca, N.Y.: Cornell University Press, 2011), 121.

7. On the ousting of Pierce, see Graeme Irvine, "A New Partnership," February 22, 1989, 2, in Folder "Partnerships," Graeme Irvine Papers, WVIA. On the tensions of the early 1970s, see "Report of the Internationalization Study Committee," 12–15. For "strict equality," see Alan Whaites, "Pursuing Partnership," 413–14. On secession, see David King, "Seeking a Global Vision: The Evolution of World Vision and American Evangelicalism" (PhD diss., Emory University, 2012), 218.

8. For "our message in the nonwhite world," see Stanley Mooneyham, *What Do You Say to a Hungry World?* (Waco, Tex.: Word Books, 1977). For "new frontier," see Graeme Irvine, "The Internationalization Journey," 1, in Volume 2 of Graeme Irvine Papers, WVIA. For "theology of internationalization," see "Report of the Internationalization Study Committee," 41–51. For "international spirit," see Irvine, "The World Vision Partnership," 4, in "Correspondence—VPIR," FY76-8, ADM/WVI 2. On international symbolism and "truly international image," see "Report of the Internationalization Study Committee," 12, 39.

9. Han quoted in Irvine, "Internationalization Journey," 4. For the task force's recommendations, see "Report of the Internationalization Study Committee," 1–51.

10. For "grand experiment," see Irvine, "World Vision Partnership," 3. For "supra-national organization," see "Report of the Internationalization Study Committee," 28. For "unilateral action," see Mooneyham, "Remarks on Aspects of Internationalization," February 1, 1978, 10, in Mooneyham Papers, WVIA. For "cast the die," see Mooneyham, "World Vision and the Future: A Continuing Growth in Partnership," 1, in Folder "Correspondence—VPIR," FY76-8, ADM/WVI 2, WVIA. On the spiritual aspects of the internationalization ceremony, see Mooneyham, "World Vision

and the Future," 11–12. On worries about secularization, see Mooneyham, "Remarks on Aspects of Internationalization," 7.

11. On the results of de-Americanization, see "Review of Structural Changes in World Vision International, 1976–1984, Interim report," September 1984, 1, in FY78, ORG/ WVI 3, WVIA. On funding and representation, see McCleary, *Global Compassion*, 117. For "children of the British Empire," see Roberta Hestenes, "Laying the Foundations: Brief Reflections on WV History from a Personal Perspective," 3–4, in "Historical Narratives" binder, WVIA.

12. For "true partnership," see "Paper III: The Feelings of the World Vision Partners about Internationalization," 1–11, in folder "Commission on Internationalization 1978–1983," WVIA. On more complaints from the Global South, see King, "Seeking a Global Vision," 273. On Latin Americans challenging "suits" from California headquarters, see David King, *God's Internationalists: World Vision and the Age of Evangelical Humanitarianism* (Philadelphia: University of Pennsylvania Press, 2019), 204; conversation with David King, September 24, 2012. On the "golden rule," see King, "Seeking a Global Vision," 241. On Australian influence, see Bernard Barron, "Memoirs of World Vision," 72, in FY03, ORG/WVI 18, WVIA; Irvine, "World Vision Partnership," 1–7; McCleary, *Global Compassion*, 117.

13. For "it became clear," see Hestenes, "Laying the Foundations," 4. On the 1986 bylaws change, see Irvine, "Internationalization Journey," 3–4. For the results of internationalization, see "Review of Structural Changes," 1.

14. On sponsorship numbers, see Rohrer, *Open Arms*, appendix. For "little permanent impact," see Barnett, *Empire of Humanity*, 123. For "a more organized . . . dimension," see Chang Uk Byun, "A Study of Rev. Kyung-Chik Han's Ministry on Domestic Mission," 491–92, in *KCHC/Theses 2*.

15. For CEPAD and "completely new dimension," see Lee Huhn, "Aglow with Victory" and "Globe at a Glance," *World Vision Magazine*, October 1979, 18–19, 22; folder "WV Nicaragua 1974 Annual Report," in FY74, ORG/NIC 1-1, WVIA. For "simply welfare," see "Feelings of the World Vision Partners," 4–8. For "twin mandates," see Stanley Mooneyham, "Development, Internationalism: Some Observations," *World Vision*, January 1974, 12–14.

16. On the limits of child sponsorship, see King, "Seeking a Global Vision," 233–36, 275–77. For "window into the community," see Robert Ainsworth, "Response to Mr. Charles G. Williams's Report," 8, in Folder "WVRO COLT Report, August '81," FY81, MIN/WVI 4-2, WVIA. For "emotional tug," see Rohrer, *Open Arms*, 151–52.

17. For comparisons of NGOs, see McCleary, *Global Compassion*, 114; VanderPol, "Least of These," 124.

18. On Barber, see "Barber Named to Development Department," *World Vision*, September 1973, 21. For "just like the West," see Rohrer, *Open Arms*, 148. For Loksado and "abstract into the concrete," see Rohrer, *Open Arms*, 152.

19. For "crisp scholar's gown," see Charles W. Hayford, *To the People: James Yen and Village China* (New York: Columbia University Press, 1990), 14–15. On Yen's conversion and religious networks, see David Hollinger, *Protestants Abroad* (Princeton, N.J.: Princeton University Press, 2017), 258. For Yen's love of coolies, see Pearl

S. Buck, *Tell the People: Talks with James Yen about the Mass Education Movement* (New York: John Day, 1945), 6–7. For Confucius, Christ, and coolies, see John C. K. Kiang, *James Yen, His Movement for Mass Education and Rural Reconstruction* (South Bend, Ind.: Self-published, 1976), 91.

20. For MEM's launch, see James Mayfield, *Go to the People: Releasing the Rural Poor through the Peoples School System* (West Harford, Conn.: Kumarian Press, 1985), x. For a description of Ting Hsien, see Kiang, *James Yen*, 115. On Yen's style of education, see Hayford, *To the People*, 125–27. For "fill the air with song" and "different air," see Hayford, *To the People*, 147. On Mao's involvement, see Hayford, *To the People*, 45. On Yen's successful mobilization, see Mayfield, *Go to the People*, x.

21. For "different air," see Hayford, *To the People*, 147. On the successes and spread of the movement, see Mayfield, *Go to the People*, 25; James Y. C. Yen, *China's New Scholar-Farmer* (Beijing: Chinese National Association of the Mass Education Movement, 1929).

22. For the description of Yen, see Kiang, *James Yen*, 99, 176. On Yen's popularity in the United States, see Kiang, *James Yen*, iv; Hayford, *To the People*, 195–97; Hollinger, *Protestants Abroad*, 260. On the "Jimmy Yen Provision," see Kiang, *James Yen*, 11.

23. For "forces of evil," see Hayford, *To the People*, 62. For "American pattern," see Pearl S. Buck, *Tell The People; Talks with James Yen about the Mass Education Movement* (New York: John Day 1945), 57. For "first conquered it," see Mayfield, *Go to the People*, 190. For "vaguely socialist leanings," see Hayford, *To the People*, 195.

24. On the spread of PRRM, see Mayfield, *Go to the People*, 29–30. On the adaptation to the Filipino context, see Juan Flavier, *Doctor to the Barrios: Experiences with the Philippine Rural Reconstruction Movement* (Quezon City, the Philippines: New Day, 1970), 6–7. On the rehabilitation of San Luis, see Kiang, *James Yen*, 13–17. On the development of the People's School System in the Philippines, see Mayfield, *Go to the People*, 36–37; Edward P. Reed, "The People's School System: An Integrated Approach to Rural Reconstruction," April 1983, Occasional Paper No. 3, 5-6, in WVIA.

25. On the *Rural Reconstruction Report*, see Kiang, *James Yen*, 165. For a description of the IIRR training center, see Kiang, *James Yen*, 156; Reed, "The People's School System," 3. On visitors to IIRR, see Mayfield, *Go to the People*, 42–50; Reed, "The People's School System," 8–21; Kiang, *James Yen*, 15–18, 159, 175.

26. On the 1978 IIRR training, see Ted Engstrom, "Monthly Memo," *World Vision*, May 1978, 17; Rohrer, *Open Arms*, 152; Reed, "People's School System," 39. On Yen's spirituality, see Stacey Bieler, "Yan Yangchu: Reformer with a Heart for the Village," 188–89, in Carol Lee Hamrin, ed., *Salt and Light: Lives of Faith that Shaped Modern China* (Eugene, Ore.: Wipf and Stock Publishers, Pickwick Publications, 2008).

27. For "euphoric days," see "The Directions for the Next Ten Years," WV in-house magazine. The article then used the Yen poem to articulate the new vision for development. See more in Rohrer, *Open Arms*, 153. On World Vision's conceptual and rhetorical dependence on IIRR, see Bryant Myers, "The Development Process: For People, By People," *World Vision*, November 1982, 12–15. For "remake villagers," see Mayfield, *Go to the People*, 43, 190. On

Yen as inspiration, see "Community Development Workers' Orientation Workshop, May 21-June 2, WVP," in "DAC Training, India," in ORG/WVI 4, WVIA.

28. On 1970s work in the Philippines, see "Philippines," 3, in Folder "WV History," ORG/ WVI 18. For descriptions of San Jose, see Gil Rebamontan and Gloria Cabacungan, "A Case Study of the 'Paaralan ng Anak-Pawis' in San Jose, Occidental Mindoro," 12–20, in "COLT/Philippines Case Study, San Jose, Mindoro," FY85, MIN/WVI 4-2; Russell Kerr, "History of the COLT Program," October 1, 1981, 1–5 and Appendix A, in folder "Community Leadership Training (COLT) Program in the Philippines," FY 81, MIN/WVI 4-2; "Community Leadership Training Program," 12–14, in "Field Development COLT," FY 79, MIN/WVI 4-2, WVIA.

29. For "better strategy," see Kerr, "History of the COLT Program," 1. On Garma and Santos, see "San Jose Community Leadership Training Project," 1–2, in "Field Development COLT," FY 79, MIN/WVI 4-2. On the Mindoran visit to Cavite, see Kerr, "History of the COLT Program," 4. For "pushed ahead," see "San Jose Community Leadership Training Project," 2. On the opening, see Kerr, "History of the COLT Program," 4. On community engagement and alumni associations, see Cabacungan, "Case Study," 59–66; Roman Garma, "COLT Program in the Philippines," October 1, 1981, and "Community Leadership Training (COLT) Program in the Philippines," 2, in FY 81, MIN/WVI 4-2. For "generous hospitality," see "San Jose Community Leadership Training Project," 2.

30. For Paaralan ng Anak-Pawis, see Charles Williams, "Report Evaluation of the Matching Grant to WVI," March 1981, 14, in "Development, Field: USAID COLT Evaluation/B. Ainsworth," FY81 MIN/WVI 4-2, WVIA. For "all factions together," see Mayfield, Go to the People, ix. For "caught the imagination," see Cabacungan, "Case Study," 49. On the Alay Lakan and success of the rondalla course, see "San Jose Community Leadership Training Project," 3.

31. On piggery production, see Kerr, "History of the COLT Program," 4. For courses in livelihood, see Cabacungan, "Case Study," 49–51. On the Flavier toilet design, see "San Jose Community Leadership Training Project," 4; Flavier, Doctor to the Barrios, 152–56. On the use of the vernacular, see Cabacungan, "Case Study," 54.

32. On the diffusion and celebration of COLT, see "San Jose Community Leadership Training Program," 3–14; "COLT Logbook, November 1978," 1, in "Field Development COLT," FY 79, MIN/WVI 4-2. On the Alay Kaunlaran, see "COLT Program in the Philippines," 15, in MIN/WVI 4-2, FY81, WVIA.

33. On the success of Supranes, see Kerr, "History of the COLT Program," 25–26; Williams, "Report Evaluation," 16, 24–26.

34. On the role of RRCs, see Cabacungan, "Case Study," 34, 46, 52; "San Jose Community Leadership Training Project," 10; "COLT Program in the Philippines," 7–12. On the division of San Jose, see Cabacungan, "Case Study," 36. For numbers of participants, see Williams, "Report Evaluation," 15–16; "1981 World Vision Philippines Annual Report," 16, in FY81, ORB/PHL 1-1, WVIA.

35. On World Vision's excitement, see Robert Ainsworth to Wil Holcomb, April 18, 1979, p. 2, in Folder "Field Development, COLT," FY79, MIN/WVI 4-2. For "zest of life," see Williams, "Report Evaluation," 27–28. On the Filipino management of WVP and

project numbers in 1981, see "WVP 1981 Annual Report," 1–2. On international observers, see Kerr, "History of the COLT Program," 5.

36. On the breakdown of the pyramid scheme, see Cabacungan, "Case Study," 57. On trainings happening along filial lines, see Ben Chitamber, "Training Courses for People in Development Projects," 3 in FY83, MIN/WVI 4-3, WVIA. On difficulties in crossing class lines, see Cabacungan, "Case Study," 76–77. For "science missionaries," see Flavier, *Doctor to the Barrios*, 58. On culturally inappropriate technology, see Cabacungan, "Case Study," 75, 78. For "individual upliftment," see Cabacungan, "Case Study," 75. For "promising start," see Williams, "Report Evaluation," 29.

37. On problems of the "poorest of the poor," see Cabacungan, "Case Study," 53, 58, 72–74. On loans, see Cabacungan, "Case Study," 58, 74. For "unintended neglect of the poor," see James M. Pines, "Compassionate Professionalism: The Challenge to World Vision," 30, in FY83, MIN/WVI 4-2, WVIA. On the Supranes' barangay, see Williams, "Report Evaluation," 26–27. On the appeal to the middle and upper classes, see Cabacungan, "Case Study," 76–77. On the market glut, see "Development Training," January 19, 1983, 2, in FY82-85, "DAC/COLT," MIN/WVI 4-3, WVIA.

38. On the slumping economy and environmental crises, see "World Vision International Partnership Annual Report, Fiscal Year 1983," 71–78; R. Tanoy, "Relief and Rehabilitation Training to Be Held Soon," *WVP Family News*, March-April 1985, 8. On the interruption of development work, see Ruth Cruz, Dinah Dimalanta, and Martejo Benares, "Christmas in the Face of Disaster," *WVP Family News*, November-December 1984, 4–6.

39. For the critical USAID report, see "World Vision Relief Organization Audit Report No. 0-000-83-63," May 12, 1983, in FY82-85, MIN/WVI 4-3, WVIA. For "organizational élan," see Williams, "Report Evaluation," March 1981. For "very high return," see James M. Pines, "Compassionate Professionalism: A Challenge for World Vision," June 29, 1982, in FY82, ORG/WVI 17-4, WVIA. For World Vision's assessment, see Cabacungan, "Case Study," 66–77; "WRVO Community Leadership Training Report, August 1981," 4, in FY81, MIN/WVI 4-2, WVIA.

40. On adjustments based on the Mindoro experience, see "WVRO COLT Report," 4; Bryant Myers, "COLT: The Next Three Years: Official Notes," November 11-12, 1982; Bob Ainsworth to Graeme Irvine, April 4, 1983, in "DAC/COLT," MIN/WVI 4-3, FY82-85. On the DAC, see Chitamber, *Introductory Rural Sociology* (New Delhi: Eiley Eastern, 1973), 107; Chitamber, "Development Assisting Centers: Transforming Villages by Living with the People," WV Staff Working Paper No. 10, January 1991, 1, in "DAC—Transforming Villages," FY91, MIN/WVI 4-3, WVIA. For the revision of the multiplier concept, see Cabacungan, "Case Study," 38, 43. On indigeneity, see "Essentials of the DAC Approach," in "Field Development," FY84, MIN/WVI 4-3-1; "DAC: First Year Report," July 12, 1985, 6, in "DAC/COLT," FY82-85, MIN/WVI 4-3, WVIA.

41. For "exact certain things," see "Meeting Notes—Bob Ainsworth and Jim Pines," 7, in "Field Development: COLT," FY83, MIN/WVI 4-2, WVIA. For the roster of WVP's board of directors, see "1979 Annual Report," in FY79-80, PHL/ORG 1-1, WVIA. On the involvement of a governor, see "DAC-CDW Seminar Workshop," September

12, 1983, in "DAC Training," FY83-4, ORG/WVI 4, WVIA. On the growing reach of DAC, see Chitamber, "DAC," WV Working Paper No. 10, 4.

42. On Area Development Programs, see *Footprints: A Brief History of World Vision India* (Chennai: WVI, 2003), 43–44; Ken Tracey, "ADPs: A Participatory Method-of-Choice," *Together*, April-June 1993, 20–23. For examples of politicians, civic leaders, and university professors working with World Vision, see "DAC Program—December 1983," January 11, 1984, 16, in "DAC—Philippine Program Plan," FY84, MIN/WVI 4-3, WVIA. On large-scale work in Ethiopia, see Rachel Veale, "From Relief to Development: Dignity amid Poverty in Ethiopia," *World Vision*, April-May 1986, 13–14; folder "Ethiopia/The Green Drought," FY88, ORG/WVI 18, WVIA; "Ansokia Famine Relief," FY86, MIN/ETH 11, WVIA; "Ethiopia Twenty Years Later: From Famine to Fullness," *World Vision*, Summer 2005. On the growth of World Vision, see Rohrer, *Open Arms*, 14, 29, 189, 204–205.

43. For "full-fledged development experts," see *Footprints*, 36. For "total Development" and the influence of WVP personnel, see "Personal Statements of Development Principles," in "DAC Training," FY83-4, ORG/WVI 4, WVIA; Kerr, "History of the COLT Program," 6. On the rigorous spirituality within WVP, see Community Development Workers' Orientation Workshop," May 21–June 2, 1984, in "DAC Training" and "DAC-CDW Seminar Workshop, Mary Hill Retreat Center," August 15, 1983, in FY83-4, ORG/WVI 4; Elnora Avarientos, "Transforming Your World Through Prayer," in folder "Philippines—Miscellaneous," ORG/WVI 18, WVIA. For an alternative view on the 1980s as weakening World Vision's evangelical identity, see Barnett, *Empire of Humanity*, 130. On post-Protestant secularism, see Hollinger, *Protestants Abroad*, 295–96.

44. On the broader development movement, see Bryant Myers, *Walking with the Poor: Principles and Practices of Transformational Development* (Maryknoll, N.Y.: Orbis Books, 1999), 14; John G. Sommer, *Beyond Charity: U.S. Voluntary Aid for a Changing Third World* (Washington, D.C.: Overseas Development Council, 1977). On growing connections with the broader development world, see Myers, *Walking with the Poor*, 2; McCleary, *Global Compassion*, 95; Tizon, "Mission as Transformation," 44. On World Vision's interaction with USAID, see Wuthnow, *Boundless Faith*, 124–25; Myers, *Walking with the Poor*, 1; King, "Seeking a Global Vision," 226; Williams, "Field Report," 7, in "Development, Field: USAID COLT Evaluation," FY81, MIN/WVI 4-2, WVIA. For "read the new development manuals at night," see Barnett, *Empire of Humanity*, 130.

45. For a description of Wheaton '83, see Tizon, "Mission as Transformation," 87–88; Myers, *Walking with the Poor*, 13–14. For "mechanistic pursuit," see Vinay Samuel, ed., *The Church in Response to Human Need* (Grand Rapids, Mich.: Eerdmans, 1987), 256. On the joint Lausanne-World Vision emphasis on the "kingdom of God," see Gene Daniels, "Holistic Ministry," August 29, 1983, in "DAC Training," FY83-4, ORG/WVI 4, WVIA. On the new ethos and language of "transformation," see Vinay Samuel, "An Evangelical Contribution from India," in "World Vision India," FY85, ORG/WVI 18, WVIA; "From Assistance to Transformation"; Wayne Bragg, "From Development to Transformation," 20–51, in *Church in Response*; Ronald Sider, *Evangelicals and*

Development: Toward a Theology of Social Change (Philadelphia: Westminster, 1982). For Majority World voices urging "equitable partnership," see Tito Paredes, "Culture and Social Change," 69; Vishal Mangalwadi, "Compassion and Social Reform: Jesus the Troublemaker," 199, in *Church in Response*.

46. On World Vision and Yen, see Myers, "For People, by People," *WVP Family News*, January 1983, 2–3. For Myers's dependence on Korten, see Myers, *Walking with the Poor*, 14, 96–99. For "better than gifted amateurs," see Myers, *Walking with the Poor*, 2. For "theology of sin" and "web of lies," see Myers, *Walking with the Poor*, 73, 88. For "truly god-forsaken," see Myers, *Walking with the Poor*, 76. For "indigenous people," see Rohrer, *Open Arms*, 159.

47. For "development journey," see Myers, *Walking with the Poor*, xviii. For "the grind of being poor," see Myers, *Walking with the Poor*, 115, 147; Jayakumar Christian, "Powerlessness of the Poor: Toward an Alternative Kingdom of God-Based Paradigm for Response" (PhD Diss., Fuller Theological Seminary, 1994).

48. On the birth of AERDO, see Amy Reynolds and Stephen Offutt, "Global Poverty and Evangelical Action," 244–48, in *The New Evangelical Social Engagement* (New York: Oxford University Press, 2014); VanderPol, "Least of These," 101–102. On appealing to both sides of the culture wars, see Gary VanderPol, "The Least of These: American Evangelical Parachurch Missions to the Poor, 1947–2005" (PhD diss., Boston University, 2010), 126; King, "Seeking a Global Vision," 248. On the dominance of the transformational development paradigm in the Accord Network, see Stephen Offutt and Amy Reynolds, "Christian Ideas of Development: Understanding the Current Theories, Networks, and Priorities of Accord Organizations," *Christian Relief, Development & Advocacy Journal* 1, no. 1 (2019): 1–14; Steve Corbett and Brian Fikkert, *When Helping Hurts: How to Alleviate Poverty Without Hurting the Poor* (Chicago: Moody Publishers, 2009).

49. For a small sampling of the new evangelical attention to structure, see Emilio Castro, "Strategies for Confronting Unjust Social Structures," *Reformed Journal*, April 1975, 17; George Fuller, "Making Business Behave," *Eternity*, May 1980, 17–22; Miriam Adeney, *God's Foreign Policy* (Grand Rapids, Mich.: Eerdmans, 1984), 71–73; Tony Campolo, "The Greening of Gulf and Western," *Eternity*, January 1981, 30–32; George Monsma, *Reforming Economics: A Christian Perspective on Economic Theory and Practice* (Grand Rapids, Mich.: Calvin College Center for Christian Scholarship, 1986). For examples of several HNGR internships that followed the transformational development model, see Tracy Swan, "Valuing Others: Motivation for Sustainable Development in India," May 3, 1996; Deborah Bragg, "A Participatory Evaluation of Community Development in Nicaragua," 1984, in HNGR Collection, Buswell Library, Wheaton College. Also see Wayne G. Bragg and Marilyn Carlson, "Third World Study and Service: A Manual for HNGR Interns," vertical file "HNGR," Wheaton College Archives. On rank-and-file interest, see Doris Longacre, *More-with-Less Cookbook* (Scottdale, Pa.: Herald Press, 1976); Ron Sider, *Rich Christians in an Age of Hunger* (Downers Grove, Ill.: InterVarsity Press, 1977).

50. "Falwell Pays Visit to Manila, Raps U.S. for 'Bellyaching,'" *Los Angeles Times*, November 12, 1985; "Falwell Praises Marcos in Visit to Philippines," *New York*

Times, November 12, 1985. On Filipino fundamentalism, see Lim, "Consolidating Democracy: Filipino Evangelicals between People Power Events, 1986–2001," 239, in David Lumsdaine, ed., *Evangelical Christianity and Democracy in Asia* (New York: Oxford University Press, 2009).

51. On evangelical participation in People Power, see Adalia Bustamante, "February 22-25, 1986: In Retrospect," *Family News*, May 1986, 6, copy in WVIA; Lim, "Consolidating Democracy," 255; "A Church Awakened," *Sojourners*, November 1983, 21; Sharon Mumper, "A Peaceful Transition," *Christianity Today*, April 18, 1986, 28–30. For "ceased to be a conservative Protestant patriot," see David Aikman, *Billy Graham: His Life and Influence* (Nashville, Tenn.: Thomas Nelson, 2007), 156. On evangelical pastors and military spending, see Axel Schäfer, "Evangelicals and Foreign Policy after World War II," lecture at University of Southampton, April 24, 2014.

52. On World Vision's conflict with Western policies on Asia and Latin America, see Whaites, "Pursuing Partnership," 415–16. On *el Consejo Evangélico Pro-Ayuda a los Damnificados* (CEPAD) and the evangelical cooperation with the Sandinistas, see Tom Minnery, "Why the Gospel Grows in Socialist Nicaragua," *Christianity Today*, April 8, 1983, 34–42; Jim Wallis, "In Defense of CEPAD," *Sojourners*, November 1981, 4–5; "A Plea from Christians in Nicaragua," *Public Justice Report*, May 1982, 3–4. On the composition of WVI's leadership, see Randy Haney, "World Vision International," 2525, in George Kurian and Mark Lamport, eds., *The Encyclopedia of Christianity in the United States* (New York: Rowman & Littlefield, 2016). On Hatfield, see McCleary, *Global Compassion*, 134, 162; "Hatfield Urges Ban on CIA Use of Missionaries," *Eternity*, March 1976, 9.

6

Almolonga 1999

Pentecostalism and the Enchantment of the North

The West is looking East for a faith.

—John Wimber[1]

The carrots were huge. Standing in a bustling outdoor market in Almolonga, Guatemala, a beaming Mayan farmer held up vegetables longer and thicker than a man's forearm. As the camera focused on the carrots, an incredulous George Otis, Jr., a senior associate with the Lausanne Committee, told viewers about the town's other agricultural miracles: beets weighing over four pounds and fast-growing radishes. "Before when we harvested the radish," explained a local farmer, "it would take up to sixty days. But when God came into town, it only took forty. Now quite often it only takes 25 days to harvest." Overall, there was a 1,000 percent increase in vegetable production in this town in the highlands of western Guatemala. In fact, American researchers were flocking to Central America to "learn their secret." According to Otis, the secret was not what the experts expected. "The wisdom that God gave the farmers in Almolonga produced better crops than the scientific methods yielded," he explained in the widely circulated 1999 *Transformations* video. "The farmers constantly give the glory to the Lord for producing the bountiful harvests."

The enormous carrots signified a broader transformation out of poverty, violence, and ignorance. In the 1970s, said Otis, Almolonga's streets had been littered with drunken men who would crawl home at nightfall to beat their wives and children. Even though four jails had been built, prisoners had to be bused to nearby villages. Agricultural production suffered from a combination of arid land and poor work habits. According to Otis, Almolongueños, descendants of the ancient Maya, also suffered from spiritual bondage in their worship of folk deities. Maximón was the most insidious. A mustachioed, three-foot mannequin with cowboy boots, Maximón stood propped up before kneeling worshippers who lit votive candles on a dirt floor. Villagers danced lewdly before Maximón and placed lit cigars in his hollowed-out clay mouth. To have any hope of good health and good crops, they had to offer money and alcohol to appease his anger.

Facing West. David R. Swartz, Oxford University Press (2020). © Oxford University Press.
DOI: 10.1093/oso/9780190250805.001.0001

This "lord of death," in the view of evangelicals, was a financial and spiritual burden.

The brutal stickup of a pastor became the catalyst for spiritual revolution in Almolonga. Images from a dramatic reenactment in *Transformations* show gang members brutally shoving a gun down Mariano Riscajche's throat—and then Riscajche's striking a bargain with God: his survival in exchange for a new dedication to revival. The pastor describes how he began fasting four times a week, leading prayer vigils, and presiding over dramatic healings. "Those being set free," Riscajche remembered, "were sometimes thrown across the room and coughed up blood." Mass deliverances from demonic oppression created a stir in Almolonga, and churches started growing. "Idolatry and superstition have fled," narrated Otis, "leaving behind a people dedicated to fervent worship and honest labor." By the late 1990s there were more than two dozen churches, and Riscajche's own congregation consisted of 1,200 joyful worshippers.

As Christian prayers rose, Almolonga itself revitalized. The town's thirty-six bars dropped to three. As the drinking slowed, violence and crime plummeted, and all four jails closed. A renewed workforce tended the valley's newly fertile fields. "Before the spiritual turnaround," explained Otis, "farmers were exporting four truckloads of produce a month. Now they leave town forty times a week." Nicknamed "America's vegetable garden," Almolonga enjoyed agricultural production of biblical proportions. Prosperous farmers paid cash for shiny Mercedes trucks accessorized with mud flaps with Christian slogans like "The Gift of God" and "God Is My Stronghold." Smiles beamed on the faces of the many new believers, who now comprised 85 percent of the town's population. "As neighboring towns celebrate the Day of the Dead, the people of Almolonga turn out en masse to honor the Living God," intoned Otis as images of huge crowds in the town square flashed across the screen.

The fast-paced, fifteen-minute film ended with a prophecy, clearly intended for American ears. "I think in many cases when we talk about community transformation, we have a battle with unbelief. Is our God and is the Gospel powerful enough to truly impact our community?" The answer, according to the film's narrator, was clear. "Almolonga teaches us yes. You had a community given to idolatry, witchcraft, alcoholism, disruptive families. And now you have a community transformed. And that's a good picture for us that, yes, God can do it there—and he can do it in my community." Three more shorts in *Transformations* sought to prove the point. In Cali, Colombia, the cocaine capital of the world, desperate believers surged into local soccer stadiums to hold all-night prayer vigils. Participants claimed that their activism broke the iron grip of drug lords over the shattered city. In Kiambu, Kenya, gatherings of prayer allegedly broke the spirit of Mama Jane, a local witch. And in Hemet, California, a hotspot for Moonies,

Scientologists, and users of methamphetamines, an Assemblies of God revival doubled church attendance as crime rates went into free fall. Hemet showed that transformation was possible in America too—at least if rationalistic, materialistic Americans could believe in angels and God enough to pray for intervention.[2]

Evangelical aspirations for Mindoro and Almolonga were not dissimilar. In fact, Otis's portrait of Almolonga—participatory, productive, and spiritually alive—seemed to be the profile of a model World Vision community. But most neo-Pentecostals in Guatemala disavowed the technocratic development methods of World Vision. Riscajche declared that there was no "program" at all, except for the communal practice of spiritual disciplines. "It is all about humbling ourselves and praying," he declared. Signs and wonders proceeding from the Holy Spirit to towns like Almolonga offered a more direct path to the Almighty God than the intricately planned social programs established on Mindoro. As C. Peter Wagner, a former missionary to Latin America, veteran of Lausanne, and leading proponent of neo-Pentecostalism, wrote to a vast North American audience, "None of the 'isms' (such as capitalism, communism, or socialism) have seemed to bring justice to the poor." He urged his readers to take seriously "the role of supernatural power in dealing with social injustice."[3]

As Americans marveled at spectacular reports from abroad, many of them, in fact, began to reconsider anew the supernatural arts. If, as one Latin American theologian observed, "Liberation theology opted for the poor and the poor opted for Pentecostalism," then perhaps spiritual warfare could also save North America. After all, the Almolonga miracle, as described by Wagner to Otis at a 1992 spiritual warfare conference in Argentina, had come "as a consequence of focused intercessory prayer," not from intellectualist methods practiced at humanistic universities. Global sources abetted both American Pentecostalism and a broader evangelical interest in spiritual warfare. As conservative Protestants in the United States bemoaned what they perceived as pervasive secularism, dropping church attendance, and other pressing problems of modernity, new attention to angels and demons enchanted the West.[4]

I. From Cessationism to Pentecostalism

Nothing about C. Peter Wagner's background suggested his future as a spiritual warrior. He was not Pentecostal. In fact, he was not even Christian. His family home in New Jersey had no Bible but did have lots of poker cards, cigars, and alcohol. After converting to Christianity in college, however, Wagner swore off drinking and gambling and devoted himself to prayer and Bible study in Rutgers University's InterVarsity Christian Fellowship chapter. His move into the evangelical orbit was completed when Wagner moved to Southern California to study at Biola (formerly the Bible Institute of Los Angeles) and Fuller Seminary. There he met key leaders of the National Association of Evangelicals, collaborated with World Vision, and wrote articles for *Christianity Today* and *Eternity* magazines. These respectable institutions instilled a suspicion of charismatic practices, such as healings and speaking in tongues, in the young seminarian, and when Wagner departed in 1956 for a seventeen-year stint as a missionary in Bolivia, he did so as a committed cessationist (Figure 6.1). Indeed, his sending agency, the Bolivian Indian Mission, would not have approved his candidacy had he believed that such supernatural acts could be practiced in the modern world.[5]

Wagner struggled in Santiago de Chiquitos. The young missionary toiled as an evangelist, an editor, and a seminary administrator, but his frantic pace did not produce many conversions. The realistic path to those conversions—healings of the sick in an enchanted Latin American landscape—was not available to a cessationist. The most he could summon, to his later chagrin, were tepid prayers of "Heal this person if it be your will." He was convinced that Pentecostal miracles were the invention of charlatans whose frantic prayers and applications of oil on foreheads only encouraged the superstitions of indigenous peoples. By the time Wagner moved to the highlands of Cochabamba in his sixth year, he had become the self-described "chief adversary of the Pentecostals in Bolivia."[6]

Figure 6.1. C. Peter Wagner strikes a classic missionary pose as he heads out on an evangelistic trip in Bolivia. Courtesy of Doris Wagner.

Wagner, however, did get curious. Though he forbade his congregants from attending a Pentecostal revival meeting in a nearby vacant lot, Wagner went himself—only to see some of his recalcitrant congregants go forward for healing. He also attended an E. Stanley Jones crusade, where the Methodist missionary's straightforward presentation of the gospel softened Wagner toward the more uncomfortable healing service that followed. Though he suffered from a painful, festering cyst on his neck, Wagner did not go forward at the invitation for healing. But he did accept Jones's prayer for him. By the next morning, he later recounted, the wound was completely healed, a miracle confirmed by Wagner's incredulous physician. Increasingly receptive to supernatural events, the missionary began to experience other strange things. One morning, while reading Paul's first letter to the Corinthians, he began to speak in tongues as an experiment. He was simultaneously intrigued and spooked—but finally savvy. He did not tell his wife, and he did not try it again out of concern that his mission agency might dismiss him for heresy.[7]

Wagner may have kept quiet, but he also kept investigating. Embarrassed to be seen consorting with Pentecostals in Bolivia, he stole away to Chile. Sitting unobtrusively in the back of charismatic worship services, Wagner at first merely observed the strange practices of waving hands in the air, dancing in the Spirit, speaking in sacred tongues, offering prophecies, and healing lame people. It was "just as if they were a normal part of the twentieth-century Christian experience," he recounted with amazement. Suggestively, these churches were much more vibrant than his own congregations in Bolivia. Wagner's remaining antagonism melted after conversations with Chilean Pentecostal leaders. He was especially impressed by the smart and personable Javier Vasquez, pastor of the legendary Jotabeche Methodist Pentecostal Church in Santiago, one of the world's first megachurches. From Vasquez, Wagner first heard a compelling scriptural justification for charismatic practices. Returning home, he declared himself an "open cessationist," still persuaded, along with his financial donors in the United States, that these spiritual gifts had ceased with the original apostles, but more open to hearing the other side. He even apologized to his old enemies.[8]

Academic study contributed to Wagner's slow embrace of Pentecostalism. Returning to Fuller Seminary for a sabbatical in the late 1960s, Wagner used the social scientific methods of his graduate school advisor, the pioneering church growth expert Donald McGavran, to chart growth rates of various Protestant groups. In the seminary's School of World Missions, McGavran had assembled faculty trained in civil engineering, education, social ethics, linguistics, agriculture, and anthropology. In fact, only one of ten had a doctorate in theology. Against a critic who asked, "Is there not a danger that sociology and computers may subtly take the place of the Holy Spirit?," one faculty member defensively explained that they were practicing "science in God's

service." Ironically, Fuller's rational calculations led Wagner toward supernatural explanations for church growth. As he constructed logarithmic tables, it
became clear that Jotabeche's spectacular growth represented broader trends
in Latin America. "Cold facts," explained Wagner, showed that Pentecostals,
enjoying a growth rate of 450 percent during the 1960s, had doubled up nearly
all other groups.[9]

When Wagner left Bolivia for good in 1971, appropriating Pentecostal supernaturalism had become his explicit goal. As a new faculty member of Fuller's
School for Missions (Figure 6.2), he sought to instruct stodgy American
cessationists in the exuberant ways of the Latin American church. Upon arrival
in Pasadena, California, he published *Look Out! The Pentecostals Are Coming*
(1973). In the book Wagner did not explicitly advocate for speaking in tongues,
but he did try to make the practice intelligible to cessationists. And most per-
suasively, he offered example after example of large Pentecostal churches in
Chile, Brazil, Ecuador, and Colombia that cultivated a "dynamic mood." Full of
the joy of the Lord, they made it nearly impossible to yawn in worship, and in
not overintellectualizing their faith, they more easily reached the lower classes
and avoided missionary paternalism. Wagner also invoked the miraculous.
Latin American spiritism is real, he contended, and demons need to be met

Figure 6.2. Wagner taught missiology at Fuller Theological Seminary for nearly
thirty years. Courtesy of Doris Wagner.

with "power encounters." Pentecostals, he wrote admiringly, "are not afraid to pit the power of God against the power of Satan." The book, compelling for its confessional and pragmatic tone, made waves in the broader evangelical world. Used extensively in seminaries and Bible schools, *Look Out!* went through four printings in the 1970s. A North American audience, indicted by Wagner for "quenching the Spirit," seemed to agree that global Pentecostals "can help us."[10]

Wagner reciprocated by speaking to the evangelical mainstream in the softer language of "spiritual gifts." Moderating his attempts at shock and Pentecostal awe, he rebranded *Look Out!* as *What Are We Missing?* (1978). In his next book, *Your Spiritual Gifts Can Help Your Church Grow* (1979), he credited "the dynamic of spiritual gifts freely operating" for Latin American growth. Wagner remained an evangelical Congregationalist, but he had also become a full-blown Pentecostal apologist who hoped to convince dogmatic cessationists at Dallas, Princeton, and Fuller seminaries to take Pentecostals more seriously. By the late 1970s, he was considered a church growth expert in his own right, and as director of the Department of Church Growth in the Fuller Evangelistic Association, Wagner spoke to thousands of pastors and missionaries each year, urging them to make use of the full array of the Holy Spirit's gifts.[11]

His colleagues in the School of Missions shared his new interest in the supernatural, and they nourished it globally (Figure 6.3). Like Wagner, this second generation of Fuller faculty had come from a cessationist background. Unlike their predecessors, who had not been missionaries themselves, they had extensive experience overseas. Dean Gilliland, an expert on the contextualization of theology, and Charles Kraft, an anthropologist specializing in intercultural communication, had come from Northern Nigeria. Eddie Gibbs, a professor of church growth, had come from Chile. Ralph Winter had come from Guatemala and others from Brazil, China, Jamaica, and Singapore. These professors had observed manifestations of demons and angels in far-away countries but had never really interacted themselves with supernatural powers. In fact, they confessed to feeling spiritually anemic, especially compared with their international students who had converged on Pasadena from over seventy nations and were yearning for discussion on how to "confront the demonic forces in their animistic cultures." Wagner himself was mortified when a twenty-year-old woman on campus nudged him aside after he could not muster up a powerful prayer for healing in a worship service. Fuller's hapless professors agreed that "we can no longer afford to send people back to the third world or out there for the first time without previously teaching them how to pray for the sick and cast out demons." Seeking insight from their behavioral science training, they analyzed tapes of people speaking in tongues in order to discern next steps. Ultimately, Fuller's provost approved a course for the winter quarter of 1982 that would investigate historical, cultural, and theological elements of the miraculous.[12]

Figure 6.3. Wagner (back row, far right), Donald McGavran (front row, second from the right), and their colleagues in Fuller's School of World Missions. Courtesy of Doris Wagner.

MC510, a doctoral-level course entitled "Signs, Wonders, and Church Growth," was an instant hit. Cotaught by Wagner and John Wimber, a house church pastor and former pianist and manager for the Righteous Brothers, it filled campus's largest classroom to a capacity of eight-five students. Some sat on the floor, and few moved during class breaks for fear of losing their seats. Each Monday at 7 p.m., Wagner began by lecturing about the history of signs and wonders in Christianity, the theology of the Holy Spirit, and the method-ology of miracles. Then, at about 9:30 p.m. the formal class concluded, and the most remarkable aspect of the course began. Wimber, whose large frame and thick bushy hair and beard radiated presence and energy, closed his notebook and declared, "It's time to do the stuff!" He invited the presence of the Holy Spirit and received "words of knowledge" about the physical needs in the classroom as people came forward to be prayed over. It was a signs and wonders clinic.[13]

News of the experimental course spread quickly. *Christian Life*, one of evangelicalism's most popular magazines, profiled MC510 in a special October

1982 issue that included nine articles about the course. The dominant theme throughout was globalism. Stories described how "Third World" students at Fuller had agitated for the course and how massive church growth abroad could be attributed to exotic signs and wonders. "The West," wrote Wimber, "is looking East for a faith." The response, both positive and negative, was astonishing. Some readers expressed outrage that Pentecostals had hijacked Fuller Seminary. Others, not close enough to take the course in person, purchased Wimber's $122.50 study course, which included thirty cassette tapes of teaching. At the seminary itself, MC510 became the most popular of the 600 courses in Fuller's curriculum. Between 1982 and 1985, 800 students enrolled. "Such was the demand," remembered faculty member Eddie Gibbs, "that guards had to be stationed at the doors to prevent gate-crashers." Wagner, pictured in *Christian Life* with a caption reading "straight-line evangelicals open to the Holy Spirit," enjoyed a stunning rise in profile nationally. Wimber, who was barely an adjunct, became the most prominent member of Fuller's faculty.[14]

MC510's very existence was telling. The trajectory of this classically Reformed, historically cessationist seminary reflected the broader pentecostalization of evangelicalism. By 1982, a startlingly high 44 percent of Fuller theology students said they considered themselves "a Pentecostal or charismatic Christian." Forty-three percent said they had spoken in tongues. MC510 also pointed to the globalization of American evangelicalism. By the mid-1980s Fuller's 2,700 students—the second highest enrollment of any seminary in the United States—represented seventy nations. The School of Missions, to be expected, housed the most concentrated group of internationals and missionaries on campus. Many of them, for whom the supernatural was just as real as the natural world, had been converted through "power encounters" with angels and demons. These foreign students and missiologists were the primary spark of Fuller's new preoccupation with the miraculous.[15]

Not everyone acclaimed this charismatic trajectory. Though young, the burgeoning seminary was symbolically important, having received the imprimatur of Billy Graham, Carl Henry, Harold Ockenga, Charles Fuller, and other evangelical luminaries in the 1950s. These men had positioned themselves theologically some distance from Pentecostalism. To be described as the "Lourdes of Pasadena" by the *Los Angeles Times* was difficult for the old guard to swallow. The School of Theology, a rival academic division at Fuller, still embraced a predominantly Presbyterian genealogy, utilized a methodology of rational apologetics, and assumed a cautionary and defensive posture toward the new emphasis. In fact, the divisive course was shut down in the mid-1980s by a new provost and the faculty senate. After a formal review and restructuring of the course, however, it returned a year later. MC510 was simply too popular, and Wagner's star was growing. At the forefront of a revived supernaturalism, Fuller was truly at home in the City of Angels.[16]

II. Exorcising the Ghost of Newton

In the decades that followed Lausanne, critics from the Global South turned the tables on the Congress's emphasis on contextualization. Billy Graham's North American associates intended to analyze the Majority World in order instruct unreached peoples with the salvation message of the Gospel. Latin Americans and Wagner, however, pushed back, using contextual strategies to reach the North with the fullness of the Gospel. As Samuel Escobar and Rene Padilla charged that Graham was missing justice elements of the Gospel, even more critics argued that the Global North was neglecting the Holy Spirit. One missionary, having lived in both the United States and Nigeria, agreed, wondering if his rationalistic sensibilities meant that he was "teaching with one hand behind [his] back." In their gloomiest moments, some even worried that they were colonizing enchanted villages in Africa with functional atheism. Among missiologists who had worked abroad, a different line of investigation developed. Instead of analyzing the "exotic Oriental," evangelical scholars began to pursue historical and anthropological inquiry of the Western Christian, whose rationalism suddenly seemed anomalous when viewed through the lens of world Christianity.[17]

American Christians, the new discourse suggested, were products of their own context. Filipino social anthropologist Melba Maggay contended that the West was "just as culture-bound" as the non-West. Fuller's Charles Kraft, also an anthropologist, explained that Americans had inherited a deistic, mechanistic view of the world from rationalists such as Isaac Newton, Jean Jacques Rousseau, and Thomas Jefferson. This worldview allowed for the possibility of the supernatural but functionally left God out of everyday life. Even American evangelicals, decidedly not deists, had been compromised by Western assumptions. Kraft located them in a nineteenth-century tradition of Scottish Common Sense philosophy that made them overly confident in their own ability to understand Scripture. He cautioned against epistemological realism, arguing that "we see reality not as it is but always inside our heads." Non-Western delegates to Lausanne argued similarly that Americans were unduly committed to nation-states, capitalism, autonomy, scientism, and other structures rooted in early modern Europe. In combining Enlightenment thought and Christianity, wrote Lesslie Newbigin, a missionary to India, American evangelicals were "just as syncretistic" as African Christian polygamists. They were puppets of their rationalistic worldview.[18]

Paul Hiebert, a former missionary in south central India, tried to show how contemporary Westerners bracketed out the supernatural. In an influential 1982 article in the journal *Missiology*, Hiebert described a man named Yellayya, who approached him for help one day. Smallpox had come to his Indian village several weeks earlier and had already killed many children. Doctors trained in Western medicine tried unsuccessfully to stop the disease, and so the village elders consulted with a diviner, who told them that Museum, the goddess of smallpox, was angry with the village. To satisfy the god, the village would have to perform the sacrifice of a water buffalo. As the elders collected money to pay for the buffalo, Christians refused to contribute. In retaliation, the elders forbade them from drawing water from the village wells, and merchants refused to sell them food. The situation was desperate, and Yellayya wanted the missionary to come with him to the town to pray for a miracle. But Hiebert was ambivalent. Though he had studied prayer in seminary, preached about the importance of prayer as a pastor, and read accounts of healings in the Bible, he felt uneasy about doing these things himself. He could not quite bring himself to pit his God against other gods.[19]

Hiebert's uneasiness compounded itself. "As a Westerner," he wrote, "I was used to presenting Christ on the basis on rational arguments, not by evidences of His power in the lives of people who were sick, possessed and destitute." He believed in the power of a high deity, but he also believed in mundane material processes described by Western science. In the article, entitled "The Flaw of the Excluded Middle," Hiebert sought to reconcile the two dimensions. He proposed a middle zone that had been ignored by Western missionaries afflicted by an epistemological blind spot. In this zone, the immaterial intervened in the material realm. "For me," he confessed, "the middle zone did not really exist. Unlike Indian villagers, I had given little thought to spirits of this world, to local ancestors and ghosts, or to the souls of animals. For me these belonged to the realm of fairies, trolls, and other mythical beings." As a Christian, he acknowledged, he should have recognized the excluded middle as the realm of angels, demons, and other real spirits. But the secularized mind of the West had hidden it from view. "It should be apparent why many missionaries trained in the West had no answers to the problems of the middle level," concluded Hiebert. "They often did not even see it."[20]

Hiebert's critique resonated. Other missiologists, Pentecostals, and American evangelical leaders cited his article exhaustively. If nothing else, it explained why Westerners plagued by the Enlightenment worldview were growing restless. David Shibley, director of missions for the charismatic Church on the Rock in Rockwell, Texas, explained that the explosion of Eastern religions and the occult in America proved that "our sterile technology has created a thirst for metaphysical experience." Disillusionment with "the impersonal, mechanistic system of scientism," Wagner echoed, "has resulted in appeals to higher, extra-human powers like the occult." Further, it suggested that a lack of spiritual power had caused the decline of the Western church. Kirk Bottomly, an associate pastor at a Presbyterian church in Thousand Oaks, California, delineated the problem in an article entitled "Confessions of an Evangelical Deist." Compared with China and Southeast Asia, where the "Spirit is moving in power" and thirty-five million people were baptized in a single year, American and European churches were in "free-fall." What could explain the "paralysis and exhaustion" of the West compared with the "astonishing growth" and "vitality" of the East? Bottomly's answer: ministries of healing and deliverance that demonstrated the "power of the gospel over rival religions." A professor from China interviewing for a job at an American seminary concurred. He affirmed the institution's faith statement, but only with the following lukewarm endorsement: "It may be adequate for a Western seminary, but not for an Asian institution." He objected that the statement did not emphasize angels, demons, and Satan. An unsatisfying scientism was excluding the supernatural.[21]

In short, global encounters seemed to expose mainstream American Christians as functional atheists who were inadvertently infecting the Majority World with rationalism. Given the evangelical war against secular humanism in the 1980s, Hiebert reveled in the delicious irony of this argument. He contended that the threat is not just " 'out there.' It has infiltrated our churches, bible schools, and seminaries." Even worse, these missiologists worried, missionary work may have corrupted the spiritual vitality of the Majority World. Recalling his "powerless" mission work in Nigeria, Kraft wrote, "Western techniques were our first choice, God was our last resort. Without meaning to, we taught our African converts that the Christian God works only through Western cultural ways." In many cases, converts simply went back to their old animistic practices because Christianity seemed to have no spiritual power. In some cases, converts practiced a syncretism that Melba Maggay called "a sandwich religion, a layer of Christian beliefs piled on top of a largely pagan slice of bread." In other cases, African converts practiced a submerged supernaturalism that remained out of sight until the Westerners left. In still other cases, Majority World leaders who came to American seminaries were persuaded by cessationism. MC510, then, was an attempt to reverse missionary rationalism. It sought to learn from international students and to prepare "typical Western, American-oriented students" for the mission field. Wagner could only hope that it would be an effective antidote to generations of Western missionaries who tragically had been "one of the greatest secularizing forces in history."[22]

There were limits to Fuller Seminary's critique of Western culture. Its missiologists enjoyed sophisticated medical care at Los Angeles-area hospitals. They also scientifically tracked potential miracles. Wagner, for example, provided a report form to everyone he prayed for over a five-year period. He asked them to wait two weeks, and then return the forms in a self-addressed, stamped envelope. The compiled results: 17–29 percent reported no healing, 22–44 percent were completely healed, and those in the middle received partial healing. These encouraging statistics, decided Wagner, were the best way to win over skeptical colleagues—and perhaps to assuage his own intermittent doubts. Those doubts, however, seemed to fade over time as Fuller's missiologists became increasingly convinced that Western culture had corrupted the gospel. They had so thoroughly contextualized themselves that it became "a personal insult to infer that someone's interpretation of the Bible is influenced by the Enlightenment," as Wagner memorably put it. These evangelical missiologists sought to exorcise the ghost of Newton.[23]

III. An Enchanted Global South

The enchantment of the Global South, in contrast to the West's arid rationalism, appeared strikingly hopeful to evangelical boosters. A vast literature of miracle narratives, suggesting that God was dramatically working salvation abroad, circulated in the United States. This, combined with the postcolonial mood of the late twentieth century, indicated that Americans had much to learn from wonderworking Latin Americans. The social transformation of Almolonga was just one of thousands of miracles that inspired Christians in America to beseech God for similar favor.

As they had for decades, miracle narratives flourished most in Pentecostal circles. They filled the testimonies of missionaries home on furlough, and they populated the pages of magazines such as *Pentecostal Evangel, Global Conquest, Good News Crusade*, and *Charisma*. From 1990 to 1997 many miracles were featured in a monthly "Ministry in the Supernatural" section in *Mountain Movers* magazine. In one representative story, Marino Shed, called "the crazy man" of Pohnpei Island in Papua New Guinea, walked around the island muttering in unintelligible grunts. At home Marino, who had fried his brain with LSD as a youth, chased his family with knives and ran about naked. Steve and Irome Malakai, associate pastors of Kolonia Assembly of God, reached out to Marino. They prayed for him, spent time with him, and finally determined to cast out the evil spirits they had identified in him. As the exorcism began, Marino miraculously began to speak. "Satan has made me like I am," he said. But "many things are going out of me." Within a week, they claimed, a legion of spirits had left, and Marino was freed of Satan's power. He began to read the Bible and attend church. Children who had once hid from him became his friends. A loving community, the report read, "marvels at the change." In fact, the healing sparked a revival, and a new church building needed to be built on the island to accommodate all the new converts. This miracle narrative characterized dozens of other "Ministry in the Supernatural" features, most of which followed a script of deliverance from evil leading to personal conversion and then a larger revival. They included miraculous rescues from Shining Path terrorists in Peru, a healed colon in China, and liberation from poverty and alcoholism in the Philippines.[24]

Miracle narratives also circulated through broader evangelical networks. In his book *The Untold Korea Story*, Bob Pierce described the power of prayer on a boy whose disabled right foot and arm were instantly healed. "You don't believe it?" Pierce rhetorically—and defensively—asked his readers. "Then . . . I am a liar," he answered, "for manifestations of this kind happened again and again." World Vision president Stanley Mooneyham, critiquing "widespread materialism and spiritual dryness" in the West, described the intensity and frequency of supernatural phenomena in the non-West to Christian Medical Society delegates at a 1975 symposium on demonology. Billy Graham told several international miracle stories, most of them from China, where his wife had been raised in a missionary family. One involved an angel saving a woman and her two young children from a tiger attack. Dramatic narratives came even from Reformed circles. Paul Long, a Presbyterian missionary to the Baluba people in Congo, described demonic power at a spirit mound. "When I stood to speak, I felt the oppressive presence and power of overwhelming evil. The utter darkness was suffocating me. I felt the cold fingers of death press around my throat and I could not speak. As I stood there in foolish helplessness, the medicine people laughed; it sounded like voices from hell." Long, who became a professor of missions at the Reformed Theological Seminary in Jackson, Mississippi, represented tens of thousands of missionaries who returned home telling supernatural tales.[25]

Signs and wonders often were linked to the missionary cause. Many observed that the world's three largest congregations in the early 1980s were all located outside the North and West. Congregação Cristã in São Paulo, Brazil, boasted 61,000 members. Jotabeche Church in Santiago, Chile, had 80,000. David Yonggi Cho's Yoido Full Gospel Church in Seoul, Korea, dwarfed them all at 200,000, up from 10,000 in 1972. Significantly, each of them was led by miracle-wielding Pentecostals. The Christian West, wrote David Shibley in *A Force in the Earth: The Move of the Holy Spirit in World Evangelization* (1997), was "becoming the minority," largely because it lacked the "supernatural orientation" of the East. Respected Christian demographer David Barrett confirmed this analysis, suggesting that 80 percent of global conversions could be linked to "charismatic witness."[26]

Cho's church was exemplary. By the mid-1980s Yoido Full Gospel, located just blocks from Korea's Parliament, had tripled in size to over 600,000 members. It was, as one champion proclaimed, "the largest church in the history of Christendom." American Pentecostals, many of whom took pilgrimages to Korea to see the explosive growth for themselves, credited Cho's practices of prayer and spiritual warfare. In fact, its founding myth was rooted in exorcism. When the church began, Cho recounted, very few came because of a "great demonic oppression over the village." But after months of prayer and Cho's casting out of a demon from a paralyzed woman, the church grew rapidly. "The sky above the village was broken open, and the blessings of God began pouring down," he remembered. Having built the world's largest church, the *Los Angeles Times* noted, the forty-five-year-old Korean pastor was "looking for new worlds to conquer." His taped sermons began airing on broadcast television at prime time on Saturday evenings in Los Angeles and New York City and on over 3,400 cable systems across the country. In just two months' time, he received over 1,200 letters from Americans, and Cho went on to function as a church growth expert and an important apostle of the Third Wave, also known as the signs-and-wonders movement, in the 1980s. He also represented a much larger groundswell of global leaders that included Ed Silvosa, Omar Cabrera, and Claudio Freidzon of Argentina; Myles Munroe of the Bahamas; and Richmond Chiundiza of Zimbabwe. These figures—some celebrities, some influential in smaller evangelical networks—made regular trips to the United States, appeared often in American print media, and were revered by American Pentecostals for their evangelistic successes and spectacular displays of "power encounters."[27]

Against critics who accused them of heresy, Pentecostals observed that charismatic practices were rooted in Scripture itself. John Dawson, director of Youth With a Mission (YWAM), identified "unseen spirits" around Jericho and Ai. The marches around city walls, he said, were spiritual maneuvers as much as military actions. Third Wavers found a similarly enchanted world in the New Testament. They cited Jesus's casting out of demons, Paul's battles with the "beasts of Ephesus," and encounters with spiritual mediums in Philippi. Scripture revealed an immanent God, not a clockmaker. In the ultimate evangelical rebuke, Charles Kraft wrote, "We may criticize liberals for leaving out certain sections of the Scriptures, but we evangelicals do the same thing when it comes to issues of spiritual power." Pentecostals proclaimed that God provides—and not just in an abstract sense. Church growth, miracles, provision in the face of poverty, and protection in the midst of violence, they said, proved the truths of Scripture.[28]

Defenders of signs and wonders extended the historical claims of Scripture. They pointed out that cessationists willfully ignored supernatural elements of postapostolic Christian history. MC510, Fuller Seminary's course on miracles and church growth, surveyed the supernatural convictions and exploits of Tertullian, Irenaeus, Martin of Tours, and Antony of the Desert. Citing historians Ramsay MacMullen and Peter Brown, Wagner and Wimber argued that people in the Roman Empire experienced divine power with "a terrifying, high-voltage quality that split and blinded." The supernatural power of God "driving all competition from the field," they wrote, should be seen as "the chief instrument of conversion in those first centuries." They also identified thousands of Catholic and Protestant miracle narratives through the Middle Ages and Reformation, the holiness movement of the nineteenth century, and turn-of-the-century Pentecostalism.[29]

In addition to usable history, many missiologists also attached the concept of indigeneity to supernaturalism. A global ethos of decolonization, the contextual spirit of 1970s Lausanne, and the indigenizing spirit of early 1980s World Vision demanded that the supernatural commitments of the Majority World be taken seriously. At Lausanne, for example, Rubén Lores asked delegates, "Are we by some stretch of the imagination agencies of a commercial enterprise directed from New York or Geneva? Let us allow the Holy Spirit to be truly Lord because the Lord is that Spirit." Taking Africans seriously meant taking demons and angels seriously. Every successful exorcism was a declaration of independence from the medicines of the imperial West. Every power encounter made Christianity intelligible in a continent already bathed in mysterious spirits and attuned to biblical concepts of blood sacrifice and atonement. Pentecostalism in Africa achieved such astonishing results, according to the new missiologists, because it minimized Western methods and mediating institutions like denominations. "This was not a diaspora of liberal resource persons," writes sociologist David Martin. Instead, it "generated an autonomous lay culture" empowered by the Holy Spirit. Indigeneity allowed ordinary people experiencing the anxieties of modernity to also experience God's power over their troubles.[30]

In some places, this stress on God's power evolved into a focus on material prosperity. The attraction of a transnational "health and wealth" movement to peoples devastated by political and economic crises was clear. In return for generous contributions, charismatic preachers offered hope and good things in this life, not only the afterlife. Critics, however, have charged superstar pastors in Asia, Africa, and Latin America with peddling a crass prosperity gospel that goes well beyond the amelioration of endemic poverty, hunger, and structural injustice. Historian Brian Stanley describes the movement as practicing "a form of religious materialism that subordinates the cross to a crude theology of divine blessing reduced to the promise of unlimited health and wealth here and now." This "incautious Pentecostal exegesis," as Nigerian scholar Ogbu Kalu puts it, places an unrelenting focus on money, numbers, and growth that makes prosperity preacher Benny Hinn look like a staid Puritan. Many of these preachers practice a personality-driven, authoritarian style that seeks to accumulate influence through burgeoning media empires. According to Kalu, "The preacher and television star become inseparable as the big man of the big God." The prosperity movement, which has registered the highest rate of growth of any Christian tradition in the last fifty years, attracts followers precisely because of its power and success.[31]

Spiritual mapping, a related phenomenon that emerged in the 1980s and 1990s, also flourished in the Majority World. Practitioners identified specific spirits that inhabited—and spiritually controlled—specific places. George Otis, Jr., described his clash with the local shaman Rigoberto Iztep and a host of territorial spirits among traditionalist Maya in Pachalum, a small town in the Guatemalan highlands. The wild climax, according to Otis, irrefutably demonstrated the material consequences of immaterial spiritual warfare:

> Pivoting to the cardinal directions, Iztep and the worshipers, some of whom were fully entranced, called forth spiritual legions to receive their oblation. As Paklom was transformed into a spiritual vortex, the arrival of unseen spirits became palpable. Suddenly, as if on cue, a pack of wild, snarling dogs appeared on the opposite side of the hill. I knew instantly why they had come. Still, watching them make a beeline for the sleeping infant sparked deep indignation. Striding toward the vicious dogs, several of whom were already tugging at the little bundle in the hay, I rebuked the controlling spirits. The effect was dramatic. In a split second the deadly spell was shattered and the snarling pack was transformed into a benign gaggle of wagging tails. Interrupted by divine power, the perverse passion play came to an abrupt halt. The child's mother, oblivious to the peril that had brushed up against her, shook off her trance and disappeared with her baby into the night.

Otis, a former YWAM missionary dubbed by Wagner as "our number one Christian espionage agent," chronicled this electrifying experience—and hundreds of others—in *The Twilight Labyrinth*, a book that became the bible of the new spiritual warfare movement.[32]

Twilight Labyrinth drew from over 35,000 pages of documentary material from nearly fifty countries on the protocols of the spiritual dimension. This deep dive into the elaborate hierarchies of incorporeal spirits that purported to rule over homes, cities, valley, and nations produced a disquieting portrait of a world "riddled with haunted drums, levitating monks, cursing owls, serpent marriages and mountain spirits" that exercised "extraordinary power over local peoples." These "tenancy rights," according to Otis, needed to be broken through an almost-technocratic application of prayer, exorcisms, and "authority transfers." Among his plethora of examples was the spirit of Maximón, who resided in Almolonga, Guatemala. Maximón, they learned from local Christians, was not a harmless mannequin. It was a spirit in cahoots with a pantheon of Mayan gods linked to the town by centuries-old spiritual pacts. Maximón had compacted with the pantheon to determine "sexual matters, treachery, and illicit schemes." For real revival to occur, power encounters had to "sever the spiritual continuum." By 1990, 400 exorcisms, thousands of conversions, and a sufficient amount of prayer had "transformed" the town, that is, delivered it from Maximón. *Twilight Labyrinth* was the first draft of the *Transformations* documentary released two years later.[33]

Scholars have emphasized the Americanness of spiritual mapping. Scholar René Holvast argues that "Plan Resistencia," a late-1980s attempt to defeat forces of evil in Argentina, was a laboratory for American practitioners. Participants themselves, however, have not concurred. Otis contended that "the most significant support for this philosophy in recent years has come from the spiritual marketplaces of the Third World." Almolongueños like Pastor Riscajche practiced spiritual mapping and authored many of the early drafts of these miracle narratives, and many Pentecostals in Latin America such as Omar Cabrera of Argentina and Harold Caballeros of Guatemala developed mapping theory as leaders in the Spiritual Warfare Network. According to this counternarrative, Otis and Wagner did not invent spiritual mapping. They were relaying the beliefs of Majority World evangelicals as much as imposing beliefs on them. As Everett Wilson, who has sought to decenter Pentecostalism from the myth of Azusa Street origins, put it: "Pentecostalism presently is not what Charles Fox Parham or any of his successors has pronounced it to be, but rather what contemporary Brazilians, Korean and Africans demonstrate that it actually is." Considerable evidence from around the world suggests that spiritual mapping was not merely a new iteration of Manifest Destiny.[34]

In fact, global encounters profoundly shaped American evangelicalism. Pentecostals from abroad, imagining Jesus as a spiritual warrior, benefited enormously from the democratization of tongues. This indigenized spirituality gave the Majority World authority to speak back to the West. The genealogy of the Toronto Blessing, an explosive revival that began at the Toronto Airport Vineyard church in 1994, traced to Argentina, Brazil, and Guatemala. Randy Clark's Global Awakening organization had roots in Colombia and Brazil, and his training materials on exorcism were taken directly from the Argentinian evangelist Pablo Bottari. Otis, like these and many other spiritual mappers, had extensive international experience and felt inspired by a lush spirituality in the Global South. Less than a century after Azusa Street, the Pentecostal diaspora had reversed.[35]

IV. An Ascending Supernaturalism

A revived supernaturalism spread far beyond Pentecostal circles. Traveling through far-flung global networks, spiritual enchantment touched mainstream evangelical, Reformed, Anabaptist, Anglican, and Catholic spaces. Contact with the Majority World forced American Christians to face the supernatural in ways that were both uncomfortable and inspiring—and sometimes transforming.

The rippling effects of global supernaturalism could be seen most clearly in the Lausanne movement. Known for its debate about social justice and methods of evangelism, the first Congress also demonstrated a subterranean concern for the Holy Spirit. Delegate registrations, which solicited topics of interest, in fact overwhelmingly emphasized the Holy Spirit. In typical responses, Robert Don Karthak of Kathmandu, Nepal, requested discussion about "the vital, dynamic role of the Holy Spirit," and Samuel Libert of Argentina urged planners to emphasize the "outpouring of the Holy Spirit." "I believe that our Lord," he wrote, "never intended to confine the outpouring of the Spirit to one historic day. . . . There must be a supernatural demonstration of God's power." Despite the interest, however, very few supernatural topics were incorporated into the Congress itself. While Article 12 of the Covenant spoke of "principalities" and "powers of evil," public talks, devotionals, and strategy papers ignored the topic. The supernatural remained only an undercurrent.[36]

Fifteen years later, in 1989, Lausanne II exhibited a newly ascendant supernaturalism. Underreported by journalists at the time and understudied by scholars since, this narrative has been obscured by the continuing fracas over social justice. But Majority World representatives, who by the 1980s comprised a substantial bloc of the Lausanne planning committee, also pushed for the inclusion of prayer, spiritual warfare, and the Holy Spirit as key topics of discussion. They were aided by North American Pentecostals, such as Thomas Zimmerman of the Assemblies of God; individuals in the Fuller–World Vision nexus like Ed Dayton and C. Peter Wagner, who had served on the planning committee since the mid-1970s; and Third Wavers like Otis and Dawson. Lausanne II's program, which suggested that Manila would be a site of intense spiritual warfare, worried the old guard. Some, according to one reporter, were concerned that "the Pentecostals were about to hijack the Lausanne Movement and evangelicalism in general." When news broke that Billy Graham would not be attending, rumors spread through the Philippine International Convention Center that advisors had convinced the evangelist that charismatics had taken over.[37]

Indeed, the difference between Switzerland and the Philippines was striking. If Lausanne I, in the heart of Europe reflected a sterile, rational context of mechanistic evangelism, Lausanne II reflected the enchanted ethos of its location in the Far East. Nearly half of delegates claimed "some kind of charismatic orientation," and more than half of the 3,600 delegates came from the Majority World to an event that *Christianity Today* called a "global camp meeting." During plenary sessions, about half the delegates raised their hands while singing, an expression of worship that was nearly absent in Switzerland (Figure 6.4). Plenary

Figure 6.4. Lausanne II in the Philippines featured a much more exuberant worship style than Lausanne I in Switzerland. Courtesy of the Billy Graham Center Archives, Wheaton, Ill.

sermons were delivered by Korean Pentecostal David Yonggi Cho and American Pentecostal Jack Hayford, who urged delegates to open themselves "to the manifestation of miraculous signs and wonders." In the afternoons, when delegates could choose among forty elective tracks, the three most popular dealt with the Holy Spirit, spiritual warfare, and prayer. Each of them, especially the Holy Spirit Track, which drew 3,200 delegates from seventy countries, featured high levels of Majority World leadership and participation. At a nearby off-site location, Wagner gathered fifty intercessors—about half charismatics and half traditional evangelicals—who prayed twenty-four hours a day during the ten-day gathering. "It was the nearest thing to a spiritual nuclear power plant we had ever seen," said Wagner. As the Congress closed, it released a "Manila Manifesto" that contained much stronger language on supernaturalism than the Lausanne Covenant had. The new accent was so pronounced that some Americans complained that Lausanne had indeed "gone charismatic."[38]

Hoping to capitalize on the spiritually supercharged Manila congress, Third Wavers launched the Spiritual Warfare Network (SWN). With large and loud events that that featured an intense internationalism, organizers intended SWN to become a "new wineskin" of Lausanne that could move evangelicals to "a higher-level kind of spiritual warfare" as the new millennium approached.

Hoping to draw on the Pentecostal successes of African Independent Churches (AIC), Chinese house churches, and burgeoning Latin American congregations, they located most events outside North America. One representative gathering, attended by 2,500 global leaders, was held in Guatemala City in 1990. Other major summits—including an "International Spiritual Warfare Consultation" in Korea in 1993 that featured Sundo Kim, the pastor of the biggest Methodist church in the world—were held in Singapore, Nigeria, and Uganda. SWN, in calculated outreach to evangelicals in the United States, also created an enormous oeuvre of literature.[39]

Most American evangelicals did not become hardcore spiritual mappers or adherents of the prosperity gospel. Many, however, did become more sensitized to spiritual realities through popular media. Billy Graham's *Angels: God's Secret Agents* (1975) sold millions of copies, and the mid-twentieth-century American discovery of C. S. Lewis led to millions reading *Miracles* (1947) and *Screwtape Letters* (1943), which featured a senior demon instructing his demon nephew on how to corrupt human souls. Many of the most compelling accounts came from outside the United States. Bob Pierce's film *A Cry in the Night* (1958), for example, featured what it said was "an actual view of demon possession" on the island of Bali. In the popular book *The Cross and the Switchblade* (1962), Nicky Cruz, a converted gangster, described his Puerto Rican childhood as the son of a satanic priest and priestess. "Satan must be unmasked," Cruz explained. "He is not a harmless caricature or a myth left over from humanity's primitive past." In numerous books and countless speaking engagements, Cruz fired salvos at a rationalistic church culture increasingly "ignorant" and "apathetic" toward Satan's threats. He and many others rode a new wave of charismatic programming on radio and television in the 1980s.[40]

Signs and wonders even penetrated the unlikeliest of evangelical circles. Thomas White, a conservative Baptist, founded Frontline Ministries after sensing satanic oppression in the jungles of Colombia. Dallas Theological Seminary, a cessationist school, fired biblical scholar Jack Deere in 1987 after he refused to renounce newly found charismatic beliefs. He became Vineyard's "international minister" and wrote a book called *Surprised by the Power of the Spirit* (1993). Chuck Swindoll, who became president of Dallas six years after Deere left, wrote a pamphlet entitled "Demonism" in which he confessed that after years of skepticism, he was "now convinced" that a Christian could be possessed. *Christianity Today* editor Harold Lindsell, who experienced a miracle that reminded him of the Book of Acts, explained that he now believed that "New Testament power is available to Christians today." In the early 1980s, Campus Crusade for Christ formally lifted its ban on tongues-speaking by staffers. The supernatural turn shaped even progressive evangelicals, many of whom had previously viewed Pentecostalism as an opiate that distracted adherents from addressing true social inequalities. In a fascinating synthesis of supernaturalism and leftist critiques of technocratic liberalism, theologian Walter Wink spoke of expelling demons and principalities from political, economic, and cultural structures.[41]

By the 2000s American Pentecostalism and its influence had reached dizzying heights. Scorching revivals in Toronto and Brownsville, Florida, spread to congregations across the nation. Missionary Heidi Baker's miracle narratives from Mozambique enjoyed a broad hearing. Cindy Jacobs, a spiritual mapping guru, became a key leader in Women's Aglow, a network of home groups that met for prayer and mutual support. John Dawson's Youth With a Mission became an important site for young evangelicals to learn techniques of spiritual warfare. Wagner continued to straddle Pentecostal and more mainstream evangelical worlds at Fuller before moving to Colorado Springs to team up with George Otis and Ted Haggard, the popular pastor of New Life Church. The high-tech World Prayer Center, funded largely from Asia and constructed on Haggard's campus in the early 2000s to function as a "Pentagon for Spiritual Warfare," became an "electronic nerve center to connect the intercessors and let each other know what they're hearing from the Holy Spirit." This collaboration produced the *Transformations* videos, which, according to its promoters, reached nearly fifty million viewers in 150 nations. As if to ratify the supernatural trajectory, Haggard was appointed president of the National Association of Evangelicals in 2003.[42]

The pentecostalization of American religion was not limited to evangelicals. Just sixteen miles from Azusa Street in Los Angeles, St. Mark's Episcopal Church launched a charismatic renewal movement in mainline circles that rose, according to journalist John Dart, "to an exhilarating peak" in the late 1970s. In the 1980s Stanley Hauerwas and William Willimon published an article in the *Christian Century* entitled "Embarrassed by God's Presence." They accused mainliners of "conducting business as if God does not exist" and challenged them to consider the works of an active Holy Spirit. In the early 2000s theologian Jürgen Moltmann offered shocking testimony at Yoido Full Gospel Church, declaring that he had been healed "under the ministry of Cho's charismatic gospel." A renewal movement also emerged within American Catholicism. Priest Tom Forrest pointed out that "if we are going to evangelize effectively, we must 'seek and expect signs and wonders.'" Jorge Bergoglio, the "bishop of the slums" in Buenos Aires, endorsed the movement in the 1990s. Elected Pope in 2013, he emphasized the existence of angels, blessed the International Association of Exorcists, and became the first pope ever to visit a Pentecostal church. Connecting many of these networks was David Du Plessis, a South African evangelist known as "Mr. Pentecost," who moved easily between evangelical, mainline, and Catholic worlds.[43]

The Pentecostal surge, most vibrant in the Majority World, profoundly shaped the American religious landscape. In 1928, the World Christian Fundamentals Association rejected Pentecostals as "fanatical" and "unscriptural." In 1942, the

National Association of Evangelicals grudgingly invited them to join. By 1999, when *Transformations* was released, Pentecostals were being embraced. To be sure, the transformation was not universal. Heirs of the old-time cessationism continued to critique tongues, miracles, and signs and wonders. But there were far fewer of them, and powerful Pentecostal voices from Latin America, Africa, and Asia had taken their places. Supernatural enchantment was part of the globalized air that American evangelicals breathed.

In the late 1980s C. Peter Wagner's first visit to Almolonga nearly ended in disaster (Figure 6.5). As the airplane, piloted by Pentecostal pastor Harold Caballeros, approached, the landing gear did not descend. Filiberto Lemus, an expert spiritual mapper waiting on the runway, saw the impending disaster and began to pray. Maximón, he felt, was trying to kill the spiritual prophets as they entered the demon's domain. Wagner described the awful landing:

> As we crashed into the runway, the belly ripped open and bushels of earth poured around us in the cabin like a waterfall! When the frightening jolts ended, cracking wings and twisting propellers, the plane was still upright, and we walked out, dirty but unharmed. We praised God for His protection, and we had no doubt that, once again, intercession had ruined the plans of the enemy.

Figure 6.5. The Wagners and Harold Caballeros moments after their airplane crashed outside Almolonga. Courtesy of Doris Wagner.

In fact just a few hours later, after climbing out of the wreckage, Wagner saw the enemy face to face. In Zunil, a town only three kilometers away, he entered the spirit's shrine, which he described as "the threshold of hell itself." There he observed five warlocks and one witch conducting "the most revolting spiritual activity I ever want to see." Wagner then toured Almolonga itself, where Maximón had been expelled. In a country where 85 percent of citizens lived below the poverty line, revival had transformed the town into a haven of faith and prosperity. Almolongueños dominated every aspect of the regional market, and bustling shops featured marquees that read "Paradise Chicken" and "Little Israel Hardware."[44]

In the 1990s Almolonga took up residence in the Guatemalan imagination. When Caballeros, founder of the megachurch El Shaddai in Guatemala City, founded a Pentecostal political party called VIVA Guatemala in order to run for national office, he declared his candidacy from Almolonga. He said, "Today I announce my victorious campaign for the president of Guatemala. [I'm announcing] here in Almolonga because Almolonga is a symbol of prosperity, of progress, of work, of productivity. . . . I dream that one day all of Guatemala will be as productive as Almolonga." He lost, but Caballeros nonetheless represented a Pentecostal surge in a nation that was already the most evangelical in all Latin America. He also continued to invoke Almolonga as a model for the whole world. At the 2006 World Congress on Intercession, Spiritual Warfare, and Evangelism hosted by El Shaddai, representatives from twenty-four nations heard from Emanuele Cannistraci, a pastor who carried around an oversized carrot as a symbol of Almolonga's piety and prosperity. They browsed a table brimming with oversized carrots and tomatoes. Farmers in traditional Mayan *traje* dress explained that the vegetables had grown so large because Almolonga was "a chosen *pueblo*."[45]

The transnational irony of Almolonga is that it made its biggest impact on the nation that had made the "city on a hill" trope its own identity. Through the advocacy of Wagner, Otis, Wimber, and Cindy Jacobs, the United States became a ravenous consumer of the Almolonga narrative, especially after Otis transformed *Twilight Labyrinth* into the evocative scenes of *Transformations*. Sunday schools across the country screened the video. It was viewed on Pat Robertson's Christian Broadcasting Network and read about in the mission publication of the United Methodist Church, *Charisma* magazine, and countless websites. It inspired many American to participate in spiritual mapping, "prayer walking," and other forms of spiritual warfare. Almolonga seemed to demonstrate that attention to the supernatural could renovate social landscapes.[46]

As its legend grew, Almolonga became an evangelical Disneyland. Spiritual tourists traveled to the enchanted town to see for themselves how immaterial realms had transformed the material. In 2004 Carol Madison, a member of an

Evangelical Free congregation in Minnesota, visited the still-booming town market with three friends to "see with my own eyes what truly could happen if God's people . . . sought Him for transformation." It was her "heart cry," she said, to see social change back home. During her visit, Madison attended El Calvario, Almolonga's biggest Pentecostal church, where she met Pastor Riscajche. She visited the downtown market to see overflowing piles of cabbages the size of basketballs. From tribal women wearing the *huipil*, an embroidered Mayan blouse, she purchased the famous oversized carrots. After smuggling the carrots through U.S. customs on her way home, she could not bring herself to eat them, and they became an object lesson for her presentations at churches in the Twin Cities. She reported, "My carrots lasted in my refrigerator for 18 months!" Many other American evangelicals made similar pilgrimages, taking "Transformations Tours" marketed to show that Maximón truly had been expelled from Almolonga. Madison called it a "backwards missions trip." "We really had nothing to offer them," she explained. "They were the ones to teach us. We in the American church have so much to learn from those who have humbly sought the Lord and experienced His healing."[47]

There are also narratives about Almolonga that do not involve spiritual lessons. While nearly all observers agree that the town has improved, if not "healed," in the last three decades, many do not attribute the improvement to revival. In the 1980s the nation finally recovered from a devastating 1976 earthquake, and the government built a paved road that linked Almolonga to markets in El Salvador and to Quetzaltenango, an economic hub in the western region of Guatemala. In the 1990s a thirty-six-year civil war that inflicted crop destruction, killings, disappearing populations, and political violence came to an end. Better seeds from Europe and North America arrived as farmers transitioned from subsistence farming to the commercial production of vegetables, fruits, and flowers. The soil, hydrated by plentiful water in the basin of an ancient volcano, was so fertile that Almolonga really could grow carrots three times the size of those in other areas.[48]

Another set of analysts also rejects the spiritual warfare explanation, even as it credits religion with the transformation. Evangelical conversion—estimates ranged from 40 percent to 95 percent—jumped significantly in the 1970s and 1980s. So did prosperity. By the early 2000s, farmers in Almolonga earned $170 a month compared with those in neighboring towns who earned only $70 a month. The three leading causes of death in neighboring villages were alcoholism, intoxication, and senility. These became so uncommon in Almolonga that they were dropped as diagnostic categories. The difference, argues scholar Amy Sherman, lies not in the expulsion of Maximón, but in the maturation of industrious citizens. "Conversion from animism to biblical Christianity," she writes, "has strengthened individual initiative, promoted the status of women, revitalized the family structure, and encouraged democracy." Two thirds of evangelicals in Almolonga reported that they became owners of their own businesses after their conversion to Protestantism. As sociologist Peter Berger put it, "Max Weber is alive and well, and living in Guatemala." What Pentecostals called the defeat of Maximón was actually, these analysts claim, the flowering of the Protestant work ethic.[49]

Still other observers offer a sharp critique. Candy Gunther Brown, contending that Almolonga's entry into the global free market may "reinforce rather than resist the problematic aspects of globalization," points out that Almolonga's booming economy does not benefit all sectors of society. Guatemalan evangelicals have been trained into an efficient workforce, but they are unwilling to challenge the social inequalities embedded in unregulated capitalism. While they have begun to use a vocabulary of social justice, or "transformation," to ratchet up their salutary involvement in mercy ministries and to participate in electoral politics at much higher levels than in previous generations, Guatemalan Pentecostals have failed to confront structural imbalances. Discounting historical factors like neocolonialism, the civil war, gang violence, rapid urbanization, and a failing infrastructure, they instead campaign for candidates with similar theological views who also believe that cumulative spiritual conversions, less alcoholism, and less adultery will produce social transformation. Almolonga, explains one such believer, "is a testimony to Jesus' ability to change an entire city from the inside out."[50]

Evangelical candidates and initiatives, however, have not fared well. Efraín Ríos Montt, a longtime lay pastor in the Pentecostal Verbo church who became president of Guatemala after a military coup in 1982, presided over the military's murder of dozens of priests, nuns, and Catholic leaders. Anthropologist Kevin O'Neill calls Ríos Montt "the architect of Guatemala's genocide." Jorge Serrano Elías, an elder at El Shaddai Church elected president in 1991 after the church fanned out to strategic "cardinal points" across the nation to "clear the way" of "strongmen" who led Serrano in the polls, was exiled to Panama in disgrace. He had illegally suspended the Constitution, imposed censorship, and dissolved Congress and the Supreme Court. Evangelicals have remained silent about the violence inflicted by their own. Pentecostal participation in politics, according to scholar Maren Christensen Bjune, has not transformed politics as much as preserved the status quo.[51]

For Almolongueños themselves, these sociopolitical critiques feel less immediate than the environmental consequences of their new prosperity. In 1996 researchers found evidence of excessive chemical applications intended to keep crops free of pests and blemishes. These pesticides, purchased from European and American agribusinesses, were applied too frequently and at much higher-than-suggested doses, even without evidence of infestations. Moreover, pesticide containers were routinely rinsed in the irrigation canals, exposing laborers to high concentrations of chemicals. Citing these environmental hazards, the United States has refused to import produce from Almolonga for decades. While malnutrition, the predominant cause of death and sickness among children in the 1970s, has decreased, there have come other health risks. In the 1990s the new leading causes of death in the town were bronchopneumonia, stillbirth, and cancer. Congenital malformations also became common. Researchers blame the extremely toxic organochlorine insecticide Gamexan and a variety of chemical fertilizers.[52]

These rational analyses of Almolonga's prosperity reflect the persistent terms of the debate. Not all North Americans have been enchanted by stories of healing and narratives of transformation emanating from the South. Los Angeles pastor John MacArthur, for example, described the practice of Pentecostal signs and wonders as "fanciful, not biblical" and criticized the "virtual pandemonium" of charismatic worship. But Pastor Riscajche—along with nearly half a billion other Pentecostals, who represent perhaps the most important religious shift of the last century—flatly rejects these critiques. "Our growth has not come because of fanaticism or ignorance," he explains. "We have had supernatural experiences."[53]

Understood by global Pentecostals and their American allies as indigenous, these supernatural experiences, ironically, have sometimes sabotaged indigeneity. Caballeros, for example, held an exorcism in which he sought to expel Mayan spirits from strategic zones around the city. At one, he killed an actual snake that stared at him with hate from an aqueduct that linked ancient Mayan ruins in the shape of a "serpent" called Quetzalcoatl. The exorcism, he said, eliminated resistance to his plans to expand El Shaddai on that site. On one hand, such activities seek to eradicate the nation's own heritage by blaming Mayan culture for negative, superstitious, and violent characteristics of Guatemalan culture. In this sense, the Majority World does not always push in local, indigenous directions. On the other hand, notes scholar Virginia Garrard-Burnett, spiritual warfare is often led not by North Americans, but by local Mayan pastors who wear traditional *traje* clothing and use the Ki'che language in their churches. In fact, many Almolongueños refuse to answer questions about the use of chemical fertilizers. They hesitate to undermine the interpretation of Almolonga as a miracle. Because spiritual warfare is to them a fiercely indigenous instinct, they own the narrative.

So do many evangelicals from the United States, who often take cues from sensational supernatural activities in Latin America, Africa, and Asia. Even those who do not practice hard-core spiritual mapping have leaned into the argument that prayer has material consequences. They believe that there is a spirit world populated by angels and demons warring over poverty, substance abuse, domestic violence, and the soul of every human being. Global encounters have demanded a North American reckoning with the supernatural.

Notes

1. Wimber, "Zip to 3,000 in 5 Years," *Christian Life* 44, no. 6 (October 1982): 22.

2. George Otis, *Transformations: A Documentary* (Lynnwood, Wash.: Sentinel Group, 1999); Otis, *The Twilight Labyrinth: Why Does Spiritual Darkness Linger Where It Does?* (Grand Rapids, Mich.: Chosen Books, 1997), 309.

3. For "the role of supernatural power," see C. Peter Wagner, *The Third Wave of the Holy Spirit: Encountering the Power of Signs and Wonders* (Ann Arbor, Mich.: Vine Books, 1988), 122.

4. For "the poor opted for Pentecostalism," see Simon Chan, *Grassroots Asian Theology: Thinking the Faith from the Ground Up* (Downers Grove, Ill.: InterVarsity Press, 2014), 27. For "focused intercessory prayer," see Otis, *Twilight Labyrinth*, 309.

5. On Wagner's move into the neo-evangelical orbit, see C. Peter Wagner, *Wrestling with Alligators, Prophets and Theologians* (Ventura, Cal.: Regal Books, 2010), 29–42, 56, 63, 73, 114–16.

6. For "if it be your will," see Wagner, *Third Wave*, 20–22. For "chief adversaries," see Wagner, *Signs and Wonders Today* (Altamonte Springs, Fla.: Creation House, 1987), 43.

7. Wagner, *Wrestling with Alligators*, 115–19; Wagner, *Your Spiritual Gifts* (Ventura, Cal.: Regal Books, 1979), 240; Wagner, *Signs and Wonders Today*, 42–43; Wagner, "MC510: Signs, Wonders, and Church Growth," *Christian Life*, October 1982, 42.

8. On his visit to Santiago, Chile, see Wagner, *Wrestling with Alligators*, 120–21. For "normal part," see Wagner, *Signs and Wonders Today*, 43.

9. Wagner, *Your Church Can Grow* (Ventura, Calif.: Regal Books, 1984), 38, 41, 45; Donald McGavran, *Understanding Church Growth* (Grand Rapids, Mich.: Eerdmans, 1970). For comparative statistics on church growth, see C. Peter Wagner, *The Protestant Movement in Bolivia* (Pasadena, Calif.: William Carey Library, 1970), xvii–xix, 188–91. For "cold facts," see Wagner, *Frontiers in Missionary Strategy* (Chicago: Moody Press, 1971), 143.

10. Wagner, *Look Out! The Pentecostals Are Coming* (Carol Stream, Ill.: Creation House, 1973), 13–4, 39, 93, 102, 106, 134, 170.

11. Wagner, *What Are We Missing?* (Carol Stream, Ill.: Creation House, 1978). For "freely operating," see Wagner, *Your Spiritual Gifts*, 14–15. On Wagner's increasing reach among evangelical leaders, see Wagner, *Your Spiritual Gifts*, 15, 23; Wagner, *Wrestling with Alligators*, 100–104.

12. Wagner, *Wrestling with Alligators*, 40, 121–28. For "pray for the sick and cast out demons," see Wagner, *On the Crest of the Wave: Becoming a World Christian* (Ventura, Calif.: Regal Books, 1983), 131. For more on the overseas experiences of Fuller's faculty, see Karen Ball, "An Evaluation by Theologians," *Christian Life*, October 1982, 64–69.

13. Wagner, *Wrestling with Alligators*, 122–31; Karen Ball, "The Students' View," *Christian Life*, 70.

14. "Yes, You Can Learn to Pray for the Sick!" *Christian Life*, October 1982; McGavran, "The Total Picture," 39–40; Ball, "Around the World," 50–63; Robert Walker, "From the Editor," 10. For "looking East for a faith," see Wimber, "Zip to 3,000 in Five Years,"

22. For "such was the demand," see Eddie Gibbs, "My Friend, John Wimber," 150–51, in C. Peter Wagner, *Signs & Wonders Today: The Story of Fuller Theological Seminary's Remarkable Course on Spiritual Power* (Altamonte Springs, Fla.: Creation House, 1987). For "straight-line evangelicals," see Wagner, "MC510," *Christian Life*, 44. On the response to the special issue, see "Readers Write," *Christian Life*, December 1982, 12. On the course's rising enrollment, see Wagner, *Crest of the Wave*, 132.

15. On the demographics of Fuller, see George Marsden, *Reforming Fundamentalism: Fuller Seminary and the New Evangelicalism* (Grand Rapids, Mich.: Eerdmans, 1987), 269. For "power encounters," see Gibbs, "My Friend, John Wimber," *Signs & Wonders Today*, 151.

16. For "Lourdes of Pasadena," see John Dart, "Return of Fuller Class on Miracles Is Delayed," *Los Angeles Times*, January 25, 1986, A14. On the return of the course, see John Dart, "Fuller to Restore Healing Class—With Revisions," *Los Angeles Times*, February 7, 1987, A7.

17. Gilliland quoted in Wagner, *Signs and Wonders Today*, 45.

18. For "just as culture-bound," see Melba Padilla Maggay, *The Gospel in Culture: Contextualization Issues through Asian Eyes* (Manila: OMF Literature, 2013), 25. On American evangelicalism as deistic, see Charles H. Kraft, *Christianity with Power: Your Worldview and Your Experience of the Supernatural*, (Ann Arbor, Mich.: Vine, 1989), 24–25, 38. For "we see reality not as it is" and Kraft's critique of Fuller's School of Theology, see Marsden, *Reforming Fundamentalism*, 239–40, 288–89. For "just as syncretistic," see Leslie Newbigin, *Foolishness to the Greeks: The Gospel and Western Culture* (Grand Rapids, Mich: Eerdmans 1986).

19. Paul Hiebert, "The Flaw of the Excluded Middle," *Missiology* 10, No. 1 (January 1982): 36.

20. Hiebert, "Excluded Middle," 35, 39, 46.

21. For "sterile technology," see David Shibley, *A Force in the Earth: The Charismatic Renewal and World Evangelism* (Lake Mary, Fla.: Creation House, 1989), 40. For "mechanistic system of scientism," see Wagner, *Signs & Wonders Today*, 76. For "free-fall," see Kirk Bottomly, "Coming Out of the Hangar: Confessions of an Evangelical Deist," 261, in *The Kingdom and the Power*. On lack of growth in certain animistic cultures, see Hiebert, "Excluded Middle," 37; Wagner, *Signs & Wonders Today*, 22. For "not for an Asian institution," see Wagner, *Third Wave*, 75.

22. For "God was our last resort," see Kraft, *Christianity with Power*, 4–5. For a dissertation on syncretism, see Wagner, *Third Wave*, 78. On submerged supernaturalism, see Kraft, "Communicating," 354. For "a sandwich religion," see Melba Maggay, *The Gospel in Filipino Context* (Manila: OMF Literature, 1987), 4. For "typical, Western students," see Wagner, *Signs & Wonders Today*, 89, 108. For "greatest secularizing forces in history," see Wagner, *Signs & Wonders Today*, 22. Also see Esther Acolatse, *Powers, Principalities, and the Spirit: Biblical Realism in Africa and the West* (Grand Rapids, Mich.: Eerdmans, 2018).

23. On tracking miracles, see Wagner, *Wrestling with Alligators*, 145. On the missiological shift, see Wagner, *Frontiers in Missionary Strategy*, 115; Kraft, *Confronting Powerless Christianity: Evangelicals and the Missing Dimension* (Grand Rapids, Mich.: Baker Books, 2002), 27–45, 98–114. See Don Williams, "Exorcising the Ghost of Newton,"

116–27, in Kevin Springer, ed., *Power Encounters among Christians in the Western World* (San Francisco, Calif.: Harper & Row, 1988).

24. On the high numbers of miracle narratives, see Gary McGee, *This Gospel Must Be Preached* (Springfield, Mo.: Gospel Publishing House, 1986), 134. On Marino's exorcism, see Tom Bozarth, "Demons Out, God In," *Mountain Movers*, February 1993, 16–17.

25. Bob Pierce, *The Untold Korea Story* (Grand Rapids, Mich.: Zondervan, 1951), 66; W. Stanley Mooneyham, "Demonism on the Mission Field," in Binder 18A, Mooneyham Papers, WVIA; Billy Graham, *Angels: God's Secret Agents*, revised and expanded edition (Waco, Tex.: Word Books, 1986), 1; Paul B. Long, "Don't Underestimate the Opposition," 129–33, in C. Peter Wagner, ed., *Engaging the Enemy: How to Fight and Defeat Territorial Spirits* (Ventura, Calif.: Regal Books, 1991).

26. On the world's largest churches, see John Dart, "Evangelical Protestants Get the Spirit," *Los Angeles Times*, April 2, 1983, B1. On Pentecostalism and church growth, see McGee, *This Gospel, Vol. 2*, 19, 31, 121, 134–37, 200, 240. For numbers of the growing Global South, see Hanciles, *Beyond Christendom: Globalization, African Migration, and the Transformation of the West* (Maryknoll, N.Y.: Orbis Books, 2008), 121–22. For "becoming the minority" and Barrett, see Shibley, *Force in the Earth*, 40, 94.

27. For "the largest church," see Shibley, *Force in the Earth*, 140. On American pilgrimages to Korea, see Wagner, *Engaging the Enemy*, 47. For "heavens open," see Wagner, *Engaging the Enemy*, 47. For Yoido Full Gospel's founding myth, see Paul Yonggi Cho, "City Taking in Korea," 117–18, in Wagner, *Engaging the Enemy*; Hong Young-Gi and Myung Sung-Hoon, eds., *Charis and Charisma: David Yonggi Cho and the Growth of Yoido Full Gospel Church* (Oxford, UK: Regnum, 2003), 4, 6, 22, 51–74, 180. On Cho's popularity in the United States, see Dart, "From Korea, Biggest Christian Church Spreads to U.S. Airwaves," *Los Angeles Times*, December 5, 1981, B13; Kate Bowler, *Blessed: A History of the American Prosperity Gospel* (New York: Oxford University Press, 2013), 231; Karen Ball, "Around the World," *Christian Life*, 50.

28. For "unseen spirits," see John Dawson, *Taking Our Cities for God: How to Break Spiritual Strongholds* (Lake Mary, Fla.: Creation House, 1989), 21. Also see Wagner, *Third Wave*, 57; Wagner, *Engaging the Enemy*, 20; Christiaan De Wet, "Biblical Basis of Signs and Wonders," *Christian Life*, October 1982, 28–34. For "criticize liberals," see Kraft, *Confronting Powerless Christianity*, 136.

29. Wagner, *Third Wave*, 82; Wagner, *Confronting*, 91–118; "Miracles through the Ages," *Christian Life*, 24–26; McGee, *Miracles, Missions, and American Pentecostalism*, 5–6.

30. Lores quoted in Wagner, *Look Out*, 157. On blood sacrifice, see Philip Jenkins, *The Next Christendom: The Coming of Global Christianity* (New York: Oxford University Press, 2006), 162–63. On reasons for Pentecostal success, see David Martin, "Evangelical Expansion in Global Society," 275, in Donald Lewis, ed., *Christianity Reborn: The Global Expansion of Evangelicalism in the Twentieth Century* (Grand Rapids, Mich.: Eerdmans, 2004).

31. For "religious materialism," see Brian Stanley, *The Global Diffusion of Evangelicalism* (Downers Grove, Ill.: InterVarsity Press, 2013), 247. For "incautious Pentecostal

exegesis" and "big man of the big God," see Ogbu Kalu, *African Pentecostalism* (New York: Oxford University Press, 2008), 108, 112–13, 268.

32. Otis, *Twilight Labyrinth*, 306–308. For "Christian espionage agent," see Wagner, *Praying with Power* (Ventura, Calif.: Regal Books, 1997), 79. On the "Otis scale" which meant to measure the spiritual condition of a city and potential for community transformation, see Otis, *Informed Intercession: Transforming Your Community through Spiritual Mapping and Strategic Prayer* (Ventura, Calif.: Renew, 1999).

33. For "riddled with haunted drums," see Otis, *Twilight Labyrinth*, 43. Otis, "An Overview of Spiritual Mapping," 29–47, in Wagner, ed., *Breaking Strongholds in Your City* (Ventura, Calif.: Regal Books, 1993). For "sever the continuum," see Otis, *Twilight Labyrinth*, 308–11. On Pentecostal appeals to evangelicals regarding mapping, see Art Moore, "Church Growth: Spiritual Mapping Gains Credibility among Leaders," *Christianity Today*, January 12, 1998, 55; Doris Wagner, *How to Cast Out Demons: A Beginner's Guide* (Colorado Springs, Colo: Wagner Institute, 1999).

34. René Holvast, *Spiritual Mapping in the United States and Argentina, 1989-2005: A Geography of Fear* (Boston: Brill, 2009), 64–67, 83, 285–92. For "spiritual marketplaces of the Third World," see Otis, *Last of the Giants*, 244. For evidence of Majority World origins of spiritual mapping, see Virginia Garrard-Burnett, "Casting Out Demons in Almolonga: Spiritual Warfare and Economic Development in a Maya Town," 216–17, in David Westerlund, ed., *Global Pentecostalism* (New York: Tauris Press, 2009); Tye Yau Siew, "Spiritual Territoriality as a Premise for the Modern Spiritual Mapping Movement" (PhD diss., Fuller Theological Seminary, 1999); Pablo Bottari, "Dealing with Demons in Revival Evangelism," 75–90; E. Lorenzo, "Confronting the Powers in Adrogué," 125–44; Omar Cabrera, "Vision of the Future," 91–105; Jane Rumph, "Engaging the Enemy in Resistencia," 143–56; and Juan Zuccarelli, "God's Kingdom in Olmos Prison," 171–84, in C. Peter Wagner and Pablo Deiros, eds., *The Rising Revival: Firsthand Accounts of the Incredible Argentine Revival* (Ventura, Calif.: Renew, 1998). Wilson quoted in McGee, *Miracles, Missions, and American Pentecostalism*, 209.

35. On the Toronto Blessing and Global Awakening, see Candy Gunther Brown, "Global Awakenings: Divine Healing Networks and Global Community," 353–54, in *Global Pentecostal and Charismatic Healing* (New York: Oxford University Press, 2011); Brown, "From Tent Meetings and Store-front Healing Rooms to Walmarts and the Internet: Healing Spaces in the United States, the Americas, and the World, 1906-2006," *Church History* 75, No. 3 (September 2006): 645–46; Pablo Dieros and C. Peter Wagner, *The Rising Revival: Firsthand Accounts of the Incredible Argentine Revival* (Ventura, Calif.: Renew, 1998), 11–13.

36. For delegate interest cards, see Box 26, Folder 3, Lausanne Collection, BGCA. On the subject of spiritual warfare at Lausanne, see C. Peter Wagner, *Confronting the Powers* (Ventura, Calif.: Regal, 1996), 15, 21.

37. For Third Wave influence on Lausanne, see Wagner to John Stott, June 29, 1982, in Box 5, Folder 2, John Stott Collection, BGCA; Dawson, *Taking Our Cities for God*, 165. For "about to hijack," see Kåre Melhus, "To Tell the Whole World," 91, in Lars Dahle, ed., *The Lausanne Movement: A Range of Perspectives* (Eugene, Ore.: Wipf & Stock, 2014).

38. For "charismatic orientation," see Shibley, *Force in the Earth*, 36. For description and analysis of the Manila congress, see L. Cryderman, "Global Camp Meeting," *Christianity Today*, August 1989, 39–40; Robert T. Coote, "Lausanne II and World Evangelization," *International Bulletin of Missionary Research* 14, No. 1 (January 1990): 10–17. For "spiritual nuclear power plant," see Wagner, *Confronting the Powers*, 18–19. For the "Manila Manifesto" and other charismatic emphases, see J. D. Douglas, ed., *Proclaim Christ until He Comes* (Minneapolis, Minn.: World Wide Publications, 1989), 26, 430–35. For "gone charismatic," see Kings, "Evangelicals in Search of Catholicity," 7.

39. For "new wineskins," see Wagner, "My Pilgrimage in Mission," *International Bulletin of Missionary Research* 23, No. 4 (October 1999): 164–68. On charismatic outreach to evangelicals, see Otis, *High Adventure* (Old Tappan, N.J.: Revell, 1971), 63, 76, 82, 185; Wagner, *Wrestling with Alligators*, 155; Kraft, *Christianity with Power*, 1; C. E. Arnold, "Giving the Devil His Due," *Christianity Today*, August 1990, 17–19. For more on the Pentecostal alliance with evangelicals, see McGee, *Miracles, Missions*, 203–206.

40. For "actual demon possession," see "Award-Winning Film Tonight," *Scope*, July 15, 1965, 1, in Folder 52, "Festival of Missions," WVIA. On Cruz, see Michelle Vu, "Ex-Gang Warlord Nicky Cruz on Why the Devil Has No Mother," *Christian Post*, January 2, 2014; David Wilkerson, *The Cross and the Switchblade* (New York: Random House, 1963); Nicky Cruz, *The Devil Has No Mother* (London: Hodder & Stoughton, 2012).

41. On Thomas White, see Wagner, *Engaging the Enemy*, 59–63. On Deere, see Russell Chandler, "Vineyard Fellowship Finds Groundswell of Followers," *Los Angeles Times*, October 5, 1990, A1, 35; Wagner, *Confronting*, 53; Deere, *Surprised by the Power of the Spirit* (Grand Rapids, Mich.: Zondervan, 1993). On Swindoll, see Wagner, *Third Wave*, 72; Swindoll, *Demonism: How to Win against the Devil* (Grand Rapids, Mich.: Zondervan, 1993). On Lindsell, see Wagner, *On the Crest of the Wave*, 128; Lindsell, *The Holy Spirit in the Latter Days* (Nashville, Tenn.: Thomas Nelson, 1983). On Bright and Campus Crusade, see John Dart, "Evangelical Protestants Get the 'Spirit' of Pentecostalism," *Los Angeles Times*, April 2, 1983, B1.

42. Heidi Baker, *Expecting Miracles: True Stories of God's Supernatural Power and How You Can Experience It* (Grand Rapids, Mich.: Chosen Books, 2007). On the significance of YWAM, see Wagner, *Wrestling with Alligators*, 157; Dawson, *Taking Our Cities*, 25–28; Holvast, *Spiritual Mapping*, 37, 122; David Stoll, *Is Latin America Turning Protestant?* (Berkeley: University of California Press, 1990), 92–94. On the Wagner-Haggard-Otis collaboration in Colorado Springs, see "Church Growth: Spiritual Mapping Gains Credibility among Leaders," *Christianity Today*, January 12, 1998, 55; Ted Olsen, "Prayer Center Construction Begins," *Christianity Today*, May 20, 1996, 78; Jeff Sharlet, "Soldiers of Christ: Inside America's Most Powerful Megachurch," *Harpers*, May 2005, 46. On funding for the World Prayer Center, see Wagner, *Wrestling with Alligators*, 225.

43. On St. Marks Episcopal, see John Dart, "Charismatic and Mainline," *Christian Century*, March 7, 2006, 22–27. For "as if God does not exist," see Hauerwas and Willimon, "Embarrassed by God's Presence," *Christian Century*, January 30, 1985, 98–100. On

Moltmann at Yoido, see Shaw, *Global Awakening*, 46–47; Moltmann, "The Blessing of Hope," *Journal of Pentecostal Theology* 13 (April 2005): 147–61. For "expect signs and wonders," see Wagner, *Third Wave*, 92. On Du Plessis, see Ogbu Kalu, "Africa," 262, in Donald Lewis and Richard Pierard, eds., *Global Evangelicalism: Theology, History and Culture in Regional Perspective* (Downers Grove, Ill.: InterVarsity Press, 2014).

44. Wagner, *Wrestling with Alligators*, 175, 187–88; Wagner, *Spiritual Warfare Strategy*; Carol Saia, "God Ends Idol's 700-Year Reign in Almolonga, Guatemala," Sentinel Group, 2009. https://www.glowtorch.org/Home/IdolatryendsinAlmolonga/tabid/2767/Default.html.

45. On Caballeros's announcement and the World Congress, see Kevin Lewis O'Neill, *City of God: Christian Citizenship in Postwar Guatemala* (Berkeley: University of California Press, 2010), 185–89.

46. For a small sample of the large body of literature citing Almolonga as a model of transformation, see Stephen Sywulka, "Guatemala: Peace Accord Amnesty Divides Church Leaders," *Christianity Today*, February 3, 1997, 76; Moore, "Church Growth: Spiritual Mapping Gains Credibility among Leaders," *Christianity Today*, January 12, 1998, 55; Harold Caballeros and Mell Winger, eds., *The Transforming Power of Revival* (Buenos Aires: Editorial Peniel, 1998); Wagner, *Revival! It Can Transform Your City* (Colorado Springs, Colo.: Wagner Publications, 1999), 54–55; George Otis, Jr., *Informed Intercession: Transforming Your Community Through Spiritual Mapping and Strategic Prayer* (Ventura, Calif.: Renew Books, 1999), 18–23; Ed Silvoso, *Anointed for Business* (Ventura, Calif.: Regal Books, 2002); Rebecca Greenwood, *Destined to Rule: Spiritual Strategies for Advancing the Kingdom of God* (Grand Rapids, Mich: Chosen Books, 2007), 75–79; Mell Winger, "Almolonga, the Miracle City," *Renewal Journal* 16 (April 2012); Winger, "The Miracle of Almolonga," *Charisma*, September 1998, 66–72; Dutch Sheets, *Watchman Prayer* (Ventura, Calif.: Regal Books, 2000), 90–91; Harold Caballeros, *Victorious Warfare* (Nashville, Tenn.: Thomas Nelson, 2001), 112; Kraft, *Confronting Powerless Christianity*, 231; Sarah Pollak, "Guatemala: The Miracle of Almolonga," CWNews, June 10, 2005; C. Peter Wagner, *On Earth As It Is in Heaven* (Ventura, Calif.: Regal Books, 2012), 58–59, 151–52; "Making Disciples amidst Transformation," *Data for Mission* 24, no. 6 (October 2012): 1–2; Charles Kraft, *The Evangelical's Guide to Spiritual Warfare* (Ada, Mich.: Chosen Books, 2015), 261.

47. Carol Madison, "Come and See What God Has Done," *Prayer Connect*, 2015; Madison, "Reflections on Trip to Almolonga, Guatemala," January 2004. https://www.prayerleader.com/longing-for-change/.

48. On recovery after the 1976 earthquake, see Garrard-Burnett," Casting Out Demons," 214. On the effects of political violence, see O'Neill, *City of God*. On the building of a road, the use of better seeds, and the shortage of land, see Sonia Arbona, "Commercial Agriculture and Agrochemicals in Almolonga, Guatemala," *Geographical Review* 88, No. 1 (January 1998): 48–50. On the transition from subsistence farming, see Oscar Horst, "Commercialization of Traditional Agriculture in Highland Guatemala and Ecuador," *Revista Geográfica* 106 (July 1987): 5–6.

49. For various evaluations on numbers of evangelicals in Almolonga, see Stephen R. Sywulka, "The Selling of 'Miracle City,'" *Christianity Today*, April 5, 1999, 23; Garrard-Burnett, "Casting Out Demons in Almolonga," 213; Timothy Evans, "Religious Conversion in Quetzaltenango, Guatemala" (PhD diss., University of Pittsburgh, 1990), 92. On Almolonga's comparative prosperity, see Garrard-Burnett, "Casting Out Demons," 212. On Almolonga as a prototype of the Protestant work ethic, see Amy Sherman, *The Soul of Development: Biblical Christianity and Economic Transformation in Guatemala*, 104, 159; Garrard-Burnett, "Casting Out Demons," 219–21. On business ownership, see Thomas Metallo, "The Sword of the Spirit: Pentecostals and Political Power in Guatemala" (PhD diss., University of Miami, 1998), 212.

50. For "problematic aspects of globalization," see Brown, "From Tent Meetings," 647. On identity politics, see Metallo, "Sword of the Spirit," 215. On the rhetoric of personal character, see O'Neill, *City of God*, 78–84. On complex historical factors, see O'Neill, *City of God*, 58–59. For "inside out," see Stuart Greaves, *False Justice: Unveiling the Truth about Social Justice* (Shippensburg, Pa.: Destiny Image, 2012).

51. On Montt, see Juanita Darling, "New Faiths for Latin America," *Los Angeles Times*, February 5, 1996; O'Neill, *City of God*, 12. On the failure of Pentecostals to challenge the Guatemalan government, see Elaine Padilla and Dale Irvin, "Where Are the Pentecostals in an Age of Empire?" 176, 184, in Bruce Ellis Benson and Peter Goodwin Heltzel, eds., *Evangelicals and Empire* (Grand Rapids, Mich: Brazos Press, 2008), 176, 184; Paul Freston, *Evangelicals and Politics in Asia, Africa and Latin America* (Cambridge: Cambridge University Press, 2001), 35, 274–76; Bethany Moreton, "The Soul of Neo-Liberalism," *Social Text* 25, No. 3 (Fall 2007): 112; O'Neill, *City of God*, 12; Maren Christensen Bjune, "Religious Change and Political Continuity: The Evangelical Church in Guatemalan Politics" (PhD diss., University of Bergen, 2016), 7, 32, 36.

52. Arbona, "Commercial Agriculture and Agrochemicals," 48, 53–57; Garrard-Burnett, "Casting Out Demons," 223.

53. For "fanciful, not biblical," see John MacArthur, *Charismatic Chaos* (Grand Rapids, Mich.: Zondervan, 1992), 130, 143. On the need to eradicate Mayan supernaturalism, see Caballeros, *Victorious Warfare*, 3–24; O'Neill, *City of God*, 97–100. Riscajache quoted in Otis, *Twilight Labyrinth*, 310. On local pastors practicing Mayan culture, see Garrard-Burnett, "Casting Out Demons," 221.

7

Mbarara 2007

An East African Critique of American Sexuality

*You remember a hundred years ago . . . Africa was taunted as a dark
continent. Now, you just believe me that darkness has shifted to Europe
and America. The passion for the gospel, the love for Jesus Christ is way
out in Africa—and we'll bring the same thing back.*
— Ugandan Archbishop Henry Orombi to
National Public Radio's Barbara Bradley Hagerty[1]

On September 16, 2007, a bespectacled preacher from suburban Virginia stood
on a rickety stage in Mbarara, Uganda. If this scene had occurred decades earlier,
observers might have assumed that this American was an evangelist sharing the
"good news" to benighted polygamists. But twenty-first century circumstances
had reversed the scenario. John Guernsey, an Anglican vicar from All Saints'
Church just outside Washington, D.C., was seeking spiritual refuge in Africa
from what he viewed as an apostate Episcopal Church in the United States. To the
throng of Ugandans in attendance, including the nation's prime minister Yoweri
Museveni and Archbishop Henry Orombi, Guernsey confessed, "In America, we
must recapture the priority of evangelism, the urgency of outreach into our communities and the need to reach young people and raise leaders of the next generations. I pray that the spirit of revival comes to us where so many are lost."[2]

For those present in Mbarara, a city in western Uganda renowned for its
long-horned cattle, America's capitulation to divorce, pornography, and most
of all, homosexuality was critical evidence of its lostness. Just four years earlier Gene Robinson, a noncelibate gay Episcopal priest, had been named bishop
of the Diocese of New Hampshire. This was the last straw for conservative
Episcopalians in America like Guernsey—and conservative East Africans like
Orombi—who began to nurture strong transnational ties over their common
views. These connections were cemented in Mbarara. In a colorful and lively
five-hour-long ceremony, more than 10,000 attendees joyfully sang an eclectic
blend of music that included African hymns and Handel's "Hallelujah Chorus."
Guernsey wore a purple shirt, flowing red vestments, and a special ring given
to him by his Ugandan benefactors. As he was consecrated as a bishop in the

Facing West. David R. Swartz, Oxford University Press (2020). © Oxford University Press.
DOI: 10.1093/oso/9780190250805.001.0001

Church of Uganda, Guernsey clutched a wooden staff and shouted in the local tribal language, "Mukama Asiimwe! Mukama Asiimwe!" which means "Praise the Lord!" The American's assignment, explained Orombi to the crowd, was to shepherd thirty-three congregations in the United States. This moment, said Orombi to applause from the multitude gathered in the open air because there were too many to fit in Mbarara's St. James Cathedral, was "an important statement to the Anglican Communion," which was countenancing impurity. "We look forward to the day when there will be a united and biblically orthodox Anglicanism in America," said Orombi.[3]

This reverse mission represented a groundswell of East African efforts in the 2000s. Three days before Guernsey's consecration, Kenyan Anglicans had consecrated American bishops to serve in Massachusetts and Texas. Simultaneously, the Church of Rwanda announced that three new bishops would be consecrated as missionaries to America by January. "This is a new order," said the Rt. Rev. Martyn Minns, a bishop newly minted by Nigerian Anglicans. It surely was. Lines of authority that for centuries had followed the pathways of the old British Empire were being redrawn by these new alliances. Going forward, Guernsey would bypass the headquarters of the Anglican Church in England and Episcopalian headquarters in Manhattan, instead taking his cues from the Church of Uganda's headquarters in the capital city of Kampala. As these relationships developed, the culture shock was palpable. When Guernsey traveled to Uganda from suburban Virginia, where the typical family enjoyed an average income of $54,000 a year, he arrived in a wholly other world where the average income was only $350 and signs at headquarters warned of a wild leopard on the prowl. While unconventional, the alliance fit the postcolonial moment. With a membership of nine million, the Church of Uganda had become one of the largest Anglican dioceses in the world, second only to the Church of Nigeria. Guernsey, flanked by Ugandans and Virginians at his consecration, vowed not only to bring the "fire of revival" to America, but also to "banish and drive away all erroneous and strange doctrines contrary to God's word." As he spoke, clouds shielded the throng from the oppressive equatorial sun. "This weather is not normal," Archbishop Orombi told the crowd. "God has done a good thing."[4]

Guernsey's consecration by Ugandans made headlines across the world. National Public Radio, the *New York Times*, the *Washington Post*, the *Los Angeles Times*, *The Times* of London, and dozens of African dailies chronicled this story of "reverse colonization." Orombi was right to say that "the whole world is watching." The world, however, articulated wildly divergent judgments of what they saw. Episcopalian loyalists in America expressed a sense of betrayal that Orombi was stealing their churches. From Lambeth Palace in London, Archbishop Rowan Williams, who had asked East Africans to desist from consecrating American Episcopalians, expressed disappointment. Nearly all Majority World Anglicans, on the other hand, expressed a quiet determination, and Guernsey's own parish in Virginia, which had voted 402 to six to align with the Ugandans, erupted in "huge excitement." At a celebratory picnic held after Guernsey returned home, a parishioner said that his new bishop's appointment was a hopeful sign that the "true church" would not capitulate to materialism and to liberal views on sexuality. When Orombi visited Guernsey's congregation a month later, they greeted the Ugandan archbishop like he was a rock star. During the 2000s, sustained challenges from Mbarara, Kampala, and beyond abetted American evangelical stands on conservative sexuality. Along with the global Pentecostal challenge to rationalist religion, critiques from members of the Majority World on what they saw as libertine sex and theological heterodoxy demonstrated that the global reflex has not always pushed in a progressive direction.[5]

As the varying reactions to Guernsey's consecration suggest, the global circulation of ideas about sexual morality is complex. Are conservative views in East Africa merely the legacy of Western colonial ideals, as many progressives from America and Europe say? Does the historical prevalence of polygamy demonstrate that there has never been a universal "traditional" sexual ethic in Uganda? Did conservative Anglicans from America truly submit themselves to the authority of the Ugandan church in the 2000s, or were they merely looking for African cover to justify homophobia? Or does such a view deny the agency of Ugandan Christians and imply that they are naïve religious actors unable to resist outside influence? How did the devastating HIV/AIDS crisis of the 1980s and 1990s shape African Christian discourse on sexuality? Whatever the answers to these knotty questions, the bonds between Guernsey, Orombi, and millions of Anglicans from the United States and around the world offer an intriguing glimpse into how far-flung religious groups made common cause on one of the most divisive and important issues of the postcolonial era.[6]

I. Bishop Orombi and the AIDS Crisis

For Guernsey, Ugandan ecclesial oversight made sense in an American setting he regarded as hostile. Having grown up in a pious Episcopalian family interested in racial reconciliation, poverty alleviation, and prayer, he did not sense this same kind of spiritual vibrancy at church. Scripture was not emphasized, and Guernsey did not feel the "supernatural reality of God" there. After experimenting with New Age practices, he sought out the Holy Spirit, which seemed to direct him toward Episcopal Divinity School. But it too was a "very, very liberal place," and Guernsey left barely believing in the resurrection of Jesus. The faculty suggested that he "should not expect God to do today what I saw Him doing in the pages of Scripture." In Guernsey's view, the outrages persisted as the Episcopal Church, which had been pushing social boundaries for decades, began to change its standards of sexual morality. In 2000 the denomination appeared to permit extra-marital sex, and then in 2003, it consecrated a noncelibate gay priest as a bishop. By contrast, Guernsey's own parish of 800 members in Woodbridge, Virginia, a conservative congregation he had led since 1988, pulsated with spiritual life and was growing fast. He also observed "vibrancy in biblical Anglicanism" throughout the Majority World. Disillusioned with his own tribe, Guernsey glimpsed a potential alliance with conservatives in Africa.[7]

Archbishop Orombi's path to Mbarara in 2007 was as different as could be imagined from Guernsey's staid mainline upbringing. Born in a hut, Orombi grew up among the remote farmer-herder Alur peoples in the Nebbi district of northwestern Uganda. His grandfathers, who practiced traditional African spiritualism, built shrines, and his grandmothers maintained them, delivering a pot of beer every month to each of the twelve gods that resided within. Orombi's father, a polygamist who converted to Anglicanism, ruled his six wives and many children with an "iron hand." These children, including son Henry, drank alcohol, smoked a strain of cannabis called *bhangi*, and sat on stools in the shrines while calling for help from the spirits. As Orombi later described it, his life was "rough, rude and difficult till I opened my heart to Jesus." His conversion, however, did not solve all his problems. He dropped out of high school in the 1960s and then failed an apprenticeship as a mechanic. At his father's insistence, he enrolled at Bishop Tucker Theological College, a missionary college near Kampala founded in 1913, to become a teacher. There his faith was quickened after hearing a visiting speaker preach about the prodigal son in Scripture. Confessing his sins, Orombi pledged himself to "light in the Lord."[8]

The young man's growing faith reflected the maturation of Ugandan indigeneity. Bishop Alfred Tucker, the namesake of Orombi's alma mater, had tried in the early twentieth century to revise the church's constitution to end British control of Anglicanism in Uganda. This met resistance in England, and so the spurned Ugandans began a low-church movement that in the 1930s merged with a broader East African Revival. In addition to historic evangelical emphases on sin, confession, and blood of Christ, the Balokole, as the revival was called, stressed the notion of "a new clan." The movement quickly grew to eighty-five million adherents as Zambia, Kenya, and Rwanda turned into Christian-majority nations. According to Anglican observer Michael Harper, "There is hardly a single Protestant leader in East Africa who has not been touched by it in some way." Driven by an aggressive indigenous evangelism, the revival transcended national divides, launched new Pentecostal-oriented religious movements comprised of African initiated/independent churches (AIC), and reshaped existing denominations. In 1962, the year of national independence, Ugandan leaders began to replace the expatriate Anglican hierarchy. In 1966 Erica Sabiti, the first native bishop, replaced Leslie Brown, the last British bishop. Mid-century revival and indigenization proved to be promising contexts for the career of young Orombi, who combined serious faith with a striking personality, a compelling baritone laugh, and a 6-foot, 5-inch frame. Anglican officials in Uganda were so impressed that they sent him to St. John's College Nottingham in the United Kingdom for further study.[9]

Upon his return, Orombi worked as a pastor in the West Nile region. The early 1970s was not an easy time in Uganda under the regime of strongman Idi Amin, and Orombi was imprisoned for assisting an underground church. This was a much lighter punishment than that dealt to his mentor, Archbishop Janani Luwum, who was martyred in 1977, reportedly killed by Amin himself. After Orombi's release from prison, his stock soared. Appointed as the first bishop of a new diocese in southwestern Uganda, he acquired a reputation as "a fiery priest with enormous persuasive, intellectual and mobilization capacity." Beginning in 1993 with no infrastructure, Orombi built schools, training centers, and rural community outreach programs that attracted international attention. He did it, Orombi explained, "by preaching the gospel fiercely." He regularly shed the archbishop's traditional purple shirt, instead wearing street clothes and his clerical collar in a style described as "civilian mufti." Often seen strumming a guitar with Anglican youth, admirers hailed him as "a counselor and friend" who passionately urged his parishioners to pursue lives of holiness and faith. This spiritual commitment to a living God superseded all other commitments. As heir of the East African Revival that stressed, in the words of Orombi, a "personal relationship with Jesus Christ" over all else, the young minister engaged in spiritual warfare against dark forces. Having experimented with devil worship as a child, he campaigned vociferously against witchcraft and child sacrifice. Orombi, however, spent most of his energies on less dramatic supernatural arts like healing with oil and quiet communication with God through prayer. Opponents would later call Orombi "the architect of African homophobia," but his Ugandan disciples knew him as the archbishop who launched a decade of spiritual growth and missions.[10]

For Orombi and other East African bishops, missions required justice. Among the continent's forty-two million Anglican descendants of the Balokole revival, the Council for Anglican Provinces in Africa (CAPA) used its organizational heft to speak with frequency and intensity about the biblical mandate of social justice. Founded in 1979, CAPA became a powerful agent for collective action on issues such as poverty, HIV, and religious conflict. These relationships culminated in a series of gatherings called "South-to-South Encounters." In addition to cultivating mutual support, they also issued series of prophetic "trumpets" to the North. The first—organized in 1994 by African bishops from CAPA—was held in Limuru, Kenya. Tellingly, the "First Trumpet from the South," did not mention sex, except for condemning "divisive sexism." Rather, it emphasized "signs and wonders," postcolonial sensibilities, justice, and poverty. In the 1990s, CAPA successfully lobbied Western Christians, including Billy Graham and Pat Robertson, to support the Jubilee movement, which called for the cancellation of debt in the Global South by the year 2000. When Orombi eventually retired in 2012, he was lauded in his own country for his attention to corruption, poverty, education, health, refugees from neighboring Congo, and reconciliation between warring parties in the north of Uganda. The same biblical hermeneutic that nurtured Orombi's conservative sexual ethic seemed also to lead him to progressive stances on economics and politics.[11]

In fact, the East African path toward an activist approach to sexuality started in part from its strong social justice sensibilities. Orombi's swift ascension in the Ugandan Anglican hierarchy coincided with a devastating health crisis caused by HIV/AIDS. By the late 1980s, one out of every six Ugandans was HIV positive. In a population of less than twenty million, the epidemic left more than two million orphans. Entire villages lacked any persons of childbearing age. A myth that having sex with a virgin could cure the disease ran rampant, which meant that young girls were targeted for rape. The nature of the crisis was all-consuming, and Ugandans, with unprecedented cooperation from religious, political, financial, and educational sectors of society, waged a war to save the nation.[12]

East African bishops fought the HIV epidemic primarily by preaching sexual holiness. As a pastor shepherding a flock that sometimes strayed, Orombi had long fought against practices—extramarital sex, divorce, pornography, and homosexuality—that the Church of Uganda deemed sinful. Offenders who had succumbed to a culture of "moral decadence," he wrote, should be treated with firm compassion, and African clergy should acclaim the beauty of heterosexual marriage. Church leaders, in fact, loudly blamed gay sex for the disease's rapid spread. Recognizing that 90 percent of new infections came through means of transmission other than gay sex, however, they also targeted drug use and heterosexual promiscuity. Danger lurked in every sexual encounter. For Ugandans living under the pall of disease and death, the crisis reinforced an ideal of monogamous, heterosexual marriage.[13]

Through the 1990s Anglican efforts broadened beyond holy living. An "ABC" prevention program began with "abstinence" and "be faithful," but also included "condoms," though Orombi worried that their distribution might be understood as sanctioning promiscuity. An "HIV summit" involving several hundred Anglican clerics from Kenya and Uganda attributed the high rate of transmission largely to ignorance, drug addiction, and poverty. CAPA developed a "Strategic

HIV/AIDS Plan," and Anglicans helped establish hospitals, facilitate research, and educate the masses through new prevention programs. "No HIV test, no wedding," became the mantra for Anglican priests in Africa. These initiatives were credited with dropping infection rates from 18 percent in 1995 to 8.3 percent in 1999. They also elevated the status of women. "When the Bible came alive during the East Africa Revival of the 1930s," explained Orombi, "the Holy Spirit convicted men of such sins of oppression and began the progressive empowerment of women that is continuing today." Specifically, he pointed out, the biblical teaching of marriage liberated women, especially those subjected to polygamy and easy divorce laws that "left many women neglected and often destitute." Evangelical Anglicans in Africa thus contended that sexual control contributed to social justice. The HIV/AIDS crisis helped spark the zealous activism against homosexuality that would emerge in the late 1990s.[14]

II. Lambeth, Gene Robinson, and Postcolonial Sexuality

East African bishops said they did not intend to address sexuality at Lambeth 1998, the decennial gathering in England of international Anglican leaders. Orombi and the rest of the Ugandan delegation planned to emphasize issues of economic injustice. Noting that Ethiopia spent four times more money on debt repayment than on healthcare, the All Africa Conference of Churches declared that "every child in Africa is born with a financial burden which a lifetime's work cannot repay. The debt is a new form of slavery as vicious as the slave trade." Debt remission, poverty, job creation, and microcredit programs were the overriding concerns heading into Lambeth. Comprising the largest regional grouping in the world, a full 30 percent of those attending, the African bishops prepared to confront their colleagues about the colonial roots of poverty in the Global South.[15]

In fact, a strong resolution on international debt remission passed, but the most hotly debated subject turned out to be homosexuality. A stunned Orombi watched a "gay lobby," led by Bishop John Spong of New Jersey, advocate a liturgy for gay marriage. Spong, who characterized African understandings of the Bible as "superstitious," had just written a book, *Why Christianity Must Change or Die*, which questioned the physical resurrection of Jesus Christ. Orombi recoiled at what he saw as brazen Western innovations. He was not alone. At Lambeth several bishops described monogamous gay marriages as "bestial." Bishop Benjamin Kwashi of Nigeria, declaring that "homosexuality is not the will of God," said that many Africans felt "oppressed with this Western problem." His colleague Emmanuel Chukwuma dramatically confronted Anglican gay rights activist Richard Kirker on the streets of Canterbury. With television cameras rolling, Chukwuma accused Kirker of "killing the church" and attempted to exorcise the evil spirit of homosexuality from him. Kirker, who had been handing out leaflets, responded, "May God bless you, sir, and deliver you from your prejudice against homosexuality." In the end, after many revisions, Resolution I.10, which declared homosexual activity as "incompatible with Scripture," passed with 526 in favor and seventy in opposition, with forty-five abstentions. Canadian Bishop David Crawley mourned that "a document whose face, a little conservative, was a face of love and compassion is gradually, bit by bit, step by step, turning into a judgment and condemnation." Orombi, who had campaigned for the harder edged version, told the *New York Times* that "we spoke for the truth."[16]

From the perspective of conservatives, liberal threats only increased in the wake of Lambeth. In 2002, Rowan Williams, who did not take a firm conservative position as activists pressed for gay ordination, was chosen as the 104th Archbishop of Canterbury. And then in July 2003, just months before Orombi's consecration as archbishop, Canon Gene Robinson, an Episcopal priest in an openly gay relationship, was consecrated (while wearing a bulletproof vest) as bishop of the Episcopal Diocese of New Hampshire. Deriving their stance from a progressive hermeneutic of scripture, deeply held moral convictions, and new scientific findings on human sexuality, many American Episcopalians believed that monogamous same-sex unions should be sanctioned. Social justice and love, they contended, should negate Resolution I.10, which had been passed five years before. Most African leaders, by contrast, staunchly disapproved, accusing liberals of holding to fashionable, not orthodox, views. In the wake of Robinson's election, Archbishop Peter Akinola, called the "Lion of Africa," threatened to leave the Anglican Communion along with his seventeen million Nigerian faithful. Similar denunciations came from Zambia and Kenya. Archbishop-elect Orombi, who was just leaving his obscure post in Nebbi to lead the second largest Anglican body in the world, immediately severed relations with the New Hampshire diocese. Several months later, he cut off the entire Episcopal Church of America.[17]

From the beginning, then, Orombi's tenure was defined by the issue of sexuality. His grand consecration on January 25, 2004, in Kampala was significant not for what actually happened, but for who was not there. No Americans accompanied the one hundred Anglican primates in full regalia as Orombi led them in a long procession up the hill toward Namirembe Cathedral, where a crowd of thousands waited. They had been disinvited by the Church of Uganda. Reports in Western religious periodicals did not discuss Orombi's lengthy speech laying out his new initiatives, which included constructing holistic development projects, mitigating the effects of HIV/ADS, nurturing spiritual growth, and working on projects of peace and justice. Nor did reporters emphasize the colorful ceremony that included the handing over of the Primatial Cross or the exuberant reception filled with dancing and singing. Instead, the reports focused on the absence of the Episcopalians, which Church of Uganda representatives were eager to defend. "They are not welcome," one declared. "Even if they come, they will not get seats."[18]

Robinson's consecration had functioned as a tripwire for Orombi, the Church of Uganda, and many other Anglican bodies around the world. It moved them from a passively conservative posture on homosexuality toward an activist conservatism. If the presence of strong LGBTQ advocates at Lambeth in 1998 had concerned them, the elevation of Robinson to such a senior position truly distressed them. Orombi's colleague Peter Akinola confronted his friend Archbishop Frank Griswold of the Episcopal Church in America. "Our hearts are bleeding," Akinola told Griswold. "You can save the communion this costly problem by putting a stop to this agenda. You can stop the consecration of a practicing gay priest." But the elevation of gay priests continued apace, and one year later Katharine Jefferts Schori, another proponent of marriage equality, was named as Griswold's successor. Orombi refused to take communion with Schori at an Anglican gathering in Dar es Salaam, Tanzania. He—and many other conservative allies—began to speak with apocalyptic language. Connecting homosexuality with the HIV epidemic, he said, "For us in Uganda, this is a matter of life and death." Griswold quoted back Scripture: "In the Gospels, Jesus says, 'I have many more things to say to you but you cannot bear them now,' which suggests to me that God's truth is always unfolding." He added, "A number of those most upset about our seemingly ignoring Scripture, though they are solidly heterosexual, have enjoyed the mercy of the church in the case of their own divorce and remarriage, which is something Jesus commented on." Other American opponents called Orombi the "architect of African homophobia" and Akinola "a fundamentalist bigot." The battle—with lines sharply drawn between the global North and South—seemed to leave no space for the historic Anglican "middle way" of compromise.[19]

African bishops denied accusations of homophobia. Orombi, for example, pledged compassionate "pastoral care" for those struggling with a wide array of "sexual temptations." They also framed their activism in terms of preserving orthodoxy. To condone homosexual practice would deny tradition and biblical fidelity. Liberal theology, they maintained, had led to equivocation on fundamental issues like the virgin birth and the divinity and resurrection of Christ. "There is a tradition on human sexuality that was passed to us by the apostles, and if we're an apostolic church, how come the Episcopal Church claims they are better than St. Paul?" Orombi rhetorically asked a *Los Angeles Times* reporter in a telephone interview from Kampala. "Why do they turn their back on the faith their grandparents brought to us?" To Orombi, the authority of Scripture was the "defining mark of Anglican identity." American conservatives cheered the critique. A *Christianity Today* editor urged Africans "to remind [the Episcopal Church] what the gospel, full of grace *and* truth, looks like."[20]

Truth took different shapes. For many liberal Episcopalians, a truer interpretation of both science and Scripture meant offering covenanted, monogamous relationships to gays. East Africans like Orombi framed their version of truth as broader than gay marriage. For them, homosexuality was the presenting issue, but they also described their critique as extending to a broader rejection of Western sexual practices. Specifically, Robinson galled many East Africans not only because of his same-sex marriage, but also because he had divorced his wife. Countless reports in African newspapers highlighted this element of the controversy. Indeed, divorce had different—and more devastating—social and economic consequences for wives in East Africa than in the United States. Orombi's homilies to Ugandan Anglicans at church meetings, revival services, Bible study groups, and youth camps also reflected a more expansive preoccupation with sexual holiness. In addition to expressing deep concern over homosexuality and rising rates of divorce, he criticized men for holding back women from educational and vocational aspirations. Orombi also criticized women for immodest dress, campaigned against abortion, pushed for the passage of antipornography legislation, and condemned adultery. He censured everyone for consuming sexualized entertainment.[21]

Some East African Christians accused the West of having exported these practices to Africa. From Addis Ababa, Ethiopia, an editorial explicitly connected libertine sexuality to the "legacy of evil left behind by the decadent spiritual civilization of Europe. . . . We have, therefore, a moral duty to resist an evil that British, French, Italian and Portuguese colonialism had planted in Africa." Ugandan bishop Nicodemus Okille told his congregation from the pulpit that he had received pre-Lambeth mailers in 1998 lobbying for the acceptance of homosexuality. Just a month later Orombi's predecessor, Archbishop Livingstone Mpalanyi Nkoyoyo, blasted Western clergy for compromising on sexuality and then dominating international gatherings with gay activism. "This cannot be allowed," he told a regional meeting of bishops at the Hotel Africana in Kampala. Voicing strong postcolonial logic, Nkoyoyo declared, "We must make certain that our voice is heard."[22]

Orombi agreed. Worrying about a second "scramble for Africa," he noted the expansion of Integrity, a gay advocacy group in the United States, into Kampala. They intended to organize a "Pan-African conference of lesbian and gay Anglicans." More generally, Orombi believed that a wealthy, powerful, and debauched Western culture was strong-arming Africans into sexual licentiousness. "The team of homosexuals is very rich," he declared. "They have money and will do whatever it takes to make sure that this vice penetrates Africa. We have to stand out and say no to them. . . . They are taking advantage of poverty in Africa to lure people into their club." When some liberals accused African leaders of being theologically ignorant, bigoted stooges of right-wing American tycoons, Orombi, in turn, condemned racist Western arrogance. In particular, he cited a 2002 Episcopalian gathering in New York City where a gay activist condemned African conservatives for "monkeying around" in the church. "All I have to say to these bishops is: Go back to the jungle where you came from!" East African conservatives conveyed deep concern over "a global totalitarian liberalism" that stressed individuality over communal obligations, personal expression over traditional customs, and Western power over a still-prostrate East.[23]

This logic puzzled many Westerners. Why did Orombi and other African conservatives view Robinson's consecration as an imperial move? The Episcopal Church, after all, did not insist that Africans preside over gay marriages. But for most Majority World Anglicans, the elevation of Robinson had poisoned the body politic. Ecclesiastical hierarchies led back to Lambeth, where communal obligations were embodied in a shared Eucharist. "Bishops in America are one part of the Anglican communion," explained Orombi. To a reporter at Lambeth, he said, "Whatever they do should be found acceptable within the wider church. If U.S. bishops are ordaining homosexuals, is it for the U.S. or the wider church? We are not local priests, we are global priests." Bishop Mwai Abiero of Kenya described the implications of Robinson's consecration more succinctly: "The entire church has been attacked." For uninitiated Westerners, these expressions of universal and communal faith often seemed baffling. But Orombi took them so seriously that he abstained from celebrating the Eucharist with American bishops after Robinson's consecration. To tolerate sin in one part of the Anglican Communion, he explained, would be to sanction it everywhere. Inevitably, sexual perversion would spread to Africa itself, just as the other strange fruits of poverty, militarism, and disease had been brought in the nineteenth century by Western imperialists. By 2006, ten of eleven provinces in Africa had declared themselves to be in "impaired communion" with the Episcopal Church. Many other provinces in India, Southeast Asia, and South America joined them.[24]

This postcolonial critique, as it emerged in the early 2000s, was met by Western ambivalence. Many establishment Anglicans, such as Canon Gregory Cameron, a leading advisor at Canterbury, sympathized with these worries about a "dark side" of Western Anglicanism that "assumes superiority over Anglicans in the developing world." He particularly indicted the U.S. church for placing "implicit obligations" on African and Asian provinces through "a NATO-style attitude of intellectual superiority." Too many Westerners, he said, failed to recognize that "the average Anglican is a black woman under the age of 30, who earns two dollars a day, has a family of at least three children, has lost two close relatives to AIDS, and who will walk four miles to church for a three-hour service on a Sunday." Sexual habits, he implied, matter. They lead to life or death. On the other hand, many Americans, even some conservatives, quailed at the intensity of antigay language that came from Orombi and others. American liberals recognized the value of indigeneity, but they objected to African homophobia. Moreover, they too felt beleaguered. Having enjoyed advances in the 1970s, gay activists suffered backlash in the 1980s. Then in the 1990s, they felt abandoned by third-way Democrats who pursued a policy of "don't ask, don't tell." Ready for a fight in the 2000s, they pushed back against conservative Anglicans holding the line.[25]

In response, East African bishops framed their views on sexuality in terms of faithfulness, leadership, and autonomy. Declaring that "the long season of British hegemony is over," Orombi predicted that "the younger churches of Anglican Christianity will shape what it means to be Anglican." Their identity would be built on three pillars: the martyrs, revival, and the historic episcopate, whose authority the Episcopal Church in America refused to acknowledge. Further, East Africa was claiming miracles, healings, and revival on a scale unimaginable in America. Even though the Church of Uganda for a time lacked working phones at headquarters, African bishops reasoned that their spiritual advantage allowed them to reject Episcopalian "dirty money," as one Kenyan bishop called it. Beginning in 2004, Orombi turned down $400,000 a year—and then triple that amount when the Episcopal Church wanted to return to communion with the Ugandans. "Do they think this church runs on money?" he asked. Emmanuel Kolini, archbishop of a Rwanda diocese desperately trying to recover from genocide, declared, "We are an independent church and we don't need any funding from America. Ours is not a begging church, it is a church that can stand on its own." It was time for Africans to "rise up," and there was compelling evidence that it already had. Uganda alone had nine million Anglicans. Africa's twelve provinces boasted seventy million, which dwarfed the Episcopal Church's declining membership of two million and average Sunday attendance of only 700,000. Inspired by this demographic triumph, African bishops readied for ecclesiastical battle.[26]

III. Reversing Mission

Conservative Episcopalians, feeling embattled as the LGBTQ movement gained steam in the United States, eyed an alliance with these African bishops. Inspired by Philip Jenkins's book *The Next Christendom: The Coming of Global Christianity* (2002), which profiled a thriving revivalist evangelical movement in places like East Africa, Guernsey wondered if bishops like Orombi could be the salvation of an apostatizing Episcopal Church. Orombi, a charismatic leader educated in the West, in fact was perfectly positioned to traverse transnational networks, and during the 2000s a relationship between Orombi and Guernsey began to take shape (Figure 7.1). Orombi was no longer a provincial tribesman, and Guernsey was not an insular Westerner. Shifting from a defensive posture in a colonial landscape to offense in a postcolonial world, African Anglicans—along with their Western allies—began to coordinate a reverse mission to America.[27]

Orombi did not operate alone. CAPA, which had coordinated efforts toward social justice in the lead-up to Lambeth in 1998, began to speak with collective force "from an African perspective" on the issue of sexuality. In the 2000s CAPA, led by Akinola, began to coordinate the breaking of member dioceses' links to the Episcopal Church during the Gene Robinson controversy. Though 70 percent of its budget came from the Episcopal Church, CAPA pledged to "take whatever action it felt necessary if the Episcopalians did not repent over the ordination of homosexuals within the next three months." As the crisis continued, twelve African archbishops met regularly in closed-door meetings to manage their relationship with the West. Canterbury felt the pressure, and Archbishop Rowan Williams, desperate to keep the Communion together, came to CAPA meetings when summoned. At one conference Williams heard passionate entreaties from the 400 bishops "to reject Western ways of tearing the church apart."[28]

Africans also sought solidarity with others in the Majority World. In the 1950s, when Ugandan evangelist William Nagenda conducted a revival tour of India, the East African Revival began to go global. Those collaborations intensified in the 1990s and 2000s as angst over homosexuality grew. Akinola reached out to colleagues from India and Pakistan upset over Robinson's ordination. Orombi strengthened ties with China and Singapore. Archbishop Datuk Yong Ping Chung of Malaysia, known as the "Asian tiger," credited the divine for these connections, saying, "Only God could bring together a churchman from Sabah (north Borneo) in Malaysia and one from Rwanda." Emerging digital networks contributed to these relationships. In particular, a website called Global South Anglican Online connected conservative Anglicans across continents. These contacts culminated in gatherings called "South-to-South Encounters." At the second meeting, which took place in 1997 in Kuala Lumpur, Malaysia, bishops issued a "Trumpet from the South." It critiqued colonialism and called for debt relief, but it also anticipated the Anglican sexual crisis. Affirming a conservative stance on sexuality and stressing "concern about mutual accountability and interdependence within our Anglican Communion," the statement concluded, "We live in a global village and must be more aware that the way we act in one part of the world can radically affect the mission and witness of the Church in another." Declarations at the next gathering—held in Egypt in 2005 in the wake of the Robinson crisis—ratcheted up the intensity even more. The "Third Trumpet from the South" condemned "the current crisis provoked by North American intransigence." Two years later, Guernsey's consecration (Figure 7.1) brought many of the same South American, Asian, and African bishops to Mbarara.[29]

Majority World activism on sexuality increasingly included like-minded Westerners who sought aid and comfort from African conservatives. These were relationships that, in some cases, had formed decades before at places like Lausanne. The prominent Anglican John Stott was especially important. From his headquarters at All Souls International Fellowship in London, Stott hosted thousands of international students preparing for national independence as the British Empire dissolved. He introduced them to the Evangelical Fellowship in the Anglican Communion (EFAC), the Alpha program, and the Oxford Centre for Mission Studies, where luminaries like J. I. Packer and Chris Sugden circulated. Stott, in turn, went on a university tour in 1962 to Sierra Leone, Ghana, Nigeria, Kenya, Uganda, and Rhodesia. His globetrotting increased through the 1970s, 1980s, and 1990s. Stott, who held to a conservative stance on sexuality, mentored many Africans, such as Festo Kivengere and David Gitari, who

Figure 7.1. In 2007 Archbishop Henry Orombi of Uganda consecrated John Guernsey, a vicar from Virginia, as a bishop in the Anglican Church of Uganda. Courtesy of Alison Barfoot.

were active in the Lausanne movement and in the same-sex controversies of the 2000s.[30]

Stott also built bridges to conservatives in the United States. Through the 1960s he maintained close ties with the Fellowship of Witness, the American branch of EFAC. In the early 1970s he helped launch the Trinity School for Ministry in Ambridge, Pennsylvania. Trinity, which became the nucleus of the evangelical wing of the Episcopal Church, also brought together Majority World Anglicans and Americans with connections to InterVarsity Christian Fellowship, Fuller's church growth movement, Rick Warren's Saddleback Church, Youth With a Mission, and evangelical elites on the Canterbury Trail. Stott built especially strong connections to Wheaton College, where some faculty and students dismayed by the liberal theology of the Episcopal Church were nonetheless drawn to its tradition and aesthetics. Other conservative Anglicans joined the reparative therapy movement. Alan Medinger, who left the Episcopal Church over same-sex marriage in 1997, was the first director of Exodus International, an organization that purported to reorient gay persons.[31]

Dense Anglican networks also connected Africa to America. Guernsey first visited the Kigezi region of Uganda in 1989. His new Ugandan friends, including Bishop Edward Muhima, reciprocated with trips to Virginia. Guernsey and his parishioners returned to Uganda at least half a dozen more times. They bonded over a conservative theology, charismatic practices, the ordination of women, and a sense of "spiritual connection." Stephen Noll, on faculty at Trinity School for Ministry for two decades, took a post as vice chancellor at Bishop Tucker Theological College, which was renamed Uganda Christian University in 1997. Many African bishops and archbishops headed in the other direction to attend Trinity. David Virtue, a prominent writer and self-proclaimed "voice for global orthodox Anglicanism," straddled the continents online. A native New Zealander, he had served as pastor of an African-American Baptist church and had ties with Trinity Evangelical Divinity School, Regent College, and World Vision International. Feeling under siege in America, Guernsey, Noll, Virtue, and other conservatives welcomed the bold, energetic activism of their distant allies. Nearly two decades after Guernsey's first visit to Uganda, the Virginian returned in 2007 to be consecrated as "an American priest canonically resident in North Kigezi Diocese.[32]

As these international relationships matured, each site contributed something to the conservative coalition. Anglicans from Europe often introduced Africans and North Americans to each other. Americans offered information. Bill Atwood, who both brought African bishops to preach and teach in the United States and visited Kampala himself, told stories about gay activism and unorthodox theology in the Episcopal Church. He described the alleged heresies of

Bishop Spong, who had proclaimed that the "view of the cross as the sacrifice for the sins of the world is a barbarian idea based on primitive concepts of God and must be dismissed." Africans contributed big numbers and righteous outrage. Archbishop Benjamin Yugusuk of Sudan was so disturbed that he cornered Atwood after one conference talk. "He had tears running down his cheeks," Atwood later remembered, "held my face in his coal black hands and began to kiss my face gently all over . . . forehead, temples, cheeks . . . and he said, 'When you spoke, God moved me. I will stand with you even against your primate.' It was one of the pivotal experiences of my life." These exchanges set the stage for the Majority World rebellion.[33]

Some of the most profound encounters occurred between parishioners. Once a year beginning in 1994, Alison Barfoot, a graduate of both Trinity and the evangelical Gordon-Conwell Theological Seminary near Boston, traveled to the Nebbi Diocese of Uganda, where Orombi was bishop. She explained that she and hundreds of others from dioceses in Virginia and Kansas returned so often because they "loved the country and people." Orombi's Ugandan parishioners traveled in the opposite direction to America. These trips, arranged by a mission agency called Sharing of Ministries Abroad (SOMA), typically took middle-aged Anglican parishioners back and forth from America and the Majority World on two-week mission ventures. Deep relationships, shaped in the crucible of mutuality, prayer, and culture shock, formed during some of these encounters. One American participant described being challenged by an African priest concerned about high rates of abortion, pornography, and sexual permissiveness in America. "By being away from my culture and separated by thousands of miles," he explained, "I got a different perspective on my own culture and I grieved. I saw what is normal at home viewed more from God's perspective. I saw this and wept and ultimately found myself in confession to this priest." These relationships, sustained by an average of eight visits each year, created strong ties between North and South.[34]

Significantly, these relationships nurtured shared sensibilities on issues other than sexuality. After Orombi led the very first SOMA mission to the United States, one report said, "These charming Ugandans proclaim, without shame, what seems to be 'pent up' inside evangelical Americans—the joy and abandonment of God." Another member of an American diocese said, upon his return from Uganda, "You've never heard children sing until you've been to Africa, you've never seen children dance until you've been to Africa; and you've never heard drums played until you've been to Africa." Miranda Hassett describes these American characterizations of Africa as the "rhetorics of idealization." Africans seemed to embody the joy of the Lord in their simplicity, nobility in suffering, and backbone in the face of liberal heresy. These descriptions—"charming Ugandans" with "coal-black hands"—often perpetuated colonial tropes of Africans as childlike, backward, and exotic. But Americans, delighting in the joyous faith of Africans and their potential to bring life to a stale and dying Episcopal Church, insisted that Westerners needed saving this time around.[35]

Salvation came at Lambeth. As historian John Maiden has demonstrated, these intimate relationships cultivated conservative networks that were solidified by 1998. At several American-funded conferences in Dallas and Kampala just prior to Lambeth—and then at Lambeth itself—American conservatives coached global primates on bureaucratic procedures and ecclesiastical etiquette. Together they orchestrated a victory at Lambeth in the face of a pliant, then stunned, liberal bloc, which did not quite grasp the implications of Jenkins's not-yet published "Next Christendom" thesis. Critics described conservative victories as a right-wing American conspiracy. American conservatives contended that they were simply supporting a minority group. Africans themselves voiced appreciation for the gift of agency. Orombi may have functioned as a usable Ugandan for American conservatives, but he nonetheless eagerly enlisted in the war for the Anglican soul.[36]

As battles raged, Majority World Anglicans began to view differently the role of America in the missionary movement. In fact, on the last day of Lambeth, Emmanuel Kolini of Rwanda and Moses Tay of Singapore rose from prayer on their knees and declared the United States, which had once sent missionaries to Africa, to be "an open mission field." Two years later they founded the Anglican Mission in America (AMiA), consecrating Charles Murphy as a bishop of the Province of Rwanda and John Rodgers as a bishop of the Province of South East Asia to launch pastoral ministries in an apostate America. Episcopal leaders were not pleased. "Bishops are not intercontinental ballistic missiles, manufactured on one continent and fired into another as an act of aggression," said one. But over the next decade, Majority World leaders launched hundreds of these missionary bishops. During one three-hour-long ceremony in 2002 at Colorado Community Church, in which Kolini of Rwanda and Chung of Malaysia consecrated four new bishops to serve in Arkansas, South Carolina, Colorado, and California, Murphy declared, "In a bold reversal of the missionary actions of the last 500 years, the churches in Africa and Asia have undertaken a labor of love and courage to renew and revitalize the Anglican faith in America." Within a few years the AMiA boasted thirty-seven congregations, seventy-five clergy, and 8,000 members across the United States. By 2007 there were 130 congregations under the auspices of the Anglican Church of Rwanda alone, which was financially independent after separating from the Episcopal Church. Conservatives, irritated by accusations of intolerance, declared, "It's hard to accuse AMiA members of being bigoted malcontents when they are, in effect, members of African churches." AMiA saw white progressives like Spong, who said Africans had moved out of animism only to fall into another "very superstitious kind of Christianity," as the real bigots.[37]

AMiA offered a reproducible model. In 2004, just one month after attending Orombi's enthronement as archbishop in Mbarara, Alison Barfoot wrote the infamous "Barfoot memo." It proposed that other dioceses follow Rwanda's example. Preferably, preexisting relationships, like those nurtured by SOMA and experienced by Barfoot herself in Uganda, could be used. If not, a match could be made through CAPA. In either case, an "offshore bishop" from Africa would provide "spiritual oversight" to American dioceses. Three months after her memo, Orombi poached Barfoot from her post as corector of Christ Church in Overland Park, Kansas, the largest in the diocese with a weekly attendance of 1,100. Her goal as the new Assistant for International Relations for the Church of Uganda was to broker partnerships with Episcopal parishes—and to massage relations with the nineteen parishes already under Orombi's spiritual care. Some American rectors reported getting "to know their Ugandan bishop better than they ever had known their American bishop." Together they sought to spark "the re-establishment of biblically orthodox faith as normative in North American Anglicanism."[38]

Many joined this missionary effort. In 2004, two large parishes in Southern California—Newport Beach and Long Beach—broke away from the Episcopal Church to affiliate with Orombi and the Church of Uganda. Within several years, the Church of Uganda was sheltering over fifty North American parishes. By 2006 observers estimated that over 200 Episcopal parishes had defected to Majority World dioceses. In 2007, as John Guernsey was consecrated as a bishop to oversee many of them, there was another flurry of missionary bishop consecrations. Nine Virginia parishes affiliated with the Convocation of Anglicans in North America, a mission launched by the Nigerian archbishop Peter Akinola. Three days before Guernsey's consecration, Archbishop Benjamin Nzimbi consecrated two Americans—Bill Murdoch and Bill Atwood—as bishops answerable to the Anglican Church of Kenya. Days later, Rwanda announced that the ordination of three American bishops would take place the next year. In 2008, the dioceses of Pittsburgh, Quincy, and Fort Worth followed San Joaquin, eighteen other congregations, and thirty-three clergy into the Province of the Southern Cone. All pledged canonical obedience to their respective African churches. Archbishop of Canterbury Rowan Williams asked the Africans to stop, but they did not comply. The scramble for America continued through the late 2000s.[39]

The hostile response of the Episcopal Church seemed to confirm the Majority World's worst suspicions. Reports of ostracism circulated widely. Liberal bishops, it was said, refused to ordain conservatives who had attended Trinity, Fuller, or Gordon-Conwell seminaries. After the Diocese of Lexington, Kentucky, refused to allow St. John's Episcopal Church to hire David Brannen, an opponent of Gene Robinson's election as bishop, the majority of members withdrew. Instead of fighting in court for the property, they abandoned possessions—including pews, prayer books, bank accounts, and buildings worth $19 million—accumulated over a 157-year history. The new congregation, St. Andrew's Anglican Church, submitted to a new authority: the Church of Uganda. In Virginia, Truro lost $10 million and The Falls Church $17 million. Frustrated conservatives complained that the Episcopal Church was running over people "like a 10-ton truck." Episcopal officials explained that they were simply carrying out ecclesiastical protocols in an effort to hold together diverse constituencies. They decried conservative dissenters who, acting as a "theological lynch mob," were defying church authority by continuing "to cross provincial boundaries and exercise authority over congregations in the U.S. without necessary consultation or consent."[40]

The conservative coalition's influence peaked in June 2008 at the Global Anglican Future Conference (GAFCON). Held in Jerusalem, a non-Western site chosen to symbolically displace Britain as the locus of Anglican authority, GAFCON emerged as a rival to Canterbury. In some ways, GAFCON was more of the same. Declaring that "we can only come to the devastating conclusion that we are a global Communion with a colonial structure," one GAFCON statement reaffirmed the Communion's conservative understandings of sexuality. Canterbury, it noted, had not followed through on Resolution I.10, which declared that the Church "cannot advise the legitimising or blessing of same sex unions." More significantly, GAFCON functioned as an "alternative Lambeth." In a gesture pregnant with meaning, 230 bishops, mostly from Africa, refused to attend Lambeth 2008 and traveled to Jerusalem instead. Since the invitation list included members of the middle and bottom of the hierarchy, GAFCON became the largest global gathering of Anglicans in history, outstripping all other Lambeths. Nearly 1,300 leaders attended (including one hundred from Uganda), representing twenty-five countries.[41]

In between pilgrimages to the Mount of Olives and prayer services on the shores of the Sea of Galilee, delegates critiqued a dying Western church and lauded a vibrant East. Invoking the Balokole revival, GAFCON leaders sought to "reassert as normative Anglican Christianity the reality we know in Uganda— that a personal relationship with Jesus Christ can bring substantive change for good in a person's life." "That's why," said one, "we're at GAFCON and not going to Lambeth." Those gathered in Jerusalem were journeying "back to the roots of our faith, to the place where Jesus was born, died, and was raised from the dead" in the middle of the Roman Empire. Two millennia later, these Eastern Christians were attempting a similar subversion, this time of the British Empire. In his closing address Akinola called for attendees to cast off the shackles of colonialism. "We are here," he declared to a standing ovation, "because we know that in God's providence GAFCON will liberate and set participants, particularly

Africans, free from spiritual bondage which [the Episcopal Church] and its allies champion." Placing the moment in historical context, Akinola concluded, "Having survived the inhuman physical slavery of the nineteenth century, the political slavery called colonialism of the twentieth century, the developing world economic enslavement, we cannot, we dare not allow ourselves and the millions we represent be kept in [a] religious and spiritual dungeon." Orombi's jubilant message back home to Uganda read, "GAFCON is not just a moment, but a movement."[42]

It was a movement, said the African archbishops, that intended to reshape the West. Akinola described their work as responding to "the vacuum created by secularism" in America. "We had no choice but to come rescue our people," said Akinola. The Church of Uganda, portraying the border dispute as a refugee crisis, described its work as an "ecclesiastical refugee ministry." It was offering sanctuary to displaced Americans. Guernsey gave thanks. "All Uganda, and the whole world," he declared at his enthronement in Mbarara, "needs to be reminded of the lifeline you courageously threw to us when a sea of secularism and revisionism threatened us with drowning." The new coalition also described its work in more aggressive terms. "Our objective is to be the Anglican mission in America," said Charles Murphy, "not the Anglican *refuge* in America." In the wake of a dying Episcopal Church, they wanted to plant new churches and make new converts. They even dreamed of a thirty-ninth Anglican province in North America that would function as an orthodox alternative to Episcopalian heresy. Barfoot put it dramatically: "Africa was once a mission field; now it is a mission force." In the face of a perceived illiberal liberalism, the old imperial pattern had been upended.[43]

Reaching out to broader evangelicalism, these Anglicans did not operate in a vacuum. They nurtured friendships with Rick Warren and other American luminaries. In 2010 Orombi served as honorary chair of the Africa Host Committee at Lausanne III in Cape Town, South Africa, where he presided over the Eucharist and the closing ceremony. His daughter Helen studied at Eastern University in Pennsylvania and worked for Ron Sider's Evangelicals for Social Action. Orombi's son Bob worked for Compassion International. Further, many of Orombi's Anglican mentors and heroes—including Stott, Kivengere, and Luwum (who having survived Idi Amin's first attack, traveled to the World Congress in Switzerland in 1974)—were participants in the Lausanne movement. Global Anglicanism both reflected and intersected with global evangelicalism. Many religious leaders pressured North American Christians to maintain conservative views of sexuality.

Lausanne III was particularly important. International delegates offered moral support to Americans who felt under siege by a rapidly changing domestic environment. At the congress, delegates noted the severe persecution of Christians in China and Algeria. "Here are people risking their lives to be Christians," said

Atwood. The implication was that, surely, Americans could withstand modest pressures on homosexuality. Issuing a statement entitled "Human Sexuality, By God's Design," a Lausanne III committee called on Christians in America and around the world to "resist the multiple forms of disordered sexuality in our surrounding cultures, including pornography, adultery, and promiscuity." It declared that God's design was a "committed, faithful relationship between one man and one woman." Not following this biblical design, continued the statement, would lead to personal loneliness and exploitation and broader social decline. Recognizing all of humanity's vulnerability to sexual sin and "Christ's pastoral compassion for sinners," it allowed for no innovation on the issue of homosexuality. In a Pew survey of the delegates, 84 percent said that society should discourage homosexuality. The numbers were especially high on the part of respondents from Asia (94 percent) and sub-Saharan Africa (96 percent) compared with delegates from North America (87 percent), Europe (72 percent), and Central and South America (45 percent).[44]

These discontinuities between East and West surfaced again several years later within World Vision. A firestorm erupted after World Vision U.S. announced in March 2014 that it would hire employees in same-sex marriages. American culture warriors such as Franklin Graham cried heresy, and donors immediately withdrew thousands of sponsorships. But the missing story in the brouhaha—and subsequent policy reversal—was international pushback. World Vision Korea, which within hours of the American story breaking received hundreds of complaints from churches and donors, immediately posted a statement of objection on its website. According to one employee, board members were "very angry." In World Vision U.S.'s announcement reversing its decision, President Rich Stearns reached out to its international partners. "We are writing to you our trusted partners and Christian leaders who have come to us in the spirit of Matthew 18 to express your concern in love and conviction," said Stearns. "We have listened to you and want to say thank you and to humbly ask for your forgiveness." Said one former World Vision worker, the organization had to "be sensitive to being a member of an international partnership. There are 50-some World Visions in the world. Especially in Africa and Asia, the position World Vision just rescinded would have been troublesome." A persistent conservative sexuality—and the internationalization of World Vision in the 1970s—made this critique possible.[45]

Through the 2000s and 2010s many Christians from the Global South forcefully inserted themselves in other ecclesiastical disputes. In 2008 Nigerian and Congolese Methodists denied "the compatibility of homosexual practice with Christian discipleship." American conservatives relished such statements. A spokesperson for the right-wing Institute for Religion and Democracy asked, "Will the UMC learn from the experience of our fast-growing UM churches in Africa . . . which preach and live the traditional Christian Gospel?" In the

United States, the United Methodist Church was losing 40,000 members a year as the already-larger African Methodist church added 100,000 each year. In 2010 Tanzanian and Ethiopian Lutherans pledged not to accept money or work with groups that "support the legitimacy" of same-sex marriage." In 2011 Mexican Presbyterians ended their affiliation with the Presbyterian Church (U.S.A.) after it began allowing clergy to perform same-sex marriages. Churches in Brazil and Peru followed a few years later. African Catholics placed similar pressure on the Vatican. Renatus Leonard Nkwande of Tanzania insisted that fellow bishops not "compromise the gospel and sacrifice divine revelation." They have come of age, said one cardinal, "and are making sure their voice is heard. . . . The fault lines at the 2014 synod don't just run left/right, but also north/south." In response to the pushback, the Vatican changed language from "welcoming" gays to "providing for" them. Debates over sexuality fractured religious bodies throughout the decade.[46]

These struggles had the secondary effect of forging new, sometimes unlikely, ecumenical relationships. Conservative Baptists, Methodists, Catholics, Mennonites, and Anglicans found common ground over sexuality and a rhetoric of anticolonialism. In 2006 Orombi, who maintained connections to Baptist pastor Rick Warren and Kevin DeYoung of the Gospel Coalition, became the first Anglican to preach at a Pentecostal church. One Ugandan Christian even pledged to work with Muslims. "Any faith that opposes the man who uses state machinery to 'ram the same sex agenda down our throats' will not escape the fire," wrote Martin Ssempa. "We need a united front of the major faiths, Christians and Muslims alike." Disputes over sexuality contributed to the realignment of global religion.[47]

IV. The Limits of Global Resistance

There were limits to this conservative reflex. Not all African Anglicans toed the line or wanted to separate from the Episcopal Church. In fact, several prominent Ugandans—including Benjamin Lubega-Musoke at Holy Trinity on Wall Street; Emmanuel Sserwadde at the Episcopal Church Center in New York; Petero Sabune, Africa Partnership Officer; and Hellen Wangusa, the Anglican Observer at the United Nations—worked for the American hierarchy. Other Anglican bishops from South Africa, such as Archbishop Thabo Makgoba of Cape Town, held to a traditional view of sexuality, yet wanted an open conversation in which both sides participated. Archbishop Desmond Tutu pushed more decisively against bishops from Uganda, articulating his "sense of shame" at belonging to an Anglican Communion that "was so unwelcoming of gay people." In the 2010s

Latin Americans emerged to defy the apparent Majority World consensus. At Lausanne III about one half of leaders from Central and South America said that homosexuality should be accepted by society.[48]

Similarly, not all American evangelicals were in tune with the scathing language of Orombi, Kolini, and Akinola. While Americans were said to have helped inspire Uganda's notorious Anti-Homosexuality Bill, most conservative evangelicals spoke out against it. Early iterations of the bill included the death penalty for some gay people, though life imprisonment replaced capital punishment in the final version that passed Parliament in 2013. Rick Warren described the bill as "unjust, extreme and un-Christian." Russell Moore of the Southern Baptist Convention declared, "Those of us who hold to a Christian sexual ethic don't want to see those who disagree with us jailed; we want to see them reconciled to God through the gospel." Such comments prompted David Zac Niringiye, a bishop in the Church of Uganda, to protest that "the international community is behaving like it can't trust Ugandans to come up with a law that is fair." Some East Africans even accused the conservative wing of American evangelicalism of drifting from orthodoxy.[49]

Nor did Americans fully comprehend the implications of the flipped ecclesiology. In 2007 All Souls Anglican of Wheaton, Illinois, invited Paul Rusesabagina, the Hutu hotel manager (played by Don Cheadle in *Hotel Rwanda*) who rescued both Hutus and Tutsis during the genocide, to speak at their church. The church's pastor, J. Martin Johnson, hoped to raise funds from the event to build a school in Rwanda. Archbishop Kolini, however, directed Johnson to cancel Rusesabagina's appearance under pressure from Paul Kagame, Rwanda's president. It turned out that Rusesabagina was a critic of Kagame. Johnson, who had little conception of the Rwandan political landscape, penitently complied with the order, saying "Truly I am horrified that we could have such a negative impact without meaning to." But it was difficult for Americans to submit to an ecclesial authority thousands of miles away. "The bigger reality for us is having to accept the whole concept of obedience, and that is a harder cultural pill to swallow than I realized," Johnson concluded. Others did not submit so penitently. In 2011 AMiA bishop Charles Murphy resigned rather than submit to Rwandan archbishop Onesphore Rwaje's demand for more oversight of the AMiA. The following year eight other bishops did the same. A common antipathy toward gay marriage was sometimes not enough to sustain the day-to-day operations and cultural challenges of these far-flung dioceses. Such episodes temper claims of American anticolonialism and North–South partnership. These relationships were sometimes marriages of convenience that faded when something substantive was demanded of the American partners.[50]

But perpetual African oversight was never the intention. In 2010, after years of planning, nearly all of the American congregations under African oversight joined the nascent Anglican Church in North America (ACNA). African leaders described the ACNA's launch as the natural progression of indigenization begun with Guernsey's 2007 consecration, which gave him jurisdiction over parishes previously overseen by ten Ugandan bishops. In essence, Africans were releasing Americans into their own natural habitat. While this reduced African influence, Americans continued to take cues from their counterparts on certain issues. At its inception, for example, the ACNA set an ambitious goal of doubling its size to 2,000 congregations within five years. According to an evangelism expert at Wheaton College, "They're following some of their southern and global Anglican churches in how they're building churches using less trained leadership." Strong networks and influences persisted.[51]

Other scholars, objecting to the notion that Africans have had much influence, suggest that conservative sexual ethics in Africa is essentially an extension of American homophobia. Jeff Sharlet has written at length about the influence of Scott Lively, Franklin Graham, T. D. Jakes, Chuck Colson, Jesse Helms, and members of The Fellowship who used their money and connections to energize the antigay movement in Uganda. A 2009 conference in Kampala, for example, was engineered by Focus on the Family, the American Family Association, and the now-defunct Exodus International. Other western groups such as Ekklesia Society, the American Anglican Council, and the Institute for Religion and Democracy also have funneled considerable money to African dissenters. If these relationships are real, charge some critics, then conservative views on sexuality may not cleanly reflect authentic African sensibilities. In this formulation, African politicians like Yoweri Museveni of Uganda and Robert Mugabe of Zimbabwe welcomed Western interference and encouraged social anxiety in order to distract voters from poor economic conditions. According to Caroline Addington Hall, homophobic language "increases internal cohesion by transferring anxiety and attention to an outside group, and it makes the leader of the country seem bigger and more powerful as he stands up to the mighty Western countries." Western pressures thus intensified a stagnant antigay movement, essentially reactivating blue laws that were on the books but generally ignored. In this narrative there is a stark difference between an earlier era of relative silence on homosexuality and the new, more strident rhetoric. In short, cherry-picking Americans, applying a postcolonial gloss selectively, drew Africans into their own culture wars. They ignored antiracist, anticolonial, and anticapitalistic initiatives in Africa while funding antigay initiatives. In this formulation, Orombi was a pawn.[52]

Critics of the critics, however, want to preserve East African agency. They point out the persistence of antigay sentiment through the 1990s and 2000s. National law in every East African nation prohibited gay sex. A 2007 poll done by the Pew Global Attitudes Project showed that 96 percent of Ugandans agreed that homosexuality is a way of life that society should not accept. Even higher numbers—98 percent opposing same-sex marriage—pervaded Kenya. Anthropologist Lydia Boyd contends that in seeing the antihomosexuality bill "as simply the result of the transposition of an American homophobia, we misrepresent Ugandan concerns as mere reflections of an American agenda and obscure the motivations of local activists." These motivations reflect profound concern about the HIV/AIDS crisis as well as a high level of respect for a conservative family model that has characterized African evangelicalism since the Balokole revival. Taking Ugandans like Orombi seriously means considering the possibility that, even amid power asymmetry between East and West, Ugandan Anglicans in the 1990s and 2000s actually believed in monogamous heterosexual marriage.[53]

Notably, these antigay provocateurs have used a postcolonial vocabulary. Functioning within an ecclesial system based in England, staffed by white, usually progressive English speakers, and run by an Archbishop of Canterbury almost always chosen from Church of England bishops, their conservative activism has been an assertion of indigeneity. Announcing the Church of Nigeria's 2003 separation from the Diocese of New Westminster, Akinola explained, "It is significant that those dioceses most tempted to indulge themselves with unilateral actions, taken without consulting the wider Communion, seem so often to be among those materially most advantaged and to be in the global north. Should this not occasion reflection? Do we not see here, in the ready assertion of superior wisdom, a new imperialism?" From the perspective of East African archbishops, the demographic triumph of African evangelicalism, after long centuries of brutal imperialism, was a long time coming. Orombi may have prayed for forgiveness for hating English missionaries as a child, but his fundamental critique persisted in old age. Turning colonial discourse on its head, he refused to bow to yet another demand for "civilization."[54]

In fact, East African Anglicans have sought to redefine civilization. In a religious agenda seen by Western liberals as bizarrely idiosyncratic, they have promoted a heightened supernaturalism, a militant defense of conservative sexuality, and progressive rhetoric of social justice. Indeed, global Anglicans at GAFCON expressed "impatience with having to spend so much time" defending traditional sexual practices. Vinay Samuel, a Lausanne veteran, told *The Guardian* that the "real passion" by delegates is "how to make a difference in society and how to deal with poverty." They campaigned for Palestinian justice, fought hard for international debt relief, critiqued laissez-faire capitalism, and pushed for the Millennium Development Goals. African lobbying helped spark Jubilee 2000, a movement recommending that Western nations and the World Bank forgive billions of dollars of debt owed by the world's forty poorest nations. Eighty percent of delegates at Lausanne III in 2010 agreed that government "has a responsibility to care for the very poor," a claim with which only 56 percent of American evangelical respondents agreed. In the end, neither side could fully claim a Global South that insisted on mixing liberal and conservative categories. One Anglican Life and Witness gathering, for example, highlighted both international debt relief and the promotion of "strong healthy families through faithful monogamous heterosexual relationships," then linked them by decrying "unbridled economic individualism" as the key threat to both. This document indicted both sides and suggested that there were limits to the notion of usable Ugandans. They simply do not follow an American script.[55]

It would have been difficult for American evangelicals in 1940s Chicago and 1950s Seoul to imagine a dark-skinned African archbishop consecrating a pale white bishop from Virginia. But Orombi's 2007 consecration of Guernsey asserted African authority over American churches. Together they chastened what they saw as the libertine sexuality, cold rationalism, and plump materialism of the United States. In the early decades of the new century, global encounters persisted and challenged Americans in many other ways. In the humanitarian realm, for example, the work of antitrafficking activists in Southeast Asia raised thorny questions about how to approach social justice. Coupled with remarkable levels of Christian migration to the United States, these encounters have begun to fashion new configurations of evangelical internationalism.

Notes

1. Barbara Bradley Hagerty, "Foreign Archbishops Flock to U.S. Congregations," National Public Radio, October 7, 2007.
2. Guernsey quoted in Raymond Baguma, "Church Consecrates American Bishop," *New Vision* (Kampala), September 2, 2007.
3. Raymond Baguma, "Church Consecrates American Bishop," *New Vision* (Kampala), September 2, 2007; Andrew Higgins, "Divided Flock: Episcopal Church Dissidents Seek Authority Overseas," *Wall Street Journal*, September 20, 2007, A1; "The Church of Uganda Consecrates Two Bishops," Church of Uganda Press Release, September 6, 2007; "What Future for Anglicanism," *Leadership* (Abuja), September 17, 2007.
4. Higgins, "Divided Flock," A1.
5. For "reverse colonization," see Barbara Bradley Hagerty, "Foreign Archbishops Flock to U.S. Congregations," National Public Radio, October 7, 2007. For "whole world is watching," see Baguma, "Church Consecrates." For "true church," see Christopher Landau, "What Future for Anglicanism?" *BBC News*, September 14, 2007.
6. On the debate over "traditional" Ugandan sexuality and the origins of anti-gay rhetoric, see Martin Ssempa, "When Faith, State, and State-Inspired

Homosexuality Clash," *New Vision*, June 3, 2005; T. J. Tallie and Jason Bruner, "Truly Ugandan: Martyrs, Pope Francis, and the Question of Sexuality," *Notches*, January 5, 2016; Jonathan Zimmerman, *Too Hot to Handle: A Global History of Sex Education* (Princeton, N.J.: Princeton University Press, 2015).

7. "The Rt. Rev. John A. M. Guernsey," Anglican District of Virginia, 2011 Bishop Nominee Information Packet, copy in author's possession. For "vibrancy in biblical Anglicanism," see "Interview with Bishop John Guernsey," *Religion & Ethics Newsweekly*, September 21, 2007. On gay activism in the Episcopal Church in the 1970s and 1980s, see Caroline Addington Hall, *Thorn in the Flesh: How Gay Sexuality Is Changing the Episcopal Church* (Lanham, Md.: Rowman & Littlefield, 2013), 43–60.

8. Nathan Etengu, "I Smoked Opium, Says Archbishop Orombi," *New Vision*, May 6, 2007; Chris Ocowun, "Orombi's Grandpa Had Small Gods," *New Vision*, August 2, 2007; Larry Stammer, "Episcopal Church Schism: A Prelate of Evangelical Intensity," *Los Angeles Times*, September 5, 2004; Mindy Belz, "Men of the Hard Cloth," *World*, December 16, 2006.

9. On the Balokole Revival, see Kevin Ward, "'Tukutendereza Yesu': The Balokole Revival in Uganda," in Zablon Nthamburi, ed., *From Mission to Church: A Handbook of Christianity in East Africa* (Nairobi: Uzima Press, 1991). Harper quoted in Timothy Morgan, "Africa's Azusa Street," *Christianity Today*, March 28, 2006.

10. On Luwuum's martyrdom, see Belz, "Men of the Hard Cloth." For "fiery priest," see Crespo Sebunya, "Orombi Becomes New Head of Anglican Church," *African Church Information Service* (Nairobi), July 14, 2003. On Orombi's work as bishop, see Belz, "Men of the Hard Cloth," *World*. On Orombi's appeal to youth, see Esther Namugoji, "Archbishop Orombi's Year of Revival," *New Vision*, October 7, 2006. For "personal relationship with Jesus Christ," see Henry Orombi, "What Is Anglicanism?" *First Things*, August 2007, Orombi, "What Is Anglicanism?" *First Things*, 23–28. On Orombi's campaign against witchcraft and child sacrifice, see Francis Kagolo, "Limit Freedom of Witchdoctors, Says Orombi," *New Vision*, June 21, 2009; "Orombi Criticises Alur over Witchcraft," *New Vision*, November 27, 2008. On the decade of mission, see Ganzi Muhanguzi, "Anti-Gay Bishops Meet in Mukono," *New Vision*, September 30, 2008.

11. For "First Trumpet from the South," see http://www.globalsouthanglican.org/index.php/archives/category/trumpets. On Jubilee 2000, see "Crushing Debt," *Christianity Today*. On refugees from Congo, see Stammer, "Episcopal Church Schism." On the progressive politics of "evangelical renewalists" of the kind represented by Orombi, see Miller and Yamamori, *Spirit and Power*, 9.

12. On the staggering impact of HIV-AIDS, see Timothy Morgan, "The War against HIV," *Christianity Today*, April 4, 1994, 70–73.

13. On the linking of homosexuality and AIDS, see Kelvin Shimo, "Homosexuality Gives Rise to AIDS," *The Post* (Lusaka), October 6, 1998; Kwame Nsiah, "Why Shouldn't HIV/AIDS Invade Us?" *Ghanaian Chronicle* (Accra), March 12, 2004; Ephraim Kasozi, "Churches Plan Demo against Homos," *The Monitor* (Kampala), August 21, 2007.

14. On Orombi's concern about condom use, see Joel Ogwang, "Orombi Decries Evil in Church," *New Vision*, September 21, 2004. On the "ABC" prevention program, see

Charles Colson, "Beyond Condoms," *Christianity Today*, June 2003, 64. For Anglican strategic planning on the AIDS crisis, see Morgan, "War against HIV," 74; "Clerics on HIV Retreat in Uganda," *The Nation* (Nairobi), August 26, 1999; "No HIV Test, No Wedding—Anglican Church," *P.M. News* (Lagos), May 5, 2004. On dropping infection rates, see Colson, "Beyond Condoms," 64. For "progressive empowerment of women," see Orombi, "What Is Anglicanism?"

15. For "born with a financial burden," see "Crushing Debt," *Christianity Today*, May 22, 2000, 39. On debt remission, see Kevin Ward, "Same-Sex Relations in Africa and the Debate on Homosexuality in East African Anglicanism," *Anglican Theological Review* 84, No. 1 (Winter 2002): 82; "The Dallas Statement," *Transformation*, April 1998, 30–32; Jason Bruner, "Divided We Stand: North American Evangelicals and the Crisis in the Anglican Communion," *Journal of Anglican Studies* 8, No. 1 (2009): 101–25.

16. On Lambeth 1998, see "Sexuality Issues Test Bonds of Affection among Bishops," *Episcopal News Service*, September 3, 1998. On Chukwuma's attempted exorcism of Kirker, see Hall, *Thorn in the Flesh*, 107. For "spoke for the truth," see "Anglican Vote Reflects Move to the Right," *Chicago Tribune*, August 6, 1998.

17. On the election of Williams, see Stan Guthrie, "New Top Anglican Receives Mixed Reviews," *Christianity Today*, September 9, 2002, 28. For a small sample of the flood of denunciations of Robinson's election, see Mwanguhya Mpagi, "Church of Uganda Sticks to Its Guns," *The Monitor*, August 10, 2003; Richard Komakech, "COU Axes U.S. Diocese," *New Vision*, August 12, 2003; "Fight Homosexuality, Says Bishop," *East African Standard*, August 12, 2003; "Anglican Church Condemns Gay Bishop's Appointment," *Times of Zambia*, August 8, 2003; Jeff Otieno, "Archbishop Nzimbi Ready to Cut Links over Gay Row," *The Nation*, July 14, 2003. For "lion of Africa," see Hall, *Thorn in the Flesh*, 156.

18. "Archbishop Orombi Enthroned at Colourful Ceremony," *Episcopal News Service*, January 29, 2004; John Abimanyl, "Orombi: The Archbishop Who Chose Not to Fight," *Daily Monitor*, June 21, 2012. For "not welcome," see Fredrick Nzwili, "U.S. Church Told to Stay Away from Enthronement," *Ecumenical News Service*, January 30, 2004.

19. On Robinson as a tripwire, see Timothy Morgan, "Global Anglicans Flex Muscle," *Christianity Today*, January 2006, 54. Akinola quoted in Douglas LeBlanc, "Out of Africa," *Christianity Today*, July 2005, 43. For "matter of life and death," see Alfred Wasike, "Orombi Boycotts Holy Communion over Gays," *New Vision*, February 21, 2007. Griswold quoted in Neela Banerjee, "Episcopal Leader Retiring amid Divisive Debate on Sexuality of Bishops," *New York Times*, June 11, 2006, A28. For "African homophobia," see Albert Ogle, "Archbishop Orombi: Architect of African Homophobic Hate," *San Diego Gay and Lesbian News*. For "fundamentalist bigot," see Belz, "Men of the Hard Cloth."

20. For "pastoral care," see Wasike, "Orombi Boycotts." On African concerns about American theological liberalism, see Sonnie Ekwowusi, "The Failure of Liberal Protestantism," *This Day* (Lagos), November 12, 2003; Dorothy Kweyu, "Uneasy Calm as Major Split Looms Large in Anglican Church," *The Nation*, July 15, 2008. For "tradition on human sexuality," see Larry Stammer, "Episcopal Church Schism."

For "defining mark," see Peter Nyanzi, "Orombi: Prelate with a Distinction," *The Independent* (Kampala), July 1, 2012. For "Africans to remind," see "Canterbury Crackup," *Christianity Today*, December 2004, 28.

21. For mentions of Robinson's divorce, see Samwel Rambaya, "Anglican Church—The Controversy in Perspective," *East African Standard*, August 18, 2003; Ropafadzo Mapimhidze, "Appointment of US-Based Gay Bishop Set to Split Church," *The Herald* (Harare), October 18, 2003; Temitope Oguntokun, "Till Sex Do Them Part," *The News*, November 3, 2003. On divorce and adultery, see Anne Mugisa, "Archbishop Orombi Warns Adulterers," *New Vision*, April 7, 2007; "Divorce Worries Archbishop Orombi," *New Vision*, July 13, 2008. On abortion and pornography, see Josephine Maseruka, "Legalising Abortion Is a Curse," *New Vision*, December 14, 2006; Joseph Mugisa, "Orombi Advises on Politics," *The Monitor*, May 5, 2006.

22. For "decadent spiritual civilization," see "An Abomination," *Addis Tribune* (Addis Ababa), November 5, 2004. On pro-gay mailers, see "Ugandan Bishop Angered by Homosexuality Debate," *All Africa News Agency*, May 11, 1998. Nkoyooyo quoted in Karyeija Kagambirwe, "Nkoyooyo Raps West over Gays," *New Vision*, June 4, 1998.

23. On Integrity, see Hall, *Thorn in the Flesh*, 47–51; John Kakande, "US Gays to Aid Ugandans," *New Vision*, August 12, 2003. For "vice penetrates Africa," see Hall, *Thorn in the Flesh*, 203. For "monkeying around," see Jenkins, *New Faces*, 16. On Western liberals looking down on Africans, see Wes Granberg-Michaelson, *From Times Square to Timbuktu: The Post-Christian West Meets the Non-Western Church* (Grand Rapids, Mich.: Eerdmans, 2013), 149. For "global totalitarian liberalism," see Owen Sichone, "Nature of Gays," *The Post*, November 3, 1998.

24. For "global priests," see Hassett, *Anglican Communion in Crisis*, 126–27. Abiero quoted in Anderson Ojwang, "'Get Ready for God's Wrath' Says Bishop Abiero," *East African Standard*, August 18, 2003. For "impaired communion," see Belz, "Men of the Hard Cloth."

25. For "dark side," see Paul Redfern, "Bishop Takes Battle for Anglican Soul to London," *The Nation*, July 6, 2008.

26. For "long season of British hegemony," see Nyanzi, "Orombi—Prelate with a Distinction," *The Independent*, July 1, 2012. For "the younger churches," see Orombi, "What Is Anglicanism?" For "dirty money," see "Anglican Bishops Back Gay Ban," *The Nation*, April 17, 2004. For "runs on money," see Belz, "Men of the Hard Cloth." On African rejections of Episcopalian money, see LeBlanc, "Out of Africa"; Joseph Mudingu, "Country to Anoint U.S. Bishops," *The New Times*, September 6, 2007; Hudson Apunyo, "Orombi Advises against Begging," *The Monitor*, October 17, 2006; Derek Otieno, "Anglicans Spurn Gay Church Cash," *The Nation*, June 9, 2005. For "rise up," see Sam Eyoboka, "Homosexuality Is Totally Unacceptable—Clerics," *Vanguard*, October 12, 2008. For Anglican statistics, see Otieno, "Anglicans Spurn," *The Nation*; Michael Gryboski, "Episcopal Church Continues Downward Trend," *Christian Post*, November 1, 2013.

27. On the significance of Jenkins for conservatives, see Bruner, "Divided We Stand," 120–24.

28. Justus Waimiri, "African Provinces Cut Links with New Hampshire," *African Church Information Service*, November 10, 2003. For "take whatever action," see "Anglican

Bishops Back Gay Ban," *The Nation*, April 17, 2004. On Williams and CAPA, see Cyprian Musoke, "Anglican Bishops Maintain Anti-Gay Stand," *New Vision*, August 24, 2010. For "reject Western ways," see Stephen Otage, "Love Your Culture, Say African Bishops," *The Monitor*, August 30, 2010.

29. On Nagenda, see Brian Stanley, *The Global Diffusion of Evangelicalism* (Downers Grove, Ill.: InterVarsity Press, 2013), 76–85. On Akinola, see Douglas LeBlanc, "Out of Africa," *Christianity Today*, July 2005, 43. Chung quoted in Belz, "Men of the Hard Cloth." On Orombi and China and Singapore, see John Martin, "Archbishop Orombi Picks a New Platform," *Living Church*, January 11, 2012; Lucille Teoh, "We Need to Go to the Cross," *Global South Anglican News*, May 19, 2006. For "mutual accountability," see "The Kuala Lumpur Statement on Human Sexuality," February 15, 1997. For the text of all "trumpets from the South," see http://globalsouthanglican.org/archives/category/trumpets.

30. On Stott's nurturing of global networks, see Hall, *Thorn in the Flesh*, 63–68; Alister Chapman, *Godly Ambition: John Stott and the Evangelical Movement* (New York: Oxford University Press, 2011), 133–54; David Neff, "The Man Who Wouldn't Be Bishop," *Christianity Today*, March 2011, 44; Orombi, "We Need to Go to the Foot of the Cross," *Global South Anglican Online*, May 19, 2006. On the critical role of Chris Sugden, former missionary to India and director of the OCMS, in mobilizing a global conservative coalition, see Hall, *Thorn in the Flesh*, 164–65.

31. On the Fellowship of Witness, Trinity, and the growing conservative movement, see Hall, *Thorn in the Flesh*, 69–71. On Trinity's ties to InterVarsity and Fuller, see Janet Leighton, *Lift High the Cross: The History of the Trinity Episcopal School for Ministry* (Ambridge, Pa.: Whitechurch, 2014), 24, 42, 104. On ties to YWAM, see Edwina Thomas, "SOMA: Sharing Renewal Overseas," 411–12, in *New Wineskins for Global Mission* (Pasadena, Calif.: William Carey Library, 1996). On ties between conservative Anglicans and Rick Warren, Joni Eareckson Tada, and Anne Graham Lotz, see Morgan, "Global Anglicans Flex Muscle," 52. On the high church appeal to evangelicals, see Robert Webber, *Evangelicals on the Canterbury Trail* (Waco, Tex.: Word Books, 1985). On conservative Anglican participation in the conversion therapy movement, see Hall, *Thorn in the Flesh*, 73.

32. For "spiritual connection," see "Interview with Bishop John Guernsey," *Religion & Ethics Newsweekly*, September 21, 2007. On the many African students at Trinity, see Kevin Ward, "Pluralism and Fundamentalism as Challenges for the African Churches: Globalisation, Neo-Colonialism and Debates about Homosexuality," 164, in Klaus Koschorke, *Falling Walls* (Wiesbaden, Germany: Harrassowitz Verlag, 2009). For the extensive writings of David Virtue, see www.virtueonline.org. For "canonically resident," see "Archbishop Orombi to Consecrate American Bishop," *Episcopal News Service*, June 22, 2007.

33. On Atwood's relationship with Africans in the lead-up to Lambeth, see Hall, *Thorn in the Flesh*, 109–24. For "a barbarian idea," see Hall, *Thorn in the Flesh*, 116–17.

34. For more on Barfoot's SOMA trips to Uganda, see Richard Kew and Cyril Okorocha, *Vision Bearers: Dynamic Evangelism in the 21st Century* (Harrisburg, Pa.: Morehouse Publishing, 1996), 91–92. For "loved the country," see David Virtue, "Alison Barfoot and the Uganda Blessing," *Virtue Online*, August 30, 2006. On the profound nature

of cultural exchange, see Thomas, "Effective Training for Short-Term Missions," 197, 201, in *New Wineskins*; Stephne Bowers, "Repentance Leads to Healing," *Sharing*, May 2005, 2. On the Africa critique of abortion and the American response, see Thomas, "SOMA: Sharing Renewal Overseas," 411–12, *New Wineskins*.

35. For "charming Ugandans" and "building partnerships," see John Maiden, "Renewing the Body of Christ: SOMA USA and Transnational Charismatic Anglicanism, 1978-1988," *Journal of American Studies* 51, No. 4 (November 2017): 1243–66. For "rhetorics of idealization," see Hassett, "Episcopal Dissidents, African Allies: The Anglican Communion and the Globalization of Dissent" (PhD diss., University of North Carolina, 2004), 359–60.

36. On the coaching of global primates, see Hall, *Thorn in the Flesh*, 185; Bruner, "Divided We Stand," 114. On the victory at Lambeth in 1998, see Hassett, *Anglican Communion in Crisis*, 106–107; Hall, *Thorn in the Flesh*, 108; "Lambeth Takes Conservative Stand on Sexuality," *All Africa News Agency*, August 10, 1998.

37. For "open mission field," see Hall, *Thorn in the Flesh*, 131. For "intercontinental ballistic missiles," see Ann Rodgers-Melnick, "Anglican Leader Refuses to Recognize Bishops," *Pittsburgh Post-Gazette*, February 19, 2000. For the numbers on missionary bishops to the United States, see "More 'Missionary Bishops' Ordained," *Christianity Today*, August 6, 2001; Alex Ndegwa, "Nzimbi to Consecrate American Priests," *East African Standard*, August 14, 2007; Grace Mugabe, "Fight Homosexuality, Kolini Tells Churches," *New Times*, December 5, 2007. For "bigoted malcontents," see Byassee, "Splitting Up," 22.

38. Alison Barfoot, "Draft Proposal for Overseas AEO," March 3, 2004, copy in author's possession. For "to known their Ugandan bishop," see "Matchmaking for Uganda," www.livingchurch.org, November 2, 2009.

39. On the Church of Uganda's sheltering of Episcopal parishes, see David Sseppuuya, "Orombi Retires to Continue Serving," *The Monitor*, January 11, 2012. On the defection of 200 Episcopal congregations, see Morgan, "Global Anglicans Flex Muscles," 54. On Murdoch and Atwood, see Caroline Wafula, "Church Ordains Bishops for U.S.," *The Nation*, August 31, 2007. On Nigerian appointments, see Madison Trammel, "Dividing the Faithful," *Christianity Today*, February 9, 2007, 19. On Rwandan appointments, see Joseph Mudingu, "Country to Anoint U.S. Bishops," *The New Times*, September 6, 2007; Hall, *Thorn in the Flesh*, 231. For Rowan Williams's response, see Paul Redfren, "Split in Anglican Faith Now Inevitable," *The Nation*, September 2, 2007.

40. On discrimination toward evangelical candidates, see Morgan, "Global Anglicans Flex Muscles," 54; Hassett, "Episcopal Dissidents, African Allies," 275. On St. Andrew's Anglican Church, see Frank Lockwood, "A Slow Exodus," *Christianity Today*, June 2004, 21. On Truro and The Falls Church, see Belz, "Men of the Hard Cloth." For "theological lynch mob," see Michael Massing, "Bishop Lee's Choice," *New York Times Magazine*, January 4, 2004. For "cross provincial boundaries," see "Archbishop Consecrates Former Episcopal Priest as Bishop," *Episcopal News Service*, September 3, 2007. For "10-ton truck," see Morgan, "Global Anglicans Flex Muscles," 55.

41. For "colonial structure," see Joanna Sadgrove et al., "Constructing the Boundaries of Anglican Orthodoxy: An Analysis of GAFCON," *Religion* 40, No. 3 (2010): 194. For "alternative Lambeth," see Tabu Butagira, "Church of Uganda Steps Farther Away Over Gays," *The Monitor*, May 18, 2008. On the size of GAFCON, see Sadgrove, "Constructing the Boundaries," 196.

42. For "not going to Lambeth," see David Sseppuuya, "We Are Back to Our Roots in Jerusalem," *New Vision*, June 26, 2008. For "shackles of colonialism," see Sadgrove, "Constructing the Boundaries," 199. For "not just a moment," see David Sseppuuya, "Anglican Church Splits over Homosexuals," *New Vision*, June 29, 2008.

43. For "vacuum created by secularism," see Sadgrove, "Constructing the Boundaries of Anglican Orthodoxy," 200. For "ecclesiastical refugee ministry," see Sheryl Henderson Blunt, "Federation Charts New Frontier," *Christianity Today*, December 2007, 15. For "needs to be reminded," see John Guernsey, "Enthronement Sermon," www.anglicanchurch.net, 4. For "not the Anglican refuge," see Trammel, "Dividing the Faithful," 19. For "mission force," see David Virtue, "Evangelical Anglican Province Has Something to Offer Africa and the World: An Interview with Rev. Canon Dr. Alison Barfoot," www.virtueonline.org, August 30, 2006.

44. For Lausanne III's statement on sexuality, see Julia Cameron, *Christ Our Reconciler: Gospel, Church, World* (Downers Grove, Ill.: InterVarsity Press, 2012), 165–66. Also see "Global Survey of Evangelical Protestant Leaders," Pew Forum on Religion & Public Life, June 22, 2011, 78, 82–83.

45. On the reaction of World Vision-Korea, see author interview with Heesoo Kim, May 20, 2014; author interview with Hoon Song, May 21, 2014, Seoul, Korea. For "humbly ask for your forgiveness," see Celeste Gracey and Jeremy Weber, "World Vision Reverses Decision to Hire Christians in Same-Sex Marriages," *Christianity Today*, March 26, 2014.

46. On Methodism, see Sarah Ruble, *The Gospel of Freedom and Power* (Chapel Hill: University of North Carolina Press, 2012), 158; Kathleen Rutledge, "Heart of Truthfulness," *Christianity Today*, July 1, 2004, 16. On African Lutherans, see "African Lutherans Press Opposition to Gay Rites," *Christian Century*, June 1, 2010, 15. On PCUSA, see Renee Gadoua, "Brazil, Peru End Partnerships with PCUSA over Gay Marriage," Religion News Service, September 23, 2015. On African Catholics, see David Gibson, "African Bishops Play a Major Role, for First Time, at Contentious Vatican Summit," Religion News Service, October 18, 2015; John Allen, "Synod Is More and More Like a Soap Opera," *Crux*, October 16, 2014.

47. On Orombi's ecumenical activities, see Jeff Otieno and John Oywa, "Campaign to Merge Churches," *The Nation*, August 11, 2003; Gaaki Kigambo, "Orombi First Archbishop to Preach at KPC," *The Monitor*, April 16, 2006; Kevin DeYoung, "Interview with Henry Luke Orombi, www.thegospelcoalition.org, June 19, 2013. For "ram the same sex agenda," see Martin Ssempa, "When Faith, State, and State-Inspire Homosexuality Clash," *New Vision*, June 3, 2005.

48. On Sabune, see Ward, "Pluralism and Fundamentalism," 170. For "sense of shame," see Ward, "Pluralism and Fundamentalism," 171. On Makgoba, see Hall, *Thorn in the Flesh*, 215. On Tutu, see Michael Battle, "Elusive Communion," *Christian Century*,

September 4, 2007, 9. On Latin American evangelical views on homosexuality, see "Global Survey," 30.

49. On American sources of the bill, see Jeff Sharlet, "Straight Man's Burden: The American Roots of Uganda's Anti-Gay Persecutions," *Harper's*, September 2010. On American evangelical opposition, see Anugrah Kumar, "Rick Warren Squashes Rumors," *Christian Post*, March 3, 2014; Sarah Pulliam Bailey, "U.S. Evangelicals on the Defense over Uganda's New Anti-Homosexuality Act," *Washington Post*, March 4, 2014. On Niringiye, see Sarah Pulliam Bailey, "Anti-Homosexuality Bill Divides Ugandan and American Christians," *Christianity Today*, December 17, 2009.

50. On the stresses of cultural difference, see Belz, "Men of the Hard Cloth." On the politics of the Rwandan genocide, see Jason Byassee, "Splitting Up," *Christian Century*, May 20, 2008, 25–26; Charles Mugabo, "If All Could Emulate Archbishop Emmanuel Kolini," *New Times*, September 30, 2007. On Murphy, see Bobby Ross, Jr., "Out of Africa," *Christianity Today*, February 2012, 16. On the resignation of eight more American bishops, see "Anglican Splinter Group Faces New Power Struggle," *Christian Century*, March 7, 2012, 17.

51. For "following some of their southern and global Anglican churches," see Heather Sells, "Anglican Fever: Youth Flock to New Denomination," Christian Broadcasting Network, December 18, 2011.

52. On The Fellowship, see Sharlet, *The Family: The Secret Fundamentalism at the Heart of American Power* (New York: HarperCollins, 2008). On the presence of American culture warriors in Uganda, see Julius Mucunguzi, "U.S. Senator Praises Janet Museveni over HIV/AIDS Fight," *The Monitor*, February 22, 2002; F. Ahimbisibwe, "Preacher T.D. Jakes to Dig Wells," *New Vision*, January 20, 2005; Colson, "Beyond Condoms," 64. On the conference in Kampala, see Robert Vanderbeck et al., "Producing Moral Geographies: The Dynamics of Homophobia within a Transnational Religious Network," *The Geographical Journal* 179, No. 2 (June 2013): 168. On Western money funding meetings of conservative African leaders, see Bruner, "Divided We Stand," 115. On the manipulation of social anxieties, see Joanna Sadgrove et al., "Morality Plays and Money Matters: Towards a Situated Understanding of the Politics of Homosexuality in Uganda," *Journal of Modern African Studies* 50, No. 1 (2012): 106, 112–17. For "increases internal cohesion," see Hall, *Thorn in the Flesh*, 201. On the new, more strident activism compared, see Ward, "Same-Sex Relations," 89–93. On the American culture wars, see Ward, "Pluralism and Fundamentalism," 157.

53. On the public rejection of same-sex marriage, see Mugumo Munene, "Big 'No' to Same-Sex Unions," *The Nation*, July 19, 2005; Joseph Mudingu, "Homosexuality Puts the Church under Siege," *The New Times*, February 24, 2007; "Pew Global Attitudes Project," October 4, 2007, 35. For "misrepresent Ugandan concerns," see Lydia Boyd, "The Problem with Freedom: Homosexuality and Human Rights in Uganda," *Anthropological Quarterly* 86, No. 3 (Summer 2013): 699. On power asymmetries, see Bruner, "Divided We Stand," 116.

54. On the persistent colonial structure of Anglicanism, see Hall, *Thorn in the Flesh*, 205. Akinola and Gomez quoted in Hall, *Thorn in the Flesh*, 212. For Orombi's prayer for

forgiveness, see Niall Griffin and Geraldine Griffin, "Identificational Repentance," *Arm Wales Magazine* (n.d.), 4.

55. Samuel quoted in Riazat Butt, "Anglican Conservative Accuses 'Relic' Williams of Colonial Mindset," *The Guardian*, June 25, 2008. On Palestinian justice, see David Sseppuuya, "We Are Back to Our Roots in Jerusalem," *New Vision*, June 26, 2008. On the Millennium Development Goals, see Hall, *Thorn in the Flesh*, 219. On Jubilee 2000, see "Crushing Debt," *Christianity Today*, May 22, 2000, 39. For "help the very poor," see "Global Survey," 31. For "unbridled economic individualism," see Hall, *Thorn in the Flesh*, 112.

PART III
DISORIENTATIONS

8

Chiang Mai 2017

A Campaign against Human Trafficking

*Defend the cause of the weak and fatherless; maintain the rights of the
poor and oppressed. Rescue the weak and needy; deliver them from the
hand of the wicked.*

—A biblical passage quoted by Gary Haugen in
Good News about Injustice (1999)[1]

Moon's childhood in Myanmar was an exotic horror show. When she was only
twelve weeks old, she was sold by her mother into slavery. At the age of three,
her owner forced her to wash dishes in a restaurant for eight hours a day. When
Moon turned thirteen, her virginity was sold to a Western businessman. She
escaped, but three months later, she was captured and locked in a hotel room
with a man who had paid 30,000 baht (about $950) for the night. Beaten with a
belt until she submitted, Moon had to be carried away and could not walk for ten
days. The emotional toll of her exploitation was worse than the physical abuse. "I
was sad and ashamed because I wasn't clean," she remembers. A year later, Moon
immigrated to northern Thailand. Expecting to work at a noodle stand, she
found herself confined in a Chiang Rai brothel. When she rebuffed the first cus-
tomer, the brothel owner stuffed a ping-pong ball in her mouth and taped it shut.
The next night, drugged and threatened with cigarette burns, Moon was forced
to submit to fifteen men. Over the next month, she was raped over one hundred
times. "I cursed every god," she said, "but in my heart, I believed someone would
come and help me."

That someone was from an evangelical ministry called International Justice
Mission (IJM). After rescuing Moon from the Thai brothel, country directors
Christa and Mark Crawford of California offered her prayer, arranged for counseling through another NGO, and introduced her to Jesus Christ (Figure 8.1).
They also helped her launch a business selling assorted nuts. When that did
not prove successful, she sold souvenirs to tourists. A marriage and two babies
later, Moon's husband started a motorcycle taxi business with $200 loaned by the
Crawfords. This, finally, was the catalyst that transformed the family's financial
condition. Soon they were making double the amount they needed for food and

Facing West. David R. Swartz, Oxford University Press (2020). © Oxford University Press.
DOI: 10.1093/oso/9780190250805.001.0001

Figure 8.1. Christa Crawford and Moon in a town on the border of Thailand and Myanmar. Courtesy of Christa Crawford.

basic needs. According to a 2007 *Christianity Today* cover story, "After years of pouring Jesus' love into the lives of Moon and her young family, the Crawfords' team is witnessing a transformation of her entire family system." They all had converted to the Christian faith, and Moon herself was training others to help survivors of trafficking. Her identity, the article proclaimed to readers across the United States, "has changed from rescued to rescuer." Indeed, Moon was a model. As she embarked on a tour of American churches and colleges, she seemed to represent evangelical social action at its most compassionate and potent.[2]

Moon's story, however, did not end in 2007. Though she returned to Thailand with a closet full of clothing from Nordstrom and promises of funding from another American supporter to attend Bible school, her life began to fall apart. After Moon and her husband divorced, conditions beyond her control militated against self-improvement. Migration policy in Thailand limited her access to healthcare and education. Corruption and a lack of sustainable employment in Myanmar kept her out of her homeland. A strong Buddhist sensibility of family obligation required her to care for three generations. Before long, Moon—along with her mother, sister, brother, several nieces and nephews, and her own children—was sleeping on the floor in a hovel next door to a notorious brothel. Responsible for supporting all of them, she sold off her expensive wardrobe, piece by piece, until she had nothing left to sell but herself. One night the

Crawfords got a call from Moon, who told them she had been working at a seedy massage parlor. It was unclear whether she had turned to prostitution, but she tearfully agreed not to ever work at a place like that again. Moon's younger sister, however, did begin working in a bar, one that had reopened shortly after IJM had shut it down. It seemed only a matter of time before she began selling more than just drinks. "1,000 baht [about $29] is too much to turn down," she explained.

There was no follow-up article in *Christianity Today*. These sordid details simply did not fit the clean narrative readers in the United States wanted. American humanitarians in Thailand, on the other hand, quickly discovered the shortcomings of Moon's redemption. As the Crawfords told me in 2017, ten years after the original story was published, Moon represents the limits of rescue. On one hand, Mark Crawford described the twenty-nine-year-old Moon as a success story. Now working as a cosmetologist at a beauty parlor in a small town on the Thailand–Myanmar border, she has rebounded again. "That is a victory," said Mark, who remembered Moon telling him she would not live past the age of twenty-five. On the other hand, the twisting paths of Moon and her sister made for a sobering story. Moon, noted Christa, had "far more resources" than most victims of trafficking. Many people helped her and prayed for her, but nonetheless she had been "pulled back in . . . pressured by economics and other factors."

The Crawfords' relationship with Moon—and their consideration of the socioeconomic pressures that impeded her escape from prostitution—suggests a shifting approach to mission. In the 1940s evangelicals saw converting lost souls as their chief aim. Social justice was ancillary, at most a welcome side effect of cumulative conversions. By the twenty-first century, however, combatting injustice had become a driving ambition for many. This broadened agenda often retained the Christian American fervor of the patriotic rally at Soldier Field in 1945. There was no better example of this than IJM. As Mark Crawford notes, "At the beginning it was the American Justice Mission. The international part was only aspirational." Though on-the-ground activism in the 2000s and early 2010s carried antitrafficking NGOs on halting journeys toward greater indigeneity, cultural sensitivity, and attention to social structures, these trajectories enjoyed only limited appeal among constituents back home in the United States, where a neocolonial discourse of rescue persists. The campaign for human rights in Thailand remains incoherent.[3]

I. IJM and Christian Americanism

Christa Foster Crawford's journey to Asia looked very different than Bob Pierce's hardscrabble rise to prominence fifty years earlier. The two occupied similar ecclesiastical locations in the tight-knit, conservative Sunbelt evangelicalism of southern California. But the Fosters, a black couple fluent in the language and social graces of the white, upper-middle class community of Valencia, launched their daughter on a fast track through elite academia. She attended Claremont McKenna College and then Harvard Law School, with plans to join the U.S. Department of Justice as a prosecutor who would enforce the gospel of bootstraps. Fighting crime and lobbying for conservative policies on social issues mattered very much to her, as they did to the other Republican students who populated her law school Christian fellowship. By the early 1990s, Crawford and other highly credentialed and accomplished evangelicals were reaching for the highest rungs of American society.

A series of spiritual and social encounters, however, redirected Crawford's aspirations. Her husband Mark felt called by God to leave the corporate world and study counseling at Southern Baptist Theological Seminary. After Southern California and Boston, Louisville was "total culture shock" for a black woman married to a white man. At the age of twenty-five, Crawford experienced outright discrimination for the first time, and as she walked to work every day, she crossed a street that sharply divided a black neighborhood from a white one. It opened her eyes to injustice, a word she "never would have used before." God, she said in an echo of Bob Pierce, "began to break my heart of the things that broke His heart." She began to see inequalities in everything, even episodes of *Law & Order*. Instead of becoming a prosecutor, she felt moved to "side with the victims" in a justice system that could not "cope with the disenfranchised." As Southern Seminary reeled during the institution's conservative takeover led by a young Al Mohler, the Crawfords felt even more marginalized and disillusioned. They moved before Mark completed his degree.

The Crawfords landed in the more moderate climes of Fuller Theological Seminary in Pasadena, California. Feeling called to overseas justice work, Mark enrolled in the School of Intercultural Studies, the same program Donald McGavran had founded thirty years earlier as the School of World Mission. He flourished in courses such as "Theology of the Urban Poor." Both Crawfords embraced a "Fuller pragmatism" that combined a winsome theological conservatism with moderate stances on politics and international issues. As Christa took a corporate law position to pay off her substantial law school loans, she began volunteering with an urban rescue mission and did pro bono work with the Pepperdine School of Law and the Christian Legal Society. The Crawfords sought to marshal their robust faith in the pursuit of social justice, particularly on issues of human rights.[4]

This focus on human rights was part of a broader push. Key aspects of the modern globalized order—the self, the nation-state, the notion of human solidarity—contributed to this investment in what Roland Robertson calls the "intensification of consciousness of the world." While those interested in missions had long imagined an international evangelical community that reached beyond the nation, efficient global bureaucracies and technologies accelerated a consciousness of human rights. To be sure, some of this new interest was disingenuous. Despite missionary concern for the civil rights movement, most American evangelicals only supported the movement decades after it started, and their commitment to religious freedom sometimes seemed grounded in identity politics more than concern for the welfare of all. But by the 1990s most elites—especially those aligned with Lausanne and the World Evangelical Fellowship (WEF)—began to frame religious freedom in terms of human rights as much as Christian solidarity. Paul Marshall's *Their Blood Cries Out* (1997), for example, did not plead on behalf of Christians only. Underscoring sobering global realities, Marshall wrote, "The persecution of Christians is a harbinger of the repression of other human rights—of political dissidents, of intellectuals, of unionists, of women, of children, of homosexuals." Numerous NGOs, including World Relief and World Vision, lobbied to loosen U.S. immigration laws to help persecuted people of all religions.[5]

With activism swirling all around in the late 1990s, the Crawfords grew restless. Finished with graduate school, bored with corporate law, and ready to confront global injustices in real life, they met Gary Haugen. A lawyer trained at Harvard and the University of Chicago Law School, Haugen had worked for the Department of Justice and had conducted investigations for the United Nations in the Philippines and Rwanda. Haugen's hardheaded analysis, Washington connectedness, and fervent spirituality were terribly absorbing to Christa. Haugen preached that social justice was a spiritual vocation. In fact, he could speak in one breath of substantiating facts and collecting evidence and, in the next breath, quote Scripture with the best of fire-breathing preachers. Hearing him speak at a Christian Legal Society conference, where he applied evangelical language like "sin," "good," and "evil" to issues of poverty, racism, and trafficking, not just to abortion, was a significant moment for Crawford. Because of Haugen, whom she saw as a prophet, Crawford assigned spiritual significance to her legal skills. God could use them to fight injustice. The attraction was mutual. Haugen's International Justice Mission, a brand-new organization founded in 1997 in the suburbs of Washington, D.C., recruited the gifted thirty-year-olds to direct IJM's first country office in Thailand. Christa would run the office, and Mark would direct operations. Landing on the Chiang Mai tarmac, Christa felt immediately at home. "This is where you belong," she felt God assuring her.[6]

A phalanx of activists heard God say the same thing. Over the next decade thousands of recruits joined IJM and other organizations to fight human trafficking. Many of these activists settled in Chiang Mai, the regional hub of northern Thailand. Described by some as "Asia's brothel," Chiang Mai attracted many johns, but also evangelicals drawn to its missionary opportunities, beautiful scenery, friendly Thai hosts, easy-to-secure visas, mouthwatering curries, low cost of living, and central location. The city was positioned within a five-hour flight of half the world's population. An especially large contingent of missionary agencies arrived in 1999 as Hong Kong prepared to come under Chinese control. But social justice–oriented evangelicals soon eclipsed them. After all, missionaries, present since the mid-nineteenth century, apparently had not done much to stop sex trafficking—or even to grow the Thai church. The flesh trade continued to prosper, and less than one percent of the Thai population was Christian. In the first decade and a half of the twenty-first century, though, missionaries and justice activists built an evangelical empire. Chiang Mai, a mid-sized city of 200,000 with over 400 NGOs and Christian agencies, became the Colorado Springs of Asia.[7]

IJM, which became the most prominent of these agencies, specialized in rescuing victims of human trafficking. Marshaling the best in high-tech hidden cameras and investigative techniques, its agents in those early years were known for hectoring corrupt local police and aggressively rescuing victims like Moon from brothels. Their work, according to some observers, was extraordinarily effective. When activists first arrived in Chiang Mai, a man at any time could flag down a taxi driver, who would arrange a sexual encounter with a woman, man, or even a very young child. By the 2010s, such exploitation was much rarer. "Eight-year-olds should not be in brothels," says Crawford. "Thank God that the sleeping evangelical giant woke up."[8]

Their methods, however, also incited controversy. According to one of IJM's Thai employees, Western investigators "kicked the doors open—like Rambo," earning a reputation as "Cops for Christ." In one of their early raids, they rescued fifteen women and placed them in a safe detention center. The women were Burmese, however, and IJM agents could not speak in their language. Nor, charged critics, had IJM consulted fully with police or planned adequately for aftercare. Observers also accused the organization of holding these trafficked women against their wills as it assessed what to do next. Cultural missteps exacerbated IJM's poor standing in the country. Some agency representatives from Washington, D.C., did not take their shoes off when visiting Thai homes and offices, did not emphasize language learning, and insisted on conducting investigative operations during the water holiday of Songkran. According to Crawford, "It was what you would expect when an American comes into a foreign context and operates with ethnocentrism. We were using American rules in another country." Among Thai police, she remembered, IJM had a "horrible reputation." Thai politicians saw them as "cowboys." One local nonreligious NGO, the sex worker union Empower, denounced IJM as "evil." Prostitutes, says Liz Hilton, were "apprehended," not rescued. Working relationships in the early 2000s frayed so badly that IJM was frozen out of certain antitrafficking networks in Chiang Mai for years.[9]

This benevolent invasion of Thailand came in the wake of 9/11. Flush with righteous fervor, evangelicals strongly articulated a case for the projection of American power on behalf of powerless victims. Gary Haugen, chronicling horrifying incidents of human trafficking in Southeast Asia in a 2005 book entitled *Terrify No More*, wrote, "As a global force, America and its people are able to generate wealth, exert governmental power, and impact the world in a way that's unprecedented in the history of nation-states. And we live here at a time when the world is full of massive and profound poverty, injustice, oppression, and suffering." "How can we," he continued, "as good stewards of American influence and liberty, turn those blessings into action on behalf of the oppressed?" In the early 2000s his efforts took the form of soft diplomatic pressure. IJM representatives explained to Chiang Mai police that the U.S. government was monitoring their activities. If they cooperated with IJM, they would receive commendations from Washington, D.C. IJM's logo, which closely resembled that of the U.S. Department of Justice, reinforced this suggestion. In fact, Thai police often mistook IJM for a governmental agency, and IJM, according to one observer, "did not disabuse them of this belief."[10]

A friendly Bush Administration encouraged IJM's global crusade. The Office of Faith-Based and Community Initiatives, established early in the administration, offered religious groups unprecedented access to federal monies. IJM, which won a $2 million grant from the Department of Labor in 2002 to work on human trafficking issues in northern Thailand, immediately partook of the new largesse. IJM reciprocated by feeding Washington data that helped determine Thailand's ranking on the Trafficking in Persons (TIP) Report, which was intended to force Thai government action by threatening economic sanctions. To be sure, not all missionaries and activists sought to project state power, but many did in ways that resembled the old-style Christian Americanism of the 1950s. Using a vocabulary of "rescue," evangelicals sought to save global innocents from their oppressors. They flexed American muscle, determined to pursue justice to the ends of the earth.[11]

II. New Methods of Social Justice

This new Christian Americanism, however, evolved in ways that contrasted with earlier Cold War iterations. Benefiting from the insights of Lausanne and World Vision—and emerging in new era of multiculturalism—the twenty-first century social justice movement took a more flexible and diverse shape. Cosmopolitans like Gary Haugen, who apprenticed with Michael Cassidy, Desmond Tutu, and other anti-apartheid activists in South Africa, began to suggest that evangelism alone could not solve social inequalities. The Crawfords, compelled by circumstances on the ground and interactions with Thai activists, learned a more indigenous approach to social justice. Interviews in 2017 with American Christians, Thai Christians, and non-Christian observers in Chiang Mai and Bangkok demonstrate that a range of evangelical humanitarians now exhibit considerable skepticism about the raid and rescue approach of the early 2000s. They express concern for cultural sensitivity, indigeneity, and a more structural understanding of the causes of and solutions to human trafficking.[12]

Seeking to distinguish themselves from early antitraffickers, Chiang Mai's evangelical activists preach the need for cultural context. IJM, said one observer, had arrived initially with lawyers and police who embodied "a very American sense of operation." They operated rationally, directly, punctually—so quickly, in fact, that many did not bother to learn the Thai language. They brought aggressive strategies, lots of money, a promotional sensibility, and a misdirected passion for rescue. This highly Western approach, dozens of informants told me, was inappropriate in a Thai context that prizes relationships and patience. One Thai employee described just how difficult the "clashing of cultures" was for her. "For me, discussing and arguing," she said, "are the same thing." Americans, by contrast, believed that the forceful exchanges of opinion produced better outcomes. The inevitable misunderstandings and confrontations in this meeting of West and East, both American and Thai activists explained, had resulted in ineffective humanitarian work—but also a new resolve to do better. Observers lauded culturally proficient organizations, whose workers learned languages and studied cultural norms of familial obligation, collectivism, and reciprocity. Progress on the complex issue of trafficking, they explained, requires much more research into inscrutable Thai cultures they increasingly understand as "other." In terms of discourse, if not always practice, Lausanne's legacy of contextual ministry has come to fruition in Chiang Mai.

Evangelical humanitarians also began to stress indigeneity. In addition to conducting their work in ways that fit local contexts, they described the importance of following the lead of Thais themselves. Many acknowledged that a combination of Asian deference and Western aggression often leaves Americans "with the last word" when Thais should be "speaking into decisions." One informant worried that "Jesus Christ is considered a big *farang*, a big white guy." To combat this image, informants spoke strongly about the importance of hiring Thai leaders who use local symbols and language. "We're in a foreign country. We need to play by their rules," said one investigator. "Ultimately, I want to turn things over to the Thais," said another. Even those organizations most often criticized for ethnocentrism voiced the logic of indigeneity. "We can't turn Thailand into America. We can't create a bunch of artificial American families," said a high-level administrator at one NGO. To be sure, dissenting voices remain unheard within some organizations, and some appear to lack the will to actually implement indigenous principles. Nonetheless, there has been movement in rhetoric and policy.

IJM, for example, reconstituted its Chiang Mai office from an all-Western staff in the early-2000s to a mostly Thai staff. By the late-2000s, according to IJM's first Thai employee, there were ten Thais and only two *farang.* "Because of the Thai voice," said one former staffer, IJM began to transition away from raids toward "helping local law enforcement enforce the law" in a background role. After being ostracized in the mid-2000s by many Thai antitrafficking activists, IJM now staffs 90 percent of its field offices with nationals. This move toward indigeneity has helped, at least somewhat, to resuscitate its moribund reputation in Thailand. Other evangelical NGOs have followed a similar trajectory, and the search for Thai counselors, administrators, and investigators is constant. Sometimes it is even competitive.

As IJM's narrative suggests, the shift toward indigeneity and contextualization came largely as a result of cultural blunders. Humanitarians bumped up against a vast and complex cultural landscape that encompassed trafficked victims from African nations, Myanmar, and Thailand itself, which included a strikingly diverse spectrum of hill tribes. True contextualization demanded attention to the intricacies of each Lahu, Akha, and Karen tribal village. As foreign antitraffickers arrived with money and passion, they were rewarded with deferential smiles, but often not real engagement. Hill tribes occasionally responded with conversions of convenience. Sometimes, however, indigenous employees, most of whom opposed the raid and rescue paradigm, took on the cultural and legal instruction of Americans, teaching them to operate in softer ways, to "beat around the bush a little," and to respect established hierarchies within the Thai government and police force. These close encounters have encouraged Westerners to assume a more culturally sensitive posture.

Americans who immersed themselves in Thai culture often made the most substantial methodological adjustments. One Gordon–Conwell Seminary graduate, for example, described a shopping trip he took in Bangkok. Searching for a polo shirt, he strode by a bar as the curtain was undrawn. Before his eyes was a half-naked woman clutching a chrome pole. Her dull eyes looked "utterly bored and hopeless," he thought. "I wish I could just rescue her with half a million dollars." His Thai wife, however, rebuked this instinct to rescue sex workers with money. Americans, she said, are naïve and resort too quickly to throwing money around as a solution. "The foreigners almost give too much. They are too nice. But it's very uncomfortable for the Thais. It's a face thing. Foreigners need to learn the best way to give and receive." While considerable frustrations remain— too many Americans "enrich themselves instead of empowering leaders here," says one Christian Thai activist—most Thai sources report adaptation. Further,

American sources seem highly motivated. Reflecting a diminishing Christian Americanism on the part of humanitarians, this new stress on cultural sensitivity extends human rights beyond identity politics and opens American organizations to international influence.

Most significantly, American evangelicals in Chiang Mai have begun to speak more fluently about social structures. Upon arrival, many passionately expressed a vocabulary and logic of the "heart." They blamed the individual sins of perpetrators for the trafficking problem and expected that the brute force of love, displays of compassion, and heroic acts of rescue would free women from sexual bondage. One recently arrived humanitarian explained, "If we boil it down to its lowest common denominator, we will see that greed and lust are the driving forces for this evil." Many veteran activists now speak much differently. Describing themselves as having been naïve when they arrived, they now see trafficked humans as survivors who are victims of social structures that left them without education, resources, or access to help. Lust, they say, thrives more or less within particular social arrangements. Fighting trafficking has become more complicated than a good guy rescuing a helpless woman from a bad guy. Activists now frequently marshal terms like systemic oppression and gender inequality to explain the causes of human trafficking and to suggest holistic solutions.

This heightened attention to social structures surfaces most clearly as Americans try to understand the bewildering reaction of those they have sought to rescue. To be sure, women locked in cages typically express deep gratitude as the dust settles from a rescue. But American antitraffickers find that most women in brothels, on the face of it, do not seem coerced at all. These women may seem bored, and they might be disgusted by their clients, but they need the money. In contrast to *Christianity Today's* story of Moon, evangelical humanitarians in Chiang Mai described a very different pattern: a Burmese daughter who crossed the Thai border in search of better opportunities, worked in a noodle shop or served drinks in a bar until she realized that she could earn much more through sex work, and then sent that money back home to parents and younger siblings living in abject poverty. As one Thai informant told me, a prostitute's earning potential is high. A coffee barista might make 10,000 baht (about $300) a month compared with a sex worker who could earn 140,000 baht (about $4,500) a month. In hushed tones, nearly all my informants explained to me that most prostitutes are forthrightly invited, not tricked, into sex work. In many cases, they said, a *mamasan* coordinates their appointments, smooths ruffled emotions, and comforts refugees. Young Burmese women may not like the work, but conditions are not as abusive as the public relations departments of NGOs portray them. High numbers of passionate, justice-seeking evangelicals from America suggest that prostitution sometimes seems to be the least objectionable option given grim social conditions.

This narrative provokes a host of questions. Does financial pressure constitute human trafficking? Is prostitution ever voluntary? Can women be "rescued" from voluntary prostitution? Why are 70 percent of traffickers women themselves? The lack of clear answers confounds assumptions. "It's so complex. It's so nuanced. There's no silver bullet," said one young American staffer at an NGO in Chiang Mai. This statement is typical of Westerners who had arrived in Thailand expecting quick solutions. "When they understand the wider issues of poverty and education," explained her Thai colleague, "they have to lower their expectations." One small NGO recently shut down for lack of interest. After years of teaching about godly femininity, emphasizing the value of women, and offering alternative jobs, their efforts continued to receive very little interest from Thai prostitutes. As an employee of the Can Do Bar, a sex worker cooperative in Chiang Mai, asked me, "Why do they come to help us? I'm just doing my job, and it feels like they're trespassing in our community." A perplexed American humanitarian, shaking her head at this logic, said, "It's pretty discouraging. All we can do is offer." Facing indifference, hostility, rapidly changing definitions of trafficking, and radically different contexts throughout Southeast Asia, many initially find themselves stunned by the complexity of it all.

As their assumptions collapse, Western humanitarians over time grow more articulate about the structural contexts of trafficking. When narrating the story of someone like Moon, most easily rattled off a laundry list of causes: broken families, lack of education, poverty, police corruption, a broken justice system, migration and dislocation, statelessness, and addiction. They spoke with sophistication about how Burmese migrants lack access to healthcare or school because they do not hold citizenship papers. A lack of citizenship rights, said a New Life Center staffer from Minnesota, "has been one of the systemic issues that feeds trafficking." The director of another small NGO similarly explained that when she arrived "she was not aware of the depth of the citizenship problem. It sets up conditions for exploitation." More than the machinations of an evil trafficker, a combination of risk factors trigger a "big chain reaction" that sends victims into a downward spiral. In fact, most of my informants identified systemic concerns more than personal failing as the primary causes of trafficking. Some, pushing hard against libertarian sensibilities articulated by constituents back home, explained that voluntary sex labor—and even exploitative trafficking—implicates unfettered capitalism as much as bad guys and loose women.

In addition to identifying structural causes, evangelical humanitarians increasingly identify structural solutions. To be sure, rescue and conversion remain planks in their platform. One young worker from Colorado explained, for example, that "a gospel presence" was the primary cure for the trafficking problem in Thailand. Activists, however, are adding other remedies. As Christa Crawford enthused at a 2009 conference at Fuller Seminary, the evangelical community is learning to go beyond "merely responding to the urgency of the need" toward creating "the thoughtfulness it takes to create long-lasting and effective change." Sean Litton, one of Crawford's successors as IJM's Thailand director, explained in the early 2010s that "when I got here six years ago, I was doing one case at a time, trying to change one kid's life." Now, he says, "I'm starting to understand that the entire system can change as the governments pick it up and use their own resources to take it on." A problem as complex as human trafficking, many Americans in Thailand explain, requires a multifaceted approach that addresses large social systems.[13]

By the late 2000s activists had settled on a strategy borrowed from the Trafficking Victims Protection Act (TVPA), signed into law by Bill Clinton in 2000. The "three P" paradigm—consisting of protection, prosecution, and prevention—was a cornerstone piece of the TVPA. First, protection would mitigate the impact of trafficking that had already occurred. In the case of Moon, IJM investigators and Thai police would raid brothels to rescue coerced victims. The New Life Center would follow up with these victims to provide therapy, vocational training, and other forms of aftercare that avoid revictimization when they reenter society. Second, traffickers must be prosecuted. When Moon was rescued, evangelical NGOs did not focus so much on prosecution, but over the next decade, they dedicated considerable resources to ensure maximum sentences. It is not enough, said IJM's Haugen, to arrest and prosecute traffickers; they must be convicted and sentenced to consistently long jail terms. Nvader, for example, specialized in identifying perpetrators, collecting evidence, and then working within the Thai judicial system toward conviction. Prevention, the third "P," seeks to stop trafficking before it begins through education and economic development. In language reminiscent of Chinese development expert Jimmy Yen, one aftercare provider urges activists to "go into the village, not to the bar." The Crawfords, for example, launched Just Food, a start-up café in which at-risk persons could get training to avoid the sex trade and receive loans to start their own microenterprises. Advocates laud prevention as far less expensive and more effective.[14]

In the mid-2010s, activists added two more Ps—partnership and policy—to their antitrafficking strategy. Though derivative of the broader antitrafficking movement, this shift also represented trends within evangelicalism. Concerned about Christian identity and purity in the early years of the movement, most groups have relaxed their efforts at boundary maintenance. The Family Connection Foundation in the southern suburbs of Chiang Mai, for example, functions as a clearinghouse and resource for Christian NGOs of all theological stripes. Some hire non-Christians and do not require employees to sign a doctrinal statement. Western investigators now work very closely with Thai law enforcement. Several of the largest organizations, such as World Vision and Hagar

International, attend quarterly meetings in Bangkok with United Nations Action for Cooperation against Trafficking in Persons (UN-ACT), a community of regional NGOs spread throughout Southeast Asia. Many smaller ones participate in the Freedom Collaborative, an online gathering place of over 400 organizations. IJM recommends supporting and learning from a wide array of organizations including Compassion International, Evangelicals for Social Action, Amnesty International, the Children's Defense Fund, Human Rights Watch, and the popular band U2. The problem of trafficking, many acknowledge, is so large and vexing that it requires broad cooperation. Out of an insular culture in which hundreds of doctrinally preoccupied organizations worked in their own silos, activists now increasingly preach a message of partnership.[15]

Finally, American NGOs began to emphasize policy. This fifth "P," which most directly addresses structural issues, deals with reform of legal systems, more precise definitions of trafficking, and consistency in the enforcement of legislation. In the United States, IJM lobbied to pass the TVPA in 2000. In Thailand the New Life Center, IJM, and others have pursued policy work on citizenship. In the mid-2010s, Nvader began hiring Thai lawyers to help judges develop standards for the sentencing of perpetrators as well as precedents for victim compensation. It also advocated treating trafficking as an organized crime. In this approach, investigators follow money through criminal hierarchies to identify kingpins instead of only pursuing expendable local traffickers. Another NGO uses digital technology to create visual representations of trafficking flows throughout Southeast Asia. It offers these charts to Thai policymakers, who can then digest big data without having to read hundreds of pages of reports. "To make a dent in Cambodia's sex trafficking industry, they first had to change the nation's institutions," explained *Christianity Today* in 2017. The new evangelical humanitarians nurture ambitions to shape national policy.[16]

The new approach represents a meaningful departure from rescue. Growing numbers of antitraffickers say that rescue does not promote long-term personal or social transformation. According to one, after a rescue the family's "younger daughter is often forced into sex work, which doubles the wounding." It also "drives the problem underground," explains a World Vision staffer. "Brothel owners just go find more and the cycle repeats itself." In a widely cited 2012 essay,[17] World Vision president Richard Stearns downplayed the role of rescue. "The real work is done when few people are looking." Progress is often difficult to see at all, Stearns continued, likening social justice to an iceberg. "The portion that we see—that gets covered in the press or promoted online—is just the tip of what we must do in order to transform lives." Stearns's admonition reflects new attention to the limits of the old narrative of rescue. Red-light activism, they say, enjoys a glamor and simplicity, but it too often reinforces systemic problems.

In addition to a broader methodology, evangelical activists are expanding their agenda. My informants almost uniformly lamented the public equation of human trafficking with sex. One director of a prominent NGO, whose work has focused almost exclusively on women in brothels, has begun to wonder about the many cases that do not fit the standard definition. "A Kenyan man is trafficked. Do we help him if it doesn't involve sex?" she asked. "Is there even another organization that will help him?" This was not a rhetorical question. This singular focus on girls at risk for sex trafficking left little attention for other trafficking issues. By the mid-2010s, however, a marked shift was occurring. NGOs began to help men enslaved in the sex trade. World Vision then led the charge on non-sex trafficking, and in 2017 IJM opened a new office in Bangkok focused on labor abuses in the fishing industry. An NGO based in Chiang Mai called Relentless worked on organ and surrogacy trafficking. Ten years after the cover story on Moon, editors at *Christianity Today* published another article on trafficking that featured important elements of this new movement. The article asserted that reality "doesn't exactly line up with most Westerners' faraway assumptions." While evangelicals still lag behind their secular counterparts—and talk more about broader labor issues than actually invest in them—their agenda is unquestionably broadening.[18]

To be sure, passion for individual souls and bodies remains. Even if the global pandemic of sex trafficking cannot be stopped through the sanctification of men's lustful minds, evangelicals demand that those minds still be purified and redirected toward true justice. As anthropologist Omri Elisha puts it, they are driven "by gravitational force" toward direct influence, relationships, personal purity, and salvation. A student studying trafficking for a semester described her time in Chiang Mai as "an Ebenezer moment." When Christa Crawford took her on a red-light district tour in 2013, her heart "completely broke for the injustice of the world." International exposure, she says, helped her "see beyond issues to human lives." Similarly, the attraction to microenterprise reflects both its social justice potential and the fact that it allows participants to maintain a long-term relationship with distant peoples. The Farmer-to-Farmer program, which pairs farmers in Iowa with farmers in Nicaragua, embodies this strategy, as does World Vision's sponsorship-driven financing of over 440,000 projects in forty-six nations of the Majority World. According to the new evangelical internationalists, impersonal campaigns to stop injustice are humanized and made better when they attend to particular communities. One Southern megachurch pastor explained, "We do not tell a community that we know what their problems are and how to fix them. We try to find out what the perspective of the community is, and we often learn more than they do." Shane Claiborne, a young prophet attentive to structural sources of injustice, speaks ardently about "people falling in love with each other across class lines." Individualism persists.[19]

The new internationalism, however, drives evangelicals to address structure as well. The student whose "Ebenezer moment" awakened her to the horrors of trafficking, for example, underwent a shift in her understanding of how to eliminate those horrors. Having watched exciting rescue movies, she began to critique that method as "not realistic" and "too simplistic." Like many of her colleagues in Thailand, she now explains how economics, culture, and politics constrain victims' lives. Problems demand structural solutions—not just protection, but also prevention, policy, and partnership. "Thailand changed how I look at injustice," she says. Significantly, it did so in ways that complicate the idea that individualist logic is conservative and structural logic is progressive. Even as progressives violate the framework by continuing to use hero myths and individual agency to assert themselves in the public sphere, theologically conservative evangelicals increasingly acknowledge systemic causes and seek structural solutions in their policy prescriptions. In addition to antitrafficking work by IJM, World Vision, and New Life Center, this is evident in activism on a host of other global issues ranging from education, poverty, hunger, gender equality, maternal health, HIV and other diseases, and environmental sustainability. More evangelicals in 2017 than in 1945 could identify structural patterns of global inequality.[20]

III. A Global Divide

Outside evangelical humanitarian networks, however, this trajectory remains largely hidden. In Thailand and elsewhere, the public reputation of evangelical activism is dismal. Cosmopolitans may nurture new commitments to indigeneity, attention to social structures, a grasp of social science research, and appreciation for complexity, but secular observers still see evangelical activists in Thailand as animated by raid-and-rescue triumphalism. At a 2017 meeting of UN-ACT, for example, most participants described evangelicals as ideologically driven right-wingers preoccupied with sexual prohibitionism. Public relations materials emanating from evangelical NGOs reinforce these outdated perceptions. They continue to publicly emphasize rescue, emotional stories, and a laser-like focus on sex exploitation. Because constituents back home in the United States relish these elements, the insights activists abroad rarely survive the long trip across the Pacific. The ocean between humanitarians in Thailand and their donors in America is deep and wide.

Humanitarians must justify their existence in a very crowded field. Hundreds of NGOs in Chiang Mai compete for American money and personnel, and so explaining social justice from Thailand presents thorny dilemmas. On one hand, they describe themselves as having been blindsided by reality. They feel compelled to talk about their work in ways that account for complexities on the ground. On the other hand, they must appeal to American donors who conceive of social justice in ways that do not emphasize cultural context and the depredations of free markets. Without compromising on their new insights, humanitarians struggle to appeal to a constituency that wants to hear compelling stories of good and evil and to feel a sense of agency in the fight against human trafficking.

In order to effectively raise support, NGOs must convince the rank and file at home that there is a crisis abroad. Many humanitarians marshal apocalyptic numbers, some claiming that there are as many as forty million trafficking victims worldwide. A Manichean vocabulary ratchets up the intensity even more. Metaphors of light and darkness and theological language of sin, evil, goodness, and redemption fill promotional materials. *Christianity Today's* article on Moon, more restrained than most accounts, heightened a sense of crisis through its use of words like "God's redemptive love," "escape," and "rescue." The very names of many NGOs—Destiny Rescue, Urban Light, Ransom, Nvader—reinforce these dualisms. Nvader's director, acknowledging how the name implies rescuers "driving black SUVs and wearing black jackets as they fight against dark forces," successfully mounted a campaign to change the name to LIFT International in 2018. "I'm *from* Nvader, and I hate the name more than you do," he told me a year earlier. That the name persisted well into the twenty-first century, however, demonstrates its long-standing appeal to a messianic donor base. The pattern that "appeals to people back home," according to an activist in Chiang Mai, is clear: "good guys, bad guys, kick down doors, show smiles on face."

Appalling stories attract American audiences. Humanitarians in Thailand might want to emphasize systemic causes and solutions to trafficking, but tales of rescue appeal to the "Western mind" back home, as an activist from South Carolina put it. According to an Indian public relations executive with high-level experience at IJM and World Vision, Americans demand "great story-telling." Contrasting action-packed, explicit Hollywood scripts with Indonesian storytelling, which deemphasizes climax, he laments that in America "every boundary is pushed." He wants to take Americans "on a deeper journey" that considers issues of poverty and citizenship, but doing so "is a much harder sell." He must tell "extreme stories just to be heard." Renarrations of *Christianity Today's* article (Figure 8.2) reflect the American preoccupation with the salacious and obscene elements of Moon's story. One derivative account printed in a popular book coopts the article's broader point about protection and prevention to make a different point about the evils of prostitution and pornography. Letters to the editor in the months that followed "Red-Light Rescue" similarly emphasized sex and underage abuses. One letter recounted a visit to Chiang Rai, where the reader observed "two or three young Thai girls, between 13 and 15 years old, [dancing]

Figure 8.2. This 2007 *Christianity Today* cover reflected growing American evangelical concern about human trafficking. Courtesy of Christianity Today, Inc., Carol Stream, Ill.

atop the bar's countertops with a catatonic look in their eyes." According to veteran antitrafficker Annie Dieselberg of NightLight in Bangkok, this strategic focus on extreme cases normalizes more mundane, yet still horrifying, forms of exploitation. She nonetheless acknowledges that focusing on the worst perversions attracts more money and activists.[21]

Injustices that involve sex hold special concern for American evangelicals. They amplify interest, justify action, and extend the distance between good and evil. Large numbers describe how their "heart broke" over sexual exploitation.

Sex work, says one, feels "more degrading" than other exploitative labor. Such feelings derive from an American purity culture that both emphasizes female vulnerability and encourages performances of masculine strength. Young Americans, according to the director of one missions agency, nurture a particular fascination with human trafficking because they are exploring their own sexuality. "They have a fetish with the exotic," he says. In an attempt to "de-eroticize" prostitutes, he tries to arrange meetings between white American youth and Majority World prostitutes in order to teach them that "women in the sex trade are not just exoticisms, they're human." The need for such efforts, however, suggests that many American evangelicals are animated by an almost-pornographic gaze at the sex lives of exploited peoples.[22]

The most effective fundraisers offer more than a gaze. They give donors a sense of agency, allowing them to intervene before these salacious narratives reach their awful conclusion. Many utilize a sponsorship program in which supporters feel like they are investing in particular children. Even small donations help, suggested a Sunday school curriculum produced by IJM. "It's about God's willingness to use perfectly ordinary Christians to perform genuine 21st century miracles of rescue and redemption," the lesson says. One of those ordinary Christians was Dawn Herzog Jewell, author of the "Red-Light Rescue" article in *Christianity Today*. A publications and training manager for a large media firm, Jewell confessed that writing about global prostitution had been the furthest thing from her mind. But she was "seeking to burst out of her comfort zone." After attending a mission event in which someone described prostitution in the Philippines, "a light went on in my head. I thought, 'Wow. That would be amazing to be a part of their journey and to tell their stories.'" Exodus Road, an organization based in Colorado Springs, recruits donors into "search and rescue teams" called Alpha (Thailand), Bravo (India), Charlie (United States), and Delta (Southeast Asia). They can join a team as "Western operatives," financially supporting "front line operatives" who marshal military and police experience abroad. Exodus Road includes language on indigeneity and partnership on its website, but the emotional intensity of its images clearly appeals to white Westerners as salvific actors redeeming helpless victims. For only $35 a month Exodus Road allows donors a close connection to "the literal rescue they are empowering."[23]

These dramatic stories flood the United States through a host of outlets. NGOs recount their efforts to bring about social justice through websites, films, social media, and traditional media. Representatives visit college campuses, write Sunday school curricula, and sponsor music festivals. Perhaps the most successful strategy has been the "vision trip" in which Westerners tour Thailand to observe firsthand the battle against human trafficking. "People want to see before they commit," explains one activist while describing an American group's visit to one of Bangkok's red-light districts. Destiny Rescue, an NGO working in Chiang Mai and Chiang Rai, shows their American visitors aftercare facilities and prevention projects, but the clear emphasis is rescue. A staffer from another NGO told me that she participated in an actual stakeout of suspected traffickers during her vision trip. Some antitrafficking veterans, though, confessed unease with the way evangelical organizations framed these two-week visits. American visitors, said one, were left with the impression that "most of the kids were tricked or happened into it." Promoting prevention, he said, "isn't a good story that communicates back home to donors and constituents." The trips, however, are such a boon for fundraising and personnel recruiting—over 40 percent of staff had been on a vision trip before signing on to a long-term commitment—that Destiny Rescue employs a full-time "team trips" director who plans itineraries and books accommodations for groups of Western visitors that arrive every three weeks. Simply put, rescue pays.

NGOs, like the traffickers they oppose, are actors in an economic market. They must appeal to constituents with many philanthropic options. "It's easy money," says one movement veteran of their urgent narratives of rescue from sexual degradation. "It pulls at North American sympathies," says another. "It's sexy," says yet another. One NGO director described Americans wanting to fund rescues or to "kick down the doors of brothels" on short-term mission trips as both "infuriating" and persistent. In a recent Facebook update, she had explained how a young hill tribe woman had finally secured citizenship after years of tedious negotiations with Thai government bureaucracies. It represented a big victory, one that gave this young woman hope for a sustainable future. The update got fifty "likes." Soon after, the director wrote a second post, an emotional and quickly written update about a rescued girl wrestling with whether to return to a brothel in order to earn much-needed money. This update received thousands of "likes" and unsolicited offers of donations. The West, as one veteran of the movement puts it, continues to "drink the Kool-Aid." A competitive market encourages NGOs to add more sugar.

Urgent tales of rescue that feed the appetites of American evangelicals, however, contradict the very message that activists want to communicate about their work. The NGO director who posts on Facebook wants to tell stories of prevention, not rescue. Exodus Road promotes rescued victims on their website, but "that's not what they really do," explained one former employee. When one IJM representative told audiences at American churches to use their purchasing power as consumers to shape practices, she was "attacked." She explained, "They don't want to look at themselves." Even though IJM's methods have broadened in some countries, its public relations machine remains "all over rescue," says a former staffer. Transformed by encounters with trafficked victims, prostitutes, and Thai law enforcement, activists want to highlight long-term prevention, but supporters back home want to fund quick rescue. Activists want to articulate complexity, but market forces compel them to tell simplistic stories. They want to preach patience and sustainability, but they feel obligated to use exaggerated numbers that feed what one critic calls a "moral panic." They want to describe indigenous Thai work that has already reduced instances of trafficking, but this diminishes a sense of urgency. Donor maintenance prevents humanitarians from fully describing on-the-ground realities.[24]

Reality includes a host of trafficking narratives that do not involve women trafficked for sex. In Thailand evangelicals tell stories about the exploitation of men and boys. They tell stories of voluntary, nonexploited male prostitutes who are law students, fathers with other jobs, young men who simply want the money so they can play more video games. "Our perception of a great need wasn't there," said one humanitarian. American donors do not hear these stories. Nor do they hear many stories about non-sex labor. As the broader antitrafficking movement extends its scope to abuses of migrants in the fishing, domestic labor, construction, and manufacturing industries, American evangelicals remain preoccupied with sex. According to a Mennonite activist in Chiang Mai, working-class issues do not resonate with his constituency. "The sympathy quits when it gets to simple overwork. Our Germanic roots don't go there." Only the oldest and most financially healthy NGOs—New Life, IJM, and World Vision—publicly address non-sex labor, and then only tentatively. Internally, they speak passionately about the structural conditions that lead to the abuse of workers on fishing boats. They echo the International Labor Organization's conclusion that a "global labor crisis" is at hand. They are even beginning to investigate the complex supply chains that implicate American consumers who purchase frozen fish at Walmart. But they acknowledge that "a thirty-year-old guy working on a fishing boat doesn't evoke empathy." By contrast, child sex work is "easy to raise funds for because it's clearly evil." The result is that every single NGO on a list of the fifty most prominent antitrafficking organizations focuses primarily on "female victims of forced sexual exploitation."[25]

As this list demonstrates, evangelicals are not the only Americans to conceive of trafficking so narrowly and dramatically. According to one regional observer, antitrafficking is also a "hot subject" for liberal mainline Christian organizations. According to sociologist Elizabeth Bernstein, "The undercover and mass-mediated model of activism that IJM propounds has become the emulated standard" in Hollywood and among many non-Christian NGOs. The vast proportion of attention and resources focuses on sexual exploitation, and activists of many stripes feel forced to publicly describe their work in ways that reinforce the old raid and rescue paradigm. In the case of evangelicals, this feeds the antipathies of secular critics, and it fails to transform benefactors at home.[26]

IV. "Rescue" and Evangelical Markets

Some blame the persistent preoccupation with rescue on individualistic American Christians who persist in conceiving of social justice without the "social." Others charge elites and on-the-ground activists, who otherwise speak with considerable sophistication about the causes and solutions of trafficking, with retrafficking victims by using disingenuous narratives in order to fund their humanitarian projects. It might be the very structure of evangelicalism, however, that most helpfully explains this global divide. As historian Nathan Hatch observed, the evangelicalization of the frontier liberated American religion with vernacular preaching, antielitism, popular appeal, and individual salvation. It fit and reinforced a rising democratic, capitalist order in the United States. The new order, though not uniform in a young nation that privileged certain racial and religious categories, did enshrine the ideal of a free market for religion in which actors operate independently. American evangelicals, resisting authority and official hierarchies, quickly adapted to the new democratic spirit. The genius of evangelicalism is that it succeeds brilliantly in the marketplace as flexible religious actors fill every niche of society. The problem, as the scattershot work of American antitraffickers demonstrates, is that radical decentralization rewards individualism, heart religion, territorialism, competition, and cowboy approaches to justice.[27]

Social justice efforts also reflect the corporatization of evangelicalism. As historian Timothy Gloege has shown, Henry Crowell turned Quaker Oats and Moody Bible Institute into branded entities that appealed to individual consumers by promising "pure" products. Parachurch organizations have followed in Crowell's wake, participating in consumer society by trademarking, packaging, and promoting its services. IJM's corporate ethos is legendary. World Vision, as David King shows, likewise maintains a professional, bureaucratized culture. Even small NGOs in Chiang Mai nurture corporate sensibilities. One young director described at length his efforts at efficiency, specialization, franchising, scaling, auditing, and branding. It should not be surprising, then, that the attraction of antitrafficking lies not only in rescuing victims from horrific conditions, but also in fueling emerging neoliberal economies in the Majority World. One IJM staffer hoped for the transformation of Svay Pak, a center of child prostitution near Phnom Penh, Cambodia, into "a nice tourist town." "Our real goal," he said, "is to bring people out of slavery into the free market." Many of my informants in Chiang Mai similarly rhapsodized about teaching prostitutes skills that could be used in entry-level jobs for the service economy. The problem, as Elizabeth Bernstein points out, is that funneling prostitutes into low-paying, dead-end jobs may bring them right back into sex labor. Taking free-market arguments to their logical end, these "rescued" women often reassert their former skills in order to earn more sustainable wages.[28]

That humanitarians have not taken this reality seriously perhaps suggests the true marketplace in which they operate. Attuned to American markets as much as their Thai location, public relations offices and fundraising teams have produced an oversupply of activists whose hearts were touched by stories of rescue. Many American men come wanting to organize stakeouts and investigations. Their goals, attentive to gendered expectations in the United States, typically are determined before they ever arrive in Thailand. The antitrafficking industry similarly, says Christa Crawford, "produces lots of middle-aged women who watch a documentary and then proclaim that 'God called me to Thailand.'" These women arrive also wanting to accomplish very particular things, usually to set up and run children's homes. The geographical distribution of children's homes, however, demonstrates that NGOs often do not address actual needs. Veterans of the movement now advise that victims should return to their home villages, but over 600 children's homes now operate in Chiang Mai alone. "If you throw a stone in Chiang Mai," says one NGO director, "you hit a missionary." In Bangkok, by contrast, there are a fraction of children's homes, almost all run by the government. After listing the many virtues of Chiang Mai—its beauty, weather, and safety— one exasperated observer remarked, "Are all of these people in Chiang Mai called by God to be in Chiang Mai?" What some call God, others call market forces. The evangelical machine, having recruited a bounty of laborers for a city already teeming with do-gooders, has not constructed a coherent strategy for Thailand.

This lack of coordination often leads to frustration. Armed with money and good intentions but not, as one observer put it, having "done research to see if there's even a need," many activists struggle to find enough children and women to fill their sparkling new safe houses. "There aren't that many orphans! And they shouldn't be in orphanages anyway!" says a manager at the New Life Center. According to a young Thai staffer, American activists "are on fire and want to change things. But they don't take the time to think about culture. Many last for no more than five years before they burn out and leave early." According to Crawford, "The reality is much harder than they expected . . . so they go home quickly with relational brokenness and big costs." The director of an influential NGO notes that many organizations "combine a corporate impulse with a missional guilt that encourages people to give everything and sacrifices staff in reckless ways." As a result, many experience high rates of turnover. At one large NGO in Chiang Rai, nearly 90 percent of staff left over a single twelve-month period in the mid-2010s.

Western leadership carries deep consequences for aftercare and prevention programs. "It really shakes the system when Westerners at high levels leave," says one Thai therapist, who has had four different direct supervisors (three

Westerners and one Thai) in her four years of work. Another Thai observer notes that Americans bring "too much Western money and management." Since promotional messages in the United States obscure difficulties on site, newly arrived humanitarians "don't know about the problems until they get to Thailand." One Thai investigator who has worked for several high-profile NGOs simply does not trust evangelical organizations, especially new ones. Calling for the Thai government to screen out bad NGOs, he worries that some of them are bent on conducting "moralistic crusades against women's sexuality." Many Thai observers, even those who appreciate compassion for victims like Moon, articulate the limits of American leadership.

In addition to rapid turnover, the decentralized nature of evangelicalism sabotages attempts at partnership. American informants in Chiang Mai preach the ideal of cooperation, but it is difficult for them to cooperate in real life. Mom and pop organizations compete for church monies in Nebraska. World Vision and IJM compete for grant monies in Washington, D.C. Overlapping constituencies and common sources of funding, says one World Vision representative, result in "so much territorialism." At the same time, NGOs often borrow each other's strategies. NightLight, for example, began a program in which prostitutes learned to make and sell jewelry. It took a long time to develop and enjoy modest success—until it received a deluge of media attention. As sales of the jewelry skyrocketed in the West, dozens of other NGOs began to launch their own handmade apparel shops. According to Dieselberg, "a tsunami of evangelical groups not willing to do their own research" oversaturated the market. Whether copycats or cowboys, some activists in Thailand display a profound lack of coordination.

The structure of evangelicalism itself—decentralized, individualized, and enmeshed in consumer capitalism—prevents a coherent approach to the problem of human trafficking. Like their sending bodies back home, religious actors span a wide spectrum. Even as organizations like IJM and World Vision mature with more Thai influence, new renegades emerge each year. There are so many organizations working in the region, says one Thai Christian, that "nobody knows who's doing what." In fact, independent charismatic actors often flourish the most as they operate without oversight far from home. Collectively, they have built an antitrafficking industry flowing with money and activity. It is an industry, however, that does not act collectively. It struggles to construct a comprehensive approach to social injustices abroad.

Significantly, some of the most trenchant critiques of the antitrafficking movement come from evangelical scholars and activists themselves. Their critiques, however, have not yet filtered out to the rank and file. "Being there" is not possible for most Americans, and for those who come for only a short time, difficult experiences may reinforce, rather than topple, tropes of Western normativity and Eastern otherness. Indeed, evangelical support of Trump's "America First" doctrine suggests that the global reflex reaches home unevenly. In some cases, it meets raw resistance.

Global encounters, though, sometimes do transform. The most important NGOs talk and act more contextually and structurally than they did twenty years ago. It is for this reason that jaded activists like the Crawfords, despite all the missteps of their religious tribe, still support American efforts abroad. These efforts have also shaped activism at home. Just as E. Stanley Jones's sojourn in India pushed him to join the civil rights movement in America, so too has American activism in Thailand sparked a campaign against the domestic trafficking of humans in Atlanta, Detroit, and Las Vegas. "Taking us out of our culture helped us contextualize ourselves," says Crawford. Conversely, Thai Christians, according to informants, are losing some of their squeamishness about addressing issues of sex and prostitution. International relationships have provoked at least a measure of mutual exchange.

These relationships are sustained not only in Chiang Mai, Mbarara, and Almolonga, but also increasingly in the United States itself. Christian immigrants from all over the world—more than half a million each year during the 2010s—arrive with a complex matrix of spiritual, cultural, and political commitments. They are beginning to reshape evangelical strongholds in Wheaton, Colorado Springs, and the American South. More surprisingly, as the final chapter shows, global migration is reconstituting Christian communities even in the heart of secular New England.

Notes

1. Gary Haugen, *Good News about Injustice: A Witness of Courage in a Hurting World* (Downers Grove, Ill.: InterVarsity Press, 1999), 155.
2. Dawn Herzog Jewell, "Red-Light Rescue: The 'Business' of Helping the Sexually Exploited Help Themselves," *Christianity Today*, January 2007, 28–37.
3. Interview with Christa Crawford, January 26, 2017; interview with Mark Crawford, February 10, 2017, Chiang Mai, Thailand.
4. Interview with Christa Crawford, January 26, 2017; interview with Mark Crawford, February 10, 2017, Chiang Mai, Thailand.
5. Roland Robertson, *Globalization: Social Theory and Global Culture* (London: Sage, 1992); Harold Fuller, *People of the Mandate* (Grand Rapids, Mich.: Baker, 1996), 108–109; Paul Marshall, *Their Blood Cries Out: The Untold Story of Persecution against Christians in the Modern World* (Dallas, Tex.: Word, 1997), 11; Marcia Pally, "Theology and Practice of America's New Evangelicals," *Radical Orthodoxy: Theology, Philosophy, Politics* 1, No. 1 (August 2012): 304–305.

6. Samantha Power, "The Enforcer: A Christian Lawyer's Global Crusade," *New Yorker*, January 19, 2009; Gary Haugen, *Good News about Injustice: A Witness of Courage in a Hurting World* (Downers Grove, Ill.: InterVarsity Press, 1999), 150; Christa Crawford and Glenn Miles, *Stopping the Traffick: A Christian Response to Sexual Exploitation and Trafficking* (Oxford, UK: Regnum Books, 2014); interview with Christa Crawford, January 26, 2017, Chiang Mai, Thailand.

7. Interview with Nate Ullrich, February 9, 2017, Chiang Mai, Thailand; Shayne Rochfort, February 11, 2017, Chiang Mai, Thailand.

8. Interview with Christa Crawford, February 23, 2017; Mark Crawford, February 20, 2017.

9. On the lack of cultural sensitivity, see interview with Jane Jinda Pawadee, February 6, 2017; Christa Crawford, January 26, 2017; Mark Crawford, February 10, 2017, Bom, February 28, 2017, Chiang Mai, Thailand. On IJM's reputation, see interview with Ralph Simpson, February 2, 2017; Christa Crawford, January 26, 2017; Liz Hilton, February 24, 2017, Chiang Mai, Thailand; Andrea Bertone, "Human Trafficking on the International and Domestic Agendas: Examining the Role of Transnational Advocacy Networks between Thailand and United States" (PhD diss., University of Maryland, 2008), iv–v.

10. For "global force," see Haugen, *Terrify No More* (Nashville, Tenn.: W Pub. Group, 2005), 100, 244. On IJM's logo, see Bertone, "Human Trafficking," *v*.

11. On IJM's grant, see Bertone, "Human Trafficking," 206.

12. I conducted ninety-one oral interviews—thirty-one of them Thai and sixty Western—in Chiang Mai and Bangkok between January and April of 2017.

13. Crawford and Miles, *Stopping the Traffick*, xv.

14. On the TVPA, see Yvonne Zimmerman, *Other Dreams of Freedom: Religion, Sex, and Human Trafficking* (New York: Oxford University Press, 2013), 167. On the importance of conviction, see Haugen, *Terrify No More*, 212. On the Crawfords, see Jewell, "Red-Light Rescue," 32–34.

15. On IJM's recommendations for partners, see Jim Hancock, *The Justice Mission: A Video-Enhanced Curriculum Reflecting the Heart of God for the Oppressed of the World* (Grand Rapids, Mich.: Zondervan, 2002), 65.

16. Kate Shellnutt, "Bringing Light to the Trafficking Fight," *Christianity Today*, June 2017, 28.

17. For "the real work," see Richard Stearns, "The Glamor of a Brothel Raid," 2012, https://www.idisciple.org/post/the-glamor-of-a-brothel-raid

18. Sen David, "Fishing Industry Traffickers Get Long Jail Terms," *Khmer Times*, May 22, 2017. For "broad-based strategies," see Shellnutt, "Bringing Light," 27–28.

19. For "gravitational force," see Omri Elisha, *Moral Ambition: Mobilization and Social Outreach in Evangelical Megachurches* (Berkeley: University of California Press, 2011), 109. On Farmer to Farmer, World Vision, and "learn more than they do," see Marcia Pally, "Theology and Practice of America's New Evangelicals," *Radical Orthodoxy* 1, No. 1 (August 2012): 303–307. On the rise in micro-enterprise, see Wuthnow, *Boundless Faith*, 83. Claiborne and the megachurch pastor quoted in Pally, "Theology and Practice," 301, 305.

20. See "Overview of the Micah Challenge," http://micahchallenge.org/overview; *For the Health of the Nation: An Evangelical Call to Civic Responsibility* (Washington, D.C.: National Association of Evangelicals, 2004).

21. Janis Ver Licuanan, "Red-Light Heartbreak," *Christianity Today*, March 2007, 10; R. C. Metcalf, *Letter to a Christian Nation: Counter Point* (New York: iUniverse, 2007), 27.

22. On evangelical gender scripts and activism, see James Bielo, "Act Like Men: Social Engagement and Evangelical Masculinity," *Journal of Contemporary Religion* 29, No. 2 (2014): 233–48; Sara Moslener, *Virgin Nation: Sexual Purity and American Adolescence* (New York: Oxford University Press, 2015).

23. For "perfectly ordinary Christians," see Hancock, *Justice Mission*, 9. For "part of their journey," see Timothy Morgan, "Sex Isn't Work," *Christianity Today*, January 2007, 10. For "literal rescue," see https://theexodusroad.com/search-rescue-teams/.

24. On exaggerated numbers, see Ronald Weitzer, "New Directions in Research on Human Trafficking," *Annals of the American Academy of Political and Social Science*, March 28, 2014; Zimmerman, *Other Dreams*, 5. On reduced trafficking and indigenous Thai activism, see Christina Arnold and Andrea Bertone, "Addressing the Sex Trade in Thailand: Some Lessons Learned from NGOs," *Gender Issues* 20, No. 1 (Winter 2002): 46.

25. On domestic work, see Bridget Anderson, *Worker, Helper, Auntie, Maid?: Working Conditions and Attitudes Experienced by Migrant Domestic Workers in Thailand and Malaysia* (Bangkok: International Labour Organization, 2016). On construction, see Rebecca Napier-Moore and Kate Sheill, *High Rise, Low Pay: Experiences of Migrant Women in the Thai Construction Sector* (Bangkok: International Labour Organization, 2016). For "global labor crisis," see Anne Elizabeth Moore, "Money and Lies in Anti-Human Trafficking NGOs," *Truthout*, January 27, 2015.

26. For "undercover and mass-mediated," see Bernstein, "Sex, Secularism, and Religious Influence in U.S. Politics," *Third World Quarterly* 31, No. 6 (2010): 1039.

27. Nathan Hatch, *The Democratization of American Christianity* (New Haven.: Yale University Press, 1989).

28. Tim Gloege, *Guaranteed Pure: The Moody Bible Institute, Business, and the Making of Modern Evangelicalism* (Chapel Hill: University of North Carolina Press, 2015). For "nice tourist town," see Elizabeth Bernstein, "The Sexual Politics of the 'New Abolitionism,'" *Differences: A Journal of Feminist Cultural Studies* 18, No. 3 (2007): 140.

9

Boston 2045

The Quiet Revival and Non-Western Immigration

Made in heaven, assembled in Nigeria, exported to the world
—Enoch Adeboye of the Redeemed Christian Church of God[1]

When Billy Graham came to New England in 1950, his boosters nurtured high hopes for an evangelical renaissance. Graham had just concluded a banner eight-week crusade in Los Angeles, and momentum seemed to be building in Boston. Six thousand people, with many more turned away for lack of space, filled Mechanics Hall to hear the young country preacher with a lilting North Carolina drawl deliver his signature invitation to spiritual rebirth. Normally jaded journalists from the *Boston Globe*, who seemed likely to mock Graham's machine-gun delivery of a simple salvation message, instead marveled at how many "hit the sawdust trail." The meetings, which extended for several weeks and eventually filled Boston Public Garden, were so successful that Graham returned several months later to the larger Boston Common, the same site where George Whitefield had preached 210 years earlier. By the end of the crusade, nearly 300,000 had attended the meetings and over 9,000 had been "born again." Harold Ockenga, pastor of the venerable Park Street Church in downtown Boston, proclaimed, "I believe that 1950 will go down into history as the year of heaven-sent revival. God is moving as he has not moved in America at least for four decades and as he has not moved in New England for two centuries. . . . You do not have to wait till next year. You don't have to wait ten years. . . . The revival is here!"[2]

Ockenga was wrong. Park Street Church might have stood as "a citadel of orthodoxy," as one Boston pastor put it. The National Association of Evangelicals may have set up office space inside Ockenga's church. But evangelicalism did not sweep New England. As it turned out, the 1950 revival waned almost immediately. By the 2000s, observers were noting that the region was only two percent evangelical. Christians from the burgeoning Sunbelt described the spiritual climate as "incalculably colder than the lowest lows of a Boston winter." Southern Baptists, once the mortal enemies of New England abolitionists, launched a missionary offensive to save the region from liberalism and secularism. But they

Facing West. David R. Swartz, Oxford University Press (2020). © Oxford University Press.
DOI: 10.1093/oso/9780190250805.001.0001

found it to be rough going. "About once every hour, I give up. It's tough, man," said Pastor Joe Souza to a CBS reporter in 2009. "It's like you found a cure for cancer and you want to give it away and nobody wants it." New England, they say, is a graveyard for church planters.[3]

That is only true, however, if the evidence consists of Anglos worshipping under white steeples. A brisk walk through Boston's South End, a historic neighborhood where George Washington once fought redcoats, reflects a different reality. On a warm summer Sunday morning in 2016, I stood at the intersection of Shawmut Avenue and Lenox Street. On three of the four corners stood churches, each pulsating with music. The Shawmut Community Church of God, a historic African American church, occupied the south corner. Fuente de Vida, a Pentecostal church founded in 2006 by Puerto Ricans, but also full of Dominican, Cuban, and Guatemalan members, occupied the north corner. The Redeemed Christian Church of God Cornerstone Miracle Center, a five-year-old Nigerian congregation, occupied the east corner.

As I entered the sparsely decorated Cornerstone Miracle Center, sixty sets of eyes turned toward me. An elegant woman, wearing a white shift-style dress with colorfully woven edging, greeted me. Clearly delighted by my arrival, she showed me to a row near the front of the large room. An elderly man seated in the row behind me wore a pale blue robe with a fez-like cap on his head. His daughter, introducing herself as Mummy Tolu, wore fashionable horn-rimmed glasses and a garment made of crisp purple fabric. A man in the row in front wore jeans and an untucked polo shirt. As he worshiped with hands high in the air, a smartphone and a Nigerian keychain rested on his chair. "We are a church of all nations," explained Pastor Yinka Aina from the stage. "When you leave, speak what you want," he said, "but now we want to speak in one language." The English-language service that followed consisted of enthusiastic singing and passionate prayer. At one point, the entire congregation, each member's arms outstretched, surrounded me as the pastor prayed that the "Holy Spirit grant the desires of his heart." A rousing sermon, also on the topic of the Holy Spirit, urged the congregation to feel and practice God's power. "We are not in the mortuary. We are in the sanctuary!" exclaimed Aina. "Sing unto the Lord a joyful song. Get ready to dance!"[4]

The intersection of Shawmut and Lenox represents the expansion of multicultural Christianity in Boston. Dozens of vibrant congregations radiate out from the Cornerstone Miracle Center through the South End. One block to the south is CrossTown Church International, a Pentecostal "apostolic epicenter" with connections to Trinidad and Zimbabwe. Another block to the east is the 1,500-member Congregación León de Judá, a Spanish-speaking Baptist congregation founded in 1982. The north end of the South End is the site of Cornerstone Boston, a Korean congregation affiliated with the Evangelical Covenant Church;

Emmanuel Disciples Fellowship, an Ethiopian Baptist church; and the South End Neighborhood Church, a congregation made up of whites, African Americans, and several other ethnicities. Of the thirty-three churches in the South End, only four are predominantly Anglo. While most worship in English, others speak and sing in Spanish, Amharic, Haitian Creole, Greek, Korean, and Mandarin. Fully one third of them were launched after 2000. They are located in hotels, community centers, and obscure storefronts. Most maintain only a rudimentary presence online. They may be hidden, but they defy conventional wisdom that Boston is unrelentingly secular.[5]

Evangelical Bostonians call it the "Quiet Revival." The number of churches, as tracked by the Emmanuel Gospel Center, a booster of this multicultural renewal, has doubled from 300 to 600 since 1969. This represents remarkable growth considering the stagnation of Boston's population and flight of white churches to the suburbs. Since the 1990s, the pace has only accelerated. In the first decades of the twenty-first century, one sustainable church was launched every few weeks. As it turns out, Ockenga's prediction about a religious renaissance in Boston was true, just accomplished in a dramatically different fashion than he expected. It was not sparked by converts following the sawdust trail at a Billy Graham crusade. It was not nurtured by successes at Harvard. Rather, immigrants fueled the growth.[6]

The global encounter continues apace. Not only do Americans continue to fan out across the world, but international Christians are also moving into the United States. Four hundred years after the Puritans, some evangelicals again see Boston as a "city on a hill." Sparked by the Immigration Act of 1965 and inspired by the southernization of global Christianity, immigration feeds a global reflex. To be sure, it was curtailed in the mid-2010s by tightened borders, and persistent cultural and spatial separation limits international influence. Indeed, I was one of only two white people—the other appeared to be a hired pianist—present at the Cornerstone Miracle Center on that Sunday morning in 2016. Nonetheless, signs of evangelical multiculturalism are emerging.

I. Emmanuel Gospel Center and the Immigration Act of 1965

Judy and Doug Hall intended to move to India, not Boston. College sweethearts at Chicago's Moody Bible Institute in the late 1950s, they embodied the revivalism that had animated the patriotic rally at nearby Soldier Field a decade earlier. As teenagers they had left their Midwestern mainline congregations, convinced by soul-winning friends that decency and going to church could not save them from their sins. After a tract-carrying coworker at a Chicagoland ice cream shop witnessed to her, Judy began praying and reading the Bible. She got baptized and began attending a fundamentalist Baptist church before enrolling at Moody. Doug experienced a similar conversion, leaving his Lutheran church in Detroit for Moody, where he led the India Prayer Band and prayed for a wife who would be "as beautiful in a mud hut as in a mansion." As their budding romance developed, the Halls felt called by God to preach the gospel in Asia. But while volunteering at a city rescue mission during seminary training at Gordon Divinity School, located just north of Boston, their attention was turned toward the city. As Doug later explained, "God seemed to say to us, 'So you want to be a missionary? Well, here is a mission field.'" The trustees of a city mission called Emmanuel Gospel Center were impressed with the "spiritual attractiveness" of the couple. They offered Doug $50 a month to serve as superintendent.[7]

The twenty-seven-year-old Halls moved to Boston in 1964. On August 4, the same day that bodies of three civil rights workers were found in rural Mississippi, they drove a black Ford Fairlane south along coastal Route 1, reversing the demographic flow of white people out of the city. Eighty-four West Dedham Street was a red brick, two-and-a-half-story storefront tucked in a row of warehouses, rooming houses, and taverns in the declining South End neighborhood. Notable for the lighted cross hanging over the sidewalk, Emmanuel Gospel Center was a mission and preaching station for the neighborhood's laboring class (Figure 9.1). For years it had deployed the "Little Church on Wheels," a replica of a New England church built on top of a car chassis that included a loudspeaker, an electric cross, and a collapsible steeple. Holding open-air gospel meetings from this platform, Emmanuel's preachers sought to persuade "the lost and the backslidden" of Boston—these included "communists, atheists, deniers of Christ, and blasphemers"—that the "wages of sin is death" and that "the gift of God is eternal life." This evangelistic ethos still permeated the mission when the Halls arrived on that steamy summer night in 1964. When they opened the mission's front door, they found an elderly woman and several middle-aged men kneeling at the altar and praying fervently for the salvation of Boston's teeming masses. Emmanuel was an old-fashioned outpost of mid-century evangelicalism.[8]

The Halls faced daunting odds. Difficult conditions had stymied a long line of mission workers, who typically lasted only a year or two. Between 1945 and 1964 a succession of eighteen superintendents passed through Emmanuel. Without a steeple or an organ, Emmanuel lacked the requisite features of white evangelical worship. It had only a broken-down piano and rooms full of old furniture and broken plumbing. The mission was also located in a difficult place. Once a culturally rich, vibrant Catholic neighborhood with the best jazz music on the East Coast, the South End by the 1950s had declined into a skid row, stricken by poverty, drugs, alcoholism, muggings, inadequate housing, and violent battles over forced busing. Middle-class residents fled to the suburbs and the Sunbelt, and the population dropped from 641,071 to 574,283. In a 1970 study that ranked

Figure 9.1. 1965. Under Judy Hall and Doug Hall's leadership, Emmanuel Gospel Center became a center of advocacy for immigrants from the Global South. Courtesy of Emmanuel Gospel Center, Boston, Mass.

Boston below Detroit, Gary, Newark, and Oakland, the Brookings Institute rated the city as a -5 on a scale of urban distress that ranged from +5 to -5. This study represented more than an intellectual exercise for Judy Hall, who survived a vicious attack near her apartment and lived with the specter of violence for years after.[9]

The spiritual condition of Boston appeared to be collapsing as well. For the first time in its venerable history, dating back to the Puritans in the 1630s, the number of churches in proportion to the population began to decline. Once-thriving Catholic and mainline congregations shut down. Doug Hall counted "at least 10 evangelical works" that had left Boston for the suburbs in the past ten years, and those remaining suffered from "lifelessness, despair and decline." If conditions did not change, Hall predicted, "we will need, in a few generations, someone to evangelize the evangelicals." Though the picture of a rapidly secularizing New England looked bleak, the Halls thrived. Living on the poverty line and eating government cheese, rice, and beans along with their new neighbors, they loved their new environment. The city seemed simultaneously "terrible" and "exciting."[10]

Full of hope, the Halls began to track signs of religious vitality. In 1969 Judy Hall scoured phone books and drove the streets of Boston in a blue Chevy station wagon. In the end, she found 300 Christian congregations, marking each of them with colored pins on a five-by-nine-foot map mounted on a giant piece of plywood. In 1975, anticipating better numbers, Emmanuel researcher Steve Daman conducted the same survey in a yellow Volkswagen bug. He found 320 churches. By 1989, Rudy Mitchell and a team of interns found 404 churches. The surveys, which conservatively counted only churches that remained, not the many that closed or merged or moved to the suburbs, demonstrated growth of less than two per year in the 1950s and early 1960s, four per year through the late 1960s and 1970s, and six per year in the 1980s. They also estimated that church attendance grew from 3 percent to 15 percent of Boston's population during these years. Astonished by the results, Emmanuel published the findings in *The Boston Church Directory* (1989), a pictorial volume that listed congregations by denomination, neighborhood, ethnic identity, language, and date of founding. The weight of the bulky directory astounded readers who had assumed that New England had secularized.[11]

Hall struggled to interpret the surprising statistics. It appeared, he wrote, that the growth had "not been orchestrated by any particular group." By 1993, however, when the number jumped to 459, patterns became discernible. First, it became clear that conservative Protestantism, especially Pentecostalism, was winning big in this historically Catholic city. Second, the black church, thriving in the midst of civil rights activism, also had contributed to the growth. In fact, Michael Haynes, pastor at Twelfth Baptist Church, became an important mentor to the Halls, and Emmanuel collaborated with nearby congregations affiliated with the Black Ministerial Alliance. The traditional black church was a crucial urban institution that helped stabilize the South End.[12]

These two observations, however, failed to capture the primary factor: immigrant religion. The clues had been around since the Halls had arrived. Just months after Judy had counted the 300 churches in 1969, she had a conversation with missiologist C. Peter Wagner about all the storefront churches she had found. "Oh," he responded brightly. "Those are your national churches!" Emmanuel, it turned out, was located at the epicenter of Puerto Rican migration to Boston, essentially giving the Halls the global encounter they never got in India. One migrant effused that "in the South End I feel like I'm in Puerto Rico." Puerto Rican farm laborers, recruited by Boston industrialists to work in factories, had come from the small town of Aguadilla. In the early 1960s, some of them started a storefront church just down the street from Emmanuel. By the middle of the decade, the South End boasted Iglesia de Dios, Iglesia de Cristero Misionera, and Asamblea de Iglesias Cristianos. By 1969 there were eleven Hispanic congregations. By 1970 there were twenty-two. By 1972 there were thirty-three.[13]

Puerto Rican migration reflected broader demographic change. After the South End's population dropped precipitously from 57,218 in 1950 to 22,775 in 1970, an influx of Brazilian, Haitian, Chinese, and Vietnamese immigrants lifted the population to 27,125 in 1990. It also turned the South End from 42 percent nonwhite in 1960 to 65 percent nonwhite in 1980. These neighborhood trends were also reflected in metropolitan Boston, where the number of Hispanics jumped from 87,014 in 1980 to 358,231 in 2000. Boston was also one of the top ten resettlement sites for immigrants from Southeast Asia in the wake of the Vietnam War. Around 20,000 Southeast Asians came to Massachusetts between 1983 and 1995. Immigrants were reenergizing local economies, enlivening the culinary scene, and jumpstarting hundreds of new Christian congregations. The spiritual geography of the South End— and of greater Boston—had transformed before the Halls' unseeing eyes. Not until the early 1990s did the Halls truly grasp the magnitude of immigrant religion. With a new church planted every twenty-two days, the widespread assumption that religion was dying in Boston was being proved outrageously wrong.[14]

The Halls were feeling the effects of the transformative Hart–Celler Immigration and Nationality Act. Popularly known as the Immigration Act of 1965, this legislation dramatically shifted the distribution of visas. Prior to 1965, 82 percent of visas went to Northern and Western Europeans, 16 percent to Eastern and Southern Europeans, and only 2 percent to the rest of the world. After 1965, European immigration slowed, and immigration from Asia, Africa, and Latin America exploded. Capping all countries at 7 percent of the annual total, it especially favored Cold War refugees, families trying to reunify, and those with "especially advantageous" job skills. The impact was staggering. By 2005, 38.4 million immigrants, 90 percent of whom did not claim European heritage, called the United States home. Together with their American-born children, they comprised about 25 percent of the U.S. population. In Massachusetts, one in every seven residents had been born in another country. In the South End, the Immigration Act of 1965 added Africans, Asians, and South Americans to the substantial population of Puerto Ricans and Haitians. It remade the face of this already-diverse neighborhood.[15]

It is also remaking the soul of America. As the white West secularizes, much of the Global South remains highly religious. At the turn of the twentieth century, less than 20 percent of Christians worldwide were nonwhite. At the turn of the twenty-first century, over 79 percent were nonwhite. By 2015, according to Gordon-Conwell's Center for the Study of Global Christianity, 84 percent were nonwhite. From 1970 to 2010, the evangelical population grew about six times faster in regions outside North America. The impact of Christian immigration to the United States has been—and continues to be—monumental. According to scholar Jehu Hanciles, himself an immigrant from Sierra Leone, nearly two thirds of immigrants are Christian. Through the 2010s, more than 600,000 Christian immigrants received green cards each year. Of course, non-Christian diversity also spiked in in the decades since 1965, but the new immigration, notes sociologist Stephen Warner, is bringing about "not so much a new diversity among American religions as diversity within America's majority religion." The striking story is that as the United States becomes less Christian by the attrition of Americans with European heritage, it becomes more Christian through non-white migration. "We're witnessing the re-Christianization of America," writes scholar Gastón Espinosa.[16]

This is especially true in Boston, a city decimated by white Christian flight. Immigrants revitalized shrinking congregations such as Dorchester Temple Baptist Church in Codman Square, located just a couple miles south of Emmanuel. Dorchester had lost many of its white members in the 1960s, but when the *Boston Globe* profiled the congregation in 1983, it was undergoing a revival. Eighty percent of its members, most of them recent immigrants from Canada, Jamaica, Trinidad, Haiti, Honduras, Iran, Vietnam, and Cuba, had joined in the last five years. "We have turned around and are on the way up," said Harold Dutton, who at the age of sixty was one of the few old-timers remaining. The most impressive growth, however, came from brand-new immigrant congregations with Pentecostal characteristics. The Lowell Renewed Baptist Church, a congregation of Brazilians in an old mill town north of Boston, began in another congregation's basement in 1994. In just ten years its 205 tongues-speaking members were bursting out of a newly purchased building. Because church became the center of immigrant life, these congregations were particularly vibrant. "I have no family but the church," said member Edelizete Silva. Passion joined with demography to spark a renaissance of religion.[17]

In the early 1990s Emmanuel began to publicize the ethnic dimensions of the spiritual surge. A report entitled *Christianity in Boston* (1993) chronicled the arrival of Korean Christians to local universities in the 1970s, the rise of the burgeoning Korean Presbyterian Church of Boston, and the growth in New England from one Korean church in the 1960s to forty-two in the 1990s. The report also documented the flight of undocumented Brazilians away from economic disaster at home in the 1980s as well as the subsequent emergence of eighty Brazilian Assemblies of God churches in Massachusetts. The authors marveled that church services in Boston and Cambridge were being held in thirty-three different languages. A third survey, called *New England's Book of Acts* (2007), charted the accelerating, cumulative effect of immigration. From 459 churches in 1993, numbers reached 483 in 1995, 501 in 2000, and 555 in 2005. This represented a net gain of one new church every forty-six days for the past thirty-five years. Noting that Boston's Christians came from over 100 nationalities, Emmanuel demographer Rudy Mitchell exclaimed, "The world has come to Boston!"[18]

Emmanuel coined the term *Quiet Revival* to describe the stunning growth. It was a revival because more churches had been recently launched than in any other twenty-five-year period in Boston's history. It was quiet because so few people had noticed, because the revival was occurring among nonwhite populations. Emmanuel itself became the go-to source on the religious effects of immigration to Boston. Journalists and activists generally took their cues from Emmanuel's research. A 1993 *Boston Globe* article entitled "Storefront Religion: Boston Sees Surge in Small, Largely Immigrant Parishes" was typical. Brazilian praise anthems were shaking stained glass windows that still bore the surnames Fitzgerald and Finnegan. The stunning rise of non-English-speaking, disenfranchised, storefront "parishes of the poor" were "bringing greater diversity . . . and breathing new life into urban churches." Emmanuel's publicity machine, spreading the notion of the "de-Europeanization of Christianity," functioned as a powerful booster of Boston's immigrant churches.[19]

II. Immigrant Activism in the South End

Emmanuel did more than document the Quiet Revival. The Halls, a white couple who raised a black child in a mainly Puerto Rican neighborhood, immersed themselves as activists in the multicultural South End. Their home was sometimes called the "Hall Hotel" because of the number of people—over 1,500 people from the 1970s to the 2000s—from the neighborhood and around the world who stayed with them for days or weeks or months at a time. These relationships convinced the Halls that non-Western spiritual vitality could renew the West. It also broadened their conception of Christian mission beyond evangelism. Learning methods of community organizing from their Hispanic neighbors, they began to call for more social action. The Halls, small-town transplants from Middle America to urban Boston, went on to sensitize parochial white evangelicals to the multiethnic dimensions of their religious tradition.[20]

The South End was an ideal social laboratory. The Boston Redevelopment Authority (BRA) declared the South End an "urban renewal" zone in 1965, calling for a large tract that included Emmanuel to be acquired by eminent domain. Full of pool halls, brothels, gangsters, and casinos, the South End, according to one document, contained "the city's most serious problems of decay and blight," including subpar sewage systems, rodent infestations, bad sidewalks, and creaky row houses. Banks were reluctant to offer loans, and insurance companies were refusing to grant policies in the area. The city wanted to rehabilitate a neighborhood that was "falling apart." Critics, however, accused the BRA of wanting to bulldoze the neighborhood to build luxury housing, create wider conduits for traffic between downtown and the suburbs, and generate a more lucrative tax base. These initiatives, it was thought, would displace the existing population, including thousands of Puerto Rican, African American, Chinese, and elderly residents, effectively "destroying the community." Activists noted that the demolition of Boston's West End had resulted in displacement and gentrification, and they resolved that their neighborhood would not suffer the same fate.[21]

The Halls joined the opposition. While they liked the BRA's proposals for new schools, parks, and the revoking of liquor licenses—all concerns of middle-class white evangelicals—their experience had exposed them to the problems of their voiceless neighbors. "It's become obvious that the South End is too valuable to be left to poor folk," complained Hall. Echoing his fellow activists, he asserted that the BRA's efforts would result in the "ruthless disruption of houses and community." To be sure, he advocated not only on behalf of his Puerto Rican neighbors but also for Emmanuel's interests. Hall, worried that the BRA wanted to "get rid" of rescue missions, wrote in 1965 that he felt "manipulated by the bureaucracy of the city." The following year, in fact, the BRA sent a letter declaring its intentions to acquire Emmanuel's property. Hall determined to fight back so that "the evangelical ministries would not be the helpless pawns of mysterious forces" bent on developing upscale housing.[22]

In the late 1960s the Halls helped reinforce a "wall of resistance." Alongside St. Stephen's Episcopal Church, Emmanuel worked with the Emergency Tenants Council (ETC) to protest the BRA's plan. Trained by community organizer Saul Alinsky, these churches and organizations in Parcel 19 of the South End held chaotic bilingual meetings, planned demonstrations in the streets, and built a tent city in which 400 people lived for three days playing guitars, bongo drums, and saxophones. Emmanuel's members—which at the time included the Halls, three other couples, four part-time workers, and twenty student volunteers from Gordon College—participated vigorously in these actions. The Halls were nearly jailed for their part in the protest. Chet Young, a radicalized Bob Jones University graduate studying urban affairs at Boston University, worked for ETC under the auspices of both Emmanuel and VISTA (Volunteers in Service to America), a Great Society program. They hosted ETC meetings, lobbied city officials, joined Mel King's People's Election Committee, surveyed residents, and proposed new urban spaces. An astonishingly diverse coalition emerged that included black protesters, recent Puerto Rican arrivals, Marxist agitators, mainline activists from St. Stephen's, and Emmanuel's contingent of tract-toting fundamentalists. "The militant people of our community," Hall later explained, "knew they could count on Christians assisting in an effort that was justly conceived and carried out." Christianity, the Halls concluded, was a "radical religion" that should include both protests and evangelistic meetings. The "battle cries of the 60s became our own," declared Hall.[23]

The protests worked. Though some parcels were razed to make room for the Central Artery road project, the neighborhood won important concessions during negotiations with the city. In the end, the BRA did more rehabilitation than demolition, and it formed and empowered a resident-driven social service agency, the Inquilinos Boricuas en Acción (IBA), which oversaw the redevelopment of the South End. The result was Villa Victoria, a project designed by John Sharratt, an architect inspired by Puerto Rican town plazas. The planned community, oriented around a colorful square filled with tables and benches and greenery, encouraged social interaction. Subsidized housing units for families, small businesses, and "the tower," a multistoried building with apartments for the elderly, surrounded the plaza. With the renovation of hundreds of buildings and the construction of 3,000 new rental units, Villa Victoria at the time was the largest urban renewal project in the country—and certainly the most attractive compared with public high-rise projects in Chicago and New York. IBA, which enjoyed high levels of participation by residents, continued its work through the 1970s, seeking to enhance Puerto Rican cultural life through community gardens, dance workshops, and neighborhood newsletters. According to a document in Emmanuel's archives, Villa Victoria represented "what the people of the Parcel want for their area."[24]

Emmanuel got a new look too. In 1972 the ministry moved into a rehabilitated building just one block from Villa Victoria that was four times larger than its previous building (Figure 9.2). Local residents had pushed hard to locate Emmanuel in this prime location because they wanted it to blend "physically and spiritually into the neighborhood." The Halls themselves were transformed during these chaotic years. They grew out their hair, shed their respectable attire, and adopted a black child. Emmanuel's board of directors, almost all of whom moved to the suburbs in the late 1960s, did not know what to make of the radicalized couple. The Villa Victoria campaign had launched the Halls, who had become "enthralled" by the success of local resistance, on a long career of activism. They declared their intent "to pour all our resources into fanning those flames."[25]

For Emmanuel, robust activism meant balancing evangelism and social justice. Against progressives, Emmanuel insisted that "social change cannot alone hope to solve the problem of a man who is himself in basic rebellion against the source of all that is good." The real innovation, though, came in Emmanuel's attack on white evangelicals fixated on individual transformation. Hall insisted that "a lack of concern" for "social degradation" is "not Christian either." In a white paper entitled "Evangelism in Urban New England," Hall noted that only 9 percent of evangelicals lived in large cities, which perhaps accounted for their

Figure 9.2. In the late 1960s Emmanuel's building was razed to make room for the Villa Victoria housing project. Courtesy of Emmanuel Gospel Center, Boston, Mass.

"negative urban bias" and their equation of the "middle class" and "Christian." In short, true faithfulness required both a rigorous evangelistic program and a strong social justice dimension. In the wake of the Villa Victoria triumph, Emmanuel continued to hold revivals but also continued to fight for affordable housing as the South End gentrified. It partnered with the Black Ministerial Alliance of Greater Boston and the Boston Ten Point Coalition on urban revitalization projects. It launched Starlight Ministries, a ministry to the homeless, and the Boston Education Collaborative. Emmanuel was committed to "social-type ministries."[26]

Most advocacy centered on the local Hispanic community. In 1970 Emmanuel established La Librería Español-Inglés, the only Spanish-language Christian bookstore in New England (Figure 9.3). It became an informal gathering place for pastors as well as a place to find housing through IBA. Emmanuel published a social service guide for immigrants called the "Shepherd's Manual," organized ESL classes, and set up Emmanuel Legal Service to help immigrants navigate the amnesty process. Emmanuel also hosted immigrant congregations until they

Figure 9.3. In 1970 Emmanuel started La Librería Español-Inglés, a Spanish-language Christian bookstore, as a site for religious instruction, immigration advice, and social services. For thirty years it served as a hub for evangélico networks in Boston. Courtesy of Emmanuel Gospel Center, Boston, Mass.

could find their own storefronts. Congregación León de Judá (Lion of Judah), for example, became one of the largest churches in Boston after incubating in Emmanuel's building. In the end, more than forty churches emerged from Emmanuel's facility. In the 1990s it also funded "ministers-at-large" to serve immigrant communities. With a staff of fifteen by 2000, Emmanuel had become the epicenter of immigrant networks across the city of Boston.[27]

La Librería reflected a growing commitment to indigeneity. Emmanuel's strategy of bringing white evangelicals in from the suburbs to rescue urban residents had not worked. Before the protests, neither had the BRA's top-down attempts to engineer the South End. Borrowing from his sociological and anthropological training at Michigan State University, from MIT systems theorist Jay Forrester, and from global evangelicals converging at Lausanne in 1974, Hall preached that transformation must happen from within. Christians must live among the people. Neighborhoods and churches alike should be self-governing. The hyperlocal Halls implemented the new strategy by requiring all Emmanuel workers to live in the South End. Instead of the "Little Church on Wheels," they hauled a new "evangelism trailer" from which East African immigrants used the music and idioms of Black Power to reach African American residents. They produced a video called "Boston Habla Español." Emmanuel sought to nurture the "living system" of the South End by empowering its residents.[28]

A 1972 riot, which still looms large in Emmanuel's mythology, demonstrates the significance of indigeneity. After a fight broke out during a Puerto Rican heritage festival at Blackstone Park, just one block from Emmanuel and La Librería, police arrived. Wearing riot gear, they waded into a swirl of floats and thousands of dancing revelers. Accompanied by dogs, they swung clubs, assaulted bystanders, and used abusive language. Roving bands of snipers retaliated. They shot at police, set buildings on fire, firebombed a cruiser, and looted stores. By morning, debris a foot deep covered the park grounds. As the riot entered its third day, went the narrative, representatives from local community agencies approached Emmanuel with a plea to help. Using a phone chain, Emmanuel mobilized hundreds of Hispanic pastors who had met at La Librería. Insisting that the police leave the park, they built a stage and held a "pray-in." More than 300 people, flying little homemade flags that read "*paz y amor*," participated in a service held in Spanish. The radicals, confessing that they could not "hit a man of God," relented, and the riot ended. The shocked Boston police department pronounced it "a miracle." The lesson, repeated for decades by Emmanuel workers, was that artificial order imposed from the outside did not work. Indigenous networks had won the peace.[29]

Emmanuel borrowed the strategy of indigeneity from missionaries as well. Numerous staffers had mission connections, and many had been shaped by Donald McGavran's School of World Missions at Fuller Seminary. In a paper entitled "What Can We Learn from Foreign Missions?" Hall described his growing belief in "an indigenous group approach where the Gospel is presented in the cultural pattern understood by the people ministered to." He criticized bureaucratic structures, rescue missions, and the "idea of the mission on the hill where missionaries live in a compound." Instead, Christian workers should drill deep into particular cultures and allow leadership to emerge from within. In a 1978 presentation to the Evangelistic Association of New England, Hall urged listeners to take their cues from missionaries. Urban workers in Boston, he wrote, should take "a world perspective on church growth patterns."[30]

Nothing, however, compelled Emmanuel more than the Quiet Revival itself. As Hall analyzed the revival, he noted that "primary relationships" cultivated by Boston's immigrants had worked better than "Western works-oriented mechanistic thinking." As religious life in the city's inner core collapsed during his early years at Emmanuel, Hall described having felt "very low about the condition of the Church" until he walked by a Hispanic storefront church. He realized it was "a place where individuals and families worshipped together nightly in one makeshift room, a place where Christ was real and radical Christian commitment was being nurtured." To wealthy white Americans, immigrants taught that "Christianity has a predisposition to the poor." To individualistic white Americans, immigrants taught "the relational element of the Gospel." To technocratic white Americans, immigrants taught how to "wage spiritual warfare" and to "pray all night." Immigrants were embodying the lessons of Lausanne and collectively demonstrating that holistic indigeneity works. "We don't even move until the indigenous leaders of the church in the city ask us to do something," wrote Hall, who began to call this approach the "Boston Model." But this term was a misnomer. These stunning levels of church vitality really had their origins in the "Caribbean Model," the "Brazilian Model," and the "Korean Model." According to Hall, they offered hope that "cities of the western world can be turned from decline to growth."[31]

The Halls sought to link these new burgeoning immigrant networks to older white evangelical ones. Mounting interest in social action naturally brought Emmanuel into contact with local members of the evangelical left such as Michael Haynes, a local minister and Democratic state legislator; Roger Dewey, a local activist on civil rights; and Steve Mott, a Gordon–Conwell Seminary professor and original signer of the 1973 Chicago Declaration of Evangelical Social Concern. Nationally, Emmanuel nurtured relationships with *The Other Side* magazine, civil rights activist John Perkins, Evangelicals for Social Action, and the Evangelical Women's Caucus. Emmanuel also linked the immigrant community to more conservative white institutions. The Halls remained faithful members of South End Neighborhood Church of Emmanuel, a Conservative Baptist congregation. They maintained connections with Moody Bible Institute, Wheaton College, InterVarsity Christian Fellowship, World Vision, the Lausanne movement, and Harold Ockenga's Park Street Church, with which they collaborated on immigrant ministries. Hall, who helped launch Evangelical Christian Urban Ministries of Boston (ECUMB) with a 1966 speech at Park Street Church, was a consummate networker and tireless promoter. As Gordon College's student newspaper put it, "Any day now, the Boston Development Authority will come in with blueprints and bulldozers. This is a crisis spot. Doug Hall wants evangelicals to know it."[32]

Emmanuel nurtured an especially close bond with Gordon College and Gordon–Conwell Theological Seminary, both located thirty miles to the north. In the 1960s dozens of students from these institutions volunteered at Emmanuel each year. In the 1970s Gordon–Conwell and Emmanuel jointly launched the Center for Urban Ministerial Education (CUME). Directed by Eldin Villafañe, a neighbor of the Halls in Villa Victoria and the former pastor of Iglesia Cristiana Juan 3:16, the largest Hispanic church in the nation, CUME brought together white faculty and students from Gordon with nonwhite faculty and students from the city to Emmanuel's new building. Within ten years CUME had granted more than 2,400 certificates and diplomas to students representing thirty-nine denominations and twenty-one nationalities. With instruction offered in Spanish, French Creole, Khmer, and Portuguese, it became a laboratory for inter-cultural exchange. By 1983, the administration consisted of two Puerto Ricans, two African Americans, and an Anglo, all of whom lived in the city. CUME's goal was to harness, "in a non-paternalistic way," the resources of a major semi-nary to serve "a traditionally disenfranchised group, comprised largely of inner-city, ethnic minority peoples." According to one evaluation, however, it was the white students who were shaped the most. For many, it was the first time they had interacted with Christians from a different ethnic background.[33]

Emmanuel became even more multicultural in the 2000s. The number of non-white staffers rose dramatically as the organization followed, in the words of Hall, "the natural networks we find here in the city." White evangelicals, when they lis-tened, heard consistent themes: that the "center of gravity of the Christian faith has shifted from the West to the non-West" and that the non-West will be the pri-mary source of Western spiritual renewal. Applying apocalyptic passages from the Book of Revelation, Hall compared American Christianity to the ancient church at Laodicea, describing it as "educated, rich, influential, well resourced" and full of "people who do good things"—but also as lukewarm and in danger of being "spit out of the mouth of God." From that same ancient text, Emmanuel also saw hope: "After this I looked and there before me was a great multitude that no one could count, from every nation, tribe, people and language, standing [and worshipping] before the throne and in front of the Lamb." Out of the ashes of white flight, said Hall, urban immigrant populations offered a vibrant religious multiculturalism for a secular New England.[34]

Boston's story, say evangelical boosters, is also the story of Atlanta, Dallas, Montreal, Minneapolis, Los Angeles, New York City, and Philadelphia. With Emmanuel's help, other organizations have replicated versions of CUME—and conducted similar surveys that reveal comparable levels of immigrant church growth. All the major denominations have experienced similar transformations. Since 1993, the Assemblies of God has shut down about forty majority-white churches each year while opening an average of eighty-seven churches, most of which were nonwhite. By 2014 overall membership was at 41 percent non-white, up from 31 percent a decade earlier. In 2016 Russell Moore, a prominent Southern Baptist working to stop the bleeding in his own declining denomina-tion, complained that most Americans think of evangelicals as "old, white pre-cinct captains in Iowa." The reality, he pointed out in a *New York Times* op-ed in response to candidate Donald Trump's nativist campaign rhetoric, is that the "thriving churches of American Christianity are multigenerational, theolog-ically robust, ethnically diverse and connected to the global church." He con-cluded, "The man on the throne in heaven is a dark-skinned, Aramaic-speaking 'foreigner' who is probably not all that impressed by chants of 'Make America great again.'"[35]

Despite Moore's activism, the notion that immigrants are transforming the face of white evangelicalism is more hope than reality. To the chagrin of anti-Trump elites trying to recover what they understand to be the best of their tradition, Christian Americanism still predominates. Doug and Judy Hall—and other white evangelicals who stayed in the city and lived next door to immigrants—are outliers whose numbers remain small compared with those who populate white congregations in Boston's suburbs. Moreover, the narrative of the Quiet Revival may claim too much, say several young Emmanuel staffers trained in the methods of social science. The most impressive data on numbers of churches has not fully considered changes in population, accounted for low attendance in some store-front congregations, or considered the problem of second-generation retention. But even skeptics acknowledge the general trajectory. Tens of thousands of immigrants have renewed what was a fading evangelical presence in the city. Evidence of a small, but growing, multiculturalism is beginning to multiply.[36]

III. Reversing Mission

Whatever the prospects of reshaping white evangelicalism, many global Christians do migrate to America carrying a burden to speak truth to apathy and apostasy. They arrive at JFK and LAX and O'Hare, the new ports of entry, ready to spiritually challenge Americans. Kwesi Ansah, Jr., a Ghanaian missionary in South Carolina, explains, "It was the Westerners, the Europeans and Americans that brought us the Gospel as missionaries to us on the dark continent of Africa. So the seed was sown, is grown, germinated, and it is now bearing fruit. So we're now here to give back." James Fadele, a Pentecostal preacher from Nigeria living in Texas, offers a more cutting version: "I'm not saying all the churches in America are fake, but . . . we have come all the way from Africa. We are engaging the people to show them the true Gospel, making sure that people are being saved and people are making it to heaven." From a model that took Christianity "from the West to the rest," a far more fluid and chaotic arrangement of "from everywhere to everywhere" now characterizes global Christian mission. The jarring result, after centuries of Christian expansion to the East, is a burgeoning phenomenon of "reverse mission." The East now targets the West.[37]

Korean Christians have been the most active. Beginning in the 1970s David Yonggi Cho, pastor of Yoido Full Gospel Church, the largest megachurch in the world, funded 600 missionaries to start churches in over sixty countries. The mission drive intensified as Korea became an economic powerhouse. In 1987 Cho and other Korean leaders hosted hundreds of Majority World mission leaders—including Patrick Sookhdeo of British Guyana, Luis Bush of Argentina, Panya Baba of Nigeria, Petros Octavianus of Indonesia, and Minoru Okuyama of Japan—in Seoul for a "Consultation on Third World Missions Advance." By 2011 more than 20,000 Korean missionaries (and nearly 100,000 from broader Asia) had dispersed across the world, and plans called for one million self-supporting missionaries from Korea by 2020.[38]

The results have been mixed. Young Nak Presbyterian Church in Los Angeles, a daughter of Pastor Han's refugee church in Seoul, boasted an average attendance of 4,600 by 1989 and ranked as the fourth fastest growing church in the country. After adding an English-speaking service in order to reach third-generation Korean Americans as well as non-Koreans, Young Nak moved into a $9 million building. By 2008 University Bible Fellowship (UBF), a Korean ministry targeting American college students, had placed 700 missionaries in 105 chapters. Described by scholar Rebecca Kim as "fervent and hyper" about "conquering the world with the gospel," UBF leaders view the United States as "a modern Rome" where churches have lost their "spirit" and missionary passion. America stands strong, however, as a geopolitical and cultural superpower, and so UBF strategically targets white Americans. In fact, Korean missionaries adjust their cultural scripts in order to revive a waning American spirituality. Mark and Grace Yoon, two of the earliest Korean missionaries, permed their hair, changed their glasses frames, stopped eating kimchi, and ate more butter. The Yoons and others, however, have converted relatively small numbers of non-Koreans. A dissatisfied Henry Koh, the senior pastor of a 6,500-member Korean Presbyterian congregation in California, rhetorically asked, "Did God plant Korean churches in America so that Koreans may build large churches, worship in Korean language, and indulge in nostalgic thoughts of homeland with fellow Koreans?" Calling for renewed efforts, he declared, "We Korean immigrants must not just enjoy the American Dream. We must pray for America's renewal!"[39]

African Christians, relative newcomers to the concept of reverse mission, also seek American converts. In a second passage to the Americas—this one voluntary—2.1 million immigrants have recently immigrated to the United States. Of the wide spectrum of religions represented in this population, the largest is Pentecostal Christianity. The Redeemed Christian Church of God (RCCG), for example, founded in 1952 by Josiah Akindayomi of Lagos, Nigeria, emerged out of the African Pentecostal revival. By 2005 it boasted close to five million members with congregations in ninety nations. Two hundred congregations had already been planted in the United States. Five years later, there were 359 congregations, and the RCCG had built a 550-acre base of American operations in rural north Texas. The tiny town of Floyd, whose most prominent feature was a water tower on which the slogan "Blackest Land, Whitest People" had been emblazoned in opposition to the civil rights movement, was an unlikely site. Pastor Ajibike Akinkoye, a former professor at the University of Lagos, upon hearing that the Ku Klux Klan was still active in Hunt County, said, "They may not welcome us, but we are not afraid of them. In fact, maybe God sent us there so we can bring them to the Lord . . . to chase them out of the darkness and to bring them into the marvelous light of God." The new complex, modeled on RCCG's headquarters in Lagos, is called Redemption City and includes a 10,000-seat auditorium, Bible college, library, restaurants, and a one-million-person-capacity pavilion. It houses Dove Media, a company that runs RCCG's television, radio, Internet, and publishing arms. Marti Garner, a local woman whose uncle was in the KKK, likes the church's multiethnic sensibilities. "It doesn't matter what color you are," she told the New York Times. In a remarkable development, Garner became an assistant pastor serving under black immigrant leaders. The RCCG, hoping to plant a church within a five-minute drive of every American, sends its best and brightest from Nigeria. One out of ten RCCG members in the United States has a Ph.D., and they are overrepresented in business, banking, and management. The aptly named Winners Chapel in Detroit, for example, is filled with Ford engineers who speak fluent English. As Apostle Albert Amoah, declared, "We have not come to establish a Ghanaian Church of Pentecost but an American Church of Pentecost." African Christians come to America on a mission.[40]

Christian immigrants also want to sanctify the converted, not just convert a secular America. Embodying diverse sensibilities, new arrivals from the Majority World nonetheless arrive with remarkably similar critiques of their new home and with imaginations that push against American categories. First, they propose supernatural solutions for a rationalist Western church. Even accounting for charismatic identification, non-Western supernatural practices dwarf those in the United States. Surveys of Lausanne participants at Cape Town in 2010 showed that much higher percentages of non-Western evangelicals said they had witnessed or experienced divine healings, speaking in tongues, and evil spirits driven out of a person. They live in a spiritually alive universe populated by demons and angels, and they seek to guide North Americans through this enchanted landscape. After a Haitian woman prayed for the Halls to conceive a child, Judy was pregnant by the end of the year. Thereafter, Emmanuel assisted Hispanics who held "Power in the City" conferences. As they faced the realities of urban life, some began to apply supernatural methodology in socially progressive ways. Eldin Villafañe, who became a professor at Gordon–Conwell Seminary, contended that "the church's mission includes engaging in power encounters with sinful and evil structures." In an arid American landscape, says one observer, Christian immigrants "may be just what the spiritual doctor ordered for many of America's newly unaffiliated and disenchanted believers."[41]

Second, immigrants demand that white Christians cultivate evangelistic urgency and spiritual fervor. RCCG's Enoch Adeboye preaches the "twelve-month pregnancy principle," that each church should give birth to another church after one year. "It is our goal to make heaven," he declared. "It is our goal to take as many people as possible with us. In order to accomplish our goals, holiness will be our lifestyle." American evangelicals, impressed by the devotional practices of immigrants, often cite Korean early-morning and late-night prayer services. Sustained by this global influence, Emmanuel's evangelistic program, which is punctuated by regular revival services and continues to use the language of "decisions for Christ," has persisted for decades. "We feel that we can do something in the United States," said the Brazilian pastor of a Baptist church in Boston. "We feel the churches here are looking for revival." Roberto Miranda, pastor of the large and influential Congregación León de Judá in the South End, contends that Hispanics function as "a renewing presence" in North America.[42]

Third, many in the global evangelical diaspora demand conservative sexual practices in what they see as an oversexed America. Hispanic members of the Assemblies of God, according to Gastón Espinosa, overwhelmingly believe that "human life begins at conception, abortion is the taking of an innocent life, same-sex relations are sinful, and that God ordained marriage as a divine covenant between one man and one woman." Eighty-five percent of evangelicals associated with the Lausanne movement say that homosexuality should be discouraged by society. Peter Akinola, the fierce Nigerian critic of homosexuality, is the subject of a saying in Anglican circles: "When Akinola sneezes, a majority of people in the Episcopal Church get a cold." There is, however, more latitude for women in church leadership—77 percent think women should be allowed to serve as pastors—compared with North American evangelicalism. This is especially true in China, where 75 percent of pastors are women, and among Pentecostals, who contend that whoever the Spirit touches should preach. But a patriarchal heteronormativity remains. Most leaders from the Global South contend that men should be the main financial providers and religious leaders in the family.[43]

There are other reasons to think that immigrants could be the future ground troops of right-wing American politics. In addition to conservative views on sexuality and a supernaturalist orientation, many global Protestants want to make the Bible the official law of the land. Some support Trump-like strongmen like Jair Bolsonaro in Brazil or Vladimir Putin in Russia. According to Southern Baptist leader Richard Land, immigrants are "social conservatives, hard-wired to be pro-family, religious and entrepreneurial." Stumping in the early 2010s for Marco Rubio, Land described the young senator from Florida as the face of a "new conservative coalition." He continued, "Let the Democrats be the party of dependency and ever lower expectations. . . . The Republicans will be the party of aspiration and opportunity—and who better to lead the way than the son of Cuban immigrants?" As their own spiritual practices intensify in a strange and hedonistic land that is not yet fully their own, immigrants sometimes subscribe to a nostalgic history of a Christian America now become a "New Rome." Like the American religious right, they mourn an apparent loss of national Christian devotion.[44]

Most evangelicals of color take issue with other planks of the religious right's platform. Al Padilla, who was the director of Gordon–Conwell's CUME, says that the migrant workers and poor laborers who fill immigrant churches "are very concerned about how the church should act in the public square, and they are progressive in social and urban issues." Immigrants, after all, often occupy a similarly marginalized space as American racial minorities. After episodes of police brutality in the 2010s, one church leader in Miami contended that he could "no longer afford to stand by while Africans are murdered and assaulted by police." African immigrants, writes scholar Jacob Olupona, have no choice but to "engage in discourse about ethnicity and racism" because "these issues impinge upon their daily lives." Immigrants may hold to the conservative theology of many evangelical churches, but they are nonetheless subjected to the whiteness embedded in American social and economic arrangements. According to sociologist Janelle Wong, this helps explain why only 25 percent of Hispanic evangelicals (compared with over 75 percent of white evangelicals) voted for Trump and Republican House members in 2016.[45]

Immigrants who criticize libertarian arrangements often frame their activism in terms of the biblical notion of "the least of these." While many express belief in the ideals of self-sufficiency and hard work, they also question whether the free market is an economic panacea. According to researchers with the polling agency Latino Decisions, "Minority citizens prefer a more energetic government, by large and statistically significant margins." Even Hispanics in the Assemblies of God, a denomination whose North American adherents largely hold to a right-wing politics, support healthcare reform, back increasing the minimum wage, and tend to vote Democratic. Eighty percent of global evangelicals—compared with 56 percent of their American counterparts—say that the government has a responsibility to help the very poor who cannot take care of themselves. Others among "the least of these" include inmates on death row. In the mid-2010s churchgoing Hispanics helped overturn the death penalty in Nebraska. Comprising about 10 percent of the state's population (but likely to reach 25 percent by 2030), they lobbied legislators to override the governor's veto of the abolition bill. The National Latino Evangelical Coalition assisted their efforts, declaring that capital punishment was "systemically flawed." Founder Gabriel Salguero explained, "All life is precious. We're pro-life: womb to the tomb." On issues ranging from capital punishment to welfare, immigrant religion holds the potential to reinvigorate an evangelical left that has languished since the 1970s.[46]

Christian immigrants are also most likely to move the dial on immigration reform. Political scientist Amy Black notes that whites who worship with immigrants are much less likely to view immigrants "as a threat." One study in California demonstrated that conservative Christians who tutored undocumented immigrants began to think of illegal aliens as not "so alien." Immigration reform for them became less of an abstract issue and more of an opportunity to keep families together. In the mid-2010s some white evangelicals joined with immigrants to mobilize against Arizona's SB 2017, one of the most restrictive immigration bills in the country, as well as Trump's announced plan to phase out the Deferred Action for Childhood Arrivals (DACA) program. This resistance surfaced with the most vigor in cities such as Boston and Phoenix, and some began to use strategies of nonviolent civil disobedience. They participated in prayer vigils, fasting campaigns, marches, boycotts, and other actions that drew from Cesar Chavez, Martin Luther King, Jr., and other civil rights leaders. As one politico in Boston put it, "The Latino vote is a beast waiting to be unleashed." Local pastor Roberto Miranda describes the ten million Hispanic Protestants in the United States as "a sleeping giant."[47]

Sounding simultaneously right-wing and progressive, diverse Christian immigrant populations do not fit America's rigid two-party system. "We're the quintessential swing voter," said Salguero in 2016. "We're religious, so people assume we're conservative and Republican. But we're Latino, so people assume we're liberal and Democrat." In fact, the electoral history of *evangélicos* swings back and forth. In 1976 most voted for Jimmy Carter, a Democrat. In the 1980s the Republican Ronald Reagan made inroads with Hispanic voters by introducing an amnesty bill. In 1988 and 1992 George H. W. Bush and in 1996 Bob Dole did little courting of Hispanics. Consequently, they helped Democrat Bill Clinton win both elections by fairly wide margins. George W. Bush, showcasing Latinas in his own family, did much better in 2000 and 2004. In 2008 Hispanics voted for Obama, though political vacillation persisted through his presidency. After dozens of face-to-face meetings with Samuel Rodriguez, Jesse Miranda, and Noel Castellenos, Obama often followed their advice on public policy issues such as immigration, healthcare, and job creation. They grew disenchanted with the president, however, because of his failure to pass immigration reform and because of his support for same-sex marriage. They also questioned the religious right's commitment to the death penalty; a laissez-faire capitalism that leaves the poor vulnerable; superpatriotic interventionism; and a xenophobic, build-a-wall mentality. "It is a wound I carry," says Roberto Miranda about his collaborations with conservative whites who are anti-immigration.[48]

Defying Republican and Democratic orthodoxies, Majority World immigrants offer new approaches. And in an era of entrenched polarization, white evangelicals who disliked both Hillary Clinton and Trump may find idiosyncratic political views from abroad more appealing. Trinity Evangelical Divinity School's Peter Cha contends, "My Anglo evangelical students are more and more willing to hear their brothers and sisters who come from other racial backgrounds—they learn why they choose to vote in certain ways." Indeed, the future of evangelical politics depends on new strategies. In the 2010s, aggrieved and embattled white evangelical Protestants, whose median age is fifty-five, declined from 23 percent to 17 percent of Americans. More broadly, white Christians now comprise less than half of the population. By contrast, religious people of color are on the rise. Sixty percent of the world's Christians now live outside the North Atlantic region, and the United States continues to be transformed by the Immigration Act of 1965. These demographic shifts are not yet reflected in the electorate, but fifty years from now historians may judge the religious right, in its tight coupling of theological, social, and political conservatism, to be the outlier.[49]

Obstacles remain. The rise of Trump—and his popularity among anti-immigration evangelicals such as Jerry Falwell, Jr., Franklin Graham, and James Dobson—suggested the limits of Emmanuel's new multiculturalism. Many whites do not interact with immigrants and consequently are less shaped by their supernaturalism, progressive social stances, and passion for immigration reform. Moreover, those who do attempt cross-cultural relationships are hampered by stark cultural differences. To the frustration of immigrant pastors, white visitors to their churches seem endlessly fascinated by African accents but "struggle to grasp the substance of the preaching." For their part, many African immigrants avoid using African American cultural markers because they fear that assimilation will result in racism against them. Moreover, immigrants who do join multicultural congregations often labor to establish a voice until they conform culturally to the white majority. Such congregations typically succeed, note sociologists Gerardo Marti and Michael Emerson, when they maintain a code of silence about race, which is seen as a disruptive subject. When such conversations do occur, multiculturalism must be framed in terms of mission work, of creating a community together, or of a "miracle motif" in which relationships are transformed through individual conversion. Nor has the rise of nonwhite populations yet translated to political clout on a national level. Though most Hispanic and Asian American evangelicals are less conservative on almost every issue besides abortion, writes Janelle Wong, they are "concentrated outside of swing states, have lower levels of political participation than white evangelicals, and are less likely to be targeted by political campaigns." The future of multiculturalism may be bright, but at present Majority World Christianity, still constrained by white culture and organizing principles, is hardly driving religious and political life in America.[50]

The story of Boston is instructive nonetheless. In the face of xenophobia, cultural differences, and power differentials, religious immigrants offer different narratives to a postmodern West mired in a spiritual malaise, yet still haunted by a desire for transcendence. Park Street's steeple still stands, but it looks much less imposing now. It is dwarfed physically by secular commercial towers—and eclipsed ecclesiastically by hundreds of immigrant churches. Spiritual and civic renewal has not materialized in the way Ockenga and Graham imagined. In the 1950s immigrants were a geographically distant curiosity. Now, Africans and Asians and Latin Americans, writes Jehu Hanciles, are "a distinct, sizable presence within and impinging on the same social space." Increasingly, this is an intentionally assertive move. The Cornerstone Miracle Center, located on the corner of Shawmut and Lenox in the South End, was "assembled in Nigeria and exported to the world," says Enoch Adeboye. Congregación León de Judá, just blocks away, ministers to hundreds of Boston's homeless, and it is courted by powerful local politicians. Though still limited, the influence of multiethnic American evangelicalism has grown remarkably since 1965.[51]

Despite sobering sociological data on the decline of organized religion, Emmanuel predicts more growth. It continues to work on ambitious plans to export the indigenous methods of the Quiet Revival to other cities. Pastor Roberto Miranda, impatient with the notion of a "quiet" revival, goes even further. Amid forecasts that the United States will become a majority-minority nation by 2045, he wants something louder, bigger, more spontaneous, and more visibly led by *evangélicos* and the Holy Spirit. The white evangelicals attending the 1945 Memorial Day rally at Soldier Field could not have imagined such a colorful future.[52]

Notes

1. Adeboye quoted in Ryan Lenora Brown, "A Top Nigerian Export: Fervent Christianity," *The Christian Science Monitor*, September 28, 2015.
2. Garth Rosell, *Boston's Historic Park Street Church: The Story of an Evangelical Landmark* (Grand Rapids, Mich.: Kregel, 2009), 106–108. For "I believe 1950," see Ockenga, "Is America's Revival Breaking?" *United Evangelical Action*, July 1, 1950, 3–4, 8, 13–15. For more on Graham's Boston crusade, see Margaret Bendroth, *Fundamentalists in the City: Conflict and Division in Boston's Churches, 1885–1950* (New York: Oxford University Press, 2005), 177–90.
3. For "citadel of orthodoxy," see David Fischer, "Park Street Church: Looking Back, Looking Ahead," *Urban Update*, Spring 1990, 8. For "incalculably colder" and for Boston's reputation as only two percent evangelical, see Rudy Mitchell, "Perspectives on Boston Church Statistics," *Emmanuel Research Review*, April 2013. On Southern Baptist missions to New England, see Carey King, "Southern Missionaries Pour Volunteers, Money into Area," *Stamford Advocate*, July 22, 2006, A12; Ruth Graham, "Re-Evangelizing New England," *Slate*, November 27, 2012. For "hard soil," see Jared Wilson, "10 Reasons New England Suffers for Mission," www.gospeldrivenchurch.

blogspot.com, March 9, 2011. For "cure for cancer," see "Evangelists Target Unreligious New England," CBS News, October 28, 2009.

4. On the Redeemed Christian Church of God on Shawmut Avenue, see interview with Tolu Aina, July 15, 2016, Boston, Mass.

5. On the religious composition of the South End, see "Knowing Your Neighborhood: An Update of Boston's South End Churches," *Emmanuel Research Review*, February 2014; "South End Churches Progress Report," January 24, 2014, EGCA (Emmanuel Gospel Center Archives).

6. For "quiet revival," see Jay Lindsay, "Greater Boston in Midst of a Quiet Religious Revival," *Boston Globe*, January 15, 2005; Rob Moll, "Boston's Quiet Revival," *Christianity Today*, January 25, 2006; Brian Corcoran, "Understanding Boston's Quiet Revival," *Emmanuel Research Review*, December 2013. For historical comparisons, see Doug Steele, "Multi-Ethnic Church Structures," B14, in Douglas Hall, Rudy Mitchell, and Jeffrey Bass, eds., *Christianity in Boston* (Boston: Emmanuel Gospel Center, 1993). On the evangelical intellectual renaissance in Boston, see Joel Carpenter, *Revive Us Again: The Reawakening of American Evangelicalism* (New York: Oxford University Press, 1997), 191–92; Molly Worthen, *Apostles of Reason: The Crisis of Authority in American Evangelicalism* (New York: Oxford University Press, 2014), 15–35.

7. Interview with Doug and Judy Hall, July 11, 2016, Boston, Mass. For "as beautiful in a mud hut," see Judy Hall, "Thirty Years of Ministry in Boston," 1995, 33, pamphlet in EGCA. For "spiritual attractiveness," see EGC Board of Trustees minutes, July 8 and July 22, 1964, EGCA. For "here is a mission field," see Doug Hall, transcript of radio interview, 1968/1969, in folder "EGC History," EGCA.

8. On the Halls's arrival to Emmanuel, see Judy Hall, "The Acts 1:8 Prayer," *Urban Update*, Winter 1995, 2; Doug Hall, *The Cat and the Toaster: Living System Ministry in a Technological Age* (Eugene, Ore.: Wipf & Stock, 2010), v, xiii, 5–8; Mark Massé, *Inspired to Serve: Today's Faith Activists* (Bloomington: Indiana University Press, 2004), 64–66. For the Little Church on Wheels, see "Little Church on Wheels to Be Dedicated Tomorrow," *Boston Globe*, July 1, 1923; Mrs. William H. Morgan, "The Little Church on Wheels, Inc.," in folder "Little Church on Wheels," EGCA; "The Founding of EGC," *Urban Update*, January 1989, 5. For "lost and backslidden," see "Alpha and Omega," *EGC News Letter*, October 1945, 2. For "wages of sin is death," see evangelistic tract entitled "The Wages of Sin," EGCA.

9. On Emmanuel in the early years, see Hall, *Cat & and the Toaster*, 7, 34; "Dedication," *Urban Update*, Fall 1972, 1. On the culture and urban blight in the South End, see Rudy Mitchell and Theresa Musante, *Neighborhood Briefing Document: South End & Lower Roxbury* (Boston: Youth Violence Systems Project, 2009), 5; "Report of the South End Study Committee," The Boston Landmarks Commission, November 14, 1983, 22, copy in EGCA. On Boston's declining population, see Rudy Mitchell, "A Portrait of Boston's Churches," B-4, in *Christianity in Boston*. On the Brooking Institute's measure of urban distress, see Ralph Kee, "Boston Is a Changed City," *Emmanuel Research Review*, October 2005. For the attack on Judy, see Hall, "Thirty Years of Ministry," 26.

10. On the decline of urban churches, see Richard Rhoades, "Urban Networks," C1, in *Christianity in Boston*. For "10 evangelical works," see "Presenting the New EGC," EGCA. For "despair and decline," see Doug Hall, "De-Evangelism," 1, in folder "ARC Regions," EGCA. For "evangelize the evangelicals," see Douglas Hall and Chester Young, "An Evangelical Approach to a Total Inner City Ministry," March 1966, 40, 58, EGCA. On the Halls' early experiences in Boston, see Doug and Judy Hall interview, July 11, 2016.

11. On the earliest surveys, see Hall, *Cat and the Toaster*, 207; Mitchell, "Portrait," B-5; Mitchell, "The Changing Shape of Boston's Church Community," *Emmanuel Research Review*, July/August 2006; Hall, "Thirty Years," 13. On later surveys, see Hall, "Thirty Years," 51; Steve Daman, "When I Survey the Wondrous Churches," *Inside EGC*, September 2005, 1–4. On the rise in church attendance, see Mitchell, "Portrait," B-5.

12. For "not been orchestrated," see Hall, "De-Evangelism: Exploring the Mystery of the Deserted Urban Church," 3, EGCA. On numbers in 1993, see Hall, "Thirty Years," 51. On the growth of conservative Protestantism, see Hall, "Thirty Years," 57. On Haynes and African American churches, see Massé, *Inspired to Serve*, 64, 68.

13. For "national churches," see Daman, "When I Survey," 4. For "feel like I'm in Puerto Rico," see Katie Kenneally and James Green, *The South End* (Boston: Boston 200 Corp., 1975), 27. On Puerto Rican immigration, see Hall, *Cat and Toaster*, 200; Mario Small, *Villa Victoria: The Transformation of Social Capital in a Boston Barrio* (Chicago: University of Chicago Press, 2004), 44–47; Marilynn Johnson, *The New Bostonians: How Immigrants Have Transformed the Metro Area since the 1960s* (Amherst: University of Massachusetts Press, 2015), 243–44. On Puerto Rican congregations in the South End, see "Iglesia Asamblea Cristiano Pentecostal," in folder "COWE Boston Study Group Materials," EGCA; "En Español Por Favor," *Inside EGC*, February 1996, 2.

14. On population shifts in the South End, see Musante, "Neighborhood Briefing Document," 14; "Discovering Your Samaria Ministry through Demographic Research," *Emmanuel Research Review*, December 2006. On the rise of Hispanics in Boston and immigration more generally, see Maynard, "New England's Hispanic Christian Community," 6; James Franklin, "Homeland Troubles Bring Brazilian Influx to Region," *Boston Globe*, February 3, 1992, 1; "Immigrants Flowing into Mass., Residents Moving Elsewhere," *Worcester Telegram & Gazette*, March 12, 1999, A2. On Emmanuel's fuller understanding by the 1990s, see interview with Rudy Mitchell, July 11, 2016, Boston; Hall, "The Church as a Healing Community," 1992, 5, EGCA.

15. On the effects of the Immigration Act of 1965, see Helen Ebaugh and Janet Chafetz, *Religion and the New Immigrants: Continuities and Adaptations in Immigrant Congregations* (Walnut Creek, Calif.: AltaMira Press, 2000), 3; Johnson, *New Bostonians*, 49–50; Jehu Hanciles, *Beyond Christendom: Globalization, African Migration, and the Transformation of the West* (Maryknoll, N.Y.: Orbis Books, 2008), 233–234; Mae Ngai, "This Is How Immigration Reform Happened 50 Years Ago. It Can Happen Again," *The Nation*, October 2, 2015; Mark Gornik, *Word Made Global: Stories of African Christianity in New York City* (Grand Rapids,

Mich.: Eerdmans, 2011), 45. On the effect in Boston and Massachusetts, see Johnson, *New Bostonians*, 55–59; "Changing Demographics," *Inside EGC*, September 2006, 4.

16. On the shift of Christianity from West to East, see Hanciles, *Beyond Christendom*, 121; Christopher Gehrz, "The Global Reflex: Toward a Transnational Turn in Evangelical Historiography," *Fides et Historia* 47, No. 1 (Winter/Spring 2015): 107. On the Christian orientation of immigrants, see Hanciles, *Beyond Christendom*, 7; "The Religious Affiliation of U.S. Immigrants: Majority Christian, Rising Share of Other Faiths," Pew Research Center, May 17, 2013. On non-Christian immigration, see Diana Eck, *A New Religious America: How a "Christian Country" Has Now Become the World's Most Religiously Diverse Nation* (San Francisco, Calif.: HarperSanFrancisco, 2001). For "diversity within America's majority religion," see Stephen Warner, "Coming to America," *Christian Century*, February 10, 2004, 23. On the attrition of Euro-Americans, see Scott Sunquist, *The Unexpected Christian Century* (Grand Rapids, Mich.: Baker, 2015), 147. Espinosa quoted in Sara Miller, "Planting New Churches: Latinos Alter Religious Landscape," *Christian Science Monitor*, February 6, 2004, 2.

17. On Protestant growth, see James Blair, "New Christian Culture Emerges as Churches Appeal to Latinos," *Christian Science Monitor*, August 28, 1997, 5. On Pentecostal growth, see Diego Ribadeneira, "Contagious Pentecostal Spirit Moves Boston Area," *Boston Globe*, April 22, 1996, 13. For "turned around," see James Franklin, "In Dorchester, a Church's Revival," *Boston Globe*, April 3, 1983, 1. Silva quoted in Miller, "Planting New Churches, 2.

18. On Korean immigration, see Doug Steele, Curtis Chang, and Jeffrey Bass, "Asian-American Churches in Greater Boston," F-1-2, and Mitchell, "Portrait," B-19-20, in *Christianity in Boston*; Jin Taek Lee, "The Korean Church in New England," 65, in *New England's Book of Acts*. On Brazilian immigration, see Johnson, *New Bostonians*, 245; Mitchell, "Portrait," B-22, in *Christianity in Boston*; Cairo Marques and Josimar Salum, "The Church among Brazilians in New England," 13–18, in *New England's Book of Acts*. On the number of languages, see Mitchell, "Portrait," B-9, in *Christianity in Boston*. For "world has come to Boston," see Rudy Mitchell, "The Boston Church Directory," *Urban Update*, Spring 1993, 4. For statistics on immigrant churches, see "The Changing Shape of Boston's Church Community," *Inside EGC*, September 2006, 1; Steve Daman, "What Is the Quiet Revival?" *Emmanuel Research Review*, December 2013; Rudy Mitchell and Steve Daman, "Research Survey of a City's Churches: Boston and Cambridge," *Emmanuel Research Review*, June 2006; "Surveying Churches III: Facts That Tell a Story," *Emmanuel Research Review*, October 2006.

19. For early usage of "quiet revival," see "If April Showers Bring May Flowers, What Does a Quiet Revival Bring?" *Urban Update*, Spring 1995, 3. On the dissemination of the "quiet revival" narrative, see James Franklin, "Storefront Religion: Boston Sees Surge in Small, Largely Immigrant Parishes," *Boston Globe*, December 24, 1993, 1. On Latinos filling empty Irish sanctuaries, see Yvonne Abraham, "Church Swells with Influx of Latino Immigrants," *Boston Globe*, March 18, 2001, B1.

20. For "Hall Hotel," see "At Home in Boston," *EGC Update*, January 2002, 1.

21. On the BRA, see Small, *Villa Victoria*, 48–55. On blight in the South End, see Margaret Supplee Smith, "Between City and Suburb: Architecture and Planning in Boston's South End" (PhD diss., Brown University, 1976), 223–24. For critics of the BRA, see Hall, "Thirty Years," 9; Mel King, *Chain of Change: Struggles for Black Community Development* (Boston: South End Press, 1981), 209; "EGC Fact Sheet,"10, in folder "EGC History," EGCA.

22. For Hall's evaluation of the BRA, see Douglas Hall, "A Study of the Effects of the BRA in Boston's South End and the Future of Our Institutions," August 24, 1965; "Planning Retreat," October 1971, 14; Hall, "Thirty Years," 9, EGCA. On the BRA's threat to Emmanuel and other evangelical ministries, see Hall, "Study of the Effects of the BRA." For "helpless pawns of mysterious forces," see Hall, "An Evangelical Approach," 52.

23. For "wall of resistance," see Small, *Villa Victoria*, 54. On Emmanuel's involvement with the ETC, see Doug and Judy Hall interview, July 11, 2016, Boston; Hall, "Thirty Years," 9; "ATTENTION!!! Announcing a Meeting," December 12, 1968, in folder "EGC Historical Materials," EGCA; "Emergency Tenants Council," 6, and "EGC Fact Sheet," in Folder "EGC History," EGCA; Mitchell and Musante, "Neighborhood Briefing Document," 5–6. For "militant people," see Doug Hall, "Beyond Contextualization," *Urban Update*, Autumn 1987, 2–3. On the demography of EGC, see "Fact Sheet Submitted to BRA," March 6, 1968, in Folder "EGC History," EGCA. For "battle cries of the 60s," see Hall, "Thirty Years," 13.

24. For an assessment of the goals of the BRA, see Margaret Supplee Smith, "Between City and Suburb," 226–29. On ETC and EGC's success, see "Spin-off Organizations EGC as Catalyst," in folder "EGC History—Mini," EGCA; Hall, *Cat and Toaster*, 14, 42, 154, 245; Johnson, *New Bostonians*, 85. For descriptions of Villa Victoria, see Small, *Villa Victoria*, 12, 44, 66. On the persistence of IBA, see Small, *Villa Victoria*, 66–68. For "what the people of the Parcel want," see "Emergency Tenants Council," 6.

25. On Emmanuel's new building, see "Remember 84 West Dedham Street?" *EGC Newsletter*, April 1973. For "physically and spiritually," see Kimberly Caviness, "Sharing Spirit at the South End Neighborhood Church," *South End News*, 12, in folder "SENCE," EGCA. On the Halls and Emmanuel's board of trustees, see interview with Steve Daman, July 13, 2016, Boston. On raising a black child in a Puerto Rican neighborhood, see Massé, *Inspired to Serve*, 74. For "enthralled," see Hall, *Cat and Toaster*, 26. For "pour all our resources," see Steve Daman, "Why Is the Church in Boston Dying?" *Inside EGC*, 2013.

26. For "social change alone cannot" and "social degradation," see Hall, "Evangelical Approach," 42. For "negative urban bias," see Hall, "Evangelism in Urban New England," 4. On Emmanuel's persistent interest in evangelism, see Halls to "Friends and Loved-Ones," Christmas 1967, EGCA; Hall to "Friends," March 1970, EGCA; "Summer Evangelism in Review," *EGC Newsletter*, Fall 1976. On Emmanuel's alliances and activism toward social justice, see flyers in folders on the Boston Educational Collaborative, Community Development Ministry, and others, EGCA; interview with Roberto Miranda, July 12, 2016, Boston Mass. For "social-type activities," see "Planning Retreat," 8.

27. On La Librería, see "Resource Center," *EGC Newsletter*, November 1971, 1; "Web & Marilyn Brower: 20 Years with EGC," *Urban Update*, Fall 1990, 1–3. On Emmanuel's social service work, see Steve Daman, "Law and Grace in the City," *Urban Update*, Autumn 1987, 1; Zerline Hughes Jennings, "Giving Them That Ol' Storefront Religion: A Fight for Souls—and Paying the Rent," *Boston Globe*, June 30, 2002, 4. On Emmanuel's hosting of immigrant churches, see "Shared Worship Space: An Urban Challenge and a Kingdom Opportunity," *Emmanuel Research Review*, January 2012; Ralph Kee interview, July 12, 2016, Boston. On Emmanuel's growth, see Hall, *Cat and Toaster*, 183.

28. On indigenous transformation, see Douglas Hall, "Understanding Defensive Sub-cultures in the American City with Implications for Church Growth," 1–5, n.d., EGCA. On living locally among the people, see Doug Hall interview, July 11, 2016; interview with Ralph Kee, July 12, 2016. On the new evangelism trailer, see "Planning Retreat," 12; "Emmanuel Gospel Center: Black Community," 5, in folder "History," EGCA. For "Boston Habla Español," see "Films for City People," 2, EGCA.

29. Steve Daman, "The Riot in Blackstone Park," *Inside EGC*, January 2009, 4–5; "Comment on the Blackstone Park Incident," February 1973, in folder "History," EGCA; "300 Attend Second Blackstone Park Pray-In," *Boston Herald Traveler*, July 24, 1972, 7, copy in EGCA; "We the Undersigned Citizens," in folder "Police Protection," EGCA.

30. On McGavran as a source of inspiration, see Hall, "A Strategy for Urban Ministry," February 19, 1972, 4, 7. For "an indigenous group," see Hall, "An Evangelical Approach," 15. For "mission on the hill," see Hall, "Evangelical Approach," 14. For "a world perspective," see "Evangelism in Urban New England," 7–8.

31. Doug Hall, "The Boston Model of Christian Development," March 1992, 1–2, 8, 26, 29. For "primary relationships," see Hall, *Cat and Toaster*, 17–8, 24. For "mechanistic thinking," see Doug Hall, "Crossing the Perception Threshold," *Emmanuel Research Review*, March-April 2010. For "don't even move," see Doug Hall, "Systems Thinking and the Urban Church," A-7-8, in *Christianity in Boston*. For "decline to growth," see Doug Hall, "EGC and the Emerging Church," *Urban Update*, Fall 1990, 8.

32. On Emmanuel's connections with the evangelical left in Boston and elsewhere, see Hall, *Cat and Toaster*, 204–205; Mitchell, "Portrait," B-11; "Remember the Poor," *The Other Side*, February 1970; EGC 1975-76 Annual Report, 4, in folder "SENCE," EGCA. For mainstream evangelical networks, see Richard Rhoades, "Urban Networks," C-2-3, in *Christianity in Boston*; "Testimonials," EGC brochure, circa 1972, 2, EGCA; interview with Rudy Mitchell, July 11, 2016; folder "History of ECUMB," EGCA. For "crisis spot," see "What about Evangelicals and the Urban Crisis?" *The Gordon*, August 1968, 4.

33. On CUME, see *CUME: An Evaluation, 1986–87*, copy in EGCA. Hall, *Cat and Toaster*, 205–206; Lee, "Urban Ministerial Education," B-59; Steve Daman, "The City Gives Birth to a Seminary," *Inside EGC*, November-December 2013. On Villafañe and Juan 3:16, see Gastón Espinosa, *Latino Pentecostals in America: Faith and Politics in Action* (Cambridge, Mass.: Harvard University Press, 2014), 14, 272–73. On interculturalism at CUME, see *CUME*, 7–8, 18, 62, 88–89.

34. On the growing ethnic diversity of Emmanuel's staff, see "Historical and Photographic Record," in folder "EGC Staff, Interns, Associates and Regular Volunteers," EGCA. On Christianity as non-Western, see Hall, "Boston Model," 41. For "center of gravity," see Elijah Kim, *The Rise of the Global South: The Decline of Western Christendom and the Rise of Majority World Christianity* (Eugene, Ore.: Wipf & Stock, 2012); Carl Racine, "Dr. Kim's Kingdom Vision for Boston," *Inside EGC*, May 2005, 4–5. On Laodicea, see Hall, *Cat and Toaster*, 83. For "a great multitude," see Gregg Detwiler, "There's Gold in the City," *Emmanuel Research Review*, November 2010.

35. On growing networks between immigration advocates in major American cities, see interview with Jeff Bass, July 12, 2016. On multiculturalism and the Assemblies of God, see Hanciles, *Beyond Christendom*, 294; Adelle Banks, "Assemblies of God Turns 100, and Looks to a Multiethnic Future," Religion News Service, August 6, 2014. Also see Russell Moore, "A White Church No More," *New York Times*, May 6, 2016; Elizabeth Dias, "The Rise of Evangélicos," *Time*, April 4, 2013.

36. On retention of the second generation, see Johnson, *New Bostonians*, 250; Grace Lee, "When the Faith of Our Fathers Collides with the Culture of Our Children," *Inside EGC*, July 5, 2010. On struggling storefront churches, see Jennings, "Giving Them That Ol' Storefront Religion," *Boston Globe*, June 30, 2002.

37. For "it was the Westerners," see Andrew Rice, "Mission from Africa: The Redeemed Christian Church of God Comes to America," *New York Times Magazine*, April 8, 2009. For "churches in America are fake," see Jason Margolis, "The Redeemed Church of God Preaches the Gospel in U.S.," PRI's *The World*, February 12, 2014. On global perceptions of American Christianity, see Rebecca Kim, *The Spirit Moves West: Korean Missionaries in America* (New York: Oxford University Press), 46–63; Hanciles, *Beyond Christendom*, 343–47.

38. On early Korean missions, see Steve Sang-Cheol Moon, "The Protestant Missionary Movement in Korea," *International Bulletin of Missionary Research* 32, No. 2 (April 2008): 59; Kate Bowler, *Blessed: A History of the American Prosperity Gospel* (New York: Oxford University Press, 2013), 102. For "Third World Missions Advance," see A. Scott Moreau, "Evangelical Missions Development: 1910 to 2010 in the North American Setting," 26–27, 35, in Beth Snodderly, ed., *Evangelical and Frontier Mission Perspectives* (Oxford, UK: Regnum, 2011). For recent numbers, see Kim, *Spirit Moves West*, 2, 28; Timothy K. Park, "History and Growth of the Korean Missions Movement," 129–34, in *Evangelical and Frontier Mission*; Hanciles, *Beyond Christendom*, 384.

39. On Young Nak, see John Dart, "Church Reflects Growing Korean Activity," *Los Angeles Times*, June 10, 1989. On UBF, see Kim, *Spirit Moves West*, 19, 48–49, 55–59; interview with Mark and Grace Yoon, July 13, 2016, Boston Mass. Also see George Thompson Brown, *How Koreans Are Reconverting the West* (Momence, Ill.: Xlibris 2008).

40. On African migration in the late twentieth century, see Deidre Crumbley and Gloria Malake Cline-Smythe, "Gender and Change in an African Immigrant Church," 158–59, in Jacob Olupona and Regina Gemignani, eds., *African Immigrant Religions in America* (New York: New York University Press, 2007). On RCCG, see Rice, "Mission from Africa"; Hanciles, *Beyond Christendom*, 231–32; Scott Farwell, "Africa's Largest

Evangelical Church Plans a New Home in Rural Texas," *Dallas Morning News*, July 20, 2005; Simon Romero, "A Texas Town Nervously Awaits a New Neighbor," *New York Times*, August 21, 2005. On the high levels of education and professionalism among African immigrants, see Hanciles, *Beyond Christendom*, 345, 356, 366; Olupona, "Communities of Believers," 41, in *African Immigrant Religions*. On the church planting efforts of the RCCG, see Gornik, *Word Made Global*, 195; Hanciles, *Beyond Christendom*, 334–38; 355. Amoah quoted in Hanciles, *Beyond Christendom*, 353.

41. On divine immanence, see Hanciles, *Beyond Christendom*, 360; Jenkins, *Next Christendom*, 123. For the Lausanne survey, see "Global Survey of Evangelical Protestant Leaders," Pew Research Center, June 22, 2011, 21–22. On the miraculous in Boston, see interview with Doug and Judy Hall, July 11, 2016; Carl Racine, "God Is Getting the Church Ready for the Harvest," *Inside EGC*, May 2006, 4. For "sinful and evil structures," see Eldin Villafañe, *The Liberating Spirit: Toward an Hispanic American Pentecostal Social Ethic* (Grand Rapids, Mich.: Eerdmans, 1993), 201. For "disenchanted believers," see Andre Tartar, "Brazilian Evangelist Has Big Plans for U.S.," *Washington Post*, April 2, 2013.

42. For "pregnancy principle" and "goal to make heaven," see Hanciles, *Beyond Christendom*, 355. On Korean prayer services, see Hanciles, *Beyond Christendom*, 361. On Emmanuel and evangelism, see Douglas Hall, "Case Study on EGC for COWE," 21, and "A Contextual Approach to Urban Evangelism in Boston," in folder "COWE Boston Study Group Materials, 12/79," EGCA. For "do something in the United States," see "Newcomers Lead a Spiritual Revival," *Boston Globe*, March 2, 1997. For "renewing presence," see interview with Roberto Miranda, July 12, 2016, Boston.

43. For "life begins at conception," see Espinosa, *Latino Pentecostals in America*, 375. On Majority World views of homosexuality and family life, see "Global Survey of Evangelical Protestant Leaders," 30. On Korean critiques of American liberal sexuality, see Kim, *Spirit Moves West*, 48. On the role of women in the global church, see "Global Survey of Evangelical Protestant Leaders," 30–31; Hanciles, *Beyond Christendom*, 249.

44. On evangelical support for political strongmen, see Mark Elliott, "Why Russia's Evangelicals Thank God for Putin," *Christianity Today*, January 7, 2015. On making the Bible the law of the land, see "Global Survey of Evangelical Protestant Leaders," 32. Land quoted in Molly Worthen, "Love Thy Stranger as Thyself," *New York Times*, May 11, 2013.

45. Padilla quoted in Moll, "Boston's Quiet Revival," 22. For "no longer stand by," see Olupona, "Communities of Believers: Exploring African Immigrant Religion in the United States," 30, in Olupona and Regina Gemignani, eds., *African Immigrant Religions in America* (New York: New York University Press, 2008). On 2016 voting patterns, see Janelle Wong, "We Are All Evangelicals Now," *Religion & Politics*, January 22, 2019.

46. For "more energetic government," see Worthen, "Love Thy Stranger," *New York Times*, May 11, 2013. On the voting patterns of Hispanic members of the Assemblies of God, see Espinosa, *Latino Pentecostals in America*, 363. On the responsibility of caring for

the very poor, see "Global Survey of Evangelical Protestant Leaders," Pew Research Center, June 22, 2011, 31. On Hispanic activism on the death penalty in Nebraska, see Aura Bogado, "Latin Evangelicals Push—and Win—on Death Penalty Abolition in Nebraska," *Colorlines*, May 29, 2015. For more on how Hispanic Protestantism is "extraordinarily diverse, complex, and multifaceted," see Mark Mulder, Aida Ramos, and Gerardo Marti, *Latino Protestants in America: Growing and Diverse* (Lanham, Md.: Rowman & Littlefield, 2017).

47. Amy Black, "Why Evangelicals Are the New Partners for Immigration Reform," *Christian Science Monitor*, January 8, 2013; Michael Jacoby Brown, "When We Meet the 'Other' Face to Face, Our Stances Shift," *Boston Globe*, October 27, 2013. On immigrants as a rising political force, see Johnson, *New Bostonians*, 228; "Student Immigrants Use Civil Rights-Era Strategies," *Brattleboro Reformer*, June 3, 2010; "Massachusetts Immigrant Group Registers 4,000 Immigrant Voters," *Berkshire Eagle*, October 17, 2012. On SB 1070, see Espinosa, *Latino Pentecostals in America*, 354–56. For "Latino vote is a beast," see Alan Lupo, "New Votes on the Bloc," *Boston Globe*, April 22, 2001. For "sleeping giant," see interview with Roberto Miranda, July 12, 2016, Boston Mass.

48. For "quintessential swing voter," see William Gallo, "Hispanic Evangelicals: The Ultimate Swing Vote?" *Voice of America*, February 27, 2016; Salguero, "Despierta! Hispanic Evangelicals and Political Ping-Pong," *Huffington Post*, November 5, 2012. On Hispanic voting patterns, see Espinosa, *Latino Pentecostals in America*, 379–99; Espinosa, "Can Obama Win the Latino Protestant Vote?" *Religion & Politics*, October 15, 2012. For "wound I carry," see interview with Roberto Miranda, July 12, 2016.

49. For "my Anglo evangelical students," see Worthen, "Love Thy Stranger." On demographic transformations, see John Judis and Ruy Teixeira, *The Emerging Democratic Majority* (New York: Scribner, 2002); Robert P. Jones, "Southern Evangelicals Dwindling—and Taking the GOP Edge with Them," *The Atlantic*, October 17, 2014; Daniel Cox and Robert P. Jones, "America's Changing Religious Identity," Public Religion Research Institute, September 6, 2017, prri.org/research/american-religious-landscape-christian-religiously-unaffiliated/

50. For "struggle to grasp," see Hanciles, *Beyond Christendom*, 368. On the limited resources of Majority World Christianity, see Hanciles, *Beyond Christendom*, 385. On the whiteness of multicultural congregations, see Michael Emerson, *People of the Dream: Multiracial Congregations in the United States* (Princeton, N.J.: Princeton University Press, 2008); Korie Edwards, *The Elusive Dream: The Power of Race in Interracial Churches* (New York: Oxford University Press, 2008); Gerardo Marti and Michael Emerson, "The Rise of the Diversity Expert: How American Evangelicals Simultaneously Accentuate and Ignore Race," 179–99, in Brian Steensland and Philip Goff, eds., *The New Evangelical Social Engagement* (New York: Oxford University Press, 2014). For "concentrated outside of swing states," see Janelle Wong, *Immigrants, Evangelicals, and Politics in an Era of Demographic Change* (New York: Russell Sage, 2018). Also see Paul Freston, "Reverse Mission: A Discourse in Search of Reality?" *PentecoStudies* 9, No. 2 (January 2010): 153–74.

51. On the West's spiritual malaise, see Charles Taylor, *A Secular Age* (Boston Mass: Harvard University Press, 2007). For "distinct, sizeable presence," see Hanciles, *Beyond Christendom*, 373–77. On the growing influence of evangelicalism in Boston Mass, see interview with Nika Elugardo, July 13, 2016, Boston Mass; interview with Roberto Miranda, July 12, 2016.

52. On immigrant life in Boston Mass, see interview with Ralph Kee, July 12, 2016, Boston Mass; interview with Rudy Mitchell, July 12, 2016, Boston Mass. For "quiet" revival, see interview with Roberto Miranda, July 12, 2016.

Conclusion

If the world is a stage, the American soliloquy is over. From Korea, Kyung-Chik Han taught social justice. From India, E. Stanley Jones brought civil rights logic. From Switzerland, Peruvian Samuel Escobar articulated a contextualized gospel. From the Philippines, Chinese humanitarian Jimmy Yen introduced new methods of economic development through civic experiments. From Guatemala, pastor Mariano Riscajche preached the power of the supernatural. By 2010 a participant of Lausanne III in South Africa was exulting, "Now the torch is being passed on from the Global North to the Global South." Following sacralized pathways from the ends of the earth, global voices resisted and moderated Christian Americanism.[1]

They also bolstered Christian Americanism. In 2005 Thomas Muthee, a Kenyan bishop, anointed future U.S. vice-presidential candidate Sarah Palin. Muthee, the star of a *Transformations* video in which Christians drove a witch out of the town of Kiambu, was invited to Wasilla Assembly of God Church, where he called on true believers to "infiltrate" key sectors of secular society, especially the so-called "seven mountains" that included education, media, government, and business. As Palin put her hands out, palms up, to receive Muthee's spiritual blessing, the Kenyan bishop asked the congregation "as the body of Christ in this valley to make a way for Sarah" as she campaigned for governor of Alaska. Muthee then prayed,

> We want righteousness in this state. We want righteousness in this nation. O Father, you will turn this nation the other way around so that the powers can be broken. We come against every hindrance of the enemy. We stand against every form of witchcraft in the name of Jesus.

In this transnational exchange, was Muthee demonstrating agency in his support for the religious right? Or was he functioning as a usable African erecting a spiritual canopy for capitalism, homophobia, and American power? Are globally mobile evangelicals who start microbusinesses, construct high-speed computing networks, and reform foreign governments merely the foot soldiers of late capitalism invading from the West? Perhaps evangelical internationalism is merely a neocolonial farce that perpetuates the whiteness of its institutions.[2]

Facing West. David R. Swartz, Oxford University Press (2020). © Oxford University Press.
DOI: 10.1093/oso/9780190250805.001.0001

Progressives too have used Majority World Christians. When Jim Wallis of Sojourners praises the activism of the Latin American Theological Fraternity at Lausanne, or when the North American CEO of the World Evangelical Alliance says that "the evangelical left in America is the evangelical middle everywhere else in the world," are they merely narrating global evangelicalism to reinforce their own progressive sensibilities? Given the particularized stories that Christians on the political left tell, historian Philip Jenkins notes that "one might easily assume that African or Asian churches are obsessed with liberation theologies, with black theology, feminism, and womanism." It is telling that postcolonial logic among progressive Christians often stops when Africans denounce same-sex marriage or when Latin Americans preach Pentecostal spiritual renewal. Americans on both the left and right have cherry-picked global voices, choosing to hear, as Jonathan Merritt puts it, "echoes of their own voices."[3]

This cynical account is true, but it is not the whole story. If power differentials often have compelled global evangelicals to follow American scripts, sometimes embodied interactions with and authentic admiration for Majority World Christianity have changed elite evangelicals in the United States. Billy Graham's travels abroad softened his commitment to American exceptionalism and his aversion to Pentecostalism. In the 1980s the evangelist devoted more of his resources to nuclear disarmament, international peace efforts, and rapprochement with the Soviet Union. Because of global pressures, Graham, Luis Palau, and other evangelists distanced themselves from the bellicosity of Reagan, Falwell, and other luminaries of the religious right. By the 2010s *Christianity Today*, publishing a much more diverse author pool, was declaring, "We live in a time when American pastors are taking cues from clergy in Rwanda, Ukraine, and South Korea." All the while, global evangelicals exercised considerable agency. Even when the Latin American Theological Fraternity was being funded by conservative American interests in the 1970s, it used that money to confront Christian Americanism at Lausanne. That phenomenon continues. In close studies of South Africa and El Salvador, sociologist Stephen Offutt contends that global entrepreneurs draw on transnational religious resources to achieve their own ends and to build their own institutions. In doing so, they have both confirmed and challenged Western assumptions about God's ways in the world.[4]

These perspectives come in complex configurations to an American population that is itself straining against established categories. Progressives are correct that most evangelical Majority World immigrants typically prefer a more energetic government, gun control, a national healthcare system, an emphasis on poverty and education, and an end to capital punishment. Conservatives are right that most also chafe against priests of secular liberalism who want to create efficient bureaucracies and defend reproductive rights. This idiosyncratic political platform intriguingly fits a growing evangelical profile. When Gabriel Salguero and others proclaim that Latinos are prolife from the "womb to the tomb," they resemble an older evangelical left whose consistent-life platform was quashed by partisan sorting in the 1970s. They also look like a growing sector of younger evangelicals who scholars have dubbed "cosmopolitan" or "freestyle." A Baylor University survey in the 2010s showed that American Christians who read the Bible every day typically oppose the death penalty, speak in the language of social and economic justice, and favor reducing consumption—but also oppose abortion on demand. Those who foresee a revitalized evangelicalism in the image of the Democratic Party will be disappointed. Global evangelicals and their politically homeless American allies crosscut categories of liberal and conservative in their views on sexuality, the exotic supernatural arts, and poverty. They insist that modern American categories cannot contain an ancient and global faith.[5]

The most conspicuous shift has occurred among evangelical elites. They were not ready for Latin American tones of liberation sounded by Gustavo Gutiérrez and René Padilla in the 1970s. But in 2000, when *Christianity Today* published an exposition of the Twenty-Third Psalm by Hannah Kinoti, editors were much more attentive to the concept of positionality. They sought nonwhite perspectives, in this case those of a woman from Nairobi familiar with refugee life, injustice, and the rhythms of agrarian life. In the article Kinoti criticized the mighty who "preoccupy themselves with feathering their nests at enormous costs to the citizenry." The article clearly implied that a person living in such conditions could offer more insight than a sixty-year-old white man from the American Midwest. To be sure, the United States remained the "presumptive hub" of global evangelicalism, according to historian Mark Noll, but a survey of magazines shows clear movement away from missionary reports toward perspectives of Christians outside the United States. And in the two decades that followed, growing numbers of articles, leaders, and conferences featuring international perspectives have been invited by Americans precisely because they were international. In fact, Western leaders surveyed at Lausanne III stated that their colleagues in Africa, Asia, and Latin America still had "too little influence." Global encounters and postcolonial insights have encouraged the descendants of Lausanne I to understand that theology is always constructed in local, physical, and historical context. It matters where voices come from.[6]

A burgeoning theological oeuvre from the East and South reinforces evangelical multiculturalism. Against a global replication of American categories, Malaysian theologian Hwa Yung calls for an authentically Asian theology that looks like a mango, not like a banana: yellow all the way through rather than yellow on the outside but white on the inside. For Fuller Seminary's Amos Yong, Asian American religious experience demands Pentecostal attention to the Holy Spirit. Others suggest that poverty and marginality lead them to an evangelical variant of liberation theology. Still others say that a communal orientation generates a different ecclesiology than individualistic formulations dominant in the West. In short, a multitude of articles and books from around the world suggest that diverse social, cultural, and geographical locations generate different readings of Scripture. They contend that Asianness, Africanness, and Latin Americanness offer hermeneutical insight.[7]

Many American theologians agree. While global perspectives were once viewed as liberal, powerful Western boosters, beginning with John Stott in the 1970s and 1980s, now advocate for the validity of otherness. Philip Jenkins, a prominent interpreter of world Christianity, writes, "Read Psalm 23 as a political tract, a rejection of unjust secular authority. Imagine a society terrorized by a dictatorial regime dedicated to suppressing the church, and read Revelation. Understand the core message that whatever evils the world may produce, God will triumph." Jenkins continues,

> Or again, read Revelation with the eyes of rural believers in a rapidly modernizing society, trying to comprehend the inchoate brutality of the megalopolis. Read Hebrews, and think of its doctrines of priesthood and atonement as they might be understood in a country with a living tradition of animal sacrifice.

Western publishers such as Regnum Books, Intervarsity Press, Baker Books, Eerdmans, and Wipf & Stock now oversee a profusion of English-language books by Majority World theologians from the African Theological Fellowship, the Latin American Theological Fraternity, and Partnership in Mission Asia. A "borderlands epistemology," in which the foundations of theology are laid by the marginalized, does not yet predominate. Many Americans still think of theology as constructed in Europe and North America—and global theology as made everywhere else. Nonetheless, evangelical theology looks much more indigenous than it did just twenty years ago.[8]

Beyond seeking global voices, increasing numbers of Americans have begun to contextualize themselves. Like E. Stanley Jones on race and C. Peter Wagner on the supernatural, a new generation of missiologists seeks to decenter Western Christianity by acknowledging their own setting. Roger Olson, a professor of religion at Baylor University, explains that

> American evangelicalism has become so Western, so American, so modern . . . that we have become a mission field for evangelicals from other parts of the world. And they are coming—to evangelize us for the gospel stripped of the cultural accretions we have put on and around it.

Those accretions, identified by internal critics as individualism, consumer capitalism, pragmatism, and the nuclear family, are interrogated at a host of seminaries. According to Jeffrey Greenman,

> Many Western students react negatively at first to an encounter with the unfamiliar Other of global theologies. But within weeks, these same students sometimes have shifted from a defensive resistance to the discomforting challenges of the Other to an uncritical and sometimes quite zealous advocacy of everything proposed by the Other, including some devastating critiques of Western Christianity.

Facing West, more white evangelical leaders are rethinking the triumphalist paradigm within which they operate.[9]

Contextualizing the West often leads to a rejection of Christendom itself. Some missiologists now call for a new missionary movement marked by incarnation, vulnerability, and dependence on God. "The power that accompanies them," contends Mark Gornik of the City Seminary of New York, "is not the state, but the Holy Spirit." He views the early Church, when Christianity was on the margins of the Roman Empire, as the model. Against some counterevidence, he contends that members of a rising East do not want to establish a "next Christendom." They are not interested in replicating Western colonialism. They do not intend to practice political expansionism, ally with state power, use the vocabulary of "a city on a hill," or participate, as Justo Gonzalez puts it, in "innocent readings of history." As the cases of Gonzalez and Gornik suggest, the most vigorous denunciations of Christendom have come from American universities and seminaries. In the 2010s faculty from Bethel (Minn.), Wheaton (Ill.), Gordon (Mass.), and Azusa Pacific (Calif.) joined a series of conferences and online gatherings called the Postcolonial Roundtable. The number of participants eventually grew to 4,000 (over one third of whom were young evangelicals from the non-West) who pressed fellow evangelicals to reread Scripture from the margins and to acknowledge that "Jesus of Nazareth was an indigenous peasant whose message critiques a European imperial power and the local elites who colluded with it." They assured observers that this was a not a "liberal project," but one that used postcolonialism as a "redemptive hermeneutical tool" to push against hegemonic Western perspectives and the "Constantinian captivity of the church."[10]

Declining Western church attendance and striking Majority World growth reinforce the sense that Christendom is over. One out of four Christians in the world lives in Africa, and the Pew Research Center estimates that that number will grow to 40 percent by 2030. Already there are three times more Hispanic Protestants in the United States than Episcopalians. Many in the global diaspora—including Soong-Chan Rah of North Park Theological Seminary, Michael Oh at Lausanne,

Tom Lin at InterVarsity, Walter Kim at the National Association of Evangelicals, and Edgar Sandoval at World Vision U.S.—are rising to positions of leadership in evangelical institutions. Boosters contend that international voices will swell to a chorus in the next century as the Global South overwhelms the North and West. They point out that in a nation growing less white, worried leaders are increasingly open to persons of color in hopes of arresting evangelical decline in the United States. These new demographic realities are leading some privileged white leaders to recover themes of marginality, pilgrimage, and lament that have always pervaded their sacred texts. There is a strong sense among some, especially missionaries, humanitarian workers, pastors, and professors, that they live in a new global age that requires a missiology of peace and a posture of submission, not a reassertion of Pax Americana.[11]

The majority of homegrown American evangelicals do not agree. When 81 percent of white evangelicals elevated Donald Trump to the presidency, many were voting for "America first." Even considering high turnout by older and more conservative voters, low turnout by younger voters, antipathy toward Hillary Clinton, and high concern for abortion, the numbers were stark—and countered the thesis that evangelicalism has shifted away from Christian Americanism. Two years after the election, 52 percent of white evangelical Protestants (compared with 39 percent of mainline Protestants and 23 percent of religiously unaffiliated Americans) said that the prospect of the United States becoming a majority nonwhite nation by 2045 will impact the country negatively. That most elites, by contrast, resisted the Trump wave suggests a fundamental divide between populists and a rival set of internationalists associated with *Christianity Today*, the National Association of Evangelicals, many mission agencies, and universities. The "scandal of the evangelical mind" posited by Mark Noll in 1994 has become less scandalous as professors have become more productive, but it has also widened the chasm between elites and a vast grassroots subculture. In order to bridge this divide, professors James K. A. Smith and John Fea have begun to speak of "scholarship for the masses" and "translation scholarship." They view populist evangelicalism as "a mission field" for evangelical scholars.[12]

Is this mission plausible? Perhaps, but the very structure of evangelicalism militates against a narrowing of the divide in the near term. Decentralized and individualized, evangelicalism has no mechanism for constructing and implementing a coherent social teaching. Charismatic (usually male) personalities rise and flame out. Lacking robust organizational structures, leaders have found it difficult to institutionalize Majority World insights in ways that filter down to the laity. Knowing the Christian American commitments of its early supporters, for example, World Vision promoted Bob Pierce over Kyung-Chik Han. Undeterred by the pleas of NGO workers, donors demanded orphan sponsorships over community development initiatives. Uninterested in the nuanced diagnoses of veteran antitrafficking activists in Thailand, the rank and file continue to demand a methodology of rescue. Despite deep resistance from establishment elites, evangelical youth are moving rapidly to embrace same-sex marriage. Though their leaders reject anti-immigration rhetoric, many older populists embrace it. When *Christianity Today* called for Trump's removal from office in December 2019, Robert Jeffress of First Baptist Church of Dallas called it "a dying magazine" that was "going against 99 percent of evangelical Republicans who oppose impeachment." Peter Illyn, a pastor and leader in the "creation care" movement, explains, "Nobody has the kind of ecclesiastical authority to say, 'I speak for everyone.' If you do that, you hear, "The hell you do. You don't speak for me." Untethered from tradition and authority, self-identifying evangelicals take their cues from cable news networks as much as their ministers.[13]

Evangelicalism, then, remains a fundamentally unstable construct. The broad coalition of born-again, Bible-believing Protestants who gathered at Soldier Field in 1945, if it ever existed in the coherent way that it claimed, has fragmented. In the 1950s Reformed, Anabaptist, and Anglican voices offered new theological ideas and cultural sensibilities. In the 1970s ecumenical conversations with Catholics began. In the 1980s charismatic revival widened the theological and political spectrum even more. By the end of the century, white Americans no longer enjoyed dominance. They were being dramatically outpaced by Pentecostalism abroad, and in the United States itself they lost considerable demographic ground, declining from 23 percent of the population in 2006 to 15 percent of the population in 2017. Robert P. Jones described support for Trump as the "death rattle of white Christian America." Yet this demographic continued to define evangelical norms in media reports, and some polls conflated "evangelical" and "white." These circumscribed definitions may inhibit use of the evangelical label among Christians of color, Majority World immigrants, and younger churchgoers, many of whom want to distance themselves from the culture wars. On the other hand, if these moderate wings choose to identify with evangelicalism, they represent the future more than aging fundamentalists who wax nostalgic for the past.[14]

Indeed, what's past is prologue. It is important to recount the exploits and outrages of evangelist Bob Pierce, Focus on the Family's James Dobson, Secretary of Education Betsy DeVos, and Pastor Robert Jeffress, who loudly performed his anthem "Make America Great Again" on the stage of the Kennedy Center in front of Donald Trump. Public liturgies of Christian Americanism demonstrate ongoing complicity in empire. So do the exclusions of Jimmy Yen, Mariano Riscajche, and Kyung-Chik Han from evangelical narratives. Resurrecting the past demands a global retelling that includes nonwhite voices engaged in both mutuality and resistance. Significantly, Han stood on a stage not only as Bob Pierce's translator, but as his interlocutor. Such exchanges, not fully recognized at the time, are multiplying as faith moves in disorienting directions. Facing West, evangelicals have their sights set on a new ends of the earth.

Notes

1. For "torch is being passed," see David Virtue, "Recalling Lausanne Congress on Evangelism 1974," www.virtueonline.org, October 12, 2010.

2. Bruce Wilson, "Palin in My Prayer Group, Says Witchcraft-Fighting 'Spiritual Warfare' Leader," *Huffington Post*, November 16, 2009; "Sarah Palin's Seven Mountains," www.youtube.com, November 4, 2008.

3. On the evangelical left's use of global voices, see Boyd Reese, "America's Empire," *Post-American*, November-December 1973, 10–11, 14; Eqbal Ahmad, "How We Look to the Third World," *Post-American*, November-December 1973, 8–9; "Is Social Justice an Essential Part of the Mission of the Church?" (debate between Jim Wallis and Al Mohler at Trinity Evangelical Divinity School), October 27, 2011; Rick Love, "A Report on Evangelicals for Peace," www.ricklove.net, October 2, 2012. For "obsessed with liberation theologies," see Philip Jenkins, *New Faces of Christianity: Believing the Bible in the Global South* (New York: Oxford University Press, 2006), 7–8, 16. For "echoes of their own voices," see Jonathan Merritt, "Follow Other Nations' Lead on Gays? Be Careful What You Ask For," Religion News Service, May 8, 2015. For a warning about "inverse colonialism" in which the West fetishizes and romanticizes non-Western Christianity as potential savior of the West, see David Congdon, "The Global-Church Industrial Complex," Anxious Bench blog, May 17, 2018.

4. On the effect of global encounters, see Heather Sells, "Anglican Fever: Youth Flock to New Denomination," Christian Broadcasting Network, December 18, 2011; Brian Howell, *Short-Term Mission: An Ethnography of Christian Travel Narrative and Experience* (Downers Grove, Ill.: IVP Academic, 2012); Ronald Morgan and Cynthia Smedley, eds., *Transformations at the Edge of the World: Forming Global Christians through the Study Abroad Experience* (Abilene, Texas: Abilene Christian University Press, 2010); Juan Martínez, "Stepchildren of the Empire: The Formation of a Latino *Evangélico* Identity," 147–51, in Bruce Benson and Peter Heltzel, eds., *Evangelicals and Empire: Christian Alternatives to the Political Status Quo* (Grand Rapids, Mich.: Brazos Press, 2008); Joel Morris, "How Western Churches Can Learn from the Far East," Gospel Coalition, the gospelcoalition.org, July 9, 2013; Greg Horton and Yonat Shimron, "Southern Baptists to Open Their Ranks to Missionaries Who Speak in Tongues," Religion News Service, religionnews.com, May 14, 2015.

On Graham and Palau, see David Stoll, *Is Latin America Turning Protestant? The Politics of Evangelical Growth* (Berkeley: University of California Press, 1990), 67. For "pastors taking cues," see David Neff, "Your Eyes on God's World," *Christianity Today*, May 2011, 4. On global entrepreneurs, see Stephen Offutt, *New Centers of Global Evangelicalism in Latin America and Africa* (New York: Cambridge University Press, 2015).

5. Deborah Fikes, "A Challenge to My Fellow Evangelicals," *New York Times*, August 19, 2016; Aaron Franzen, "Survey: Frequent Bible Reading Can Turn You Liberal," *Christianity Today*, October 2011, 32; *For the Health of the Nation: An Evangelical Call to Civic Responsibility* (Washington, D.C.: National Association of Evangelicals, 2004).

6. Hannah Kinoti, "In the Valley of the Shadow of Idi Amin: An African Perspective on Psalm 23," *Christianity Today*, June 12, 2000, 78. For "presumptive hub," see Mark Noll, "The View of World-Wide Christianity from American Evangelical Magazines, 1900–2000," 367–86, in Geoffrey Treloar and Robert Linder, eds., *Making History for God: Essays on Evangelicalism, Revival and Mission in Honour of Stuart Piggin* (Sydney, Australia: Robert Menzies College, 2004). For "too little influence," see "Global Survey of Evangelical Protestant Leaders," Pew Research Center, June 22, 2011, 35.

7. Yung Hwa, *Mangoes or Bananas? The Quest for an Authentic Asian Christian Theology* (Eugene, Ore.: Wipf & Stock, 1997). For emphases on the Holy Spirit, see Amos Yong, *The Future of Evangelical Theology: Soundings from the Asian American Diaspora* (Downers Grove, Ill.: InterVarsity Press, 2014); Samuel Escobar, "Doing Theology on Christ's Road," 83, in Jeffrey Greenman and Gene Green, eds., *Global Theology in Evangelical Perspective* (Downers Grove, Ill.: InterVarsity Press, 2012); Amos Yong, Vinson Synan, and Kwabena Asamoah-Gyadu, eds., *Global Renewal Christianity: Spirit-Empowered Movements Past, Present and Future* (Lake Mary, Fla.: Charisma House, 2016). For theology of the marginalized, see Ken Gnanakan, "Some Insights into Indian Christian Theology," 214, in *Global Theology*; Jung Young Lee, *Marginality: The Key to Multicultural Theology* (Minneapolis, Minn.: Fortress Press, 1995); Zaida Maldonado Pérez, *Latina Evangélicas: A Theological Survey from the Margins* (Eugene, Ore.: Cascade Books, 2013); Jayakumar Christian, *God of the Empty-Handed: Poverty, Power, and the Kingdom of God* (Monrovia, Calif.: MARC, 1999); Yohanna Katanacho, *The Land of Christ: A Palestinian Cry* (Eugene, Ore.: Pickwick Publications, 2013); Mitri Raheb, *Faith in the Face of Empire: The Bible through Palestinian Eyes* (Maryknoll, N.Y.: Orbis Books, 2014). For other important examples, see Justo González, *Santa Biblia: The Bible through Hispanic Eyes* (Nashville, Tenn.: Abingdon Press, 1996); Kosuke Koyama, *Water Buffalo Theology* (Maryknoll, N.Y.: Orbis Books, 1974); Mercy Oduyoye, *Introducing African Women's Theology* (Cleveland, Ohio: Pilgrim Press, 2001); John Jusu, *Africa Study Bible* (Wheaton, Ill.: Tyndale House, 2017); Simon Chan, *Grassroots Asian Theology: Thinking the Faith from the Ground Up* (Downers Grove, Ill.: InterVarsity Press, 2014); and the Majority World Theology Series from Eerdmans launched in 2014. Also see academic journals such as the *Asia Journal of Theology, Journal of Theology for Southern Africa*, and *Journal of Latin American Theology*. On the growth of global Christian higher education, see Rick Ostrander, "In the Developing World, a Renaissance in Christian Higher Education," *Chronicle of Higher Education*, October 10, 2013; Joel Carpenter, Nicholas Lantinga, and Perry Glanzer, *Christian Higher Education: A Global Reconnaissance* (Grand Rapids, Mich.: Eerdmans, 2014).

8. For "read Psalm 23," see Jenkins, *New Faces*, 182–83. For other examples of Western advocacy, see Gene Green, ed., *Jesus without Borders: Christology in the Majority World* (Grand Rapids, Mich.: Eerdmans, 2014); Miriam Adeney, *Kingdom without*

Borders: The Untold Story of Global Christianity (Downers Grove, Ill.: InterVarsity Press, 2009); Keith Augustus Burton, *The Blessing of Africa: The Bible and African Christianity* (Downers Grove, Ill.: InterVarsity Press Academic, 2008); Mark Noll, *From Every Tribe and Nation: A Historian's Discovery of the Global Christian Story* (Grand Rapids, Mich.: Baker, 2014); Susan VanZanten, *Reading a Different Story: A Christian Scholar's Journey from America to Africa* (Grand Rapids, Mich.: Baker, 2014); Timothy Tennent, *Theology in the Context of World Christianity: How the Global Church Is Influencing the Way We Think about and Discuss Theology* (Grand Rapids, Mich.: Zondervan, 2007).

9. For "so Western, so American," see Roger Olson, "The Future of Evangelicalism, Part I," lecture at George Fox Seminary, March 11, 2013. For "many Western students," see Jeffrey Greenman, "Learning and Teaching Global Theologies," 247, in *Global Theology in Evangelical Perspective*. Also see Randolph Richards and Brandon O'Brien, *Misreading Scripture with Western Eyes: Removing Cultural Blinders to Better Understand the Bible* (Downers Grove, Ill.: InterVarsity Press, 2012); Soong-Chan Rah, *The Next Evangelicalism: Freeing the Church from Western Cultural Captivity* (Downers Grove, Ill.: InterVarsity Press, 2009); Graham Hill, *Global Church* (Downers Grove, Ill.: InterVarsity Press, 2015); Collin Hansen, *Blind Spots* (Wheaton, Ill.: Crossway, 2015).

10. For "not the state," see Mark Gornik, *Word Made Global: Stories of African Christianity in New York City* (Grand Rapids, Mich.: Eerdmans, 2011), 215. For "city on a hill" and "innocent readings of history," see Arlene Sánchez-Walsh, *Latino Pentecostal Identity: Evangelical Faith, Self, and Society* (New York: Columbia University Press, 2003), 151; Justo González, *Mañana: Christian Theology from a Hispanic Perspective* (Nashville, Tenn.: Abingdon Press, 1990). For "an indigenous peasant" and "redemptive hermeneutical tool," see "Introduction," 26, in Kay Higuera Smith, Jayachitra Lalitha, and Daniel Hawk, eds., *Evangelical Postcolonial Conversations: Global Awakenings in Theology and Praxis* (Downers Grove, Ill.: InterVarsity Press, 2014), 26. For numbers of participants in the round table and "liberal project," see Joseph Duggan, "The Evolution of the Postcolonial Roundtable," 241–42, in *Evangelical Postcolonial Conversations*. For "Constantinian captivity of the church," see Mabiala Kenzo and John Franke, "The Future of Evangelical Theology in an Age of Empire," 275, in *Evangelicals and Empire*.

11. For demographic numbers, see Wes Granberg-Michaelson, "Think Christianity Is Dying?" *Washington Post*, May 20, 2015. On the importance of pilgrimage and lament, see Jehu Hanciles, *Beyond Christendom: Globalization, African Migration, and the Transformation of the West* (Maryknoll, N.Y.: Orbis Books, 2008), 391. On lament, see Soong-Chan Rah, *Prophetic Lament: A Call for Justice in Troubled Times* (Downers Grove, Ill.: InterVarsity Press, 2015), 24.

12. John Fea, *Believe Me: The Evangelical Road to Donald Trump* (Grand Rapids, Mich.: Eerdmans, 2018). On white evangelical anxiety about demographic change, see "American Democracy in Crisis: The Challenges of Voter Knowledge, Participation, and Polarization," Public Religion Research Institute report, July 17, 2018. Smith and Fea quoted in "Evangelicalism as a Mission Field for Evangelical Scholars," The Way of

Improvement Leads Home blog, September 27, 2017. https://thewayofimprovement. com/2017/09/27/evangelicalism-as-a-mission-field-for-evangelical-scholars/

13. Christian Smith, *Christian America? What Evangelicals Really Want* (Berkeley: University of California Press, 2000), 57; Janelle Wong, *Immigrants, Evangelicals, and Politics in an Era of Demographic Change* (New York: Russell Sage, 2018), 69; Lydia Bean, *The Politics of Evangelical Identity: Local Churches and Partisan Divides in the United States and Canada* (Princeton: Princeton University Press, 2014), 113. Illyn quoted in Lydia Bean and Steve Teles, "Spreading the Gospel of Climate Change: An Evangelical Battleground," policy paper for New America's Political Reform Program, November 2015, 14–15.

14. Mark Labberton, ed., *Still Evangelical: Insiders Reconsider Political, Social, and Theological Meaning* (Downers Grove, Ill.: InterVarsity Press, 2018). For "death rattle," see Robert P. Jones, *The End of White Christian America* (New York: Simon & Schuster, 2017), 248. Also see Eliza Griswold, "Evangelicals of Color Fight against the Religious Right," *New Yorker*, December 26, 2018.

Index